TRANSLEITHANIAN
PARADISE

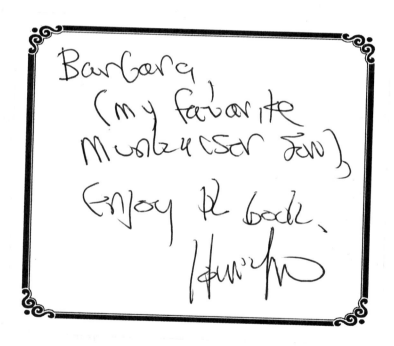

Barbara,
(my favorite
Munkacser Jew)
Enjoy the book.

Central European Studies

Charles W. Ingrao, founding editor
Paul Hanebrink, editor
Maureen Healy, editor
Howard Louthan, editor
Dominique Reill, editor
Daniel L. Unowsky, editor
Nancy M. Wingfield, editor

The demise of the Communist Bloc a quarter century ago exposed the need for greater understanding of the broad stretch of Europe that lies between Germany and Russia. For four decades the Purdue University Press series in Central European Studies has enriched our knowledge of the region by producing scholarly monographs, advanced surveys, and select collections of the highest quality. Since its founding, the series has been the only English-language series devoted primarily to the lands and peoples of the Habsburg Empire, its successor states, and those areas lying along its immediate periphery. Among its broad range of international scholars are several authors whose engagement in public policy reflects the pressing challenges that confront the successor states. Indeed, salient issues such as democratization, censorship, competing national narratives, and the aspirations and treatment of national minorities bear evidence to the continuity between the region's past and present.

Other titles in this series

Finding Order in Diversity: Religious Toleration in the Habsburg Empire, 1792–1848
Scott Berg

*Unlikely Allies: Nazi German and Ukrainian Nationalist Collaboration
in the General Government During World War II*
Paweł Markiewicz

*Balkan Legacies: The Long Shadow of Conflict and
Ideological Experiment in Southeastern Europe*
Balázs Apor and John Paul Newman (Eds.)

*On Many Routes: Internal, European, and Transatlantic
Migration in the Late Habsburg Empire*
Annemarie Steidl

Teaching the Empire: Education and State Loyalty in Late Habsburg Austria
Scott O. Moore

TRANSLEITHANIAN
PARADISE

A History
of the Budapest
Jewish Community,
1738–1938

Howard N. Lupovitch

Purdue University Press, West Lafayette, Indiana

Cataloging-in-Publication Data is available at the Library of Congress.

978-1-61249-780-8 (paperback)
978-1-61249-779-2 (hardback)
978-1-61249-781-5 (epub)
978-1-61249-782-2 (epdf)

Cover photo: istock.com/florin1961

For my parents, Aaron and Rochelle Lupovitch

Contents

List of Tables

Preface

THIS BOOK, A HISTORY OF THE BUDAPEST JEWISH COMMUNITY FROM 1738 through 1938, grew out of two seemingly unrelated encounters. The first took place when I visited Budapest for the first time. Walking the streets of the Jewish part of the city, I was surprised to learn that Theodore Herzl, the quintessential assimilated Hungarian Jew, grew up right next door to the Dohány Street Synagogue, the hallmark of Jewish communal life, but rarely attended; and that the Dohány Street, Rombach Street, and Orthodox Kazinczy Street Synagogues, the "Jewish Triangle" formed by the main synagogues of three different religious denominations, were located just a few blocks from one another. In both cases, I was struck by the close proximity of such different Jewish outlooks and that, despite the thematic distance that separated Herzl from the Dohány Street Synagogue and the two synagogues from each other, they were all located within a single square mile.

The second encounter took place when I was teaching an undergraduate seminar called "Jews and the City." Each week, the students and I situated Budapest Jewry and other leading European Jewish communities in a comparative framework that distinguished these cities geographically between Eastern, Central, and Western Europe; and culturally between more traditional communities such as Warsaw and Vilnius and more assimilated communities such as Vienna and Budapest. At one point, a student who hailed from Istanbul noted a "European paradigm" common to all of these Jewish communities in major cities across Europe from London to Lvov and from Vilnius to Vienna. Drawing on an extra-European perspective of geography and history, the student argued that the similarities between urban European Jewish communities far overshadowed the geographical and cultural differences between them; all, he concluded, evinced a common set of European urban Jewish characteristics.

My student's extra-European perspective and the compact diversity of Budapest's Jewish neighborhood have remained with me through years of research and writing, and, in tandem, were a helpful guide in formulating and pursuing what became one of the central themes of this book: the concentration of a large, diverse population of Jews in a compact urban space is something that Budapest Jewry shared in common with large Jewish communities in other large European cities. Like other Jewish communities in larger urban centers, the rise of Budapest Jewry was inseparable from the rise of the city that housed it. The rapid growth of Jewish communities in Budapest and other urban centers during the nineteenth century was a symptom of these cities redefining the urban space—political, economic, cultural space—available to groups like Jews who hitherto had been largely excluded and, at most, only selectively included. Key aspects of the rise of Budapest Jewry during the long nineteenth century were no less important in the rise of other large Jewish communities. Examples abound, beginning with the sheer size and rapid growth of Budapest Jewry. In 1800, a Jewish community of 5,000 or 10,000 was considered large; a century later, Budapest Jewry, which had exceeded 200,000, was one of a dozen European Jewish communities approaching or in excess of 100,000. No less important a similarity was the dispersal of this large Jewish population all over the city with the largest concentrations in an older, original Jewish neighborhood inhabited by less acculturated, less affluent, more recent Jewish arrivals; and a newer Jewish neighborhood for upwardly mobile, acculturated Jews, native-born Jews—Terézváros and Lipótváros in Budapest, Leopoldstadt and Alsergund in Vienna, Marais and Montmartre in Paris, and in the United States, the Lower East Side and Washington Heights in New York City.

The other theme of the book is the distinctly Hungarian aspects of Budapest and its Jewish community. The rise of Budapest and Budapest Jewry was shaped by the rhythms of its distinctly Hungarian and East Central European context. The most striking example, and another central theme of this book, is the particular juxtaposition of the old and the new, of change and continuity. Budapest Jewry was regarded as one of the most highly acculturated Jewish communities in the world, while housing a large and diverse array of Jewish communal organizations that included dozens of synagogues, schools, a world-class rabbinical seminary, newspapers, voluntary organizations, kosher butchers. Other communities had one or the other—for example, the Jewish community of Vienna was highly assimilated with a smaller traditional enclave; the Jews of Warsaw had a vibrant traditional Jewish life with a minority of acculturated Jews. Budapest had both.

The juxtaposition of the old and the new as constituent elements of Budapest Jewry is a central focus of this book. To this end, the book focuses on the two centuries from 1738 through 1938, using 1838 as a fault line between these two periods in the rise of Budapest Jewry.

More specifically, following the introductory chapter that contrasts the modern and the premodern city, chapters 2–4 explore the creation of social and cultural space for Jews in heretofore inaccessible Pest, though a combination of royal or magnate protection, urban expansion, and changes in the legal status of Jews; the emergence of Terézváros as the heart of Pest Jewry; and the contrast between Jewish communal leadership in Pest and Óbuda as an indicator of the transition from an older, corporate community to a new, economically defined space for Jews. The point of departure is the market town beginnings of what eventually became Budapest Jewry. The modern

Jewish community in Budapest began neither in Pest nor in Buda but in Óbuda, the third (and often forgotten) town that was later amalgamated with Pest and Buda to form Budapest. At a time when the remnant of Buda's premodern Jewish community was dwindling down to zero and no Jews lived in Pest, the Jewish community that emerged in the market town of Óbuda was rooted in the symbiotic relationship between local magnates and their Jewish subjects; and this relationship laid the basis for Jews to live in Pest, too. This situation was not uniquely Hungarian, but an important aspect of urban Jewish life in Poland and the Czech Lands, too.

Chapters 5–7, the second part of the book, focus on the rapid growth and development of Pest and of Pest Jewry, the heart of what eventually became Budapest Jewry, from 1838 to 1914, amid the reconstruction, expansion, and development of the city of Pest during the long nineteenth century. Here the urban dimension of the rise of Budapest Jewry comes to the fore. In the aftermath of the Great Flood of 1838, a more inclusive Pest polity and society was complemented by an expanding network of Jewish communal institutions that helped Jews navigate the tension between the allures of a more open society and the aim of maintaining a sense of communal cohesiveness; and by the concurrent emergence of Lipótváros as a secondary neighborhood for more upwardly mobile, more acculturated Jews. This part of the book explores the way that Budapest Jewry, like Jewish communities in other large cities, navigated a combination of centrifugal and centripetal forces. That is, Jewish life in Budapest was defined by a tension between the openness and vibrancy of the city, drawing Jews away from the Jewish community, and an array of institutions and organizations whose vitality allowed the Jewish community to flourish despite the challenges of disaffection and drift. The city and its Jewish community became, at once, a home for observant, committed Jews no less than for a barely affiliated Jew like Herzl. The final chapter of the book considers how the synergy between Budapest Jewry and Budapest was challenged by the difficulties of World War I and its aftermath and by the new realities of post-Trianon Hungary; and how Budapest Jewry confronted and coped with these changing conditions and tried to preserve the scope of Jewish space and the fluidity between the Jewish community and the city.

While structured more or less chronologically, the book is not simply a narrative history of Budapest Jewry. Instead, the book focuses less on aspects of this story that other historians have covered, and more on those aspects that have received less scholarly attention. Thus the book devotes less attention to changes in the political and legal status of Jews, the rise of a Jewish *haute bourgeois* commercial and industrial elite, the widespread acculturation and Magyarization of Budapest Jewry, and the contributions of Budapest Jews to the culture of the city. Older historical works on Budapest Jewry such as those by Sándor Büchler and Zsigmond Groszmann, along with the more recent scholarship of Vera Bácskai, Nathaniel Katzburg, Mary Gluck, and Miklós Konrád explored these issues in great detail. Instead, building on and engaging the more recent work of Julia Richers and Ferenc Laczó, the book focuses more on external developments such the expansion of Pest beyond the walls of the inner city; the reconstruction and reconceptualization (and "rebranding") of Pest, in particular, in the aftermath of the flooding of the three cities in 1838; the marginalization of Budapest after World War I; and on internal factors such as the emergence of Jewish neighborhoods in the Terézváros and Lipótváros districts and the construction of an array of Jewish institutions that formed the backbone of a vibrant Jewish life—notably the burial society and other voluntary associations, the Pest Jewish Women's Association, community education and vocational training, the Jewish hospital, the Dohány Street Synagogue and other synagogues, and the Rabbinical Seminary. These external and internal developments allowed Jews in Budapest to live with one foot in the Jewish community and the other in mainstream society, seamlessly and unself-consciously.

The chronological parameters of the book follow from these aims. The book begins with the Zichy family formally recognizing the Jewish community of Óbuda and encouraging other economically productive Jews to settle there and join the nascent Jewish community, the first step in the creation and expansion of urban space in all three towns. The book ends in 1938, when anti-Jewish laws began eroding and ultimately curtailing this space. While the Jewish community remained more or less intact until 1944, after 1938 the situation deteriorated rapidly, creating a different set of dynamics that lie outside the scope of this study.

Parts of the book appeared in previously published articles. Part of chapter 1 appeared as "Jews and the Zichy Estate: A Case Study in Magnate-Jewish Relations" in *Jahrbuch des Simon Dubnow Instituts* 7 (2008). Part of chapter 2 appeared as "Beyond the Walls: The Beginning of Pest Jewry" in *Austrian History Yearbook* 36 (2006). Part of chapter 8 appeared as "It Takes a Village: Budapest Jewry and the Problem of Juvenile Delinquency" in *Juvenile Delinquency and the Limits of Western Influence, 1850–2000*, edited by Lily Chang and Heather Ellis (Palgrave Macmillan, 2014).

A NOTE ON PRIMARY SOURCES

In writing this book, I relied on a variety of archival and printed primary sources. The archival sources include, first and foremost, minute books, that is, transactions of the periodic meetings of the Jewish communities of Pest and Óbuda and of two Jewish organizations in Pest: the burial society and the Hevra Shas. The lion's share of the content of these books deals with the mundane minutiae of day-to-day exchanges between communal officers and institutions, and the mainly intracommunal disputes that local Jewish tribunals adjudicated. The challenge in analyzing these sources is to cull from this large pile of ordinary occurrences the successes and disappointments of these in-stitutions. These minute books were written in Hebrew, Yiddish-Deutsch, German, and Magyar, the last being used exclusively by the beginning of the twentieth century. In addition, I used the correspondence between Jews and various government officials in the two cities—local magistrates, the high sheriff and deputy high sheriff (*főispán* and *alispán*) of Pest County, and the Lord Lieutenancy (*Helytartó*). For the later pe-riod covered by the book, I relied also on reports in a burgeoning Jewish press, mainly from the liberal Budapest Jewish weekly *Egyenlőség* (Equality), the journalistic arm of the Pest Neolog community. I focused on weekly news reports and not on polemical essays so as to minimize the level of bias. These weekly reports included firsthand de-scriptions and summaries of the activities of local institutions. Finally, in the chapter on the interwar period, I used the testimony of Budapest–born and raised Holocaust survivors, focusing on their recollections of the years prior to 1938.

ACKNOWLEDGMENTS

The completion of this book provides an opportunity to express gratitude and appre-ciation to those who provided assistance in one form or another through the years. Primary sources for the book came from archival collections in three cities: the Jewish Theological Seminary in New York; in Budapest, the Jewish Archive (Zsidó levéltár) and the Budapest Municipal Archive (Budapest Fővárosi levéltár); and in Jerusalem, the Central Archive for the History of the Jewish People. My gratitude to the archivists and other staff members whose assistance was, at all times, generous and invaluable, in particular, Jerry Schwarzbard at JTS, Hadassah Assouline at the Hebrew University, and Toronyi Zsuzsanna and István Garay in Budapest. I am equally indebted to nu-merous other colleagues who read parts or all of the manuscript at various stages of its development or provided useful perspective in conversation about the subject, in-cluding Robert Nemes, Rebekah Klein-Pejsova, Shaul Stampfer, Adam Ferziger, Tim Cole, Glenn Dynner, Rabbi Baruch Oberlander, John Gardon, and, as always, my be-loved mentor István Deák. Ongoing conversations and exchanges with my colleagues at Wayne State University, especially Tracy Neumann and Saeed Khan, have always pro-vided me with supported, useful feedback and comparative perspectives. Thanks also to Justin Race and the staff and editorial board of Purdue University Press and to the peer reviewers who provided invaluable suggestions and criticisms on an earlier draft of the manuscript. My family has supported me at every turn. My parents, Dr. Aaron and Rochelle Lupovitch, waited patiently for me to finish this book over the course of a decade. Their stories of growing up on Dexter in downtown Detroit whetted my ap-petite to explore the intricacies of Jewish life in a big city. Their periodic gentle nudges have always been a very helpful reminder to keep going, and my mother proofread the entire manuscript with her typically remarkable thoroughness—this book is dedicated to them. My wife, Marni, and daughters Dahvi and Hanny inspire me every day to strive for nothing less than excellence. All three, especially Dahvi, have been indispensable in helping to make the flow of the book more streamlined and coherent, identify the more important and interesting parts of the story, and complete the last chapters of the book while we were quarantining together at home. They remind me every day how lucky I am to be part of this family and to do what I do.

Part I

Beginnings, 1738–1838

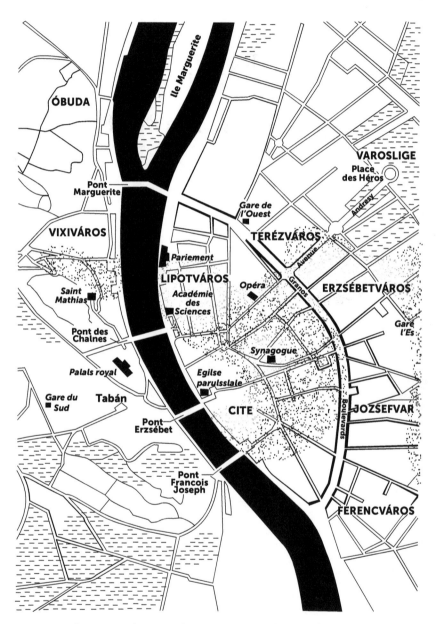

Budapest in 1900. (Source: Catherine Horel, *Historie de Budapest* [Fayard 1999].)

I

Introduction:
Budapest as a Laboratory
of Urban Jewish Identity

T HE JEWISH COMMUNITY OF BUDAPEST IS ONE OF THE GREAT URBAN JEW-
ish success stories of the long nineteenth century. Until the end of the eighteenth century, the Jews of Pest, Buda, and Óbuda—the three towns that amalgamated in 1873 to form Budapest—were small, insignificant enclaves on the periphery
of the Ashkenazic world that paled in comparison with the more prestigious Jewish
communities of Prague, Cracow, and Amsterdam; these locations were situated in three
towns that were unimportant and virtually nonexistent in comparison with the larger
and more established towns of Pressburg and Vienna. Prior to 1686, Buda had been
an important city in medieval Hungary and a significant eastern outpost of Western
Christendom, and then a significant western outpost of Ottoman rule in Southeastern
Europe; but it had declined to a position of irrelevance following the Habsburg recon-
quest of the Balkans at the end of the seventeenth century. Likewise, the Jewish community of Buda had been an important center of Jewish learning and a way station
between the Ashkenazic and Sephardic worlds during the century and a half prior to
1700, but had dwindled after the eviction of the Jews in 1686 and largely disappeared by
1749. Pest and Óbuda at the beginning of the eighteenth century were little more than
fishing villages adjacent to or across the Danube from Buda.[1] Pest had no permanent
Jewish residents before 1780, and fewer than one thousand in 1800. At the beginning
of the nineteenth century, the combined Jewish population of Pest, Buda, and Óbuda
still barely totaled four thousand, the majority of whom lived in the least prominent
of the three towns, Óbuda.

By 1914, the population of Budapest approached one million, the majority of whom lived in Pest. This rapid growth was one of the factors that led, in 1892, to Budapest joining Vienna as one of the two *Haupt- und Residenzstadte* of the Austro-Hungarian Empire. The Jewish population grew at an even faster rate, exceeding 200,000, 90 percent of whom lived in Pest, the heart and soul of an amalgamated Budapest. In 1800 Jews made up less than 5 percent of the total population of the three towns; a century later, nearly one in four people in Budapest was Jewish. Budapest and Budapest Jewry were not the only city and Jewish community to experience this dramatic growth during the nineteenth century. The populations of more than a dozen cities in East Central Europe increased manifold during the nineteenth century; even among these, Budapest was one of the fastest growing cities. Only the population of Berlin increased at a faster rate during the nineteenth century than Budapest.

Still overshadowed at the end of the 1880s by Vienna in terms of size and culture, by the end of the century Budapest challenged the economic and cultural dominance of the other Habsburg capital, not least of all in the eyes of its proud Magyar inhabitants. Budapest Jewry was one of a handful of rapidly growing Jewish communities situated in a burgeoning European metropolis, along with the Jews of Warsaw, Berlin, Vienna, Moscow, Saint Petersburg, Odessa, Breslau, and Kiev. Like Budapest, none of these

TABLE 1. POPULATION GROWTH,
1800–1890, BY PERCENTAGE (%)

Berlin	818	Paris	343
Budapest	809	London	339
Munich	775	Hamburg	334
Glasgow	631	Saint Petersburg	333
Sheffield	611	Lyon	300
Brussels	602	Prague	327
Leeds	591	Marseille	263
Liverpool	572	Milan	214
Manchester	571	Madrid	213
Warsaw	511	Copenhagen	210
Birmingham	507	Rome	177
Vienna	453	Moscow	151
Breslau	429	Amsterdam	90
Torino	347	Naples	36

Source: Gusztáv Thirring, *Budapest székesföváros a Millennium idejében*
(Budapest: Pesti könyvnyomda, 1898), 7.

cities had more than a handful of Jews in 1700 and more than a few thousand in 1800. By the beginning of the twentieth century, all of these cities had large Jewish communities whose populations were approaching or exceeding 100,000. By 1910, Budapest Jewry had grown into one of the largest Jewish communities in Europe, second only to Warsaw.[2]

By the turn of the twentieth century, Budapest had blossomed into one of the most vibrant and diverse centers of urban life and culture. The city was situated at the crossroads of Europe, in relative proximity to Eastern and Western Europe and other parts of Central Europe. This contributed to the rapidly expanding diversity of the city's population. At the beginning of the nineteenth century, most of the residents of the three cities were ethnic Magyars and Germans, with small enclaves of Greeks and Jews. By the end of the nineteenth century the city was one of the most diverse in Europe. As Julia Richers noted, Budapest was among the most heterogenous multiethnic locales in Europe, "where more and more ethnicities, faiths, and cultures lived together in a confined space, creating an increasingly pluralistic culture."[3]

The diversity of the city, moreover, was paralleled by a different sort of diversity within the Jewish community. The vast majority of Jews in Budapest were Ashkenazic Jews from a relatively compact area of East Central Europe—Hungary, the Czech Lands, Poland, and western Ukraine. In terms of religious observance and outlook, Budapest Jewry was more diverse, a mixture of more acculturated, westernized Jews from Central Europe and less acculturated immigrants from Eastern Europe. Budapest Jewry combined, in the words of Viktor Karády, "an eastern density with the dominance of western Jews," evincing at once a powerful trend toward assimilation by a majority of Jews and a tenacious resistance to assimilation by Orthodox Jews and *Ostjuden*.[4]

For some Jews, the diversity of the city and its Jewish community was part of the allure that attracted Jews to Pest by the thousands during the second half of the nineteenth century. Jews in Pest, one of many ethnic and religious minorities, felt less like outsiders, as Richers notes: "Jewish immigrants were outsiders among other outsiders."[5] The range of Jewish identities in Budapest, moreover, was reflected by and resonated with Neolog, the predominant Jewish outlook. For some Jews, Neolog seamlessly combined a commitment to traditional Jewish observance with an equally strong or even stronger inclination to embrace Magyar as a language and culture and to immerse oneself in mainstream society. In tandem, these two meanings described not only the Jewish outlook and communal connection of the majority of Budapest Jews but also the eclectic range of identities of Budapest Jewry. This range of identities found expression most vividly in Neolog institutions such as the Budapest Rabbinical Seminary and publications such as the *Magyar Zsidó Szemle* (Hungarian Jewish Review) and the annual yearbook of the *Izraelita Magyar Irodalmi Egylet* (Hungarian Israelite Literary Society); but also in the synergy that the myriad of synagogues, schools, and voluntary societies that filled the organizational landscape of Budapest Jewry fostered between the Jewish community and mainstream society.[6]

To be sure, the rapid rise of Budapest and its Jewish community was more tortuous than smooth. As Richers and other historians have pointed out, the growth of Budapest Jewry elicited a recurring and almost chronic backlash from certain elements within the city's populace. This backlash continued even during the dualist era, the half-century leading up to the First World War that some have regarded as a golden age (*aranykor*) for Hungary and Hungarian Jewry. While Richers is correct to be wary of an overly Pollyannaish view of the rise of Budapest Jewry, the resistance to it underscores further the tenacity of Jews of Budapest in the face of local resistance to Jewish communal expansion and development. This tenacity is further evidenced by the ability of Budapest Jewry to maintain much of the integrity and vitality of the Jewish community through most of the interwar period in the face of surging antisemitism and other difficult challenges.[7]

Given this growth and vitality, it is not surprising that the rapid growth and diversity of the city and its Jewish community elicited various comparisons between Budapest and other cities. Budapest is one of several cities described as "Paris of the East."[8] This sobriquet refers, first, to the city's seamless blending of older and newer architectural styles, modern technological accoutrements, and proud national flavor—Budapest defines Hungarian culture as Paris defines French culture; and, second, to the role of the city as a metropole attracting a diverse array of migrants, in this case, from all over the Habsburg monarchy. Others have portrayed Budapest as gritty, loud, and boisterous, less akin to a *mitteleuropa* city like Vienna or Berlin, and more like Warsaw or a North American city like New York or Chicago. Writing shortly before the First World War, for example, Lajos Hatvany-Deutsch described Budapest as "the Chicago of the Balkans." Budapest, in the recent words of Mary Gluck, evinced "a brash entrepreneurial spirit that caused contemporary observers to remark—not necessarily in a complimentary spirit—that the city resembled an American rather than a Central European Metropolis." More recently, Máté Tamáska described the rapid development of Budapest after 1867 as "an accelerated style of urban development termed 'American.'"[9] Accordingly, comparisons of Budapest and New York have been more frequent than comparisons of Budapest and its twin, the Habsburg capital city of Vienna.[10]

The rise of Budapest Jewry also elicited varied appraisals from contemporary intellectuals and politicians. Some observers lamented the hyper-Jewishness of Budapest and other cities as a sign of decline and social decay. The most well-known of these responses was the epithet attached to Budapest and its Jewish community by Karl Lueger, the openly antisemitic mayor of Vienna at the turn of the twentieth century: "Judapest." Lueger coined this derogatory epithet to underline the (in his mind unacceptably) favorable position of Jews in Budapest as evidence of everything about the city he saw to be decadent and corrupt, and therefore inferior to Vienna.[11] Other contemporaries celebrated the full immersion and acceptance of Jews in Budapest society and regarded Budapest and its Jewish community in exceptionally favorable terms. Most dramatically, perhaps, were several Zionists addressing the First Zionist Congress in Basel in 1897. Even as they raised doubts regarding the future of a viable Jewish life in the diaspora, they continued to see Budapest as a "Transleithanian paradise," in the words of Alexander Mintz, and "an oasis in the Anti-Semitic desert," in the words of Budapest native Theodore Herzl.[12] Seen together, these comparisons and appraisals point to the inexorable link between the three towns that formed Budapest and their Jewish communities. As such, crucial to understanding the transformation of the premodern cities of Pest and Buda into the modern city of Budapest, and the Jewish communities of the three towns into Budapest Jewry, is understanding the differences between premodern and modern European cities.

Premodern European cities were defined primarily as corporate entities. In order for a particular locale to be defined as a *civitas* (city) rather than *oppidum* (town), the residents needed a legal charter from a powerful authority—temporal or ecclesiastical—that conferred the privileges associated with living in a city. Foremost among these privileges was the right to decide who was allowed to live and work in the city. A combination of economic and theological considerations led city leaders to permit only a select group of people to enter the city at all, and an even more select group to remain overnight and for an extended period of time. As the medieval German proverb "*Stadtluft macht frei nach Jahr und Tag*" (City air makes you free after a year and a day) connoted, residence in a legally chartered city was a highly coveted privilege that was equated with freedom itself.[13] These cities were demographically and culturally homogeneous, exclusive to a carefully defined population. Symptomatic of the exclusivity of the medieval city was the *privilegium de non tolerandis judeus* (the right not to tolerate Jews). Beginning in the sixteenth century, this privilege entitled chartered cities in Europe to minimize and often outright prevent Jews from settling there, even temporarily. As a result, most of these cities were largely *judenrein* until the end of the eighteenth century. In Paris, for example, the number of Jews from the final expulsion of Jews in 1394 until 1789 did not exceed 100.

The modern European city, by contrast, is defined less in legal and corporate terms than as a geographic, demographic, economic, and cultural concept. Since the eighteenth century, major European cities typically span a minimum number of square miles, have a larger and denser population than that of the surrounding area, and function as a regional or national hub of politics, commerce, industry, and culture, or some combination thereof. These cities are more inclusive spaces, where virtually anyone with the economic wherewithal can reside and where residence and other possibilities are

defined by a mishmash of economic, cultural, and social factors. Lacking these characteristics, present-day enclaves will often be designated as towns or villages.[14]

Jewish communities in these cities arose when the elimination of local residential restrictions on Jews allowed the Jewish community to increase in number, and then the
openness of the city allowed Jews to join the city's social mainstream. The processes of
change did not unfold in the same way in every European city. Historians have generally described the removal of urban restrictions on Jews in terms of three patterns of
change. The most oft-cited pattern focuses on legal restrictions barring Jewish settlement being removed by legislative acts that were symptomatic of a broader state-wide
triumph of liberal aims over antiquated privileges. Such was the case in Paris, Vienna,
Berlin, Breslau, Kiev, and other cities where the rise of urban Jewish life not only coincided with the age of emancipation, but was often a prominent symptom of it.[15] More
recently, several historians suggested an alternate paradigm for Jews in port cities such
as Amsterdam, London, and Livorno, where the increase in the number of Jews resulted not from legislative acts but rather from a pervading mentality that elevated
commerce and profit as a prerequisite for settlement above other considerations, including religious affiliation.[16]

Other historians, focusing on early modern East Central Europe, focused on market towns where restrictions on Jewish settlement were not removed through specific
legislative acts or the pragmatic pressure of maritime commerce, but rather through
a gradual process of erosion by a combination of urban expansion and imperial, royal,
or magnate intrusion. In some cases, this process took place in cities that were the seat
of a powerful royal or imperial authority who wanted to settle taxpaying Jewish subjects without undermining the privileges he had extended to the city *Burghertum*. The
sovereign in such cases settled his Jewish subjects in an area adjacent to the city. In
Cracow, for example, Jews who had been excluded from the city itself settled under the
aegis of the royal crown in the adjacent town of Kazimierz; when the city expanded
and incorporated the adjacent town, the Jews there became residents of the heretofore
inaccessible city under royal protection.[17] Similarly in Prague, Jews who had settled
in the *Judenstadt* under royal and then imperial protection became residents of the
city when this area was incorporated. In Warsaw and Vilnius, the intrusion of Polish
magnates into city politics eroded residential restrictions, allowing Jews in Warsaw to
settle in *Jurydcki*—areas of the city under magnate control—and in Vilnius, in the
magnate-controlled area known as Castle Court.[18]

To date, much of the historical scholarship on Budapest Jewry has emphasized the
first pattern, presenting the appearance of significant Jewish life in the Hungarian capital through a series of legislative acts beginning in the late eighteenth century that
eroded and then eventually struck down the rights of the burgers of Pest and Buda to
exclude Jews. "Only in 1783," wrote Nathaniel Katzburg, "did the situation [for Jews]

improve when Emperor Joseph II nullified the discriminatory laws directed against Hungarian Jewry, and the gates of the 'free' cities, including Pest, opened to Jewish settlement."[19] Accordingly, the Jewish right to reside in Pest and Buda and the expansion of Jewish life in Pest, in particular, were set in motion first by Joseph II's ephemeral reforms of the 1780s, and then by the more permanent reforms of the Hungarian National Diet in 1840 and the emancipation edict of 1868, culminating with the Reception Law of 1895, which placed Judaism on an equal footing with other religions, facilitating a larger role and presence for Jews in the city and encouraging an increasingly widespread embrace of Hungarian language and culture.[20] This narrative continued into the twentieth century, as the legal and political space of Jews in Budapest and Hungarian Jewry generally was curtailed by a *Numerus Clausus* in 1920 and, more seriously, by a series of more draconian anti-Jewish laws beginning in 1938. These laws disenfranchised the Jews of Budapest, thus reversing the political gains of the previous century. As such, the rise of Budapest Jewry from several small enclaves of Jews on the periphery of the Ashkenazic world into one of the largest and most vibrant Jewish communities a century later has been presented as exemplifying the broader emancipation and then disenfranchisement of Hungarian Jewry.

In fact, the rise of the of the Jewish community in Budapest combined elements of all three patterns. Like Jewish communities in port cities, Budapest Jewry arose virtually from scratch during the eighteenth century, with little or no connection to the small premodern Jewish community of Buda. The small enclave of Jews in eighteenth-century Buda was little more than a handful of Jews who lived precariously under military and royal protection. Once the military presence in Buda diminished in a shift toward peacetime administration, Maria Theresa withdrew this protection and expelled the remaining Jews from Buda at the end of the 1740s—in effect, a belated implementation of the 1686 edict of expulsion.[21] Like Jewish communities in market towns, moreover, the first century in the rise of Budapest Jewry, from the 1730s through the 1830s, was driven largely by the sponsorship and protection of magnates who facilitated the migration of a relatively small number of Jews until the end of the 1830s and a rapidly increasing number of Jews thereafter.[22] Magnate protection allowed a comparatively small enclave of Jews in Pest to become the nucleus of a much larger Pest Jewry—and, after 1873, Budapest Jewry; thereafter, the reconstruction and rebranding of Pest that followed in the aftermath of the flooding of the three towns in 1838 transformed Pest into an urban space with an array of economic, cultural, social, and political opportunities for Jews that expanded continuously until the end of World War I.

As impediments to Jewish settlement disappeared and these new opportunities materialized, the Jewish community of Pest increased not only in number but in diversity. By the end of the nineteenth century, most Jews in Budapest had embraced some degree of acculturation, acculturating first toward the German language and Viennese culture and then, from the 1870s on, increasingly toward the Magyar language and culture. Historians of Budapest Jewry have tended to foreground the putative sharp dichotomy between an unacculturated minority of Jews and a rapidly increasing acculturated Jewish majority whose degree of assimilation was unmatched elsewhere in Hungary, indeed, in much of Europe. Along these lines, historians have often presented urban Jewish life as an either/or proposition between fully immersing in or rejecting mainstream society. They depict a mature Budapest Jewry as inherently inimical to traditional Jewish identity, overwhelmingly Magyarized, disaffected from the Jewish community, and immersed in the social mainstreams, with new arrivals resisting assimilation only temporarily and a smaller Orthodox or Ultra-Orthodox subcommunity rejecting mainstream society entirely.[23]

This view of Budapest Jewry reflects a broader view of cities that was propagated most notably by the Chicago School of urban studies. Accordingly, Jews and other ethnic groups were able to sustain their traditional community and culture within the nurturing, protective confines of immigrant neighborhoods; once they relocated to new areas of settlement, however, the opportunities and pressures of urban life eroded and then undermined this tradition and culture. As Bettina Hitzer and Joachim Schlör noted, until the 1980s the big city was viewed as "the birthplace of religious indifference and distance, if not outright hostility to church and synagogue."[24] This dichotomy between immigrant neighborhoods and secondary settlements reflects a recurring historiographical tendency to analyze the urban ethnic experience in a decidedly compartmentalized fashion, drawing sharp boundaries between various elements within a particular urban ethnic population. To this end, a sharp line is often drawn between the urban experience of unacculturated, first-generation immigrants and their more acculturated, native-born children as a way of making a distinction between traditional and cosmopolitan elements of a particular ethnic group.

This historiographical tendency has been no less prominent with respect to the Jewish community of Budapest. Historians have conventionally distinguished between the old-fashioned, parochial outlook of unacculturated lower-class *Ostjuden* living in the crowded conditions and social isolation of the immigrant enclave of Terézváros (Theresa District) with the cosmopolitan *Weltanschauung* of native-born, upwardly mobile children and grandchildren of the *Ostjuden* who managed to escape from the old neighborhood and relocate to Lipótváros (Leopold District). Most recently is Julia Richers's in some ways pioneering study of Budapest Jewry that, while grounding the rise of Budapest Jewry in the complexities and nuances of Jewish neighborhoods and institutions as a measure of an expanding urban space, winds up with a Budapest Jewry whose connection to the city and immersion in the social mainstreams overshadows the concurrently thriving Jewish community.[25]

There is no question that a sizable portion of Budapest Jewry was highly Magyarized and religiously indifferent at the beginning of the twentieth century—perhaps the majority. Emblematic in this regard was Theodore Herzl, the assimilated Budapest-born Jew who is conventionally described as having little or no Jewish identity or connection to the Jewish community prior to his encounter with antisemitism and ensuing embrace of Zionism.[26] Yet Jewish communities like Budapest illustrate not only the path away from the Jewish community but rather a combination of centripetal and centrifugal forces that facilitated defection and drift while providing a large, diverse constituency for a broad range of institutions that continued to reinvigorate communal solidarity and identity. This juxtaposition of the centripetal and centrifugal dimensions of urban life is epitomized by the proliferation of a wide variety of Jewish organizations and associations—some specifically Jewish and other not—whose diversity paralleled that of Budapest Jewry itself: synagogues, a Jewish hospital, kosher butchers, Jewish bookstores, charitable organizations, on the one hand; casinos, coffeehouses, and vocational training organizations, on the other; and by the coexistence of Orthodox and Neolog communities in relatively close proximity on a scale unmatched in any other Hungarian Jewish community—indeed, in few communities anywhere in the world. This large-scale coexistence underscores the peculiar relationship between Orthodox Jews with their non-Orthodox Jewish neighbors in Budapest. In Budapest, the Orthodox subcommunity was still a minority at the beginning of the twentieth century within the large Neolog-dominated Jewish community. Nonetheless, it was considerably larger than not only any Orthodox community elsewhere in Hungary, but any Jewish community in Hungary.[27] The complete picture of Budapest Jewry extends beyond a putative sharp divide between traditional, unacculturated immigrants and more acculturated native-born Jews; it illustrates that a Jewish community as large and diverse as Budapest Jewry includes significant numbers of Jews all along the spectrum of Jewish identity.

The expanding array of possibilities that Jews encountered in big cities like Budapest was especially important for Jewish women, who were often excluded from public life and public Jewish life until the beginning of the twentieth century. The dynamic character of the big city, coupled with the size and diversity of the Jewish community, eventually created new possibilities for Jewish women as well as men. The conventional divide between the Jewish home—where women were expected to devote the lion's share of their time and energy—and public Jewish life was eroded in the big city, as the complexity of the city blurred the line between public and private. It was not clear, for example, where a new gathering spot like a coffeehouse or a casino fell on the spectrum of public and private; thus it was not clear whether or not women could participate in these new centers of culture and intellectual discourse. Against this increasingly blurred divide between public and private, the Jewish Women's Association, a hallmark of many Jewish communities in big cities and small towns, discovered a broader range of possibilities in the big city. Charity, for example, was a pillar of the activities of this organization. In the big city, particularly after the decline of the church and prior to the rise of municipal social welfare networks, the philanthropic role of Jewish women took on greater importance.

The new opportunities that arose for Jews, however, did not appeal equally to all Jews. Even at its largest, Budapest was home only to a minority of Hungarian Jews. At the turn of the twentieth century, when nearly one-quarter of Hungarian Jews lived in Budapest, three-quarters of all Hungarian Jews lived elsewhere in Hungary. For many of these Jews, the decision not to relocate to Budapest resulted in part from the belief that the city was less amenable to the way of life they wanted to lead. This reluctance at times extended to newly arrived Jewish settlers in a big city like Budapest. Like other urban Jewish communities, Budapest Jewry was comprised of immigrants, in-migrants, and their children from smaller towns and villages; at any given time, a sizable portion of Budapest Jewry was a generation or less removed from small-town life. Larger cities such as Budapest presented these Jews with opportunities and challenges, and allures and temptations, that were unfamiliar if not unimaginable. For these Jews, transplanting to the city the outlooks and institutions of small-town Jewish communal life was a necessary way to adapt to a radically new set of conditions. Large cities like Budapest, moreover, were generally pivotal intersection points between the Jewish community and the non-Jewish world. Intellectual exchanges between Jews and non-Jews often took place in a major city; and Jewish communities in large cities often mediated between the larger Jewish population and the state. All of this required individual Jews and the Jewish community in a large city like Budapest to navigate one of the central challenges of urbanization, a challenge that Ferenc Erdei termed "*városiasodás*—an on-going expansion of one's cultural character and one's social relations with other urban residents," which challenged communal leaders—and especially defenders of traditional Jewish life—to counter such novelties with more dynamic and fulfilling communal activities and institutions.[28] This meant more than simply balancing Jewish life and the allures of the mainstream. Rather, it constituted what Árpád Tóth has described as a bifurcated interaction between communal institutions and the city: "On the one hand, the need for dynamic urban development facilitated and encouraged the formation of voluntary associations; while, at the same time, these associations shaped the urban society in which they developed."[29] At different times, Jews regarded the challenges and opportunities of a big city like Budapest differently; some with great enthusiasm, others with deep ambivalence. Prior to the 1840s, for example, Pest was not seen as a place that was suitable for raising Jewish children; and Orthodox Jews remained aloof from Pest for a half-century thereafter.

This ambivalence toward the city was neither novel nor unique, neither with respect to Jews nor Budapest. It dates back centuries and was embedded in the varied political and intellectual matrix out of which European society was constructed. Greek philosophers such as Plato regarded the city favorably as a focal point and gathering place of the most virtuous and most ethical individuals. Only in a city, Plato suggested, would enough virtuous and moral individuals be able to live in close enough proximity to one another to combine individual virtue and morality into a collective virtue and morality that would exceed the sum of its parts. Accordingly, as individual inhabitants achieved moral perfection, the city as a whole approached moral perfection. Commenting on Plato, the Muslim Aristotelian philosopher Ibn Rushd (aka Averroes) offered more practical reasons why cities were necessary and beneficial. First, he suggested, the benefits of a collective virtue and morality could only be achieved and maintained in a place where many people could get hold of adequate food, shelter, and other daily needs; a city was best suited to accomplish this task. Second, the city's larger population facilitated division of labor, thus allowing each person to perform those tasks that provided the best result and the most happiness. In other words, in a rural village, everyone had to farm; in Plato's ideal city, theoretically only people who were good at farming and enjoyed farming would farm.30

Christian teachings associated with the city were more mixed. Some Christian leaders, echoing Plato and Averroes, recognized the communal nature of Christian life and the practical advantages of a larger enclave of Christians living in close proximity to one another. Others associated the city with decadence and moral turpitude. Revelations 17:5 described urban life, epitomized by the ancient city of Babylon as "the great mother of prostitutes and of the abominations of the Earth." This was the basis of a common trope through which Christians who were suspicious of cities and wary of their seductive influences could express their disdain for urban life.

The Jewish view of the city combined aspects of Plato's and Averroes's idealistic view with the Christian conceptualization of urban decadence. According to one rabbinic saying, "Ten measures of wealth descended on the world, nine on the city of Rome and the tenth everywhere else." A similar saying taught that "ten measures of beauty descended on the world, nine on Jerusalem, the tenth everywhere else." Rome and Jerusalem exemplified two central aspects of the city: wealth and beauty. Other Jewish views of the city were more practical and functional. One of the most common metaphors for a city in rabbinic tradition is *"Ir va-em be-Yisrael"* (lit. a city and mother in Israel, aka a mother-city).31 The notion of "mother-city" was elaborated by subsequent Jewish thinkers. The sixteenth-century commentator Rabbi David ibn Zimra explained the phrase *"Ir Va-em"* as "a big city that sustains the smaller nearby villages; just as small villages are called the daughters of the big city." Along these lines, Jewish tradition required that every city maintain a level of social justice. Sanhedrin 56a explained the biblical term "*Va-yetzav*" (And he commanded) to mean "*Elu ha-dinin*" (This means establishing justice). An early rabbinic legal text mandated that each city set up "a soup kitchen available all day and a charity box available all week; and that both be available to all residents of a city on an ongoing basis." A city that lacked these basic elements and thus a basic system of social welfare was likened in *Bereshit Rabba* to the quintessentially evil cities of Sodom and Gomorrah.[32]

Later Jewish impressions of the city were more varied, even when reflecting on the same city. Two nineteenth-century Yiddish sayings about Odessa, for example, conveyed opposite impressions: "*lebn vi got in Odes*" (living like a god in Odessa) suggested the city as a epitome of the good life; "*zibn mayl arum Odes brent dos gehenem*" (the fires of hell burn for seven miles around Odessa) described the city as a focal point of depravity, immorality, and corruption. Living in Budapest reflected in this regard the dichotomy that Scott Ury drew between the disorder and chaos embedded in the fluidity and openness of a big city like Budapest, and the order, structure, and institutional framework provided by the Jewish community.[33]

In the face of such ambivalence, one of the central aims of the leadership of Budapest Jewry was constructing an array of institutions that would help newly and recently arriving Jews navigate the challenges and opportunities that they encountered in the big city. In response, Jewish leaders created a network of communal institutions that balanced the task of serving the needs of the Jewish community and preserving Jewish identity with the insurmountable allures of the big city. In retrospect, it is possible to distinguish two overlapping strata in the construction of this institutional array. In eighteenth-century Óbuda and nineteenth-century Pest, the two communities each erected the conventional institutions of Jewish communal life, including a community council, cemetery, new synagogues, an expanded rabbinate and school network, an ever-growing array of voluntary and charitable societies, and in Pest, a Jewish hospital. This array of Jewish communal institutions was modeled after the array of Jewish institutions that Jewish migrants transplanted from other, smaller communities; but, especially in Pest, the eventual scope of these institutions and their prominence in the broader urban institutional landscape exceeded that of other communities. Paradigmatic in this regard was the Dohány Street Synagogue—Pest Jewry's central house of worship. In some ways, this synagogue was a much larger version of synagogues elsewhere, and especially Neolog synagogues, where rabbis and cantors delivered the highest quality weekly sermons and elevated synagogue liturgy and music to its zenith. Yet the size and grandeur of this edifice not only reflected the wealth and self-confidence on the part of Pest Jewry by the end of the 1850s, unmatched anywhere in Hungary and in much of Europe; it also exemplified the inexorable link between the transformation of the city of Pest and the concurrent expanding urban space for Jews there.[34]

The prominence of this synagogue in the architectural and visual landscape of Budapest, moreover, marked a transition to a second stratum of Jewish communal institutions that were created more deliberately to mediate between a connection to the Jewish community and participation in the urban life and culture of the city. These newer institutions began appearing during the 1840s and, as Julia Richers noted, created the medium for Jews and non-Jews to engage together in activities that were not specifically Jewish, and combined existing Jewish communal aims with more novel aims such as Magyarization.[35] Notable among these were the Magyar Israelite Crafts and Agriculture Association (MIKÉFE), the Pest Jewish Women's Association, and the Magyarization Society. The creation of these more novel Jewish organizations complemented the more traditional ones but did not replace or displace them; the Budapest Talmud Society, founded at the end of the 1860s primarily for Orthodox Jews, was typical of the older institutions.

All told, the expansion and increasing complexity of Jewish communal life and especially Jewish communal institutions created ways for these Jews to remain connected to the Jewish community. As this larger and more diverse array of communal institutions attracted not only single male Jewish adventurers and entrepreneurs—initially the lion's share of Jews moving to Pest—but also families with children and observant and Orthodox Jews, the gradual and incremental pace of growth during the first three decades of the nineteenth century accelerated after 1838 into the twentieth century. As such, the rise of Budapest and Budapest Jewry into a major city and a major Jewish community not only paralleled each other but impacted each other. In Budapest, this transformation began in Óbuda with the expanding relationship between Jews and the Zichy family.

2

The Óbuda Kehilla and the Magnate-Jewish Symbiosis

"THE JEWISH COMMUNITY OF ÓBUDA," WROTE LOCAL JEWISH EDUCATOR J. Lipót Berger in 1896, "is regarded as not only the oldest but at the same time among the most distinguished in our country." This sentiment was echoed nearly a decade later by another rabbi and Jewish educator, Bernát Mandl, who noted in 1903 that "after Pressburg, the Jewish community of Óbuda was the most populous and most prestigious of all Hungarian Jewish communities."[1] When Berger and Mandl made their respective comments, however, this observation was already decades out of date. By the beginning of the 1830s, the Jewish community of Óbuda was well on the way toward becoming a satellite of and ultimately being absorbed by the rapidly growing, larger Jewish community of Pest that, by this point, was emerging as the new center of Jewish life in the Hungarian capital.

Hitherto, however, the Jewish community of Óbuda had been, for nearly a century, one of the leading Jewish communities in Hungary, predating the vast majority of Hungarian Jewish communities. At the turn of the nineteenth century, only a handful of Jewish communities in Hungary boasted even the most meager array of communal institutions. Óbuda Jewry had, by this point, already developed into a fully developed and operational Jewish community for a generation.

Like other market town Jewish communities in eighteenth-century Hungary, Poland, and the Czech Lands, the growth of Óbuda Jewry was exemplified by a mixture of stability, incremental growth, continuity, and gradual change. The Jewish community of Óbuda in 1848 bore a similarly striking resemblance to its iteration at the beginning of the nineteenth century, numerically and in terms of its institutional array.[2]

The eventual ascendance of Pest and the ensuing relative paling of Óbuda, therefore, does not eclipse the fact that, for decades heretofore, Óbuda Jewry had been one of the preeminent Jewish communities in Hungary. More than any other prominent Jewish community in turn of the nineteenth century Hungary, the Jewish community of Óbuda's successes had a singular impact on the rise of Hungarian Jewry, not least of all by laying the foundation for the rise of Pest Jewry. The relationship that Óbuda Jewry established with the convoluted hierarchy of municipal, country, and state government, coupled with the community's institutional array, would become a template for the subsequent rise of Pest and other new Jewish communities during the course of the nineteenth century. As such, the rise of the Jewish community of Óbuda linked the decline and disappearance of the Jewish community of Buda with the rise of a new Jewish community in Pest—the first step toward the rise of Budapest and its Jewish community.

The foundation of the Jewish community of Óbuda began with its relationship with the Zichy family, the magnate family that owned and controlled the town. This relationship emerged during the eighteenth century, supplanting an older relationship between Jews and the Hungarian royal crown that had largely run its course by the end of the seventeenth century. Magnate patronage of Jews in eighteenth-century Óbuda, as in other market towns, would prove to be a decisive element in the rise of large Jewish communities in the metropolitan centers of East Central Europe a century later. As the relationship stabilized between Jews in Óbuda and the Zichy family, the Jews constructed an array of communal institutions that managed virtually all facets of Jewish life in the town. The operation of these institutions, ostensibly under Zichy supervision, exemplified the Zichys' administrative strategy that combined meticulous regulation of taxation with the extension of broad latitude to the Jews in other facets of communal life. As long as Jews paid their taxes and provided their magnate benefactors with the requisite gifts, they were left largely undisturbed.

During the second half of the eighteenth century, an added dimension was adjoined to the relationship between the Jews of Óbuda and the Zichy family by the transfer of the town of Óbuda from the Zichy estate to the jurisdiction of the royal crown. Until 1766, the Zichys had taxed and protected Óbuda Jewry, along with other Jews on the Zichy estate, as *földesúr* (lord of the estate, *Grundherr* in German), with virtually absolute sovereignty and with little or no intrusion from the Habsburg crown.[3] From 1766 on, Count Zichy governed Óbuda and its Jewish community as high sheriff (*főispán*) of Pest County on behalf of the Habsburg dynasty in its capacity as royal crown of Hungary; that is, not as a magnate benefactor per se, but as what R. J. W. Evans termed a "bureaucratized magnate."[4] Despite Óbuda's change of jurisdiction and Count Zichy's change in official capacity, the situation of Óbuda Jewry remained largely unchanged. The patent that the Zichy family gave to Óbuda Jewry in 1765, the latest renewal of the original patent to the Jews in 1738, remained in effect long after the town and its Jews came under royal administration.[5] This patent anticipated many of the commercial and residential reforms legislated by Joseph II and was left largely undisturbed by the latter's patent to the Jews of Óbuda.

Indicative of the complexity of the Jews' relationship with the Zichys was an ostensibly minor incident that took place in the spring of 1788, when a fire consumed much of Hunfalu, a village in Pest County. The fire impoverished the town's thirty-eight Jewish families, depriving them of the means to pay their share of the Toleration Tax for the 1787 and 1788 fiscal years. Facing the possibility of losing their residence permits and being evicted, the thirty-eight families asked the Jewish community of Óbuda to intervene with the royal treasury on their behalf. The Jews of Óbuda, in turn, petitioned the high sheriff of the county, Count Károly Zichy. Count Zichy, noting the intervention of Jews from Óbuda, forgave the debt of the thirty-eight families for the two years.[6] Nor was this an isolated occurrence. From 1787 to 1790, the Jews of Óbuda appealed for assistance to Count Zichy nearly a dozen times, and for a variety of reasons. Most dramatically perhaps, in 1790 the Jews of Óbuda asked Count Zichy to intervene on behalf of the family of a deceased Jewish woman who had been converted to Christianity postmortem in the hospital where she died before the family had been able to retrieve the body for proper burial.[7] These events reflected how the Zichy family—much like other magnate families such as the Eszterházy, Batthyány, Pálffy, Károlyi, Csáky, and Erdődy families—provided protection and periodic exceptional treatment to their Jewish subjects in the face of burdensome royal obligations such as the Toleration Tax. Jews on the Zichy estate had maintained this sort of relationship with the Zichy family since the end of the seventeenth century; Jews in Óbuda since around 1715.[8]

That magnate politics rather than Habsburg reforms were more decisive in Óbuda suggests a need to rethink the triangular relationship between Jews, magnates, and the Habsburg dynasty in eighteenth-century Hungary, particularly the impact of Joseph II's Edict of Toleration in light of the preexisting relationship between Jews and magnates. Historians have conventionally contrasted Joseph II's efforts to remove occupational and residential restrictions from Hungarian Jews, especially during the 1780s, with the austerity of magnate rulers in market towns. Jews under magnate rule, it is argued, languished as "sojourners, their presence problematic to the minds of the surrounding population."[9] Accordingly, Joseph II's Edict of Toleration for Hungarian Jewry is regarded as a key moment in the longer political trajectory of Hungarian Jewry: a seminal, albeit short-lived first step toward the civic amelioration and eventual emancipation of Hungarian Jewry—a false dawn that presaged the more lasting, comprehensive reforms of the 1840s and the 1860s. By the same token, the negation of Joseph II's patent by Law 38 of 1790, through which the Hungarian National Assembly reinstated much of the pre-Josephinian status quo, is generally regarded as a setback for Hungarian Jews. A retrograde Hungarian nobility, historians have argued, undermined an attempt by an enlightened absolutist to improve the plight of Hungarian Jews, thus delaying any real improvement in the status of Hungarian Jews for nearly a half-century.[10]

To be sure, there were instances in which the austerity of magnates was undeniable, particularly in Transdanubia. The harsh restrictions that, most notably, the Eszterházy family placed on their Jewish subjects in Sopron County remained largely unchanged between 1694 and the 1830s. In such cases, Joseph II's Edict of Toleration gave the Jews a brief reprieve.[11] By the end of the eighteenth century, however, the austerity of Transdanubian magnates was increasingly the exception in the broader context of magnate-Jewish relations in Hungary. This was due in no small part to a shift in the demographic center of Hungarian Jewry from Transdanubia to central Hungary beginning in the second half of the eighteenth century, a demographic shift that was reflected, among other things, by the rise of Óbuda and its Jewish community to prominence. The vast majority of Hungarian Jews continued to reside in magnate-controlled market towns well into the nineteenth century. Yet more and more lived in the market towns of central and northeastern Hungary, where the pressing need to repopulate towns and rebuild commerce prompted ruling magnate families to implement some of the same changes on their own estates that Joseph II would later impose on a kingdom-wide basis in a single, dramatic act of legislation.

These magnates incrementally diminished restrictions on Jewish residence, travel, and trade. They allowed Jews to settle in virtually all the towns and villages on their estate, to travel freely under magnate tutelage, traffic in a much broader range of commercial goods, engage in crafts, distill and sell alcoholic beverages, absorb newcomers, build new homes and synagogues and rebuild decaying ones, and establish a full array of communal institutions. For these Jews, the dimensions of Joseph II's patent that removed residential and occupational restrictions merely glossed an expanding array of magnate-sponsored opportunities with a royal stamp of approval. Moreover, in contrast to Joseph II's concerted attempts to refashion the internal leadership and administration of the Jewish community, Count Zichy's administration of Óbuda remained largely aloof from internal Jewish matters. To be sure, Óbuda Jews had lost the right to issue a *Herem* (writ of excommunication). Yet, by maintaining the remaining elements of communal administration, the Jewish community of Óbuda remained largely intact.

In one important respect, though, Count Zichy's enhanced role as a royal official augmented the influence of Óbuda Jewry: the ability to intercede on behalf of Jewish communities located outside the Zichy estate. This would prove crucial in 1791 when the Jews of Pér, a small town in Transylvania, asked Óbuda Jewry to intercede on their behalf with the royal crown when faced with a blood libel accusation. The complex dynamics of the ensuing negotiations between Óbuda Jewry, the Zichy family, the magnate owners of Pér (who were also royal officials), and the Habsburg dynasty enabled Óbuda Jewry to extend its influence from Hungary proper to Transylvania—no small feat amid Habsburg efforts to treat these two regions virtually as separate possessions. This incident, relatively minor in the broader history of Hungarian Jewry, would prove to be an important rehearsal for the Jews in Óbuda to intervene on behalf of Jews in Pest; and, more importantly, for Budapest Jewry to intervene on behalf of Hungarian Jewry.

ZICHYS AND JEWS:
FROM TRANSDANUBIA TO ÓBUDA

The Zichys were a prestigious noble family whose pedigree dated back to the thirteenth century. They were one of a handful of magnate families allowed to use a title, their title being count. The Zichy family entered the ranks of the magnates at the end of the sixteenth century with the appointment of György Zichy to the office of deputy-sheriff of Moson County in 1580, a position he held for eleven years. A member of the Zichy family held this office for much of the seventeenth century, until István Zichy was appointed high sheriff in 1682. The same year, István Zichy was appointed high sheriff of Szabolcs County and the chief captain of the town of Zsámbék in Pest County. His son Péter was appointed as an advisor to Habsburg monarch Joseph I in 1694. A year later, Péter was allowed to inherit his father's positions in Szabolcs County and Zsámbék. Later, he was awarded in perpetuity the position of high sheriff in neighboring Pest County. Unlike István, who lived mainly in Oroszvár (Karlburg), Péter lived mainly in Zsámbék, where he would eventually relocate the center of the estate. In 1708, he married Zsuzsanna Bercsényi, who bore him two sons, László and Miklós. The latter married Erzsébet Berényi in 1734 and assumed leadership of the estate during the 1740s.[12]

Count István Zichy, the family patriarch at the end of the seventeenth century, was the first to govern Jewish subjects. In 1676 he issued a *privilegium* to the Jews of Oroszvár, a well-established Jewish community in Habsburg-controlled western Hungary. Although not as elaborate and detailed as the *privilegium* that the Eszterházy family would grant to the Jews of Sopron County two decades later, the Zichy patent anticipated the austere tone of the latter.[13] At the heart of the Zichys' administration was an attempt to obtain the highest economic productivity from their subjects while keeping the number of economically undesirable subjects at a minimum. This dual aim was common among magnates in Hungary and elsewhere. The singular influence of a powerful Polish, Czech, or Hungarian magnate over a market town that the family not only ruled but owned, overwhelmed the demands of the local townsfolk to exclude Jews. This mandate allowed the ruling family to invite and even encourage Jews to settle largely for commercial reasons, with little or no objection from the local Christian population that was largely powerless in the face of the magnate's absolute authority.[14] As Gershon Hundert noted regarding magnates in Poland: "Very frequently the motivation behind the actions of a magnate should be understood as related to his material interests, especially to the expansion of his share of lucrative patronage positions."[15]

Likewise, the 1676 patent encouraged settlement by Jews who could provide substantial revenue to the estate treasury, while discouraging any significant increase in the number of less affluent Jews. To this end Count Zichy granted privileged status to a select group of Jews who were "born or protected here in Karlburg, to engage in any kind of commerce commonly done by Jews." He also allowed them to worship and perform Jewish rituals, bury their dead, and conduct weddings, all "without hindrance." These privileges came at a very high fee, which Zichy spelled out at the conclusion of this patent: "Whereas the above-mentioned Jews promise to obligate themselves to comport themselves in a true, sincere, and righteous fashion, they will remit annually fifteen gulden per person."[16]

In order to maximize the revenue paid by Jews to the estate treasury, Zichy exempted Jews from typical obligations to state or county governments, including annual gifts and taxes, service obligations, and billeting soldiers. The Zichy family's emphasis on protecting the economic viability of their Jewish subjects remained at the heart of this relationship. Annually, and sometimes semiannually, Count Zichy met with the Jews of Oroszvár to settle existing debts owed by the Jews to the estate and, based on the outcome of this meeting, to determine the tax and gift obligations for the coming year.[17]

The aim of limiting Jewish settlement while welcoming affluent Jews remained at the heart of Zichy administration in Oroszvár. In 1728, for example, Károly Zichy leased a large apartment complex known as the Polish Manor to the Jews of Oroszvár and promised to pay for necessary repairs: "If some unexpected event occurs such as a fire breaking out or storm blowing (or whatever God will do) and the house or courtyard is damaged in any way, the Jews shall not be charged, rather the estate shall bear the expenses; if the aforementioned community puts up money to undertake repairs ... the cost will be deducted from the annual fees owed by Jews." At the same time, Zichy allowed only select Jews to reside in this domicile: "Lest the aforementioned Jewish community better accommodate itself with an increase of Jews from neighboring towns and villages [lit. suburban Jews] and gain further advantage in commerce, only the abovementioned [i.e., already privileged] Jews are permitted to reside or trade in the abovementioned courtyard."[18] This aim included protecting economically desirable Jews from criminal prosecution. In 1714, a Jewish subject of Péter Zichy was accused of murdering two other Jews and injuring a non-Jew, Simon Wolfgang. The accused was arrested and ordered to pay restitution to the victims' families and to Wolfgang. At this point, Zichy intervened and tried to relieve his subject from this obligation. When Habsburg monarch Charles VI/III intervened, ordering the Diet of Komárom County to enforce the payment, Zichy relented.[19]

Other instances, though, revealed the limit of the Zichys' willingness to protect Jewish subjects. In 1715, Péter's brother Károly Zichy contracted with Isaac Hirschl of Győr to sell grain from Oroszvár to the estate treasury. According to the terms of this contract, "the aforementioned Hirschl the Jew will pay annually four hundred and fifty Rheinish forints, and will provide the lord of the estate with all the beer he needs at a cheap rate." In addition, Hirschl was permitted to sell beer "only in the aforementioned house, and nowhere else in Moson County," and was required to use the estate's designated miller to procure grain for beer. The last clause of this contract underscored the limits of Zichy protection: "If a fire breaks out accidentally in the brewery, the damages will be assumed by the estate and not by the brewers; if however, the fire is caused by contraband or illegally brewed beer, the brewers will be held responsible for damages." Hirschl's brewery, in other words, was protected and insured for fire damage by the estate only insofar as it brewed or sold beer for the benefit of the estate.[20]

As the Zichy estate expanded from Moson to Pest County, Zichy policy toward Jews extended to the three nascent Jewish communities there: Palota, Föleges, and Zsámbék. In 1717, János Zichy concluded an agreement with Samuel Isaac Löbl of Palota to deliver 1,000 units of corn from Palota to Zsámbék. This agreement included an assurance by Zichy to provide an armed escort for those transporting the grain.[21] In Föleges, the Zichy estate leased to the Jews a portion of the local cornfields—an early example of a Jewish type of merchant later known as *Kornjude*—with the provision that, while Jews would not farm the land, they would receive the revenue from the sale of the corn.[22] Zsámbék, newly reestablished at the end of the seventeenth century, replaced Oroszvár at the discretion of Péter Zichy as the commercial and administrative center of the Zichy estate. The subtle differences between the Zichy administration of Jews in Zsámbék and Oroszvár anticipated Zichy rule in Óbuda. In Zsámbék, the Zichys encouraged, first, an increase in the Jewish population; and second, a more developed and extensive Jewish communal organization to help count and tax Jews.

From the outset, Péter Zichy shielded the dozen Jewish families who settled there during the 1720s from unduly harsh treatment. In 1728, he allowed them to forego paying any taxes for three years. When a county commissioner attempted to impose an annual tax of seventy-five forints on the twelve Jewish families, the Jews petitioned Count Zichy to intervene on their behalf: "As the praiseworthy county has never received a single request from twelve families, we hope and have the utmost trust in his esteemed, vested, sheriff of this laudable county, where we have lived under the aegis of his excellence Count Zichy. Thus we hope not to be refused, as we have lived in Zsámbék in estate households thus far, else it would cause discomfort to the estate."[23]

At the behest of the count, the tax was reduced by 80 percent, a far cry from the much steeper tax obligation that the Zichys had imposed on the Jews of Oroszvár. These measures were codified in a contract between the Jews of Zsámbék and Countess Zsuzsanna Bercsényi-Zichy in 1732 that included provisions for the construction of a synagogue and the designation of land for a Jewish cemetery. In addition, the countess allowed additional Jewish settlement, but only with her permission. Thereafter, a growing number of Jewish migrants settled in Zsámbék, increasing the Jewish population from 90 in 1735 to 283 in 1785.[24] This comparatively less austere magnate administration was not unique to Zsámbék, but detectable elsewhere in central and northeastern Hungary. The Eszterházy family, for example, gave significant tax breaks and imposed comparatively few restrictions on the Jews of Edelény, the family's commercial outpost in Borsod County. They allowed these Jews to trade in a wider range of commercial products.[25]

The charter that Count Sándor Károlyi gave to the Jews of Nagykároly reflected a similar mentality. As was the case in Zsámbék, this charter reflected a decidedly positive view of an increase in the Jewish population of Nagykároly. The initial charter, given to the Jews in 1723, bore a striking resemblance to those given by Polish magnates. Rather than imposing high fees for residence and trade, Károlyi sold arrendator licenses to ten Jews for an annual fee of 300 Rhenish forints. In exchange for this fee, these Jews received from Károlyi "my estate authority and power, the right to judge . . . such that they can proceed in the way in which they are accustomed." He also allowed each to operate a Jewish wine tavern for an additional payment of 500 forints, as a security deposit "lest they are secretly selling wine other than Jewish wine openly to residents or outsiders; if they sell or provide even a bucketful, they will be charged a fine of 500 forints." In addition, Károlyi invited the Jews to "form . . . a school so that they may educate their children; similarly, a suitable cemetery, for which they will pay 300 forints to the estate." In clear contrast to the patents given to Jews by magnates in Transdanubia, Károlyi concluded this letter with an invitation for additional Jews to settle: "More houses can be erected, and Jews other than those listed above can settle and reside in them. Each household will pay three forints annually. Anyone who settles in a noble or resident house other than those built by me can find shelter under my wing by paying five forints annually. Those who keep these obligations I shall protect against everything."[26]

This last clause was put to the test nearly two decades later, when a fire destroyed ten Jewish houses. Károlyi not only permitted the ten houses to be repaired but also twenty new ones to be constructed. "Although I initially contracted in 1723 to protect a certain number of Jews, I became aware of the felicity that I could gain by tolerating not only those already permanently residing, but from an increase." At this point, Károlyi added several privileges, allowing the Jews to be master craftsmen and to sell alcohol to the non-Jewish population for an annual fee of twenty forints. He also allowed Aaron Löebl, the ritual slaughterer licensed by the estate, to sell meat to Christians. He allowed the communal tribunal to assess and collect taxes, and to make rulings on internal civil and criminal matters.[27]

ZICHYS AND JEWS: ÓBUDA

This more welcoming approach to governing Jewish subjects would define from the outset the way that the Zichys governed the Jews of Óbuda. By 1700, the Zichys had acquired the town of Óbuda and relocated their main residence to the town's central square, as well as the estate board of exchange and house of council. This was a major acquisition that brought close commercial and political connections to Buda and, later, to Pest; Óbuda quickly replaced Zsámbék as the capital of the Zichy estate.[28]

From the outset, the Zichys encouraged extensive settlement in Óbuda by peasants, artisans, and Jews. The Zichys promoted a more diversified economy that combined commerce, agriculture, manufacturing, and artisanal trades, thus creating a wider range of opportunities for Jews and other settlers. Óbuda's economy, more than that of Pest or Buda, had closer ties to local agriculture, a growing manufacturing sector, and a more diverse array of artisanal trades. For many recently settled peasants, viticulture in Óbuda was a primary source of income, rather than an auxiliary source as in Pest and Buda.[29] The number of households supported by viticulture increased from 129 in 1720 to 504 by 1780. Manufacturing in Óbuda was more significant than in Buda, stirred by the infusion of capital during the 1770s by Joseph Beywinkler and Jacob Höpfinger, two Vienna silk manufacturers whose factories in Óbuda soon outproduced their counterparts in Vienna.[30] In addition, many artisans settled in Óbuda because the master craftsmen in Pest and Buda prevented them from joining guilds and practicing their trades.[31]

By abrogating the Hill Tax (hegyvám), moreover, the Zichys made it easier for peasants and artisans of limited means to settle. Count Zichy also gave all residents of Óbuda the right to own a house, courtyard, and vineyard, thus making Óbuda an even more attractive place to settle. The number of urbarial households in Óbuda increased rapidly from 166 in 1720 to 650 in 1770.[32]

Óbuda Jews, too, benefited from this varied economy, especially in comparison to Jews in nearby Buda and Pest. Jewish settlement began as early as 1715, when Jacob Flés was provided armed protection to transport two gold forints' worth of fabric to Óbuda.[33] From the outset, Jews in Óbuda could buy and sell a large array of agricultural products, including sugar, wool, and animal hides. The Zichys endorsed an array of artisanal trades for Jews that included not only more established trades such as coppersmiths, tinsmiths, and glaziers but also newer trades that were generally unwelcome in Pest and Buda, including turners, button makers, tailors, stocking weavers, cutlers, rope makers, locksmiths, and saddle makers. These newer trades were often more open to Jews than more established trades. By 1744, there were twelve registered Jewish artisans in Óbuda: five tailors, three cobblers, two soap makers, one furrier, and one glazier. Not surprisingly, Óbuda Jewry increased more rapidly during the half-century between 1737 and 1787 than any other Jewish community in Hungary. In 1727, twenty-four Jewish families residing in five houses enjoyed the protection of Countess Zichy in exchange for a tax that alternated annually between three and eight forints. By 1737, the Jewish population of Óbuda surpassed that of Buda, and Jews owned ten houses near the Zichy Palace. All told, the number of Jews increased concurrently from 24 families and 88 Jews in 1727 to 56 families in 1744, 59 by 1752, 109 by 1767, and 320 by 1787.[34]

Historians typically attributed the growth of the Jewish community after midcentury to the expulsion of the Jews from Buda by Maria Theresa at the end of the 1740s. As Sándor Büchler noted more than a century ago: "Around this time the Jews who were expelled from Buda settled in Óbuda, where previously only a few Jewish families had lived. . . . Óbuda Jewry increased following the expulsion of Jews from Buda. . . . Even before the expulsion it was more numerous than Buda but did not play as significant a role."[35] In fact, this increase resulted primarily from the efforts of the Zichy family to attract Jews to Óbuda. On the heels of the expulsion from Buda, Countess Bercsényi-Zichy, wife of Count Zichy, invited the expelled Jews to settle in Óbuda, acknowledging that the presence of Jews facilitated an orderly and rational urban development and commercial expansion: "Everywhere order is that which is desired above all . . . and is that which the jurists of the Óbuda Jewish community have adhered to. Their camaraderie and harmony toward each other, coupled with their loyalty and sense of duty to this estate, will insure that order and justice will be preserved."[36] The countess's *privilegium* to the Jews of Óbuda reflected the Zichys' overall administrative outlook for the town of Óbuda, articulated by her husband, Count Miklós Zichy, in his patent to the burghers of Óbuda: "Because order is demanded in all things, I am instructing the Óbuda magistrate, council, and populace how to behave in order to enhance fraternity among them." Just as Count Zichy set up a permanent council, whose authority derived from his and was binding on all communal affairs, the countess's invitation established a permanent Jewish community council that owed homage to the Zichy family.

The expanding opportunities and stable situation for Jews in Óbuda were consolidated and codified in the *privilegia* given to Óbuda Jews by the Zichy family. The 1737 patent was issued by Countess Zsuzsana Bercsényi-Zichy, wife of Péter Zichy;[37] this patent was renewed in 1746, and then renewed again and expanded in 1765 by Bercsényi-Zichy's daughter in-law Countess Erzsébet Zichy-Berényi, wife of Miklós Zichy. This last charter maintained and solidified the Zichys' overriding balance between facilitating Jewish productivity and maintaining an orderly relationship between Jewish and non-Jewish residents of Óbuda and among the Jews themselves. It formalized the privileges that Óbuda Jewry had enjoyed since the 1730s and added many others.[38]

These privileges laid the foundation for the most elemental aspects of Jewish life, and for the basic responsibilities and jurisdiction of the community's Kehilla (an officially recognized community). The 1737 patent reiterated the status of Jews as protected subjects of the Zichy estate, and warned all others not to disturb them in their rituals and customs. Jews were also warned against "the audacity to act against Christian rituals and customs." The patent, while warning that the homes of Jewish residence were not to be disturbed or molested, added that this protection could be withdrawn if "it would come to pass that one of the occupants commits even a petty crime against an-other." In this case, the domicile would no longer be sacrosanct. The patent maximized the ability of Jewish merchants to turn a profit by allowing them to pay a reduced fee in order to participate in local trade fairs. They were even permitted "to do business and sell their wares in the free and royal cities" under the protection of the Zichy estate. In addition, Jews were exempt from quartering troops, but expected to maintain law and order in their part of the city by "working toward the regulation of morals, commonly known as *Policay-Ordnung.*"[39]

Furthermore, the patent invited the Jewish community to establish the basic insti-tutions of communal life: to purchase the plot of land on which their synagogue would eventually stand, along with an adjoining manor to be used as a communal administra-tion center; to purchase a plot of land for a cemetery and, for a surcharge of twelve fo-rints, to bury the deceased from other towns and villages; to set up a slaughterhouse; to establNished a burial payment for non-native Jews so they could be buried in Óbuda, which laid the foundation for a steady influx of Jewish immigrants; and to enlarge and renovate the synagogue, as long as they did not quarrel or fight inside. In order to en-sure that Jews followed these instructions, the charter imposed fines on anyone who violated the terms of this patent, ranging from 30 to 300 forints.[40]

Above all, these patents authorized Jews to form a Kehilla. The establishment of an officially recognized Jewish community in Óbuda beginning in 1738 culminated the community's incremental beginning. A decade and a half after the first Jew settled in Óbuda in 1712, the eighty-eight Jews who were there came under the protection of the Zichy family in 1727. A decade later, Countess Zichy laid the foundation for a perma-nent, recognized Jewish community by granting Jews the right to bury their dead in Óbuda and granting them land for a cemetery.[41]

Thereafter, the foundation stone for the internal, institutional development of the Óbuda Jewish community was laid by clauses in the 1737 and 1767 patents that autho-rized the Jews of Óbuda "to elect new judges, jurors, and deputy-judges annually or to reinstate existing ones, who will . . . have jurisdiction over lawsuits between Jews and Christians and between Jews. Ultimate authority, however, will reside with the crown." From the outset, Countess Bercsényi-Zichy allowed the Jews to elect their commu-nal officers with no outside interference, as long as they kept her apprised of the elec-tion results, with one exception: she instructed the outgoing president to remain *ex of-ficio* as a member of the tribunal (*bet din*) for at least one year. Communal elections proceeded accordingly into the nineteenth century. In 1769, for example, the Kehilla elected a new slate of officers except for the presiding officer. The slate was submit-ted to and approved by Countess Zichy-Berényi, the daughter-in-law and successor of Countess Bercsényi-Zichy. Similarly, in 1773 the list of officers, "compiled in the pres-ence of community Rabbi Nathan Ginsburg who certified the election," was signed by Ginsburg, Pest County prefect Franciscus Xavier Ferber, and three Jewish council members: Jeremiah Kopel, Abraham Israel, and David Boskovitz. In 1787 and 1794, the list of a newly elected twenty-one-member council was submitted to and approved by the countess. This protocol continued at least until 1809.[42]

The patent held communal officers "responsible for preserving a sense of order," and instructed them "to be discreet and impartial, to dismiss indiscreet and biased members, and to ensure that Kehilla members refrained from quarreling in the synagogue." Kehilla leaders were to "make certain that communal taxes be assessed and collected justly, and that the Jews keep precise accounts."[43] All of this laid the groundwork and set the parameters for a functioning Kehilla leadership and for an associated *bet din*—comprised initially of lay leaders and eventually including the community rabbi. The *bet din* was tasked with adjudicating mainly intracommunal civil disputes, and at times disputes between Jews and non-Jews. The members of the tribunal were authorized to impose penalties, ranging from the withdrawal of synagogue privileges (for example, being called to the Torah, serving on the Kehilla board), to public shaming, and in extreme cases, to corporal punishment (which was later banned by Joseph II).

The patent also empowered the Kehilla board to impose taxes on the members of the community and to appoint judges for the community's tribunal from a slate of thirty-three candidates approved by Countess Zichy. In addition, the patent allowed outsiders to join the Jewish community as long as they were registered. Unregistered residents were not to be honored by being called to the Torah. All Jews who resided in Óbuda were eligible and expected to join the Kehilla. As was the case elsewhere, membership was divided into three categories based on the annual fee that a particular household was able to pay. The benefits of membership increased steadily from the 1740s on; membership provided access to an array of communal institutions that operated under the supervision of the Kehilla.

The earliest documented meeting took place in the spring of 1769. At this meeting, the presiding officer reported on the annual budget, including a careful rendering of revenue from donations and communal taxes and expenses. The latter included standard expenses such as the salaries of communal employees, and recurring expenses such as the cost of repairs to the synagogue, cemetery, and other community buildings and property.[44] By the end of the 1780s, the Jewish community of Óbuda was the leading community in Pest County. Not only did the Jews of Óbuda pay the largest single share of the annual Toleration Tax, the leaders of Óbuda Jewry negotiated annual discounts in the payment of the tax for themselves and for other Jewish communities in Pest County. These discounts for individual communities ranged from 20 to 40 percent of the total tax payment. For Jewish communities whose tax payments were in arrears, the Jews of Óbuda obtained an extension on the deadline for payment and convinced county authorities not to assess fines on unpaid or truant tax payments.[45]

The Kehilla council not only supervised communal affairs but was also, by the end of the 1760s, a reliable source of employment in Óbuda for Jews and non-Jews alike. Per the 1737 patent's instruction that the Jews of Óbuda police the Jewish quarter of the city, the Kehilla hired several night-watchmen who patrolled the streets, sometimes alone and sometimes in pairs.[46] The Kehilla also engaged the services of chimney sweep Johannes Mohl several times a year at an annual cost of forty-three forints.[47] In addition, during the 1780s, flour miller Salamon Bohl had a contract with the Kehilla to provide 100 centners (5,000 kg) of flour annually at a cost of five forints per centner.[48] Apart from these ongoing contracts, the Kehilla also engaged local contractors and day laborers on an ad hoc basis. When lumber was needed for construction or renovation projects, local lumber merchant Mihály Konyha provided lumber and related materials such as nails.[49] When repairs to the synagogue foundation required redigging part of the foundation, the Kehilla engaged the services of ten day laborers for five days at a cost of five forints each.[50]

In general, the Jewish community's ability to enforce its own preexisting statutes was more easily implemented and enforced when they echoed one or more of the statutes in the charter, as evidenced by two areas of communal administration: absorbing newcomers and protecting Jews outside the Zichy estate. The 1737 charter granted Óbuda Jews the right to settle, travel, or relocate anywhere on Zichy lands with estate protection, and, for a fee of one gold coin, protected anyone who married a resident of Óbuda. The charter also required any Jew who wanted to leave the estate to obtain permission from and negotiate an exit fee with both the Zichy estate and the Jewish community.[51] Moreover, the charter required nonresident Jews seeking to join the Jewish community to secure a letter of protection from the estate and to negotiate an entrance fee with the Jewish community. When Eliezer Segal wanted to relocate to Óbuda from Tétényi, about ten miles northeast of Székesfehérvár, his petition to settle in Óbuda without the permission of the Jewish community was rejected.[52] In order to protect Jewish merchants, the 1765 charter prohibited nonresident Jews from opening a store or stall prior to obtaining a letter of privilege.[53]

At the same time, the 1765 charter explicitly permitted Jews to house strangers, a clause that the Jewish community used as the basis for allowing or denying Jewish outsiders to settle or even visit. This required a would-be Jewish settler to obtain permission from the Jewish community, as well as permission from the city of Óbuda. Officially the latter meant petitioning the town council; in practice, it meant securing permission from Count Zichy in his capacity as lord of the estate prior to 1766, and as sheriff of Pest County from 1766 on. The end result was a *Hezkat Iranit*, a writ of legal residence:

> Let it be said that the above mentioned is worthy to live as one of us as a resident of our community . . . to reside and trade, to import merchandise without impediment

or interference. He, his wife, their progeny, and the children yet to be born are covered in perpetuity by this *Hezkat Iranit* with the approval of our most merciful Lord. They are thereby legal residents of the city and of this land. They have access to all seats in the synagogue.[54]

An applicant's chances for acceptance depended on multiple factors, including the applicant's extant residence status and place of origin, the extent to which his inclusion was regarded as beneficial to the greater good of the Jewish community, and the endorsement of Count Zichy. A representative example was the case of Mordechai Feldsherr, who applied for a residence permit in 1778: "At this assembly, the officers discussed the petition of Mordechai Feldsherr from Kompaltz, a doctor ... who, having received training from the medical faculty in Prague, had proof of an imperial privilege. ... Owing to his skill at his craft and that he is an expert in many things ... the Kehilla has determined that he can practice here and is allowed to reside here along with his wife, and to have the house with the alley." The endorsement of Count Zichy was especially crucial in the case: "There are reservations among the officers, but the support of the most gracious ruler helps us reach a more immediate consensus."[55] The most straightforward requests were from those applicants who already lived under Zichy protection and who asked to relocate to Óbuda from elsewhere in Pest County or on the Zichy estate; typical in this regard was Samuel Rosenthal, a protected Jew in Vasvár, who successfully petitioned the Jewish community and Óbuda royal crown for permission to relocate to Óbuda.[56]

While welcoming many Jews who wanted to settle in Óbuda, the community nonetheless took measures to prevent member families from housing unauthorized guests: "[The *Sculklopfer*] shall go from house to house to warn the members of our community against hosting any guest without the knowledge and approval of the kahal, subject to punishment and fines, and to warn authorized guests that they are subject to the same regulation."[57] By the 1780s, the growing presence of illegally residing Jews prompted Jewish communal leaders to work together with the Zichy estate to curb this problem:

Despite prior warnings from the estate not to abet any stranger if they do not pass through in a few days or less and act with the proper demeanor, there is as yet no supervision of this statute. ... and the members of our community have for half or even an entire year housed outsiders and quartered men, women, and children on various pretexts ... and have provided them and their wives and children flats like a member of our own community. ... The leaders of the community are obligated to "burn the thorns from the vineyard" [*le-va'er ha-kozim min ha-kerem*]. To this end, a deputy of the Kehilla will issue each visitor an overnight pass [*nacht zettel*], which

will allow them to remain for a few days, thus relieving them from the harsher penalties from the estate.[58]

Jews in Óbuda, along with other residents, were instructed by the County Lieutenancy's Council (*helytartótanács*) to "watch out for alien and dubious individuals
... especially itinerant Jews [*herumziehenden Juden*] hiding in privately owned domiciles." This concern was especially pronounced during time of war when there was a concern that itinerants might be intelligence operatives for foreign states. Despite attempts
to crack down on illegal settlement, all Jews in Óbuda, whether residing legally or illegally, were considered part of the Jewish community to some extent.[59] This was aided by
the fact that the tribunal of the Jewish community, though authorized to adjudicate all
cases between and involving Jews, was part of the broader judicial hierarchy of Óbuda
and Pest County. Jews in Óbuda who disagreed with the decision of the tribunal periodically exercised the option of appealing its decision to one of several state courts, including the county magistrate, the county high sheriff, and the Zichys' manorial court.

Disputes that came before the tribunal in Óbuda would not infrequently drag on for
an extended period of time. For example, when Abraham Israel sued Hirschl Löbl for
damages in a civil dispute, the tribunal ruled in favor of Israel. Löbl appealed the case
to the Zichys' manorial court, which ruled in his favor. Israel then appealed the case
to the county magistrate, who overturned the decision of the manorial court and reinstated the decision of the tribunal, which ordered Löbl to pay Israel the 200 forints he
claimed, plus a fifty-forint late fee and three forints to cover Israel's cost of appealing. All
told, the case lasted from the spring of 1783 until the fall of 1786.[60] Similarly, an equally
contentious civil dispute between Moses Bernwald and Abraham Oppenheimer in
1791 eventually wended its way from the tribunal to the manorial court, to the county
magistrate, and then back to the manorial court until the original decision of the tribunal was upheld.[61]

Marriage and inheritance disputes that came before the Óbuda tribunal could be
equally contentious and protracted. In one case, Abraham from Hunfalva arranged
for his son Naftali to marry the daughter of Óbuda Jew Aron Kitzer. Kitzer broke
the engagement, claiming that "he never wanted it to happen and his daughter finds
the groom to be nauseating." When the tribunal ruled in Kitzer's favor, his rival from
Hunfalva appealed to the county magistrate. After a witness affirmed that Kitzer's version of the story was correct, the magistrate ruled in Kitzer's favor. Abraham appealed
the case to the manorial court, who dismissed the appeal, rendering Kitzer the victor.[62]
Inheritance disputes could be just as contentious and prolonged. The will of recently
deceased Simon Löbl left instructions that his close friend David Kornitzer be the executor of his estate. Two of Löbl's relatives, the brothers Israel and Moses (probably his
sons), claimed that Kornitzer was biased against them and would prevent them from

properly claiming their share of the estate. The tribunal rejected their petition to re-move Kornitzer. On appeal, the brothers claimed that the judges of the tribunal were biased against them. The county magistrate rejected this claim and, after nearly two years, the estate was divided up, per the deceased's instruction, with Kornitzer as the executor.[63] An equally contentious court battle took place between Gitl Austerlitz and her father, Reb Mordechai. Austerlitz claimed that her father had wrongfully denied her the inheritance that her maternal grandmother, Ceperl Herzlemann, had promised her. When the tribunal ruled in the father's favor, the daughter appealed to the mano-rial court, which ruled in her favor.[64]

A NETWORK OF INSTITUTIONS

From the outset, the Kehilla created a network of Jewish communal institutions. The first synagogue, founded in 1738, would remain the community's main synagogue un-til 1820, when a larger synagogue was completed on Lajos utca, designed by famous ar-chitect András Landherr. This latter synagogue was regarded as one of the most beau-tiful in Hungary and the Habsburg monarchy prior to the construction of the Dohány Street Synagogue at the beginning of the 1860s. When seats in the original synagogue were put up for sale, the community's officers chose their seats first, followed by Jews who had paid their annual membership dues according to the level of dues they paid. Thereafter, per a community statute renewed in 1774, "All remaining seats in synagogue, in the men's and women's sections, will be auctioned off to individuals residing here permanently first and then to those residing here temporarily . . . yet it should also be made known to all who pass through that, for anyone who needs additional seats, an arrangement will be made with those seats that were acquired in order that everyone be able to find his place peaceably."[65]

By the 1780s, the synagogue became not only the main space for Jews to pray com-munally but a central hub for meeting and exchanging information reflected by the va-riety of announcements and messages that were written on a placard near the door of the synagogue. At one point, the list of announcements included the following: the Zichy estate reminding the Jewish community that they were prohibited from hous-ing transients in the synagogue, even for one night; regulations for family celebrations that take place in the synagogue; a forthcoming auction for a kosher wine lease; an of-fer of child care; a reminder to those in arrears to pay their taxes promptly; a request to register all leeches, "examined and unexamined," with local physician Dr. Claudius; an appeal by the local prefect to use Abraham Krautner as creditor; and several lost and found notices, including a soldier's gold watch, a master sergeant's silver item, and a candleholder missing from the Franciscan Church in Buda.[66] The synagogue's role as communal hub was complemented by the emergence of a respected rabbinate. The community hired its first rabbi in 1752, Matityahu Nathan Ginsburg, and his successor thirty-one years later, Moshe Münz. Münz came to Óbuda after serving as community rabbi and *rosh yeshivah* in Brody and being recommended by the noted Prague rabbi Ezekiel Landau. In 1793, the Jews of Óbuda petitioned the county magistrate to appoint Münz as the rabbi of Pest County. Once the Jewish communities in the county approved, Münz was appointed.[67]

In 1770, members of the Kehilla founded a local Hevra Kadisha (Jewish burial society). Initially, this organization took charge of preparing the deceased for burial and ensuring that the burial ceremony and subsequent mourning of the dead followed the proper protocol. By 1772, the Hevra Kadisha had expanded its activities to include providing hospice care for those close to death and, eventually, hospice care for the Jewish community. The first Jewish hospice in Óbuda, run by the members of the Hevra Kadisha, was founded in 1772 next to the synagogue. It had sixteen beds in two wards, and hired two local physicians to care for the infirm as well as to make house calls.[68]

One of the main accomplishments of the Jewish community of Óbuda was its improvement of communal education. The first Jewish school, founded in 1742, was a *heder* with a limited Ashkenazic curriculum. Less affluent Jewish children attended this traditional *heder* with a limited Jewish curriculum and substandard teachers; affluent children received first-rate homeschooling by private tutors engaged by their parents. This situation changed in 1784, when, per the instruction of Emperor Joseph II to Óbuda Jews and to other leading Jewish communities in Hungary and elsewhere in the empire, the Jews of Óbuda founded a *Normalschule*. The stated goal of this school was providing a broader, higher quality education to all Jewish children in Óbuda. Implicitly this meant reproducing the education of the wealthy in a way that was accessible to all. Modeled after the Pressburg Jewish *Nationalschule*, the Óbuda *Nationalschule* was to be available not only for Jewish children in Óbuda but throughout Pest County. In exchange, thirteen Jewish communities in the county raised 70 gülden and 50 krajcar to help maintain the school.[69]

The original contract for the school was signed by county chief clerk Michael Ebert for the state, Óbuda *Judenrichter* Abraham Frankel, and three members of the Kehilla board—Moses Oesterreicher, Löbl Holitscher, and Abraham Bobeler. Accordingly, the community acquired a building near the main town square for 2,900 *Wiener Wendung*. Per the agreement, the building would house not only the school but also lodging for teachers. The agreement also stipulated that it was only valid if the school educated Jewish boys and girls, one of the earliest efforts to provide communal education for Jewish girls in Hungary or elsewhere in Europe.[70] At the dedication of the school on June 22, 1784, prominent local Jewish leader Moses Oesterreicher delivered a rousing speech in the presence of "numerous local dignitaries." The opening of the school generated such interest that members of the Jewish community stood outside the school watching and listening to the teachers through the windows. According to one observer, the noise and din created by the onlookers was disturbing to the point that the head of the Jewish community hired a local gendarme (*hajdú*) to disperse them with a cane. This did not diminish the enthusiasm for the school. By June 1785, the Jewish communal record noted that 119 boys and 19 girls had enrolled (though the city's official account listed 56 boys and 5 girls).[71]

Despite the shared good intentions of the state and the Jewish community, the new school faced a series of difficulties during its early years. By 1790, the building that housed the new school was rundown and in need of serious repair, prompting a debate over whether the building was salvageable or whether the community needed to buy or lease a new building; and, if the latter, whether the local authorities would permit it. In the end, the decision was reached to repair the existing building.[72]

More serious was the reluctance of affluent parents to send their children to the school. Most chose simply to continue educating their children at home with private tutors. This meant that the school educated predominantly the children of the poor and orphans. The lack of participation from the wealthy made it more difficult to raise money from private Jewish donors, which was badly needed to maintain the building and support the teachers. The situation worsened in 1789 when several wealthy Jewish families attempted to set up a more exclusive Jewish private school in Óbuda. This threatened to draw students away from the *Nationalschule* during its fragile, formative period. In response, the Kehilla leadership, endorsed by the county, prohibited Jews from forming any other school in Óbuda, though homeschooling with private tutors was still allowed.[73] They claimed that rich and poor students alike would benefit from the added knowledge the school would provide and, in particular, took pride in the fact that the school provided instruction in German and Latin. They noted that this school was the first to be approved by Dr. Manes Osterreicher—a communal leader, the first Hungarian Jew to graduate from a Hungarian medical school, and a man who was highly respected in and beyond the Jewish community—who reveled in the fact that "everyone has performed satisfactorily." Finally, they noted that general studies teachers in the school used a state curriculum and methodology.[74]

The problem of attracting affluent parents was further aggravated by conflicts with dissatisfied teachers. Joseph Hebrandt complained to communal judge Lazar Osterreicher that his teaching salary had been withheld, leaving his family in dire financial straits; the Kehilla intervened and he was paid immediately.[75] A more serious challenge to the school's image took place when the school's first and most reputable teacher of Jewish subjects, Abraham Hirsch Kohn, left the school over a salary dispute and returned home to Trencsén. The community struggled to replace him.[76] In response, the school implored Kohn to return to Óbuda and resume teaching, and offered him a 50 percent increase in salary. Kohn agreed on condition that the Kehilla reimburse him not only for the costs of moving back to Óbuda but also retroactively reimburse him for what he had paid to move to Trencsén. The community agreed, and Kohn returned. Once Kohn returned from Trencsén, the Kehilla was able to convince another top teacher, Kohn's colleague Abraham Hirschel Breslauer of Trencsén, to accept a teaching position at the *Nationalschule.*[77]

The Óbuda school suffered another significant setback when the Hungarian National Diet repealed the reforms of Joseph II, including state support for the *Normalschulen.* Thereafter, the community had to raise the money to keep the school going. As a result, the school never reached the size or prominence that its founders had expected during the 1780s, and enthusiasm for the school waned. This last problem was resolved by a generous endowment from the Goldberger family, after whom the school was then named. Once the money was in place, it became easier to offer first-rate teachers a competitive salary. Consequently, the school managed to overcome these "birth pangs." In 1820, the Óbuda *Nationalschule* was still the best Jewish school in Pest County, indeed the best anywhere in Hungary east of Pressburg.

STABILITY AND TENSION: SUPERVISING KOSHER MEAT AND KOSHER WINE

Even more than its role in managing the school, the Kehilla council's ability to influence institutions and mediate intracommunal conflicts was exemplified by its control over two central aspects of Jewish life: the preparing and selling of kosher meat and kosher wine. The 1737 and 1765 patents codified the privileges of Jews to produce and sell kosher meat and wine, less out of a sense of religious toleration or ecumenicism than as a reflection of the Jews' increasingly indispensable role in the local economy: "Whereas Christian butchers are unable to meet the community's demand for meat, such want would cause suffering. Thus the Jews may establish private slaughterhouses that can sell all kinds of meat to Jews or Christians, whether beef or pork. They can engage private Christian butchers who can prepare meat according to their laws, and who can prepare kosher meat for Jews."[78] Per the 1765 patent, moreover, Jews were permitted to import and sell kosher wine, except on Saint Andrew's Day, for an annual payment of 150 forints; and only those ritual slaughterers licensed by the Jewish community and endorsed by the estate could practice their trade.

The first license to slaughter and prepare kosher meat in Óbuda was granted to the Jewish community by Countess Anna Zichy-Berényi in 1737, which, in exchange for the payment of an annual fee, permitted a particular slaughterer or group of slaughterers to set up a *fleischbank* along the Danube River to ensure proper disposal and minimize sanitary concerns. That the proper regulation of the slaughter of kosher meat was seen by Countess Zichy-Berényi more as a civic than a religious issue is indicated by her concern for the impact of ritual slaughter on urban hygiene. To this end, the patent held Jews responsible for "removing the refuse from the slaughterhouse without impeding access to or along the Danube."[79] Initially this contract was renewed and renegotiated annually; the Jewish community licensed two Jewish slaughterers each year to provide kosher meat. By the 1770s, the number had increased to four, then to six at the beginning of the nineteenth century.[80]

To be sure, the right to license specific Jews to procure kosher meat and wine was more complicated than simply employing individuals. The Kehilla's responsibility of licensing Jews as purveyors of kosher meat and kosher wine periodically situated community leaders squarely in the middle of intracommunal squabbles, not least of all because providing kosher wine and meat raised one's social status. For a kosher slaughterer, in particular, a community-issued license was an invaluable source of income and status. From a commercial standpoint, the licensed slaughterers had a monopoly on the slaughter of kosher meat in a given area. Nonlicensed slaughter not only violated a commercial statute enforced by the Zichy family, but also a religious statute. Only the meat of a licensed slaughterer was deemed kosher; the meat provided from an unlicensed slaughterer, regardless of how meticulously and stringently he observed the rabbinically mandated procedures, was by definition not kosher; any Jew who consumed or even purchased this meat was deemed in violation of the Jewish dietary laws and appropriately censured.[81]

The challenge of the Kehilla board and tribunal in these instances was to balance two competing interests of the community as a whole: assuring that only the most capable and reliable individuals would be providing kosher meat and wine, while keeping infighting between competitors to a minimum. As these licenses became more lucrative, the Kehilla board's control over them enhanced the board's influence over communal affairs; concomitantly, the decisions of the Kehilla board came under greater scrutiny. By the 1780s, disputes over the licensing of kosher meat and wine had become chronic, with virtually every meeting of the community's tribunal including several disputes of this sort. This was not only a consequence of the economic implications of licensing decisions. It also reflected that the Kehilla's right to license kosher meat and wine was a venerated, centuries-old responsibility that often crossed the perilous divide between the financial and spiritual needs of the community. Taxes on kosher meat and wine were not only a source of revenue that supported communal institutions and charitable funds, but also an integral part of the traditional lives of most Jews, in Óbuda and elsewhere. The communal obligation to ensure that all Jews had access to kosher wine

for the Sabbath and festivals, in particular, prompted the custom of reciting the kid-
dush prayer in the synagogue on Friday evening, lest even one Jewish family lack the
means to procure wine and welcome the Sabbath properly.[82]

Obtaining a license to brew and sell wine, and renewing an existing license required
the approval of both the Jewish community and the Pest County magistrate. The Jewish
community vetted the applicants and then petitioned the county to approve their
choice to grant or renew. Typically this transaction proceeded smoothly, though not
always. In 1789, for example, the magistrate rejected the community's choice of wine
producers because they doubted the licensees would be able to pay the wine tax reliably
for more than two years. When the Jewish community guaranteed payment of the tax
in the event the individual licensee went into arrears, the application was approved.[83] In
another instance, the county magistrate raised the annual wine tax three times during
the 1770s. This prompted the Jewish community to petition for a freeze on the tax for
the ensuing three years, complaining that it was becoming difficult to find individuals
willing to incur the tax. When the magistrate refused, the Jewish community appealed
to the deputy sheriff (alispán) of Pest County. To their disappointment, the latter told
the Jewish community to cease complaining about the wine tax, lest the community
forfeit the privilege to brew kosher wine entirely.[84]

Despite the increase in the wine tax, Jews in Óbuda continued to vie with one another for licenses to brew wine. This was due in part to the growth of the Jewish community during the 1780s and 1790s, which increased the weekly demand for kosher
wine. By the mid-1780s, the Jewish community was granting or renewing, with state
approval, three licenses annually. Though there was no explicit prerequisite to obtain
a license, typically licensees were not only economically viable and commercially capable, but also related to a member of the Kehilla board.[85] Providing meat was less urgent—consuming meat as part of the Sabbath meal was more a preferred custom than
an actual requirement.[86] The lack of meat did not preclude the possibility of a minimally suitable Sabbath meal. Still, most Jews aspired, at least, to serve meat with dinner
on Friday evening. Often the status of a Jewish family within the Jewish community
was gauged based on the frequency with which the family served meat to their guests
and the quantity and quality of the meat they served.[87]

By the end of the 1780s, expectations regarding licensed butchers had been codified.
When the Kehilla board approved the application of Franz (Ephroim) Reiss, his specific duties, privileges, and responsibilities were spelled out and included the following: (1) Licensed butchers were expected to be meticulous in slaughtering and preparing meat in accordance with Jewish law and custom; and, more importantly, willing to
defer to the community rabbi whenever there was suspicion or doubt as to the fitness
of the meat in question. (2) Each butcher would receive a fair and reasonable annual stipend from the community that enabled the licensed butcher to provide for his family

without driving up the price of kosher meat beyond what community members could afford. (3) Each licensed butcher would receive an annual bonus during the Hebrew months of Tishrei and Nissan (when the holidays that fall during these months raised demand for kosher meat). (4) Licensed butchers were expected to maintain a proper level of decorum and piety, attending services regularly and refraining from improper behavior.[88] Applicants seeking a license to slaughter and sell kosher meat were required to demonstrate that they met these criteria and supply letters of approbation, either from a member of the local Kehilla board or from a dignitary from another Jewish community. More often than not, one of the support letters came from a rabbi. Applicants also indicated some measure of commercial acumen as well.[89]

The complexities associated with obtaining a license to provide kosher meat or wine were further complicated by questions relating to the sale of meat and wine in Óbuda. The intricacies of these questions surpassed the specific rules listed in the patents, and thus required the Jewish tribunal to interpret these rules so as to apply them equitably and reasonably. Related to the Kehilla contracting and engaging the services of individual members of the community, two additional disputes arose that not only tested the Kehilla's ability to adjudicate these specific matters, but also shed light on the community's liminal relationships with the general population of Óbuda and, beginning in the 1790s, with the emerging neighboring Jewish community in Pest.

With regard to the former, the questions emerged: Can unlicensed Jewish butchers and wine producers in Óbuda prepare and sell nonkosher meat and wine to non-Jews? At issue was the fact that the regulations governing the licensing of kosher meat and wine fell under the broader category of religious pursuits of the Jewish community. Nonlicensed individuals claimed that, since the sale of nonkosher meat and wine had no religious dimensions, it did not fall under the jurisdiction of the Kehilla, but rather under the larger right to engage in commerce that the Zichys had granted to the Jews of Óbuda.

An important test case came in 1776 when those licensed to prepare and sell kosher wine and meat petitioned the Kehilla to bundle the preparing and selling of nonkosher wine and meat with kosher wine and meat. The *bet din* deliberated the case for more than six months and then ruled in favor of the licensees. At this point, unlicensed plaintiffs appealed their decision to the county magistrate, who upheld the decision of the Kehilla, on condition that licensed vendors could meet the demand for kosher and nonkosher wine and meat. Consequently, by the end of the 1770s, the Kehilla had effectively asserted a communal monopoly over all sales of wine and meat, kosher and nonkosher, by Jews in Óbuda.[90] This decision stood for more than a decade until it was tested again in a lawsuit brought by Karl Rupp. By this point, the population of Óbuda had increased to the point where local wine vendors were not meeting the demand for nonkosher wine. Rupp saw in this situation an opportunity to import nonkosher wine, and challenged the earlier ruling. The Kehilla's tribunal modified its decision to allow nonkosher wine to be imported, but upheld its earlier decision to prohibit the importing of kosher wine.[91]

The other issue regarding kosher meat and wine had to do with whether or not kosher meat or kosher wine could be imported from other Jewish communities in Óbuda. This issue arose when kosher meat became available in Pest, first briefly during the 1770s, then permanently during the 1790s. Here the issues were not only whether the meat or wine was kosher and the matter of commercial competition by a neighboring Jewish community, but also about Jews in Pest, hitherto an unofficial satellite of Óbuda, asserting autonomy vis-à-vis the parent community, not only regarding meat and wine but more broadly in all communal affairs. As such, seemingly minor disputes over meat and wine measured the larger impact of the rise of Pest Jewry on its older, more established neighbor across the Danube.[92]

UNDER ROYAL ADMINISTRATION

When Óbuda was transferred by Countess Zichy to the royal crown in 1768, a newly legislated royal patent added a royal rubber stamp to decades of magnate patronage. This is attested to by the fact that the Jewish community continued to operate under largely the same privileges and obligations. The Jewish community continued to present to Count Zichy qua high sheriff annually a list of nominations for communal office; following communal elections, the Jews solicited the count's approval for a list of elected officers.[93] Jewish communal leaders, moreover, continued to negotiate with county and royal officials in terms of the *privilegium*:

> The following matter came before the office of the crown estate, in the presence of court treasury commissioner and prefect Johann Josef von Kollier, together with Samuel Jeszinovszky, the Óbuda crown estate comptroller: a petition by principal assessors Simon Löbl and Simon Spitzer on behalf of the Óbuda Jewish community, *in which they petitioned according to the 1764 communal protocol decisions,* points 630 and 631, . . . to modify the by-laws from 1764.[94]

More impactfully, the shift from estate to royal jurisdiction facilitated the ability of Jewish leaders in Óbuda to act as *shtadlan*, or intercessor, not only on behalf of Jews in Óbuda, but elsewhere in Pest County and beyond; and, in one dramatic instance, as far away as Transylvania. In some cases, this meant coming to the assistance of local Jews who habitually violated local regulations. In 1768, for example, the son of Óbuda resident Isaac Landesmann was arrested by the Court Chancellery in Vienna for illegal commercial transactions. Later the same year, the Royal Chancellery in Vienna convicted Landesmann for tax evasion. In both cases, when royal officials arrived in Óbuda to arrest the younger Landesmann, the Jews of Óbuda appealed to Count Zichy; in both cases, Zichy intervened and the matter was dismissed.[95]

In some cases, the Jewish community was forced to take sides in lawsuits between legal Jewish residents. In one instance, Moses Bernwald and Israel Abraham refused to accept the ruling of the Óbuda *bet din*. The latter had ruled in favor of Bernwald, who had sued Abraham for civil damages, but awarded him less than he believed he was owed by the defendant. When Bernwald appealed the decision to the Zichys' manorial court (*Úriszék*), the Jewish court asked that the manorial court uphold the Jewish court's decision.[96] A more complex case took place in 1791 when Óbuda Jew Mikhel Mathis (*sic*) refused to accept the decision of the Jewish tribunal that had ruled against him in a civil suit, and then assaulted one of the judges.[97] When Mathis appealed his claim to the manorial magistrate, the latter not only upheld the decision of the Jewish court but also fined Mathis eighteen forints for assaulting a judge and disrespecting the Jewish court. The Jewish court, in turn, ordered that the fine be paid to the local Jewish orphanage.[98]

More serious were incidents that involved not only state but also ecclesiastic authorities, specifically cases of Jews who were pressured or coerced into undergoing baptism. In 1790, the recently baptized hitherto Jewish mother of a two-year-old girl named Johanna, who had died at the local hospital, attempted to baptize her deceased daughter at the hospital. The child's Jewish father objected and appealed to the Óbuda Jewish community for assistance, who appealed to the head of the Óbuda town council to intervene. The latter, acting on behalf of the Zichy estate and the royal crown, prohibited the mother and the local diocese from going forward with the baptism.[99] A similar case took place when the local priest attempted to baptize a recently deceased Jewish woman posthumously. In this case, the Jewish community petitioned Count Károly Zichy, the high sheriff of Pest County, to ban the priest from performing this rite. The count intervened and the priest relented.[100] The same year, a priest in Pest attempted to baptize three recently orphaned Jewish children whose mother had died in the city hospital, on the grounds that, in the absence of a parent, the church had the right to claim custody over the children. In response, the Óbuda Jewish community asked the Pest County high sheriff to instruct the Pest municipal magistrate that the three small children should neither be placed in the custody of any church nor baptized, but rather placed in the custody of their relatives, "who can ensure a well-to-do, proper upbringing."[101]

More complex were attempts by the Óbuda Jewish community to intervene on behalf of Jews in Pest and Buda where, even during the more tolerant reign of Joseph II, city officials in these two towns and especially in Buda obstructed efforts by Jews to reside or do business.[102] In 1784, the Óbuda Jewish *bet din* petitioned the Buda city magistrate and council on behalf of Óbuda Jews who wanted to participate in seasonal Buda trade fairs. When the initial petition was first ignored and then dismissed, the Jewish community asked Count Zichy to intervene in his capacity as county high sheriff. At this point, the Buda magistrate relented and allowed Jewish merchants to sell their wares—including handicrafts, household items, and agricultural products—in designated places in Buda.[103] Three years later, when Jewish merchants were temporarily banned from participating in Pest trade fairs, a joint petition from the Óbuda Jewish community and the local diocese to the Royal Chancellery in Pest successfully asked that the city lift this temporary injunction.[104] Three years after that, a dispute broke out between Jewish carriage drivers who transported people to Buda and Pest. City officials in the two towns claimed that the Jewish drivers were gouging their customers and wanted Jewish drivers banned from the two towns. When the Jewish drivers asked the Óbuda Jewish community to intervene, the county high sheriff fixed the fares that the drivers could charge, dispelling this conflict.[105]

A more challenging situation arose when Jews got into trouble with the local authorities. In the autumn of 1788, when two Jews from Óbuda were convicted of theft and arson and sent to a prison in Pest County, the Óbuda Jewish community petitioned Pest County on behalf of relatives of the two inmates, Óbuda Jews Áron Schönberger and Löbl Politzer, and asked that the two inmates be provided kosher food during the approaching Jewish holidays.[106] Intervening on behalf of Jewish criminals was more difficult when they had committed crimes or had been arrested in the royal free cities of Pest and Buda, where Jews had no legal standing. Such was the case with Jesája Wolf, a Jew from Óbuda, who "came to a house there [i.e., in Pest], stole a silver spoon, and then lied about it, causing all the doors to be locked in the neighboring houses." The Jews of Óbuda successfully appealed directly to the magistrate, citing the protection of the Zichy estate: "And thus the magistrate ruled that he should never again enter the city of Pest lest he be prosecuted there . . . and the head of the Kehilla instructed that he avoid the city of Pest. . . . thus the distinguished, revered leader of our Kehilla interceded [hishtadel] with the magistrate, who agreed not to pursue this case on condition that the perpetrator no longer set foot in Pest, and to expunge the crime itself."[107]

Yet the most elaborate instance of intercession by the Jews of Óbuda took place in 1791 when the Jews of Pér (later renamed Szilágypér) in Közép-Szolnok County in Transylvania (today Romania) faced a blood libel accusation. On February 20, when the body of a dead Christian child was discovered, András Takács, a local barber, was invited to examine the corpse and determine the cause of death. Takács claimed that the blood had been completely extracted from the body of the deceased. He accused Ábrahám Salamon, a Jew from Pér, of murdering the child and extracting the blood by means of a secret elixir. During an ensuing investigation by local officials, Salamon's wife and five-year-old son testified that Salamon's whereabouts at the time of the murder were unknown. Furthermore, it was discovered that two rabbis had convened a special prayer service at the time of the murder. The local court found five local Jews guilty of murder.[108]

At this point the Jews of Pér appealed for help to the Jews of Csenger, an important town on the estate of the Károlyi family in neighboring Szatmár County.[109] When the Jews of Csenger appealed to the Károlyi family for assistance, a representative of the Károlyi family refused to intervene because of two jurisdictional barriers. Pér was not in Szatmár County, where the Károlyi family had significant influence, but in Közép-Szolnok County, where they held little influence. In addition, Közép-Szolnok County was part of Transylvania, which had a different constitutional relationship with the royal crown than Szatmár, which was located in Hungary proper.

Having failed to find assistance from the Károlyi family, the Jews of Csenger turned to the Jews of Óbuda. When the Jews of Óbuda asked Count Zichy to help, the latter, as a magnate, faced the same jurisdictional impediments that had dissuaded the Károlyi family from intervening. At this point, though, Count Zichy resorted to the Zichy family's standing and influence within the royal hierarchy: sheriff of Pest County—the highest-ranking high sheriff in the royal government—and sheriff of Szabolcs County. The latter bordered Szatmár County, and Nyiregyhaza, the seat of county government where Zichy administered Szabolcs County, was less than 100 miles from Pér. Using the influence of these two royal positions, Zichy convinced the royal court in Közép-Szolnok County to reopen the case. The higher court determined that the barber's testimony was not credible, and that the testimony offered by Salamon's wife and son had been extracted through torture. Salamon and the other Jews were exonerated.

In the end, intervention in Csenger was a relatively minor affair involving a remote community. At the same time, this incident was more important as a rehearsal for the Jews of Óbuda to intervene on behalf of Jews who wanted to relocate to Pest and on behalf of those already there. Óbuda Jewry's connection to the Zichy family would provide enough leverage for Jews to overcome the resistance of the Pest burghers at the moment when new, unregulated space was becoming available to outsiders.

More broadly, the importance of the Zichy family's style of governance lay not only in what they allowed Jews in Óbuda to do but in the motivation behind allowing them to do it. The Zichys did not govern the Jews according to an ideology of political or social reform, but rather as the sum total of three generations of estate building and family politics. This difference was crucial, especially with respect to internal Jewish affairs. Whereas the Habsburg dynasty, and particularly Joseph II, self-consciously tried to reshape Jewish communal administration by eroding the influence and authority of Jewish communal leaders, the Zichys remained largely aloof from internal Jewish communal matters. Jewish communal leaders in Óbuda, whether under the aegis of the Zichys or the royal crown, retained control over virtually the entire repertoire of communal institutions and activities. Jews preferred the ad hoc, incremental improvements enacted by the Zichys to the sweeping reforms of Joseph II—the latter came at a much higher price. The seamless transition from Zichy qua magnates to Zichy qua royal officials allowed for a sense of stability that facilitated the task of building an array of communal institutions that would manage the lives of Jews in Óbuda for the next half-century and lay the groundwork for the Jewish community of Pest.

3

Terézváros and the Pest
Jewish Community

URING THE FIRST QUARTER OF THE NINETEENTH CENTURY, THE JEWISH
communities of Óbuda and Pest exchanged places as Pest Jewry superseded
its counterpart across the river in terms of both their mutual relationship and
their relative prominence within Hungarian Jewry. This change was not unique to the
Hungarian capital but a reflection of a broader transition in Jewish urbanization in
East Central Europe from magnate-controlled market towns to hitherto inaccessible
cities.[1] This transition reflected a change not only in political and legal status but also
in Jewish communal organization and function. The Jewish community of Óbuda, like
other market towns, was officially recognized by the imperial, royal, or magnate authority who owned and ruled the town, thus the leadership and institutions of the community were empowered with real authority. The Jewish community of Pest, by contrast,
operated largely off the grid for several decades, that is, without official recognition,
until the 1830s. Centered in Terézváros (Theresa District), Pest Jewry coalesced gradually from a loose amalgam of individual Jews living in this recently constructed bor-
ough into a more coherent Jewish community.

The parallels and contrasts between these two communities suggest a need to reconsider the meaning of *Kehilla*, the term often used to refer to a paradigmatic Jewish
community whose formation was, in the words of Jacob Katz, "a social act intended
to articulate the religious and cultural ties that linked individual Jews to one another."[2]
During the last several decades, historians have qualified Katz's archetypical notion of
Jewish community, not least of all by noting that, while his notion of Jewish communal organization was an accurate representation of Jewish communal life in late medieval Spain and along the Mediterranean, it was less applicable to Jewish communities

in Italy, Central Europe, and Poland, prompting the elemental question: What does "community" mean?

This question, originally posed regarding the sixteenth-century Italian ghettos, pertains also to Hungarian Jewish communities at the end of the eighteenth century, and it is especially useful in delineating not only the parallels but also the differences between the Jewish communities of Óbuda and Pest.[3] Complicating this question from the outset is the vocabulary that historians have at their disposal to describe the nature and structure of a Jewish community: *Kehilla, Gemeinde, Kultusgemeinde, Gemeinschaft*, and, for historians of Hungarian Jewry, *hitközség*. Historians often regard the first two terms as largely synonymous, describing a premodern, Katzian autonomous Jewish community; and the latter three terms as describing a Jewish community whose jurisdiction and authority were truncated in exchange for or as a precondition to emancipation. Yet the record keepers of Jewish communities like Óbuda and Pest often used these terms casually and even interchangeably, seemingly indifferent to and unself-conscious about what, if anything, each term reflected about the political status of the Jewish community.

Given this lack of precision, it is not surprising that, at first glance, the two Jewish communities appear to be similar to each other, variations of a paradigmatic Katzian Kehilla. Each community consisted of a leadership structure that organized, supervised, and supported an array of institutions—*bet din* (tribunal), synagogues, communal charity, rabbinate, schools, cemetery, and Jewish voluntary associations and confraternities. These institutions guided and regulated the lives of ordinary Jews and Jewish households on a consistent ongoing basis.

Further complicating the comparison between Óbuda and Pest is the fact that, prior to the 1830s, not all Jews in Pest had the same legal status. The 20 percent who were legally registered had a status and relationship with the authorities not unlike that of their co-religionists across the river in Óbuda. The other 80 percent were illegal residents (*commorans*). This intracommunal distinction meant that the vast majority of Jews in Pest lived off the grid, for better or worse. For these Jews, forming a community or participating in an existing one meant constructing a bottom-up framework of kinship and interactions, without presuming the existence of or easy access to a conventional Jewish community in the classical, Katzian sense of the term.

In this sense, the Jewish community of Pest paralleled the city itself: each was an amalgam of stability and fluidity. Like the largely unchanging population of the *belváros* (inner city), the number of legally recognized Jews in Pest remained around one thousand between 1800 and 1830. Like the growing population of the *külváros* (outer boroughs), the illegal Jewish population of Pest increased from close to zero in 1800 to more than four thousand by 1830. This frenetic growth anticipated the dramatic increase of Pest Jewry from barely a thousand Jews in 1800 to more than ten thousand by midcentury—Pest Jewry in 1850 barely resembled its counterpart from a half-century earlier—and to nearly two hundred thousand Jews a half-century after that. As such, the difference between the frenetic growth of the Jewish community of Pest and the stability of Óbuda Jewry were symptomatic of the differences between officially recognized and unofficial Jewish communities in eighteenth- and early nineteenth-century Europe. In Óbuda, an officially recognized Kehilla played a central role in creating communal institutions. In Pest, a loosely connected assemblage of institutions eventually coalesced into a community presided over by a Kehilla.

TERÉZVÁROS

The beginnings of Pest Jewry are closely connected to the growth of Terézváros as a residential center and a hub of local commerce and culture. Budapest's original Jewish neighborhood was in Óbuda, yet the area most well known as the Jewish neighborhood of Budapest for the longest duration was Terézváros. Like the classic Jewish neighborhoods of other cities—Leopoldstadt (aka Mazzesinsel) in Vienna, Kazimierz in Crakow, Podiacheskii in Saint Petersburg, Duke's Place in London, the Lower East Side of Manhattan, Dexter in Detroit, Squirrel Hill in Pittsburgh, to name a few—Terézváros was *the* Jewish neighborhood. Indeed, it is difficult if not impossible to tell the story of Pest Jewry without mentioning Terézváros, and vice versa. The beginnings of Pest Jewry and Terézváros are inseparable. Neither existed prior to the 1780s. At the beginning of the 1780s, Terézváros along with the rest of the *külváros* had not yet been constructed. Pest was virtually *Judenrein*, a situation tersely summarized in the 1768 census: "Jews do not live in the town of Pest."[4] Five years later, the city's updated letter of privilege reiterated that no Jews resided there.[5]

Jews were denied entry into Pest until 1783, when Joseph II's patent allowed Jews to settle freely in Pest and other royal free cities. This privilege was sharply curtailed by Law 38 of 1790. This law, while barring royal free cities from evicting Jews wholesale, allowed these cities to evict all Jews who had not obtained legal residence by January 1, 1790. As Vera Bácskai pointed out: "After the death of the emperor, the Pest council wanted to expel [the Jews] and only a special order by the palatine made possible Law 38 of 1790, according to which Jews who had settled before 1790 could not be expelled from the city." Law 38 defined the parameters of Jewish settlement in Pest and other royal free cities until 1840, when the National Assembly enacted Law 29, allowing native-born and naturalized Hungarian Jews to settle freely in Pest and other royal free cities.[6]

By placing Pest in the context of other royal free cities, the scholarly emphasis on these legislative acts accounts for the limited presence of Jews in Pest prior to 1790 and the virtual absence of Jews prior to 1783. The exclusion of Jews from cities like Pest was the hallmark of the governing *Burghertum*, rigidly maintaining the stable character of the city populace. In Pest and other Hungarian royal free cities, the effort to exclude outsiders took on additional importance as these cities were inundated with an influx of noblemen refugees from Ottoman-occupied Hungary at the end of the seventeenth century, and later by an influx of non-nobles.[7] Pest, a royal free city since 1703, had only 114 Jews as late as 1787 — a typical feature of most royal free cities in Hungary and other parts of Central and East Central Europe during this period.[8] Yet the focus on legal status overlooks the accelerating growth of Pest Jewry during the half-century between the annulling of Joseph II's patent annulling the restriction on Jewish residence in 1790 and Law 29 of 1840, which reopened royal free cities like Pest to Jews. From a community of 114 in 1787, the number of Jews in Pest exceeded 1,000 by 1799, and then approached 4,000 by 1823 and 8,000 by 1840. During the first half of the nineteenth century, this rate of increase was almost unparalleled.[9] The bulk of this growth was in Terézváros, though a smaller number of Jews settled in Lipótváros. By 1830, nearly one-quarter of residents in Terézváros were Jews.

To some extent, this increase was part of the overall growth of the city's population. In 1790 Pest was not much more populous than other Hungarian towns, and it was

TABLE 2. JEWS IN PEST BY DISTRICT

	MEN	WOMEN
BELVÁROS	70	69
LIPÓTVÁROS	438	327
TERÉZVÁROS	2,238	2,199
JÓZSEFVÁROS	—	—
FERENCVÁROS	4	4
TOTAL	2,535	2,599

TABLE 3. TERÉZVÁROS BY DENOMINATION

	MEN	WOMEN
ROMAN CATHOLIC	8,509	9,159
LUTHERAN AND CALVINIST	696	366
GREEK ORTHODOX	108	59
JEWISH	2,023	2,199

Source: József Patachich, *Szabad Királyi Pest Városának Leírása* (India: Pranava Books), 25.

still overshadowed by Buda and Pressburg. By 1840, Pest was nearly twice as populous as Pressburg, the second largest city, and was emerging as one of the leading cities in Central Europe. In all, the population of Pest increased from under 30,000 in 1790 to over 70,000 by 1840, despite the fact that the town council was controlled by burghers dead set against this sort of expansion.[10] Pest Jewry, though, increased twice as quickly as the total population of Pest, comprising under 5 percent in 1799 and over 10 percent by 1843.[11] The rapid influx of Jews during the half-century before 1840 thus belies the centrality of legal developments in the rise of Pest Jewry. Barely 100 Jews had settled in Pest by 1787, that is, during the first four years that Joseph II's patent was in effect; most of the Jews who did were illegal residents. After 1790, moreover, an increasing number of Jews lived in Pest as *commorans*—temporary denizens whose residence permits were not transferable to their children—in effect, as illegal aliens. Already by 1799, less than 30 percent of Pest Jews had obtained letters of toleration. This percentage fell steadily during the first third of the nineteenth century. Of the more than 5,000 Jews who lived in Pest in 1830, nearly 80 percent resided illegally, beyond the authoritative grasp of the city government and its privileged status.[12]

This situation was epitomized by the case of Bernard Schlesinger. Schlesinger lived in Pest during the entire seven-year period during which Joseph II's patent of 1783 was in effect, but he passed up the opportunity to obtain a residence permit. Ultimately, Schlesinger lived in Pest illegally for more than a quarter of a century, despite repeated efforts of the city council to evict him in accordance with a royally sanctioned city ordinance.[13] Schlesinger's seeming indifference to the 1783 patent and his extended illegal tenure in Pest embodied the ebb and flow of Jewish settlement in Pest after 1783.

More intriguing than Schlesinger and the growing number of Jews who resided in Pest illegally were the more than one thousand Jews whom the city recognized as legal residents between 1790 and 1840, despite its efforts to limit the size of the Jewish population. From the vantage point of legal status, these Jews represent perhaps the most enigmatic aspect of the problematic rise of the number of Pest Jews. Why did the mass influx of Jews begin only after Jews lost the legal right to settle in Pest? Why did the leaders of Pest, empowered with a royally sanctioned privilege, fail to check Jewish settlement and allow a large number of Jews to reside in Pest legally?

When one looks beyond legal status and considers the larger development of the city of Pest, the rapid increase of Pest Jewry after 1790 appears less problematic. At the heart of this transformation were three interconnected developments that created the basis for Jews and other heretofore excluded groups to reside in Pest and, indeed, in other hitherto inaccessible European cities. First, the massive expansion of the city beyond its walls increased the size of the city tenfold. This created a physical space beyond the authoritative grasp of city government that was large enough to house an influx of immigrants. As Vera Bácskai has shown, the initial influx of immigrants into Pest arrived

in two waves: a smaller wave of nobles who came to Pest as state and county administrators to help manage the city's physical expansion and expanding role in Hungarian
politics and culture; and a larger wave of non-nobles drawn to Pest by economic expansion, who found employment as day laborers, construction workers, and porters.[14]

The expansion of Pest included the construction of Terézváros, where 80 percent of
Pest Jews resided by 1820. The physical expansion of the city, moreover, superimposed
the growing social, ethnic, and religious diversity of the population on a concomitant
division between the inner city (*belváros*) and outer city (*külváros*). The former was
inhabited predominantly by permanent residents who were noble and Catholic. The
latter housed the mass of non-noble, non-Catholic transients. In this regard, the rapid
influx of Jews into Pest was part of a larger process of diversification that began decades before Jews settled there, with the arrival of other heretofore excluded groups:
non-Catholics, peasants, day laborers.[15]

Second, as Pest emerged as a commercial hub, economic viability superseded corporate privilege as the overriding prerequisite for residing in Pest, at the moment
when Jewish merchants replaced Greek Orthodox merchants from the Balkans at
the forefront of commerce and trade. Like commercially burgeoning port cities
such as seventeenth-century Amsterdam, eighteenth-century London and Trieste,
and nineteenth-century Odessa, Pest was increasingly characterized from the mid-
eighteenth century on by an increasingly diverse and transient population interested
primarily in trade and profit. The influx of Jewish settlers into Pest after 1790, and
the ensuing predominance of Jewish merchants, followed a half-century of settlement and commercial dominance by Greek Orthodox merchants from the Balkans,
and was thus the latest shift away from the city charter's original aim of excluding
non-Catholics.[16]

Finally, the city of Pest's charter was eroded by growing royal indifference and noble intransigence. This subordinated Pest to the interests of the royal crown and, after
1790, to those of leading members of the nobility—most notably the Zichy and Orczy
families. After 1790, it became increasingly clear that the city's right to exclude Jews,
no less than any other privilege, was only effective insofar as the royal crown was willing to enforce it and the nobility was willing to abide by it. Once the royal crown and
leading nobles decided that a Jewish presence in Pest would be in their respective best
interests, Jewish settlement proceeded virtually unabated. In turn, the give and take
between Jews and the city ceased to consist simply of Jews requesting the right to reside and the city granting or denying such requests, but was a more complex series of
negotiations between Jews, the city of Pest, Pest County, prominent noblemen, and
the royal crown. Symptomatic of the convoluted character of Hungarian politics, the
city and its Jewish petitioners negotiated up the same corporate hierarchy. After 1790,

as the growing commercial predominance of Jews further encouraged royal and noble support for Jewish settlement in Pest, this hierarchy increasingly favored Jews over burghers. After 1800, the burghers of Pest tried in vain to stem the influx of Jews, finally turning even to the "legal" Jews of Pest in a final act of desperation.

The construction of a new urban space, widening commercial opportunities, and royal and noble protection created new opportunities for Jewish settlers. However, the impact of these developments varied between more and less affluent Jews. For Jewish settlers who came to Pest with substantial means, noble or royal tutelage more than adequately provided access to the expanding commercial possibilities that Pest had to offer. Many among the nascent Jewish economic elite were members of elite Jewish families from Óbuda who had relocated to Pest with the aim of expanding their family's commercial enterprises. Often they settled in Pest under the aegis of the Zichy family, the landlords of Óbuda. The tutelage of the Zichys thus complemented the material means of the new economic elite.

For less affluent Jews, evading restrictions on settlement did not guarantee the ability to earn a livelihood. An entrepreneur wanting to obtain a commercial license in Pest in the late eighteenth or early nineteenth century needed property worth 30,000 forints to conduct wholesale trade, 15,000 forints to buy and sell foodstuffs or textiles, 12,000 forints for a hardware store, 10,000 to sell leather goods, 5,000 forints to sell paper, or 2,000 forints to run a small grocery store. For the class of Jews who lacked the means to obtain a commercial license, noble protection was essential, particularly from the periodic attempts by the city to evict the economically unproductive.[17] As most Jewish settlers were neither from Óbuda nor from some other Zichy-owned town, the more sweeping protection provided by the Orczys was crucial. The Orczys' support for Jewish settlers combined the Zichys' economic pragmatism with a moderate liberalism, thus motivating them to protect Jews regardless of their place of origin or economic situation. To this end, the Orczys transformed Terézváros into a haven for all Jews—wealthy and poor, legal and illegal, from Óbuda and from elsewhere—by erecting the Orczy House.[18]

By 1800, Pest Jews divided into two distinct groups. A minority were affluent Jews from Óbuda living in Pest under the protection of the Zichy family, who formed much of the Jewish economic elite. They regarded Pest Jewry as an extension of Óbuda Jewry, their hometown Jewish community. The majority were less affluent migrants from Pest County and neighboring counties. These Jews were often younger than the members of the economic elite and were drawn by a sense of adventure to the boomtown atmosphere of Pest, and by the absence of an organized, authoritative Jewish communal leadership. In 1800, this group included most of the 80 percent of Jews in Pest who were between seventeen and forty years old.[19]

A CITY IN TRANSITION

Pest was exceptional among royal free cities in Hungary in terms of local initiatives to create a physical space for Jews. More typical was the case of the eastern Hungarian town of Debrecen, where the first Jewish residents settled in an adjacent, noble-controlled hamlet that later became part of the city itself, much like the case in Cracow and Prague.[20] The town closest to Pest that had a substantial Jewish population was Óbuda, which was separated from Pest by the Danube. Until the second half of the eighteenth century, this topographical barrier encouraged Jews in Óbuda to regard Buda and not Pest as a preferred place to trade. Rather, the creation of space for Jews in Pest resulted from a newly constructed extension of the city itself. The emergence of Terézváros as a point of entree for Jews into the commercial world of Pest compensated for the absence of a Jewish community in a town or village that was adjacent to Pest.[21]

The construction of Terézváros was part of the overall expansion of the city outside the walls of the inner city that began during the reign of Maria Theresa. Construction began in 1730s with Lerchenfeld, later renamed Józsefváros (Joseph District). It accelerated when the 1746–1747 census revealed a staggering number of homeless individuals in the inner city, convincing the royal crown that new settlements were necessary in order to house a growing number of day laborers and unaffiliated craftsmen.[22] By the end of the 1770s the newly built outer city was divided into upper and lower parts. The upper part was Terézváros, the most populous part of the city by the beginning of the nineteenth century. The lower part was Józsefváros and an area that would eventually become Ferencváros (Franz District). The outer city and, in particular, Terézváros were ideally suited for new immigrants. The number of households in the outer city grew far more quickly than the number in the inner city. While the latter remained stable during the second half of the eighteenth century, the number of houses in the outer city increased to 859 by 1769, 1,111 by 1781, and 1,276 by 1792. More than 70 percent of these new houses were in Terézváros.[23]

What's more, Terézváros was far less physically attractive than neighboring suburbs. As Sándor Büchler noted: "For Jews, its narrow, dirty streets were reminiscent of the Prague and Pressburg ghettos."[24] Its apartment houses were not arranged in rows but haphazardly around courtyards and gardens. These apartment complexes measured between 3,000 and 11,500 square feet, and most of the flats were adequate for a single man or even for a couple with a small child. Until the end of the 1770s, the majority of Terézváros residents were cottagers, day laborers, and small-scale artisans who could not afford anything better. From the beginning of the 1770s, Terézváros became increasingly populated by immigrants, and especially by Jews.[25] The first tolerated Jews in Pest relocated from Óbuda, including members of the Berliner, Boskowitz,

Hirsch, Leidersdorfer, Oppemheimer, and Schönstein families.[26] Beginning in 1786, Jews were allowed to rent apartments in Terézváros between Király utca, Károly körút, and Dohány utca; they were allowed to open shops but not to display signs. By 1796, there were fifty tolerated Jews in Pest; by 1799 there were 111 Jewish families.[27]

The city of Pest, moreover, lacked the administrative apparatus to locate and evict even those residing illegally in the inner city, let alone in the suburbs. For most of the eighteenth century, administration of the outer city was handled by two commissioners and two jurors, who dealt primarily with smuggling and crime prevention. These jurors were appointed for life, thus they were not driven by the need to impress their superiors. Initially, these officials were able to manage the newly constructed suburbs. However, as the size and population of the suburbs grew from 865 households in 1769 to 1,276 by 1792, these officials became hopelessly ineffective, lacking the resources and mandate to pursue and evict illegal residents. When the city convened a commission in 1790 to deal with problems in suburban administration, the commission dealt only with ways to maintain law and order, not with the growing number of illegal residents.[28] The inability of city officials to stem the influx of Jews into Terézváros reflected the underdeveloped character of city government in general. As late as 1792, there was only one Pest prosecutor to handle the myriad of lawsuits, including those aimed at evicting illegal aliens. Until 1813, the town council doubled as the town judiciary. The physical expansion of the city beyond its walls far outpaced the development of a city government that had been forged in an age of stability.[29] By the time an effective administration was put into place, Terézváros was firmly established as a neighborhood for immigrants, non-Catholic Christians, and Jews. Much of Pest remained around 90 percent Catholic during the first half of the nineteenth century, including the inner city, Józsefváros, and Ferencváros. Terézváros was never as overwhelmingly Catholic, largely as a result of the rising Jewish presence. As Jews spilled over into neighboring Lipótváros (Leopold District), its percentage of Catholics fell, too, from 90 percent in 1800 to 70 percent by 1847.[30]

The emergence of Terézváros as a largely Jewish neighborhood epitomized the impact of urban expansion on the ethnic makeup of Pest. What had been the city of Pest at the beginning of the eighteenth century became the inner city, ringed by newly constructed districts whose residents the city government struggled in vain to regulate. In this respect, the influx of illegal Jewish immigrants into Pest at the end of the eighteenth century paralleled other illegal immigration movements, such as the decades of illegal Chinese immigration to the United States—albeit on a much smaller scale. What Erica Lee pointed out regarding illegal Chinese immigrants in the United States described the illegal immigration of Jews into Pest: "The government lacked an efficient and centralized bureaucracy to handle the steady flow [of illegal immigrants] and to expose the strategies they used to get around the exclusion laws."[31]

The expansion of capital cities complemented royal protection of Jews, particularly when royal or imperial intervention was sufficient. It is useful in this regard to contrast Pest with Vienna. In Vienna, prior to 1848, Jews evaded restrictions on settlement through a special exemption from a royal or noble patron. *Hofjuden,* or court Jews, were allowed to reside in Vienna because their imperial benefactor deemed them special cases. Emperor Leopold I's 1703 patent allowed the *Hofjude* Sámson Wertheimer and his personal entourage to remain in Vienna despite an imperial edict that had expelled the Jews in 1670; until 1848, the Jewish community of Vienna was little more than an extension of this and similar special exemptions.[32] There were no *Hofjuden* in Pest; such Jews generally preferred Pressburg, Buda, or some other western Hungarian city over upstart Pest. This lent additional importance to royal and noble support for Jews in Pest. As certain key state institutions moved from Pressburg and Buda to Pest, the royal and noble presence increased accordingly. Like czarist endorsement of Jewish settlement in Saint Petersburg, royal and noble support for Jews in Pest reflected the subordination of city politics to the interests of the central government. In Saint Petersburg, the czarist policy that restricted Jews to the Pale of Settlement until the end of the 1850s precluded the need for a law that categorically excluded Jews. When Alexander II allowed certain Jews to leave the Pale, cities like Saint Petersburg had no law barring Jewish settlement, facilitating czarist efforts to settle select Jews in the imperial capital. In Pest, the royal crown and leading nobles vitiated the local law barring Jewish settlement to the point where the city of Pest was as ineffective as Saint Petersburg in stemming Jewish settlement.[33]

The emergence of Terézváros as a haven for Jews was crucial in this respect. Like the Podiacheskii area of late nineteenth-century Saint Petersburg, Terézváros became a haven for Jewish settlers, legal and illegal, born of an anemic city government and an enlarged noble presence. In effect, the growing presence of Jews under the protection of noble patrons transformed Terézváros into a miniature market town adjacent to the walls of the inner city.[34]

ROYAL AMBIVALENCE

The success of Catholic burghers in Pest in excluding non-Catholics—Protestants, Jews, and Balkan merchants—depended on the attitude and policy of the royal crown toward each of these groups. The city's original charter, granted by Leopold I in 1703, was typical of those granted by Habsburg monarchs during and after the Counter-Reformation. This charter limited burgher status in Pest explicitly to Catholics: "No one who is not truly of the Roman Catholic faith, may under any pretext be accepted as a burgher."[35] The Catholic burghers enforced the statute most effectively with respect to Protestants

and Jews, contesting even the slightest attempts by members of either group to settle in
Pest. Upon discovering that Lutheran leader Pál Ráday had purchased a house in Pest
in an attempt to found a Lutheran congregation, the burghers claimed the building for
administrative purposes and insisted that Ráday sell it to them for a fair price. Ráday appealed to the palatine, who ordered Ráday to cede the house but only on condition that
the city compensate him with a comparable house in Pest.[36] The burghers then appealed
to Archbishop Ágost Keresztély, asking him to preserve the Catholic character of Pest:

> How fortunate that, since Pest was retaken from the Turks, only the Catholic re-
> ligion is blossoming there. This is threatened by the efforts of Lutheran dignitar-
> ies. . . . even before the fact, it is apparent that this house will be the continuous res-
> idence of Calvinists and Lutherans, indeed, in time a prayer house will come into
> being and from whence heretical teachings will be disseminated.[37]

The appeal succeeded. Henceforth, the closest Protestants came to gaining access
was in 1738, when a Lutheran preacher obtained permission to preach to Lutheran soldiers stationed in Pest, largely due to the intervention of a local regiment commander
on behalf of his Lutheran officers.

The closest Jews came to settling in Pest took place at the end of the 1750s. In an
oft-cited incident, the commander of the local regiment, after three failed attempts, secured a lease from the city for three Jews to run a canteen, over the objections of the
city council. Jewish butchers were not allowed to slaughter meat in Pest, so they either
imported it from Óbuda or used space in city butcheries to provide kosher meat twice
a week. By 1780, the kosher canteen had expanded into an inn. The first Jewish innkeepers—Baruch Abelsberg, Moses Liebner, and Markus Sachsel—came from Óbuda.
Beyond allowing individual Jews to settle in Pest, the question of whether or not to establish a Jewish quarter was a matter of debate between the magistrate and the county
főispán (high sheriff). The city petitioned főispán József Majláth in 1785 that the Jews be
permitted to settle only in the külváros. Majláth granted this request, calling attention
to the fact that Jews crowd together, so they should be excluded from the inner city.[38]
Even this minimal and limited presence of Jews in Pest angered the local burghers, who
complained to the royal chancellery and to the high sheriff of Pest County that Jews in
Óbuda would use this contract as a pretense to settle in Pest. The high sheriff supported
the council's efforts at "keeping out those who harm the holy name of our lord." With
this support in hand, the council canceled the Jews' lease.[39] The Jewish presence in Pest
was so minimal prior to the enactment of Joseph II's 1783 patent that even requests by
Jews to trade at local markets or remain overnight were seen as major violations of the
town charter. One observer noted with alarm in June 1766 that two or three Jews had
obtained permission to trade in the central market square.

In contrast to Jews and Protestants, Balkan merchants flourished in Pest, despite the objections of Catholic burghers. Since the end of the seventeenth century, Balkan merchants had dominated trade in counties that had been located along the Habsburg-Ottoman border, and many remained after the Ottoman retreat. Initially, as they trickled into Buda and Pest during the first quarter of the eighteenth century, Balkan merchants met with little resistance from local burghers. As the number of Balkan merchants increased, the royal crown acknowledged—at times tacitly, often overtly—their central role in rebuilding Hungarian commerce following the end of the Ottoman occupation.[40] The crown recognized that Balkan merchants had certain commercial advantages that allowed them to trade more freely and sell their merchandise at a lower price than their Catholic competitors. They traded at fairs not accessible to Catholics from Buda and Pest. They imported Ottoman goods deemed superior to those produced in the Habsburg monarchy including furs, cotton, pipe tobacco, sugar, coffee, tropical fruits, and spices. In addition, they claimed exemption from local taxes on the pretext that they were Ottoman subjects exporting goods to the Ottoman Empire, even when they sold the goods in Hungary. Increasing wealth and prominence enabled Balkan merchants to dominate trade in Pest. The number of Balkan merchants doubled between 1720 and 1735. In 1731, the Royal Governor's Council (Helytartótánács) ordered the Pest city council to accept Balkan merchants into the ranks of the burghers, although it did not allow Balkan merchants to be elected to either of the city's councils.[41]

By 1750, the growing presence of Balkan merchants alarmed Catholics, who complained to the governor that the commercial dominance of the Balkan merchants was forcing Catholic merchants into bankruptcy, and that the majority of Balkan merchants were residing in Pest illegally. In 1760, Catholic burghers complained to the governor that merchandise owned by Balkan merchants was flooding the city, limiting Catholic storekeepers to daily revenues as meager as four or five forints. Balkan merchants, the complaint continued, sold merchandise along every major city street and next to every city gate, and all the merchants in Sebestyén tér (Sebastian Square)—the largest market—were Balkan merchants. The commercial presence of Balkan merchants peaked during the economic expansion of the 1770s. By this point, three out of every four merchants in Pest were Balkan merchants and more than fifty Balkan merchants had acquired land. Most important, by the end of the 1770s Balkan merchants comprised two-thirds of the town council.[42]

The attempts by Jews, Protestants, and Balkan merchants to live in Pest, while yielding dissimilar results, revealed the extent to which the exclusion of non-Catholics by the burghers of Pest depended on the attitude of the royal crown. What's more, the town council and its non-Catholic adversaries seldom negotiated directly, turning instead to the royal crown or one of its subsidiaries. When non-Catholics petitioned the city

directly and they were refused, they routinely appealed this decision to a higher authority. The centrality of royal support in determining the effectiveness of the charter in Pest
is further illustrated by contrasting the situation of Balkan merchants and Jews in Pest
and Buda. In Buda, Balkan merchants received little or no support from royal officials.
The burghers confined Balkan merchants to the Tabán district with little or no protest
from royal officials. Even after Balkan merchants in Buda attained a measure of success, they were still physically isolated. This limited their involvement in city politics. [43]

As royal policy toward non-Catholics shifted from the 1770s on, the situation of
Balkan merchants, Protestants, and Jews in Pest changed accordingly. The first hint of
this shift was Maria Theresa's 1771 letter of privilege, which marked a subtle change in
royal policy. The letter reiterated the Habsburgs' commitment to preserving the exclusively Catholic character of Pest. It barred non-Catholics from entering the ranks
of the burghers because of their refusal to participate in the Catholic observance of
Corpus Christi:

> Since every man's pressing obligation requires, first and foremost, that he promote
> respect for and fear of God, so this assemblage of merchants and storekeepers are ob-
> ligated to endeavor to live a Christian life; further, burghers and artisans should, like
> their counterparts elsewhere, participate in the annual Corpus Christi procession
> with spiritually uplifting devotions. This applies to merchants, storekeepers, appren-
> tices, and assistants, regardless of the denomination to which they belong. Anyone
> absent without just cause, whether merchant, storekeeper, assistant or apprentice
> will be fined one pound of white or yellow wax. [44]

That she allowed Protestants to pay a fine rather than face eviction was a step forward.
They could buy the right not to be expelled.

For Balkan merchants, a decisive shift in royal policy followed the Peace of Pas-
sarowitz in 1772. By removing some of the custom fees on trade between the Habsburg
and Ottoman Empires, the treaty narrowed the economic advantage of Balkan merchants. In 1774, the royal crown asked Balkan merchants to swear an oath of allegiance to Maria Theresa as a prerequisite to trade freely, thus disavowing that they
were Ottoman subjects. Those who refused to swear were restricted to trading in foodstuffs. In 1780, at the request of Catholic merchants, the governor forbade selling commercial licenses to Balkan merchants unless the number of Catholic and Balkan merchants was equal, and prohibited Balkan merchants from entering into a commercial
partnership with Ottoman subjects. In retrospect, these changes signaled the beginning of the commercial decline of Balkan merchants in Pest and, indeed, in Hungary. [45]

By the beginning of the 1780s, Catholic burghers in Pest had regained much of their
predominance. Royal policy in Pest, long since favoring Catholics over Protestants and

Jews, now favored them over Balkan merchants as well. This situation, however, was short-lived. Beginning with Joseph II's 1783 patent, Catholic burghers in Pest lost the unqualified support of the royal crown. Like other enlightened absolutists, Joseph II had the primary goal of undermining the antiquated corporate privileges of chartered towns like Pest in such a way as to make his non-Catholic subjects more productive. In Pest this meant eliminating residential and occupational barriers that impeded the commercial activities of non-Catholic merchants. To this end, the patent removed religious-based restrictions on settlement, thus allowing non-Catholics to reside legally in Pest.[46]

In retrospect, the impact of the patent was limited by the particular circumstances of its beneficiaries. The patent did not slow the recent decline of Balkan merchants, and it merely rubber-stamped the presence in Pest of those who had weathered the deteriorating economic conditions of the 1770s. For Protestants, the patent created a new possibility to settle in Pest. Most Protestants, though, were deterred by the availability of viable alternatives. Neither Joseph II's patent nor Laws 26 and 27 of 1790, which allowed Protestants who had settled before 1790 to remain, led to a significant increase in the number of Protestants. Protestants, it seems, preferred to settle as first-class citizens in one of several Protestant-dominated Hungarian towns, an option not available to Jews or Balkan merchants. Debrecen, for example, was not only comparable to Pest in 1800; its reputation as the "Calvinist Rome" made it preferable. In 1800 such towns were no less inviting than upstart Pest.[47] Such alternatives preempted an influx of Protestants well into the nineteenth century. In 1806, only 1 percent of Pest Christians were Protestants. By 1847, the percentage of Pest Christians who were Catholic had dropped by 15 percent, due largely to the increase in the number of Jews, but the percentage of Protestants was still barely more than 1 percent. The number of Protestants increased tenfold between 1806 and 1847, but this increase was due to their virtual absence at the beginning of the nineteenth century.[48]

For Jews, the 1783 patent created new possibilities, which some Jews were quick to exploit. Even the rumors of the pending patent encouraged Jews to challenge the burghers. On February 18, 1782, David Moses of Óbuda requested permission from the royal chancellery to open an inn in Pest. Six months later he requested further that the inn be allowed to remain open year-round, so that "Pest will become Hungary's leading commercial town within the next few years." The emperor allowed the inn to operate year-round, as long as the proprietors paid the city 150 forints annually.[49] In response, the city council took measures to regulate the new inn, but did not oppose it outright. The council asked that suspicious Jews be lodged only in rooms where they could be watched, and that Jews stay overnight at the inn only during fairs. More extended stays, the burghers argued, would harm the local Christian economy and public morale. In

March 1783, the palatine allowed the inn to rent rooms to Jews even when there was not a fair. Because Jews did not eat Christian food, he asserted, they would not harm burghers. In October 1783 four Jews from Óbuda reached an agreement with Pest to operate the inn for four years at 550 forints per year.[50]

Nonetheless, despite allowing the inn, the burghers continued to oppose Jewish settlement. They discovered more creative and at times cruel ways of opposing and preventing Jews from settling. The burghers distinguished between the inner and outer city of Pest as suitable places for Jews to reside. In July 1786, the town council asked the governor to bar Jews from settling in the inner city. The governor ruled that it was up to the town council to determine where Jews would be allowed to reside.[51] That so few Jews settled in Pest during the 1780s, though, was less the result of such initiatives than the limited economic opportunities for Jews in Pest. Even after a decade of commercial decline, Balkan merchants still dominated commerce and trade in Pest, and they virtually monopolized the more lucrative forms of trade. After 1790, as the decline of the Balkan merchants created new economic opportunities for Jews, Jewish settlement began in earnest.

It should be noted that neither the impact of Joseph II's patent nor subsequent royal policy were intended primarily as a blow to burgher control or as a boon to non-Catholics, but aimed at serving Habsburg interests. Habsburg officials after the death of Joseph II, while never challenging the burghers' corporate privileges as directly or aggressively as Joseph II had, continued to erode these privileges when they deemed it beneficial to the crown. In 1791, Palatine Alexander Leopold wrote to his brother Emperor Leopold II in support of Jewish settlement: "Regarding the Jews, we have decided to treat them humanely and allow them to remain in the cities they inhabit, except for the fortified cities of Croatia that have never allowed Jews."[52] The underlying goal of Habsburg policy was to attract Jewish wholesalers who had an annual income of at least 10,000 forints. Francis I (II), over the objections of the town council, allowed tolerated Jews in Pest to establish factories and guilds and to employ servants. To a large extent, this strategy worked. By 1812, 50 out of 163 wholesalers in Pest were Jews, among them the Mauthner and Kadisch families, who founded a textile factory, and the Ullmanns, who established Pest's first commercial bank and built the first railway.[53]

In some cases, Habsburg policy worked to the Jews' detriment. Palatine Joseph, who succeeded Alexander Leopold in 1795, cracked down on shady Jewish business practices. On several occasions, he ordered the arrest of Jews who were passing false currency, and, in response to complaints regarding Jewish speculators and smugglers, instructed his underlings to take all necessary measures to impede the illicit activities of the so-called *Kornjuden*.[54]

NOBLE INTRUSION, JEWISH INCLUSION: NEGOTIATING THE CORPORATE LADDER

The endorsement of royal officials for Jews to settle and trade in Pest shifted the balance between Jews and the burghers in the Jews' favor. The balance shifted further in this direction after 1790, as the Zichy and Orczy families exerted more influence in Pest. Seen together, the ways the two families aided Jews in Pest reflected a key discrepancy between nobles in Western and Central Hungary at the end of the eighteenth century. The Zichys and the Orczys had holdings in the less developed, frontier reaches of Eastern Hungary, respectively, Szabolcs and Zemplén Counties. In both counties, the Jewish population and the tax revenue paid by Jews had increased during the eighteenth century; the Zichys and the Orczys acknowledged that they could benefit by enlarging the number of Jews in Pest who were under their tutelage. The efforts of the Orczys and Zichys to augment the Jewish presence in Pest thus reflected a broader effort to import the benefits of frontier practicality into the stodgy, corporative world of the capital.[55]

The difference between the Zichys and the Orczys also reflected a broader difference among noblemen. Typical of leading Hungarian nobles, the Zichys were motivated to help Jews in Pest largely by a desire to reap the economic benefits of urban development. During deliberations of the Habsburg court in 1794, Count Zichy attributed the prevailing economic backwardness in the monarchy to the retrograde commercial practices of privileged towns. He suggested that towns be governed like the enclaves of Balkan merchants: "The Greeks have civic privileges, and when they do not adhere to each of these privileges they forfeit all of them. Even when they do adhere, they must still be subjected to our laws." More succinctly, he later remarked, "Perhaps it is necessary to fashion a new type of city." Such comments presaged his efforts to settle Jews in Pest.[56]

In some instances, Zichy intervened directly on behalf of his subjects. In 1793, the aforementioned Bernard Schlesinger received an eviction notice from the city council after having lived in Pest illegally for eleven years. In his appeal to the county magistrate, Schlesinger invoked the protection of his powerful patron, Count Zichy—the noble landlord of Vörösvár, Schlesinger's hometown. Schlesinger asked the magistrate "to seek the counsel of Count Zichy, who should be invited to investigate and rule on this matter." The council, seemingly loathe to involve Count Zichy, appealed the matter instead to the Royal Chancellery, which upheld Schlesinger's request to remain in Pest.[57] In 1801, Schlesinger, still residing illegally, turned from petitioner to sponsor, securing Count Zichy's support on behalf of Samuel Glass, a fellow Jew facing eviction; after Zichy intervened, Glass was allowed to remain for an additional year. In 1810, Schlesinger and Glass were still living in Pest as illegal residents.[58]

Once the 1783 patent introduced the possibility of Jews participating in the Pest market fairs, Count Zichy championed the right of Jews from Óbuda to attend the fairs. This was a direct challenge to the city's efforts to limit the scope of the patent to Jews who resided legally in Pest. Annually between 1784 and 1788, the Pest magistrates rejected the petitions of Jews from Óbuda to attend the fairs.[59] They also denied the request of Joseph Fattier, a Jewish merchant from Vienna.[60] As late as 1792, Jews still complained that the city was impeding their right to participate in Pest fairs.[61] At this point, Count Zichy intervened, and Jews from Óbuda, Zsámbék, and other Zichy-owned towns were allowed to attend the fairs. Having failed to prevent Jews from attending the fairs, the burghers challenged the Jews' right to sell kosher food and wine there. When the Jews secured the right to sell food and wine, the burghers opposed the opening of a kosher canteen. When the canteen finally opened in 1792, the burghers assaulted the wine-sellers.[62]

Zichy's patronage of Jews, however, seldom extended beyond his Jewish subjects from Óbuda, making the support of Baron Orczy all the more important. The Orczys were more progressive than the Zichys. Count Miklós Zichy was a conservative reformer whose interest in the Jews was largely economic. The Orczys were more liberal in their desire to undertake reforms, especially brothers József and László who owned the Orczy House, a large apartment complex in Pest. Both were members of a freemason lodge and liberal enough for the palatine to suspect them of revolutionary activity during the 1790s: "Count Ladislas Orczy, vice-treasurer and high sheriff of Abaúj County: a rich, powerful man who dispenses much money to arouse others and to form a party. . . . a violent, dangerous man at whose home take place, for the most part, subversive assemblies. . . . József Orczy, the aforementioned's brother, is as dangerous as the aforementioned but more talented, prudent, and surreptitious."[63]

The Orczy family's most important contribution to consolidating the Jewish presence in Pest was allowing Jews to use the Orczy House. This square-block complex of apartments and office space, situated at the boundary between Terézváros and the inner city, was purchased by Baron József Orczy in 1795, and soon became the heart of Jewish life in Pest. The Orczy House attested to the importance of noble patronage facilitating the efforts of Jews to settle in Terézváros, further undermining the influence of city government there.[64] In this way, the Orczy and Zichy families provided protection in a lawless, boomtown environment. In 1786, Orczy intervened on behalf of Löbl Pollák when the latter, accused by a Christian woman of extorting 200 forints from her, was threatened by the town with eviction.[65] In 1790, shortly after Law 38 went into effect and dozens of Jews faced eviction, Zichy secured the release of a two-year-old child of Óbuda Jews who had been kidnapped and was being held by missionaries at a Pest hospice.[66]

Ultimately, the patronage of Zichy and Orczy, coupled with the emergence of Terézváros as a poorly regulated Jewish suburb, intensified the give and take between

Jews and burghers. From the outset, the burghers distinguished tolerated Jews, whom they allowed to remain, from untolerated ones, whom they tried repeatedly to evict. Without directly challenging the legitimacy of the 1783 patent or Law 38 of 1790, the burghers limited the impact of these laws by interpreting them stringently and disputing their implementation on a case by case basis, forcing Jews to litigate for each new privilege. In 1789, the town asked the governor to evict all Jews from Pest on the grounds that most were there without permits, that Jewish businesses were bankrupting Christian businesses, and that Jews were luring Christian youth into the field of money-lending. When Pest Jews submitted a counter-petition, the governor ruled that, because excluding Jews would be detrimental to local commerce, Jews were free to settle and trade anywhere in Pest. Further, he ruled that eviction of Jews from towns was, from this point on, a matter for the National Diet to decide. Later that year, the governor reminded Pest burghers not to confiscate the property of Jews until the National Diet and the royal crown resolved the issue of Jewish settlement.[67] In 1799, the town council petitioned the governor to prohibit Jews from renting apartments in the newly constructed suburb of Lipótváros. The governor denied the petition on the grounds that the sixty Jewish families living in Lipótváros were indispensable to this new area's construction and development.[68]

In 1804, a new city ordinance allowed only one child from each family to inherit the tolerated status of the parents. Accordingly, younger children and their families had to leave or be designated illegal residents. In 1807, the council asked the palatine to evict married children of legally residing Jews. The palatine rejected both of these proposals, extending legal residence to children and wives of legal residents. He added, however, that children of tolerated Jews who opened their own business would forfeit their legal status. He also allowed the city council to refuse settlement to any nonresident Jew whose daughter was married to a legal resident.[69] While fueling burgher efforts to stem the influx of Jews, however, Law 38 of 1790 guaranteed a Jewish presence in Pest by providing a legal basis for certain Jews to remain. For the next thirty years, the burghers tolerated this Jewish presence, but made every effort to contain it by cracking down on illegal Jewish immigration in the name of enforcing Law 38. Occasionally such efforts resulted in multiple evictions; in September 1794, for example, several dozen Jews were evicted for not having permits.[70]

Subsequent municipal legislation tried to facilitate eviction procedures but often resulted in drawn-out court battles instead. In one case, Löbl Wolf Ferber, a subject of Count Zichy, had been accused in 1808 of residing illegally since 1794. Pest burghers, still trying to have him evicted in 1814, invoked not only Law 38 of 1790 but also municipal law 17424 of 1808, which gave the town council the right to carry out evictions. In 1820, though, Ferber, the "un-tolerated Jew," was still living in Pest, underlining the inability of the town to expel even illegally residing Jews.[71] In another case, the burghers

challenged the legal status of Herschel Fleischer, another subject of Count Zichy, arguing that he had falsely claimed the right to be tolerated under the 1790 law. Although
the council tried to evict him according to the 1808 municipal law, Fleischer was able
to remain in Pest into the 1820s.[72]

The upshot is that noble support made legal residence less essential, spurring a rise
in the number of temporary and illegal residents. The latter, it should be noted, included prominent and affluent Jewish immigrants. Of the Jewish heads of household
who had relocated to Pest from Óbuda, more than half had lived in Pest as untolerated residents for five years or more prior to 1797. Wolf Boskowitz, a leading rabbinic
scholar and a member of one of Óbuda's elite families, lived in Pest for nearly a decade
without permission.[73] For affluent and impoverished Jews alike, there were incentives
to living in Pest even without official toleration. Temporary residents at times found
ways to avoid sharing the burden of Pest Jewry's annual tax obligation. In one instance,
when tolerated Pest Jews tried to coerce illegally residing Jews from Óbuda to contribute to this tax, the latter refused on the grounds that they were officially part of Óbuda
Jewry, and hence exempt from being taxed anywhere else.[74]

The growing number of illegal residents prompted legally residing Pest Jews to aid
burgher efforts to stem illegal Jewish immigration, partly as a way of ridding themselves of the burden of looking after impoverished Jews, but also as a way of limiting
economic competition from other Jewish merchants. Affluence and ties to the Óbuda
Jewish elite were the factors most helpful in winning the endorsement of Pest Jews, but
even these were not always enough. The overriding consideration in Pest Jews endors-
ing a Jewish request for residence was whether accepting the would-be resident would
benefit the tolerated Jews who were already there.[75] At times this meant excluding affluent, accomplished merchants. In 1802, Abraham Ullmann, a merchant from Pressburg,
asked the Jews of Pest to sponsor his petition for toleration. The Jews of Pest refused.
They claimed that there were already more than enough Jews in Pest, and that allowing Ullmann in would set a bad precedent. On their recommendation, the town council rejected Ullmann's application. Ullmann appealed to the governor, who granted
his petition after a two-year legal battle.[76] In other instances, tolerated Pest Jews went
to great lengths to assure that certain Jews be allowed to settle regardless of economic
standing. In 1797, when the town council petitioned the magistrate to evict a certain
illegal Jewish resident, tolerated Pest Jews came to his defense, explaining to the magistrate that the Jew in question was to serve as rabbi, ritual slaughterer, and teacher for
tolerated Jews. In the end, efforts by burghers and Jews to limit Jewish immigration
were, for the most part, ad hoc and poorly coordinated, but the burghers, at least, succeeded in one key respect: they kept at a minimum the number of Jews who settled in
the inner city, the *sanctum sanctorum* of Pest burghers. In 1804 and in 1820, only 1 out
of every 20 Jewish men in Pest lived in the inner city.[77]

A COMMUNITY COALESCES

Amid the fluidity and uncertainty of Jewish settlement, the gradual emergence of a structured Jewish community provided much needed cohesiveness for what was otherwise a diffuse collection of individual Jewish families. The creation of an organized community was the culmination of decades of ad hoc incremental, chaotic formation of individual institutions. According to Marcus Sechsel, fourteen Jews gathered in prayer at his home beginning in 1774. The Pest municipal authorities did not sanction "synagogues" and shut down this private prayer group by the decade's end. Once Jews were officially permitted to reside in Pest, a second weekly prayer service met unofficially in the Hauszlir House on Király utca; it was formally recognized in 1796.[78]

By 1805 the first semblance of an organized Jewish community appeared in Pest with the founding of the Pest Burial Society (Hevra Kadisha).[79] The function of this organization underlines the parallels and differences between the Jewish communities of Pest and Óbuda. Like its counterpart in Óbuda, the Hevra Kadisha in Pest assisted individual grieving Jews by taking care of the burial and helping to mourn the deceased. The Pest Hevra Kadisha, too, took on broader health care issues soon after its founding, forming a Jewish hospital in Pest at the end of 1805. Initially, the hospital had one room with four beds and was situated in the Orczy House—the heart of the Jewish community. Four years later, the Hevra Kadisha rented a space in an adjacent building to accommodate a growing number of patients. By 1815, this space, too, had become too small, and the Hevra Kadisha relocated the community hospital to Kazinczy Street. In 1825, the Jews of Pest petitioned the Habsburg government to open a new municipal hospital. Since the Jewish community of Pest had not yet been formally recognized, the petition was denied. Instead, the Jews rented a larger space on Nagy Diofa Street in 1827.[80]

Supervising burial and mourning, and running the hospital, though, were not the sole responsibilities of the Pest Hevra Kadisha. In the absence of a regular Kehilla, the leaders of the Hevra Kadisha coordinated the activities that in formally recognized communities, such as the Jewish community of Óbuda, were managed by the Kehilla, including the synagogue and the disbursement of charity. In 1796, Jews in Pest had obtained permission to build a new synagogue in the Orczy House, on the corner of Károly Boulevard and Király Street. This synagogue had a larger room for men and a smaller room for women. The increase in the size of the community eventually necessitated the opening of a larger synagogue in a more suitable room in a first-floor wing of the Orczy House.[81]

By 1810, the Hevra Kadisha, in lieu of a Kehilla, had taken charge of collecting the annual Toleration Tax from registered Jews in Pest, and the tribunal of the Hevra

פנקס

דחבֿ"ק דנ"ח דקק

פעסט

נעשה

עֿ אלופים אֿומֿיר נבֿאֿים

דחב"ק דנ"ח ∴ הה הקצ'ין הרֿ"ר

יֿעקבֿ בֿערלין ∴ וההֿתֿורנֿ מוהֿרֿ

יוסף גֿרוֿנֿא נֿ"י ∴∴ וֿעֿ אונֿטֿ"ר

גֿבֿאֿים הֿ"הֿ הֿרֿ"ר אֿ"יזק פֿעֿצֿיל

והֿרֿר אֿבֿרֿם פֿאלאק והרֿר וֿואלֿף

קן

בֿשֿנת **תֿקֿסֿה** לֿפֿק

Cover page of the *Pinkas de-Hevra Kadisha* (Minute Book of the Pest Burial Society).

Kadisha began to adjudicate cases for non–Hevra Kadisha Jews in Pest, too. These two pressing tasks led to a division of responsibility within the leadership of the Hevra Kadisha. The three-member tribunal was drawn from the *borrerim* (arbitrators) of the Hevra Kadisha, while the *gabbaim* (trustees) took charge of collecting the tax. The broadening range of responsibilities led to a more extensive involvement in communal affairs, reflected by the number of Pest Jews who were officers of the Hevra Kadisha and the breadth of disputes that came before the tribunal. The only people who attended the initial meeting in 1805 were officers, including five *borrerim* (Yosef Hirsch Petzel, Leib Pollak, Yoseh Haim Wechsler, Ya'akov Pollak, and David Osterreich), three *gabbaim* (Ya'akov Berlin, Anshel Mautner, Zelki Arlis), three *unter gabbaim* (David Zaks, Meir David, Moshe Leib Reinitz), and two *ro-ey heshbonot* (comptrollers) (Itzik Preisach, Wolf Katz). The agenda of this meeting included the renewal of officers, an accounting of dues and charitable donations collected by the Hevra Kadisha, and an accounting of charitable gifts given by the Hevra Kadisha to the families of infirm Jews in Pest.[82] A decade later, in 1815, the slate of officers had increased to fifty-seven.[83]

The range of disputes that came before the tribunal of the Hevra Kadisha also increased in complexity. Initially, the *bet din* heard primarily disputes about lapsed or late payment of membership dues and unfair distribution of tasks such as sitting vigil over the deceased before burial and visiting the home of the mourners. By 1815, the tribunal had begun arbitrating commercial disputes, both between its members and between a member and other Jews in Pest; and disputes over the allotment of seats in the synagogue, especially as the number of available seats struggled to keep pace with the increase in the number of Jews in Pest.[84]

It is instructive to compare and contrast the influence and authority of the Kehilla's tribunal in Óbuda with that of the Pest Hevra Kadisha. By 1820, Jews in Pest had begun bringing civil disputes to the tribunal of the Hevra Kadisha, which meant that both tribunals addressed disputes relating to commerce, inheritance, marriage, and divorce.[85] At the same time, the decisions of the Óbuda tribunal, under the aegis of an officially recognized communal leadership, carried greater authority and gravitas than those of the Pest Hevra Kadisha. The latter had little or no recourse in the face of a recalcitrant plaintiff or defendant, apart from withdrawing the benefits of membership. Though these benefits carried great weight as the organization expanded, there were still Jews in Pest who did not belong to the Hevra Kadisha and were beyond the authoritative reach of its tribunal. In this sense, the two tribunals illustrate what one recent scholar has described as "the essential distinction between a communally established *bet din* and an *ad hoc* tribunal selected by the litigants. . . . An established *bet din* [like the one in Óbuda] has the right to summon any person subject to its jurisdiction and to compel his appearance," while an ad hoc tribunal like that of the Hevra Kadisha "derives its authority from the consent of the litigants," the distinction between the two being "roughly parallel to that between an agreement to be bound by the decision of an arbitration panel and submission to the jurisdiction of a court."[86] This distinction was especially crucial for illegally residing Pest Jews, who lacked the luxury of appealing the decisions of the Hevra Kadisha's tribunal. Appealing a case to a government official introduced the possibility of exposing themselves as illegal residents and risking the possibility of eviction. Thus few if any cases of any kind that came before the tribunal of the Hevra Kadisha were appealed or dragged on for a protracted period of time. In short, the decisions of the ad hoc tribunal of the Hevra Kadisha wound up, ironically, being more final and less contested than those of the more established tribunal of the Óbuda Kehilla.

SHEDDING THE YOKE OF ÓBUDA: EDUCATION AND THE RABBINATE

Until the turn of the nineteenth century, Jews in Pest had largely lived in the shadow and under the tutelage of the more established Jewish community across the river. This relationship began to change with the first sharp disagreement between the Jews of Pest and Óbuda, when Pest Jewry looked to hire a rabbi for the first time. The immediate source of this disagreement was the extent of the new rabbi's authority in communal affairs. The larger issue was whether Pest Jewry would be subordinated to the more established and prominent Óbuda Jewry.

The search for a rabbi in Pest grew out of a growing concern that food served at the Jewish inn be prepared according to Jewish dietary restrictions. Prior to the founding of the Hevra Kadisha, the inn had been the closest thing to a Jewish communal institution in Pest. Although primarily an economic arrangement, running the inn had religious overtones. The inn served food to Jewish merchants and thus required dietary supervision by a *mashgiach*, a designated supervisor of dietary propriety. The need for a *mashgiach* underlined the absence of a rabbi in Pest. Law 38 of 1790, however, precluded Pest Jews having a rabbi since there had not been one in 1790. Pest Jews circumvented this prohibition by claiming that the man they would hire as rabbi would be a "ceremonial leader and sexton" (*Sermunial* [sic] *Vorsteher und Versorger*).[87]

The search by Pest Jews for a rabbi lasted several years and took place in two phases. The first phase was dominated by Jews with strong ties to the Óbuda Jewish community. These Jews took it for granted that the rabbi would be from Óbuda. The major source of conflict was which Óbuda rabbi to hire, Moses Münz or Wolf Boskowitz. Both were competent scholars who had served on the *bet din*, or Jewish tribunal, of Óbuda. Since 1789, Münz had provided religious guidance and legal rulings for Pest Jews. Boskovitz, though, was a member of a leading, well-connected Óbuda Jewish family. The confrontations between Münz and Boskowitz while the two were competing for the Pest rabbinate revolved almost entirely around the supervision of food preparation at the Jewish inn. In 1785, Boskowitz acquired the inn contract and disqualified Münz as *mashgiach* in accordance with a local ordinance that prohibited an outsider from supervising the inn. He then named himself *mashgiach*. In response, Münz challenged Boskovitz's credibility, declaring that "certain Jewish restauranteurs in Pest behave contrary to our laws, violate the Sabbath, and act scandalously with regard to forbidden food and drink." Münz ordered the holder of the inn contract to solicit instructions regarding the kashrut of the inn from the Óbuda tribunal. In retrospect, what dissuaded Pest Jews from hiring either candidate was not a lack of scholarship, propriety, or family pedigree, but the fact that Pest Jewry was neither candidate's primary concern. Both candidates regarded the position as a vehicle for personal prestige and advancement. Münz saw the Pest position as a way of solidifying and expanding his control over the Óbuda community, and as a stepping-stone toward being appointed rabbi of Pest County. Boskowitz wanted to be named Pest rabbi as a way of eventually replacing Münz as rabbi of Óbuda. Ultimately, Pest Jews divided over which candidate was preferable and rejected both.

The conflict between Münz and Boskovitz, moreover, brought to the surface larger tensions between Pest Jews who had come from Óbuda and those who had not. "It seems," noted one Pest Jew, "that Jews from Óbuda do not want concord among Pest Jews. After all, our quarreling for the last fifteen years has been the result of them cleverly orchestrating disputes." Echoing this sentiment, Pest Jews complained to the city council, claiming that Jews from Óbuda had intruded in the internal affairs of Jews outside Óbuda Jewry's jurisdiction, had threatened law and order in Pest by not letting local Jews manage their own affairs, and, most damningly, had discouraged Jewish merchants from trading in Pest by undermining the stability of the community. Fed up perhaps with this seemingly endless dispute, the royal governor's council intervened at this point, asking Pest Jews to choose someone other than Boskovitz or Münz.[88]

At this point, the situation changed. In 1796, Pest Jews completed construction of a new synagogue in the Orczy House. Noting that the population of Pest Jewry had exceeded 1,000 and that an influx of nonresident Jews during market times doubled the Jewish population for as much as two weeks, Pest Jews obtained permission to hire Israel Wahrmann to officiate at the newly constructed synagogue. Wahrmann was an ideal candidate. Although he was born in Óbuda, he had established his rabbinic reputation while rabbi in Zemplén County. His sermons, published in 1814, reflected a humble, peaceful person who was not interested in controversy. He was well suited for a lay-run community interested in a spiritual leader more than in a religious authority figure. Wahrmann's hands-off approach to the rabbinate was preferable to Boskowitz's or Münz's desire to claim authority over Pest Jewry.

When Münz tried to challenge Wahrmann's appointment and to intrigue for the post, even Pest Jews who had sided with Münz against Boskowitz now sided with Wahrmann.[89] The decision to hire Wahrmann over Münz or Boskowitz was indicative of the changing character of Pest Jewry. From 1800 on, an increasing number of Pest Jews came from other parts of Hungary. The entrepreneurial impulse and sense of adventure that brought these Jews to Pest was in direct conflict with the Jews from Óbuda who wanted to forge strong ties between Pest and Óbuda Jewry. Wahrmann's first initiative as Pest rabbi was to open a new community school, further solidifying the religious independence of Pest Jews from Óbuda Jewry.

SYNAGOGUE AND SCHOOL

By the end of the 1810s, the growth of the Jewish community presented two new challenges to its ad hoc leadership: a shortage of seats in the synagogue and the need for communal education. Two problems arose regarding the synagogue. By the second half of the 1820s, there was a chronic shortage of available seats in the community synagogue in the Orczy House. In response, small groups of Jews had begun to organize prayer meetings in private homes and storefronts. This prompted a concern, both among affluent Jews in Pest and city and county officials, that these local prayer services, if unregulated and unsupervised, might become a public nuisance. Second, after a certain point not all Jews in Pest were in complete agreement regarding the conduct of the service, specifically as to the level of decorum in the synagogue. These Jews were increasingly bothered by aspects of traditional Jewish behavior during the service—especially arriving late, gossiping, conducting business, and especially spitting. They wanted a more dignified service.

In response, an ad hoc council of prominent wealthy Jews met with the leadership of the Hevra Kadisha and fashioned a two-pronged strategy to deal with these problems. This ad hoc council included Rabbi Wahrmann, Marcus Sachsel, Naftali Rosenthal, Salomon Bauer, Moses Ullmann, Isaac Schlesinger, Moses Breitner, Isaac Breisach, Adam Mauthner, Judah Schwarzenberg, Joseph Schwarzenberg, and the leaders of the Hevra Kadisha.[90] It would eventually evolve into a newly recognized Pester Gemeinde Council a decade and a half later.

For the moment, though, the main problem the ad hoc council faced in addressing the shortage of seats was obtaining permission from the city to designate more space, in the Orczy House or elsewhere in the neighborhood, for public prayer. The challenge stemmed from the fact that, officially, there were still only one thousand Jews in Pest and that the official number of Jews in Pest had not increased for nearly thirty years. From the vantage point of city officials, there was no reason why the synagogue space allotted to the thousand Jews living in Pest a generation earlier would no longer accommodate the current number of Jews. In order to circumvent this disjunction between perception and reality, Jews in Pest began to raise funds and petition the city for permission to construct a new synagogue in the Orczy House. The ostensible goal was not to create more space per se but to create a more dignified space for Jews who by this point were more affluent. City officials approved this plan and this synagogue, completed in 1830, had 585 seats situated on two stories, one for men and the other for women.

In addition, the council encouraged those groups of Jews who wanted a service with greater decorum to found "private synagogues," which were really prayer groups in private homes. Unlike the prayer groups that previously had popped up spontaneously and were difficult to supervise, these "private synagogues" would be registered with the city clerk and thus be more easily regulated so as not to disrupt the public atmosphere of the neighborhood. The most prestigious of these private synagogues was located initially in the Fehér Lúd (White Goose Club) on Király utca. Founded and run by the Chesed Neurim Society, a voluntary charitable society created by more progressive members of the Jewish community, this popular service attracted new participants quickly and soon expanded into the Cultus Synagogue. The service in the synagogue was modeled after the Vienna Kultustempel, with a first-rate orator, cantor, and choir.[91]

The establishment of these new synagogues, however, did not diminish the problem of other, less decorous private prayer groups popping up in and around the Orczy House and on neighboring streets. These were often conducted and participated in by newly arriving illegal residents. In 1830 the Chesed Neurim Society, several of whose leaders now also served on the new Gemeinde Council, asked the municipal authorities to prohibit them and close them down.[92] Their success in this regard was limited, symptomatic of the larger challenge of regulating the arrival of illegal Jewish migrants into Terézváros. All told, the establishment of new synagogues, coupled with the hiring of Wahrmann, allowed Pest Jewry to assert its independence from Óbuda Jewry.

The establishment of new schools complemented and furthered this accomplishment. Prior to 1820, the problem of addressing educational needs was not very pressing, in no small part because a disproportionate number of Jews in Pest were young men and women without children. Consequently, there was little demand for communal education prior to the 1810s. This situation changed with the founding of a new school by the rising Jewish community of Pest. The project of establishing a communal school in Pest was the first joint venture of the Hevra Kadisha and the communal elite (there was overlap between these two groups). In March 1812, a royal decree instructed all Jewish communities to found a community school. In August of the same year, János Boráros, the county inspector of schools, noted regarding Pest that "since this numerous Jewish community exists with as yet no schools, the community should be pressed to found one. Bringing this mandate to fruition is to be the highest priority." [93] In fact, the Pest Jewish community council had already begun to look for a space to house existing institutions—synagogue, Hevra Kadisha, and hospital—that would also house a new school. For this purpose, they secured a loan of 38,760 bankó-czédula (= 1,938 forints). At a meeting in March 1813 attended by community leaders and all tolerated (i.e., legally residing) Jews, those in attendance reached the decision that that new school must be modeled after the *Nationalschule* in Óbuda.

Initial attempts to secure a plot of land for the building proved difficult until one was finally secured in the spring of 1814. In order to raise the funds necessary to purchase this plot of land, community leaders imposed a tax of one-half krajcar on all purchases of kosher meat from May 1814 through April 1815. [94] This decision was the first recorded incident of the leading Jews in Pest acting as an ad hoc community council; in retrospect, it anticipated the establishment of a formal community council just over a decade later. For the moment, the ability of this ad hoc committee to impose the tax was made possible by a general consensus regarding the necessity of having a new school and community building, fortified by the new state requirement to educate their children.

The newly formed school committee named the school Bet Hinuch Ne'urim Le-To'elet Yaldei Bnai Yisrael. [95] The school opened in the fall of 1814. Annual tuition was staggered based on household income, four forints for some families, two forints for less affluent families. A year later the tuition was halved to two forints and one forint. [96] Indigent families were eligible for free tuition by registering at the community building on Sunday morning between ten and noon. In June 1814, the school committee, tasked with presiding over and running the school, approved 2,579 forints to remodel a large room on a second-story court of the Orczy House as the new school's classroom, and to hire Károly Kohlmann as the main schoolteacher for an annual salary of 1,000 forints. In 1816, the committee added five teachers and two teaching aides, causing the cost of operating the school to balloon abruptly to more than 3,300 forints. [97]

During the first academic year, there were seventy-two students in the first grade, thirty-four in the second grade. The original curriculum, finalized in 1814, called for seven hours of daily instruction (8 a.m.–noon, 2 p.m.–5 p.m.) to be devoted to a broad range of subjects, including reading Hebrew ("without stammering and in a grammatically correct fashion"), prayer ("learning the morning and evening services in a way that is pleasing to God and man"), Hebrew language comprehension, German alphabet and spelling, proper penmanship in Yiddish-Deutsch, Latin, German and Fraktur, morals and ethics, etymology of German words, and arithmetic. More advanced and capable students, per the recommendation of the instructor, were eligible to pursue more intense Jewish subjects: *Mishnah, Gemara*, biblical and rabbinic commentaries such as those of Rashi and other commentators, and the *Shulchan Aruch*. [98]

By 1821, the school was well on its way toward emerging as a centerpiece of the Jewish community, with a reputation for excellence beyond Pest. In 1823, a friend of Shlomo Yehuda Rapoport of Prague, while assessing the quality of Jewish education in East Central Europe, included Pest on his list of communities (along with Vienna, Prague, and Lemberg) where "founders of schools have provided a solid foundation for young Jews to acquire knowledge and wisdom and ascend to great heights."[99] The school continued to expand throughout the 1820s. By 1828, the school had four grades and 182 students, taught by eight teachers.[100] The curriculum had expanded into three-tiered courses of study, divided by the three languages of instruction—Hebrew, German, and Hungarian. In this sense, the school was remaining in sync with the broader cultural trend of the city of Pest: German was still the main vernacular language of instruction, Magyar was a second vernacular language amid the revival of the Magyar language and Magyar literature.

TABLE 4. CURRICULUM OF THE PEST SCHOOL, 1828[*]

GRADE	HEBREW	GERMAN	MAGYAR
1	Religion, alphabet, spelling, reading the Siddur and Bible, composition	Moral philosophy, alphabet, penmanship, composition, German numbers	Reading, vocabulary drills with words from daily life
2	Religion, Book of Genesis, reading legal texts, dictation exercises	Moral philosophy, biblical history, writing and spelling exercises	Reading, writing, expressions and idioms
3	Religion, Book of Exodus and Leviticus, language, aural comprehension, pronunciation and inflection	Moral philosophy, writing in Latin characters, dictation, biblical history	Literature, composition, grammar and syntax
4	Religion, Numbers and Deuteronomy, language and translation to German, literature, aural comprehension	Moral philosophy, reading Latin and Fraktur, German grammar, biblical history, arithmetic	Literature, aural comprehension, grammar and vocabulary

Source: Bernát Mandl, "A Pesti Izraelita hitközségi fiu-iskola monográfiája" [Monograph of the Pest Jewish Community's Boys School]; Jónás Barna and Fülöp Csukási, eds., *A Magyar-Zsidó felekezet elemi és polgári iskoláinak monográfiája* [Monographs on the Elementary and High Schools of the Hungarian Jewish Denomination] I (Budapest, 1896).

TABLE 5. EMPLOYEES OF THE PEST SCHOOL, 1814–1834

EMPLOYEE	POSITION	TERM OF EMPLOYMENT
Károly Kohlmann	Teacher/headmaster	1814–1816
Bernát Heller	Headmaster	1816–1834
Yeshias Trank	Teacher	1814–1815
Ignácz Schreier	Teaching assistant	1815–1817
N. Grünnagel	Teacher	1816–1820
N. Jacob	Teacher	1816–1826
József Mestitz	Teacher	1821–1834
Farkas Rothschild	Teacher	1821–1834
Áron Reinitz	Teacher	1826–1834
M. Sonnenfeld	Teacher	1826–1828
S. Drach	Teacher	1826–1828
Ruszicska	Magyar teacher	1826–1828
Dávid Freidenhaus	Teacher	1828–1834
Lipót Herz	Magyar teacher	1828–1830
Lipót Leitner	Teacher	1828–1834
Mózes Kunitzer	Rabbi/teacher	1828–1834
Ignácz Braun	Magyar teacher	1830–1834
Jónás Kohn	School attendant (Iskolaszolga)	1814–1834

*Ibid., 21–22.

FROM UNOFFICIAL TO OFFICIAL

Beginning in the mid-1820s, Pest Jews began to take steps to formalize what had here-tofore been a loose confederation of institutions into a single integrated, conven-tional Jewish community. Precisely when the transition took place is not entirely clear. According to the Minute Book of the Pest Jewish Community, the first meeting of a new organization, the Pest Gemeinde, took place on July 1, 1828. However, in 1925 the Pest Jewish community commemorated the thirtieth anniversary of the Reception Law of 1895 and the centennial of the founding of the Pest *hitközség* (the Hungarian equiv-alent of *Gemeinde*).[101]

In either case, by 1828 the Pest Gemeinde consisted of a council that varied in size from seven to twelve members. The council began to meet regularly at the request of the "esteemed county magistrate," suggesting for the first time a Jewish communal organization in Pest operating with state recognition. The new Gemeinde Council met frequently—eighty-eight times from July 1828 through August 1829. While there was some turnover in the composition of the council, there were several members who attended virtually every meeting, notably Salomon Rosenthal, Gerson Koppel, Selig Mandl, Wolf Abeles, and Samuel Ullmann. From the outset, the primary functions of the council were to register newly arriving Jews who had settled in Pest legally and to collect the Toleration Tax. At the end of 1829, though the council had also taken over supervision and administration of two other communal institutions—synagogues and schools—it was nonetheless still defined officially as an ad hoc organization. Two developments, in particular, at the beginning of the 1830s would solidify its status resulting in official recognition as the Pest Kehilla/*hitközség* in 1833: the impact of the cholera epidemic of 1831, and the broader recognition of the problem of illegal Jewish migration to Pest and settlement in Terézváros.

The cholera epidemic that swept across Hungary in the summer of 1831 was part of a larger pandemic that had originated in India in 1819. It reached Russia in 1826, Galicia by the beginning of 1831 and eventually extended as far west as Paris and London by the end of 1831. Historians have noted that, unlike cholera outbreaks later in the century, in 1831 most physicians still did not know how the disease spread, how to contain it, and—above all—how to treat it. As a result, though not a fatal disease per se, the number of fatalities from cholera were still comparatively high in 1831.[102] Pest, Buda, and Óbuda were not exceptions in this regard. Between July 18 and August 31, 1831, 1,198 men (897 civilians, 301 soldiers) and 601 women died from cholera.[103] Pest County ranked fourth among Hungarian counties with 10,016 fatalities and 9,682 infirm, behind Abaúj, Nyitra, Moson, Sáros, and Zemplén Counties. Pest had the second highest rates of fatalities and infirm among Hungarian cities; only Debrecen had more.[104]

City officials attributed the high number of fatalities to the lack of efficient, effective government regulation and supervision; the inner city, where government regulation was the most extensive, suffered the lowest number of fatalities. The central concern among Hungarian officials at all levels of government was the porous border between Hungary and Galicia; many believed, not entirely incorrectly, that the epidemic had been brought to Hungary by immigrants crossing the border from Galicia into Hungary. Symptomatic of this concern was the preponderance of illegal Jewish residents in Pest. Though most had come from central and northwestern Hungary and few from the northeastern counties adjacent to Galicia, the frantic atmosphere that pervaded Hungary during and after the epidemic allowed the presumption to outpace the demographic reality.

In response, these officials looked to address the problem of illegal Jewish migration and settlement in Pest. This was not a new problem, to be sure; such concerns dated back to the 1790s. Yet the added urgency placed on this issue by the epidemic stirred them to act decisively and immediately. The response of city officials, however, was not to oppose or try to prevent future settlement. They had concluded accurately that Jews who resided legally in Pest had not worsened the epidemic but rather had helped to diminish its deleterious effects. The Hevra Kadisha, in particular, had joined in local efforts to contain the epidemic and had provided invaluable assistance. Days after the epidemic reached Pest in July 1831, the organization raised 200 forints for the purchase of new, uninfected clothing for those afflicted with cholera. At the end of July the leaders of the Hevra Kadisha allocated all disposable revenue to help deal with cholera victims and housed victims in the Jewish hospital.[105]

The solution to the problem of illegal Jewish residents, officials posited, was to register them as legal residents, and register new arrivals as well. The limited number of officials who dealt with Terézváros, however, led to the conclusion that a recognized Jewish community acting in cooperation with city officials would have the best chance of solving the problem of illegal residency among Jews in Pest. The result was official recognition of the Jews of Pest as the Pester Israelitische Gemeinde (in Hungarian, Pest Hitközség) on January 2, 1833.[106] From the vantage point of the city of Pest, the reasons for recognition were transparently clear and woven into the newly crafted statutes of the newly recognized community:

> Since the number of Jews has exceeded five thousand in the last few years, and as the dearth of regulations ... and the inability to make decisions on communal affairs has led to disobedience and disorder ... so it follows naturally that without proper order, the reputation of the head of the community and the heads of households [*Besitzer*] has diminished, and disrespect for community obligations by many Jewish residents has increased causing discord, friction, and rancor, which has led to perniciousness among Jews residing in Pest and for unpleasant negotiations between Jews and the local authorities.[107]

The problem was not simply the number of illegally residing Jews but also the lack of a permanent leadership council. Rather, day-to-day leadership left in the hands of the Hevra Kadisha, which tended to be more democratic in its decision-making, had led to chaotic town hall–type meetings that accomplished relatively little:

> What now must be clear is that the exceedingly large number of local Jewish residents who participate in communal assemblies and are directly involved in the negotiation and management of community affairs has typically reached four or five hundred. And despite the fact that they are generally suitable individuals who have been authorized to live here and who generally show consideration for their elders,

they are not able to improve the community without consulting the hitherto tumultuous assembly, leading to the resulting current hostility and complaints, which have continued to virtually sanction an exacerbated and increasingly spiteful situation.[108]

The conclusion drawn from the impeding effects of this cacophony was to create a smaller, more effective leadership body: "Thus the president of the local Jewish community, in cooperation with the city magistrate, has created a council to examine the petitions and requests [from] the Pest Jews, and to create a set of bylaws to administer religious and economic affairs of a Jewish community made up of all the Jews who live in this locale."[109] To this end, the members of the community (i.e., Jews residing legally by this point) elected a board that consisted of a five-member executive committee and a twelve-member inner council. The board and council appointed a committee of thirty electors who would annually nominate subsequent boards and executive committees. This committee would also nominate candidates to be the two directors of the orphanage, the two hospital administrators, and the fifty-one-member outer council. All of these nominations were to be approved by the executive committee and the inner council before the membership at large voted to approve the slate.[110] An immediate concern that was addressed right away was the potential for elite families to dominate these positions. This had been a prevalent trend in the ad hoc committee during the preceding decades—members of four or five affluent families dominated its makeup. To limit the influence of these families without excluding them, father, son, and brother from a single extended family were permitted to serve simultaneously on the executive committee and inner council.[111]

At this point, membership in the community was extended to every "local, reliable, tax-paying, native-born resident" of Pest. New arrivals were encouraged to apply for legal residence, a prerequisite to official membership in the newly organized Jewish community. Community members were divided into three tiers: affluent [*wohlhabende*], well-to-do [*bemittelt*], and indigent [*unbemittelt*]. This allowed all but the most indigent Jewish residents to become legally registered members of the Jewish community. More importantly, it allowed the rank and file membership of the Hevra Kadisha, not all of whom were propertied, to merge seamlessly with the Jewish community.[112] The new official Jewish community assumed control over communal institutions and the appointment of clergy, including the rabbi, preachers, *hazzan*, and "ritual assistants" (beadle or shamash).

One of the rules governing the appointment of rabbis and preachers, in particular, revealed two important aspects of Pest Jewry's outlook. The electors were required "to give great consideration to make sure that candidates for the positions of rabbi and preacher have doctorates and ordination based on legitimate references." The

preference for rabbis and preachers with rabbinic and secular training suggests an overall moderate and centrist outlook, ranging from moderately traditional to moderately
progressive. Indeed, the rabbis and preachers whom the community employed for the
next century would for the most part meet this description.[113]

Second, the willingness to articulate specific and exclusive preferences for potential
clergy suggests that, by this point, Pest Jews were coming to realize that theirs was no
longer a remote, marginal Jewish community that would be lucky to attract any rabbi
or preacher. On the contrary, by the 1830s, as the community and the city came of age,
Pest Jews were willing to compete for top rabbis and preachers more aggressively.

This change of attitude regarding the rabbi epitomizes the broader changing relationship between the Jews of Pest and Óbuda. Both Jewish communities lost their first
prominent rabbinic leader within a few years of each other. Israel Wahrmann, the religious leader and later rabbi of Pest since 1796, died in 1826. By the time of his death,
his reputation for excellence had extended beyond the Jewish community. He was eulogized in *Vereignigte Ofner Pester Zeitung* on July 2, 1826, as a first-rate spiritual leader
"who labored tirelessly for the moral and intellectual training of schoolchildren." A generation earlier, it would have been difficult for Pest Jews to imagine replacing him with
a comparable rabbi willing to come to Pest. By 1826, they replaced him with minimal
effort with Moses Kunitzer. Born in Óbuda, Kunitzer was trained at the Prague yeshiva and was educated at Breslau University—the very sort of rabbi the new communal statutes instructed the community to find.[114] Several years later Moshe Münz, rabbi
of Óbuda, was among the victims who died from cholera in 1831. The Jews of Óbuda
were unable to replace him for several decades. Even Kunitzer, though born in Óbuda,
preferred Pest by the end of the 1820s—a measure of how much Pest had overtaken its
erstwhile parent community from a generation earlier.

Ironically, the burghers' meticulous enforcement of Law 38 of 1790 may have facilitated the increase in the Jewish population and the emergence of an official Jewish
community. The burghers refused to allow Pest Jews to organize into an official community. Instead, by 1802 Pest Jews, when they acted in concert, were permitted to refer to themselves as *Communitas Judaica, Pester Juden, Judaei Pesthienses* but prohibited from using terms such as *Gemeinde* and *Gemeinschaft* that acknowledged their
communal status. As late as August 1820, the city council rejected petitions from Pest
Jews simply because the latter signed "*von der Pester Gemeinschaft*" and "*von der Pester
Juden-Gemeinde.*"[115] Until the late 1820s, moreover, there was no officially acknowledged Pest Jewish community, thus no registry with which opponents of Jewish population growth could monitor the size of the Jewish community. The lack of official
recognition allowed Jews in Pest to settle quietly and inconspicuously. By the time the
Pest Jewish community was officially recognized, the Jews in Pest numbered nearly five

thousand. By this point, the town had decided that any Jew who had lived in Pest for ten years or more, had his own business, and lived respectably could remain in the city if he petitioned the town council.[116]

More broadly, the emergence of Terézváros as a haven for Jewish and other immigrants epitomized the differences between the inner city and outer city. It was in Terézváros that Pest Jewry began as an extension of Óbuda Jewry under Count Zichy's protection and as a haven for other Jews under Baron Orczy's protection. The fluid environment of Terézváros, though, made such protection less necessary. Thus it was no surprise that, at the moment Pest Jewry began to come of age, Pest Jews threw off the yoke of Óbuda Jewry.

For the burghers, the decision to recognize Pest Jews as a community was not a concession. It was a final, desperate attempt to curtail the influx of Jews by coopting the assistance of the Jews themselves. Unwittingly, the burghers caused immigration to increase, just as they had earlier when they had refused to recognize Pest Jews as a community. This ironic twist exemplified the way Pest and Pest Jewry had changed during the first quarter of the nineteenth century. In 1790, Pest attracted Jews who were only too willing to trade the comforts of organized Jewish life for the adventure and excitement of a boomtown. By 1828, Pest was less of a boomtown. For Jews the establishment of a recognized Jewish community complemented the material possibilities the city had to offer, making Pest an ideal place for established, conservative Jews. The burghers' decision, moreover, culminated a half-century of negotiations and confrontations between burghers and Jews. As happened in so many previous engagements, both sides came away with a partial victory. Jews obtained the right to build a community. The burghers found satisfaction in the fact that, although Pest had the largest Jewish community in Hungary by 1828, very few Jews had penetrated the inner city.

In the end, the ability of so many Jews to evade legal impediments resulted from the ways in which the city itself changed during this half-century. From a small town bounded by walls, physical and legal, it had developed into a more fluid collection of neighborhoods ringing the inner city. In the disjunction between urban expansion and legal stasis, Jews established a foothold that quickly grew first into the largest Jewish community in Hungary and then one of the largest in Europe. The rise of Pest Jewry preceded the removal of legal restrictions by the Diet of 1839–1840 by nearly half a century, suggesting that Pest Jewry was not forged by the rhetoric of political reform but by the mortar of urban expansion. In this sense, the expansion of Pest and the emergence of Pest Jewry reflected the broader expansion of Hungary and Hungarian Jewry. From the eighteenth century onward, the rise of Hungarian Jewry was most visible in those parts of Hungary rebuilt during the eighteenth century after being depopulated by the Ottoman Wars. Terézváros and its large Jewish community represented in microcosm the appearance of dozens of new Jewish communities east of Pest. The role of

noble families like the Zichys and Orczys showed how the reconstruction of the former Hungarian frontier dovetailed with the expansion of Pest. The Zichys and Orczys
brought new ideas and administrative strategies from the provinces to the capital, and
forced the entrenched elites to recognize their benefits. Pest Jewry was, in many ways,
the result.

By the end of the 1830s, Óbuda was still highly regarded and revered by other Jewish
communities in Hungary, including Pest. Indeed, the two Jewish communities were
still more or less comparable in size and in the quantity and quality of their respective
arrays of communal institutions. Yet the two communities were moving in different
directions. Pest Jewry was on the rise, taking its first steps toward becoming the centerpiece of Hungarian Jewry. Óbuda Jewry was remaining the same. Relative to the accelerating growth of Pest Jewry, this meant receding in prominence. Both Jewish communities, having weathered the difficulties of the cholera epidemic, would be tested at
the end of the 1830s by a far more challenging and destructive natural disaster—the
Great Flood of 1838.

Part II

Coming of Age, 1838–1873

4

Washing Away the *Ancien Régime*: The Great Flood and the Rebranding of Budapest, 1838–1873

A zsidóság olyan, mint a só, kell belőle mindenbe egy csipetnyi, de sok belőle árt az ételnek. [Jews are like salt: you need a pinch with all of your meals, but too much spoils the food.][1]
— FERENC DEÁK

WHEN FERENC DEÁK, A PROPONENT OF MODERATE REFORMS AND EVENTUALLY one of the leading proponents of civic equality for Jews, made this comment at the end of the 1820s, he encapsulated the prevailing attitude of the Hungarian populace toward Jews generally and toward the Jews of Pest in particular: a limited number of select Jews are needed to help expand commerce and further urban development; a mass influx of Jews was neither desirable nor acceptable. Until the end of the 1830s there was no vision of a large, expansive Jewish community in any of the three towns that would later form Budapest. During the ensuing generation, this vision was sharply critiqued, an important step toward both the emancipation of Hungarian Jewry and the amalgamation of Budapest. The first murmurs of the critique had resonated during the decade prior to the Flood, particularly during the cholera epidemic of 1831. The lack of preparedness by the city governments of Buda and Pest to respond to the *Nagy Árvíz* (Great Flood)—the flooding of Buda, Óbuda, and Pest in 1838—intensified and galvanized this critique into a sweeping reconsideration of the future of the capital cities and, more broadly, Hungarian society as a whole—including the status of Hungarian Jews.

The transformational nature of the Great Flood, for the cities and for the Jews there, was etched in the collective historical memory of Budapest Jewry. Writing in March 1938 on the centennial of the Flood, Jenő Erdődi and Zsigmond Groszmann each recalled a key aspect of this difficult episode. Erdődi noted that Jews in Pest played a part in the city's efforts to overcome the direst natural catastrophe in its history: "The Pest Jewish community hurried to offer assistance.... Anyone who did not give food or clothing sent money immediately to alleviate the misery. . . . Each man gave according to his ability. No one saw the religion of his people, but rather there was only one goal: to help, to help." Groszmann reflected on the ways that the Flood transformed the city: "The place where the floodwaters once engulfed the Orczy House a century ago, today boasts a towering skyscraper, proclaiming the triumph of human industry." In tandem Erdődi and Groszmann captured the pivotal nature of this watershed moment in the history of Budapest and its Jewish community. It was, as Erdődi described it, a moment of great solidarity between Jews in Pest and the surrounding population, one of the first such moments for Pest Jews; and, per Groszmann, the first step toward the rapid nineteenth-century growth and development of what would eventually become Budapest and its Jewish community.[2]

In this sense, the Great Flood of 1838 delineated two distinct periods in the history of the cities of Buda, Óbuda, and Pest and their Jewish communities. In the aftermath of the Great Flood, efforts to rebuild the three towns once the waters subsided engendered a new sense of what these towns could become. The reimagining of Pest, in particular, as a more open, fluid, and inclusive city meant that Jews there were no longer regarded as a tolerated enclave of outsiders, most of whom lived illegally in Pest. Rather, they were increasingly welcomed into mainstream Pest economy and society, and regarded as integral and indispensable participants in the reinvention of Pest—and, later, Budapest—as a modern metropolis.

THE FLOOD AS A TOOL OF HISTORICAL ANALYSIS

That the transformation at the end of the 1830s began with the three towns submerged underwater for six months points to the role of natural disasters not only as agents of change but also as a lens through which to understand larger historical changes. As one historian recently noted:

> The 1838 flood interrupted, but did not reverse Pest's rise from a relatively insignificant town in 1800 to a major municipality by the century's end. Memories of the flood were soon eclipsed by the 1848–49 revolution and the Compromise of 1867 by which Hungary became Austria's political partner. Particularly after the latter event, the 1871 unification of Pest, Buda and Óbuda led to the creation of Budapest, which became one of two capitals of Austria-Hungary and by 1900 the sixth largest city in Europe. . . . For the Austrian government and its representatives in Hungary, the timing of the 1838 flood was highly inopportune. The catastrophe exposed inadequacies of the governmental precautions to spare the city from a clearly foreseeable danger.[3]

Along similar lines, other historians noted the impact of flooding on urban life generally:

> A major flood, like an epidemic, is an unpredictable event. But just as the cholera ep-
> idemics that struck large cities in the nineteenth century could not have occurred
> without the overcrowded housing, dirty streets, and polluted water supplies associ-
> ated with rapid urbanization, the severity of flooding . . . was a product of its drainage
> and water management technology and infrastructure. The flood-prone parts . . . of
> most cities, were the site of working-class neighborhoods, with more affluent peo-
> ple occupying larger houses on higher and drier ground. . . . In studies of disease and
> flood control, urban and environmental historians have increasingly sought common
> ground, whereby the city is conceptualized as a hybrid space or an urban ecosystem
> of natural and built elements. . . . Situating floods in their natural and historical con-
> texts allows historians to show how floods are the product of human and natural fac-
> tors, how the risk of flooding is differentiated over space and time, and how some
> groups are rendered more vulnerable to "natural" hazards than others. . . . Reactions
> to and recovery from such disasters are historically and socially contingent, reflect-
> ing governance structures that involve complex sets of relationships between the
> state and non-state actors.[4]

In other words, floods and other natural disasters—epidemics, earthquakes, fires—are
useful tools of historical analysis, for several reasons. First, natural disasters are unse-
lective in whom they strike; they cut across the lines of wealth, privilege, class, religion,
gender, and ethnicity. Moreover, attitudes toward natural disasters measure the balance between faith and reason, as victims and observers ponder the cause of the natural disaster and the best response, particular in societies such as that of the early nineteenth century in the midst of a transition from tradition-driven society to a society
guided more by science, practicality, and reason. Third, during natural disasters, the
urgency of the moment often supersedes legal restrictions as more and more resources
are directed toward responding to the crisis. This often not only requires contemporary officials to look beyond legal rights and restrictions of a particular group to a more
fundamental level of exigent circumstances and immediate social necessity, but also
facilitates efforts by later historians to look beyond the legal parameters of a particular time and place to a more fundamental level of social reality. Consequently, natural
disasters were often agents of change; often, the urgency of the crisis and the swift response it demanded separated the wheat from the chaff—in the case of the flooding of
Budapest, the efficient from the inefficient.

  In this regard, focusing on natural disasters is especially pertinent to nineteenth-
century Central Europe, that is, to unraveling the overlap between the hodgepodge of
old and new ideas: vestiges of feudalism (the survival of privileged nobles, chartered

towns and guilds), eighteenth-century absolutism (all-powerful centralizing states combating feudal privileges) and nineteenth-century liberalism—notions of individual rights, right of property, careers open to talent—and the city as a place where these novel ideas can flourish to the benefit of all. Hungary is a case in point. In Hungary, not only did the nobility survive into the twentieth century, it dominated all aspects of Hungarian politics well into the twentieth century. In addition, political currents ordinarily associated with an attack on noble privilege elsewhere were introduced into Hungary, in modified form, by the upper ranks of the nobility itself. While the Hungarian magnates rejected the absolutist politics of the Habsburgs, they implemented many of the same ideas on their own estates as local absolute monarchs, and in county administration. Similarly, the leaders of the liberal opposition in the Hungarian parliament were nobles of various ranks, who agreed that non-nobles should receive some rights, provided that noble supremacy and privilege not be compromised. As a result, tracing political change in places like Hungary can be difficult, because there are individuals and groups advocating progressive and traditional ideas that are simultaneously outmoded.

The Great Flood of 1838 is equally useful as a medium through which to appose center and periphery in Hungarian politics, specifically Frederick Jackson Turner's frontier thesis. Accordingly, the transformation of Budapest after 1838 was driven in no small part by Hungarian magnates from the Hungarian hinterland such as Miklós Wesselényi, who brought to the Hungarian capital an outlook that had helped reconstruct central and northeastern Hungary. Nobles like Wesselényi, without relinquishing their own privileged status, increasingly acknowledged that the privileges of urban burghers—not least of all *de non tolerandis Judeus*—impeded the pressing need to expand to improve the efficiency of government on all levels, to stimulate commerce, and to fashion an urban society that harnessed the best elements of Magyar culture. The Great Flood created an opportunity for Wesselényi to import this outlook into the Hungarian capital.

In conventional histories of Hungary, the Flood of 1838 is usually mentioned as a precursor to the amalgamation of Buda, Pest, and Óbuda into Budapest several decades later, and as a sidebar to the construction of a series of bridges across the Danube that connected Buda and Pest.[5] In this respect, the impact of the Flood clarifies an anomaly regarding bridge construction. The construction of a bridge connecting Buda and Pest was first proposed in 1836, and the first bridge was completed in 1849. Yet Pest and Buda were not amalgamated until 1873—thirty years after the two cities were connected. Once Pest and Buda were connected by bridges, why did it take another thirty years before the two cities were officially amalgamated?

The answer lies in the fact that amalgamation was not simply a result of eliminating the physical barrier presented by the Danube River, but also the larger political and cultural barriers between Pest and Buda. In the same way that the Brooklyn Bridge, for example, not only linked Manhattan and Brooklyn physically, but also connected two different populations (some of whom are still learning to accept the fact that they live in the same city), the Great Flood, too, cut across physical and cultural barriers.[6] During the flood, Buda and Pest were submerged under the waters of the Danube, facing common threats and challenges that, afterward, downplayed the larger political and cultural differences and barriers that separated the two towns.

Historians of Budapest Jewry too, have been reticent about the Flood, focusing far more on the political reforms enacted two years later by the National Assembly. Sándor Büchler, in his 500-page history of the Jews of Budapest, devoted a single paragraph to the Flood:

> The surging of the Danube inundated Óbuda on March 13, 14, and 15. According to the Hebrew instructor J. H. Kohn, the water entered the synagogue where the homeless were housed. In the cemetery, moreover, the bodies were washed away, and gravestones destroyed. The destruction of property and impoverishment of the poor caused by the flood forced the Óbuda Jewish community to call on other Jewish communities for assistance. In Pest, where the water level did not cause as much hardship to Jews as it did in Óbuda, the Evangelical minister Mihály Láng attested to the dignified behavior of the frightened Jews. The Jewish residents of the submerged Király utca fled and remained unscathed by the waves by remaining in the evangelical church, where the minister had graciously provided them shelter.[7]

Subsequent historians, typically using Büchler's history as a point of departure, followed suit, devoting little or no attention to the Great Flood. More recently, historians Michael Silber and Julia Richers pointed out the significance of the Flood as a turning point for Pest and Pest Jewry. Silber noted the impact of the Flood on the relative importance of Óbuda and Pest:

> The year 1838 proved a turning point in the history of the community. A flood in the spring of that year swept away buildings, including that of the school, and brought ruin to many. When two years later the last impediment to settling in the cities was removed by Law 29 of 1840, it only affirmed the resolve of Óbuda's wealthier families to move to Pest. From that point on, the number of Jews in the community began to plummet in sharp contrast to the spiraling population of Pest, and its institutions fell into decline.[8]

Richers noted the Flood as a turning point both for Pest and Pest Jewry: "It was remarkable that the Jewish population never abandoned the city during the Flood or the

months that followed. . . . For anyone noting the upheavals of the time it is significant
to note the great demographic changes that followed the Flood of 1838."[9] What historians of Budapest Jewry have yet to examine in any thoroughgoing fashion is the significance of the flooding of Budapest per se and not only as a prelude to the political
reforms of the early 1840s; and the role of post-Flood repair and reconstruction in the
rebranding of Pest as a more inclusive, fluid urban setting.

THE ÁRVÍZ

On the eve of the Flood, Pest was the fastest growing of the three towns. After sur-
passing Buda at the turn of the nineteenth century, the population of Pest was nearly
double that of Buda by 1827 and more than double by 1838; by 1827, 60 percent of the
population of the three towns lived in Pest. Political preeminence during the 1830s
had yet to catch up with demographic reality. Most royal and county officials and the
royal residence of the Habsburgs still resided in Buda, which was still officially the
Hungarian capital.

This disjunction was more than a matter of location. The political importance
of Buda reflected the broader backwardness of Hungarian politics and government,

TABLE 6. THE THREE TOWNS ON THE EVE OF THE ÁRVÍZ

	PEST	BUDA	ÓBUDA	TOTAL
1809	32,980			
1812		22,272		62,458
1817			7,206	
1819	45,472			
1821		27,471		80,272
1822			7,329	
1827	56,577	30,001	7,535	94,113
1838	64,374	31,245	7,712	103,331
1846	100,000	40,500	7,690	148,190
1851	119,391	53,614	12,174	185,179
1857	136,566	55,230		191,796
1869	202,293	67,000	16,002	285,295

Source: Pest, *Buda és Óbuda népességgyarapodása 1809–1869 között.*

epitomized by the three towns' limited ability to deal with the recurring flooding of the Danube.[10] Smaller floods had taken place almost every decade, in 1775, 1809, 1811, and 1830. The last prompted Pest city captain József Patachich to warn of the possibility of something far more destructive and lethal:

> If there is considerable standing ice between Pest and Buda during the winter, when it melts in the spring it will overrun canals and spill over into streets along both sides of the Danube . . . leading to significant damage like this year in Vienna, where flooding caused one million forints worth of damage; and may in the future overrun other cities along the Danube. Pest, too, will suffer this misfortune.[11]

Patachich's ominous prediction came to fruition in the Great Flood of 1838. The flood began with the convergence of a cold winter and a surge in the water level of the Danube. As the Pest correspondent to the *Allgemeine Zeitung des Judenthums* summarized, the Flood "followed a winter that was exceptionally strong throughout, because of the unusually high water-level of the Danube, steady ice floes, and enormously frequent snowfall." More specifically, in January 1838, a surge in the Danube flooded the Buda side of the river. The lower streets of Buda along the Danube were submerged by January 12. At this point, the water receded by a full meter.[12]

Had the situation not gotten worse, it could have wound up as just another flood. Heavy snowfall and dropping temperatures, however, aggravated the situation. Óbuda, further upriver on the Buda side, was submerged by mid-January 1838. The northern end of Csepel Island froze all the way down to the bottom of the river, obstructing the already increased flow of water. As the flow of the Danube backed up, major flooding began, first in Buda and Óbuda, and then in Pest. By February 26, the outer districts of Buda—Víziváros (Watertown) and Tabán—were traversable only by boat. By March 13, the main streets of Buda were completely flooded, with water reaching ground-floor apartments. To this point, Pest was still spared destruction caused by the flood. This gave the town time to mobilize laborers to build dams, which they erected up to the water level of the 1775 flood. This time, though, these measures proved insufficient. By mid-March, the water level had exceeded the high point of the 1775 flood by nearly a meter. By the end of March, Pest was completely flooded.[13]

A Jewish chronicler in Óbuda described the situation more poignantly:

> The 3rd day of Tevet in 1838 was an unusually cold Sabbath day. So much so that for days there were blocks of ice floating in the Danube. Eventually it piled up so much to our amazement that the Danube's water overflowed its banks; no one was able to explain this scene. Many believed that the gates of heaven had opened and all of the water flowed into the Danube. And people did not know how they would escape.

We had to acknowledge that no one had any idea what tomorrow would bring, and our ideas are not the ideas of the Almighty. The water level rose so much that by Thursday, the seventh of Tevet, waves engulfed the streets of the city. Great apprehension gripped those who lived along the banks of the river. By the morning of the 8th of Tevet, the eve of our holy Sabbath, many houses were under water. As the danger became more acute, people got their children and possessions out, but the problem worsened because it started to snow and it became impossible for many to rest on the day of rest. Those who lived near the river were able to rest, but not to sleep. They were so exhausted after an entire day of toil, sleep did not come to their eyes. Seasoned old-timers shook their heads in amazement saying that this was a new thing in nature. They never saw or heard such a thing that in the middle of winter that water would flood our streets, and never heard of such a thing from their forbears. Surely, they said, this is an entirely anomalous act of the Almighty. . . . The week before Purim the water again multiplied and reached the streets of the city such that it was impossible to come and go. Once again, the fields were flooded with water and waves again reached the houses. At this time every part was already overwhelmed. Dread and horror caught hold of us. The danger increased at every moment.[14]

A century later, Groszmann echoed this description with equal poignancy:

Entire rows of houses were destroyed leaving thousands of residents homeless to endure three days of gruesome devastation before the water began to return to its normal level. The difficulties afflicted Pest Jews, too, who, once the rising reached the Orczy House and its environs, were left without room and board. Many fled to the neighboring palace, whom the communal minute book referred to as "a not insignificant exodus of Jewish families." The flood left Lipót Bauer dead and his widow with three orphaned children.[15]

Initial rescue efforts by the city government, which was sorely unprepared to deal with a crisis of this magnitude, amounted to very little. Far more impactful were the efforts of private individuals and groups, Jews included. The palatine, living in Buda, used his personal boats to ferry flood victims from Pest to Buda, where the flooding had begun earlier and began receding earlier.

Other prominent individuals followed the palatine's example, most notably Miklós Wesselényi. Wesselényi, who hailed from Transylvania and was the head of one of the leading magnate families in Hungary, made it his personal mission to aid as many people in distress as possible, yet also noted the difficulty of this mission: "Among the debris, ruined houses, ice floes, furniture, beams, and every other obstacle, one could hardly traverse the narrow streets only with the most concerted effort. . . . One needed and wanted to go ten different ways at once, but alas could go only one way. One could

Nagy pesti árvíz 1838-ben [Flooding of Pest] (1838).
(Source: *Cultura* magazine, https://cultura.hu/aktualis/a-nagy-pestiarviz-1838-ban/.)

help only one-third of the hundreds of people in danger, while leaving the rest in the jaws of death." Despite painful and debilitating physical ailments, he spent most of the first week of the Flood personally and often singlehandedly rescuing flood victims. His heroic rescue efforts earned him the sobriquet "Boatman of the Danube."[16]

Jews, too, came to the assistance of those in distress. As city official János Trattner observed: "They neither stopped nor rested as they helped their fellow men in peril. Owing to divine providence and being part of a magnanimous people, they let not one person's life be taken in this time of misfortune. Especially praiseworthy were Moses Österreicher and Lázár Hirsch, who waded into the water up to their waist where boats could not go, where their help was most needed, and worked most of the night to help rescue those in danger and their belongings." Trattner noted further that this assistance across denominational lines went both ways, describing how the Lutheran pastor Mihály Láng had allowed Jews fleeing from the floodwaters to find refuge in his church. As a show of gratitude, once the water subsided the head of the Jewish community, silver dealer Herman Lőwy, donated a silver chalice to Láng's church.[17]

The travails caused by the Flood were noted not only in Buda and Pest but elsewhere, too. Celebrated Hungarian composer and pianist Franz Liszt, living in Vienna, wrote in his diary on March 21, "There is much to say about the gruesome ill-fate of

Miklós Wesselényi, the "Boatman of the Danube."
(Source: *From Hungary with Love*, https://fromhungarywithlove.wordpress.
com/2020/03/06/baron-mikloswesselenyi-the-boatman-of-flood/.)

Pest. Ah, how much happier things might be had someone been able to mitigate the situation. . . . If I want to help in some way, I must act. I think first of charity, thereafter I am determined to use my ability in the best and greatest way to this end, thus it is my hope that we will succeed in gaining the help of God." To this end, Liszt scheduled a series of special performances to raise money for the victims, the *árvízi hangversenyek* (Concerts for the Great Flood). Jews in Vienna responded to Liszt's plea for assistance. The commercial firm of Arnstein and Eskeles donated 5,000 forints and, in addition, Bernhard Eskeles personally donated an additional 1,500 forints.[18]

Jews on both sides of the Danube experienced adversity caused by the Flood. The hardest hit Jews were those in Óbuda, which itself was devastated by the rising waters. Prior to the Flood, many Jews lived illegally in Újlak—a neighborhood on the border of Buda and Óbuda (today it is located on the boundary between Budapest Districts II and III)—which was a local center of Jewish trade, where fifty-five Jewish merchants had resided for decades. All told, seventy Jewish families in Újlak and nearly three hundred Jews were displaced by the Flood.[19] Óbuda Jews experienced 194,515 forints' worth of damage in the 1838 Flood out of an overall 679,034 forints' worth of damage. Subsequently, the Jewish merchants would prefer either Pest or Buda as a place for commerce.[20] On the Pest side, the inner city, though closer to the river, was less affected than much of the outer city. Pest city officials had constructed an elaborate network of embankments along the banks of the inner city, but little or nothing comparable for any other part of the city. In addition, the inner city had the only thing resembling a sewage and drainage system anywhere in Pest. Consequently, the districts outside the walls suffered more extensive damage, Terézváros in particular.

TABLE 7. PERCENTAGE OF HOMES DAMAGED
OR DESTROYED BY THE FLOOD, 1838

	SHATTERED	DAMAGED	DESTROYED
CASTLE DISTRICT(VÁR)	—	—	100
KRISZTINA DISTRICT	—	—	100
TABÁN	2.3	2.9	94.8
WATERTOWN (VÍZIVÁROS)	3.6	19.4	77.0
ORSZÁGÚT	1.0	8.3	90.0
ÚJLAK	37.7	13.2	49.1
BUDA(TOTAL)	6.5	8.4	85.1
ÓBUDA	54.0	35.3	10.7

Source: *Pest-budai árvíz* [Flood in Pest-Buda], ed. Tamás Faragó (Budapest, 1998).

In this regard, Terézváros was indicative of the limits of the Pest government in the Kulváros. Even though Terézváros was farther away from the river than was the inner city and outer districts that abutted the river, it was hit hardest by the floodwaters, due mainly to limited government and the largest number of housing units per square mile and residents per unit. Most of these units were poor-quality, low-income immigrant houses that the raging floodwaters demolished. Consequently, Terézváros suffered more damage than any other district, and the greatest number of homes were damaged or destroyed there. This meant that Jews in Pest, the vast majority of whom lived in Terézváros in 1838, wound up bearing the brunt of the damage caused by the flood.[21]

TABLE 8. NUMBER OF HOUSES IN PEST BEFORE
AND AFTER THE FLOOD, 1838

	PRE-FLOOD	SURVIVED THE FLOOD	% SURVIVED	1847–1848
BELVÁROS	695	456	66	679
LIPÓTVÁROS	394	256	65	466
JÓZSEFVÁROS	1,253	249	20	1,544
TERÉZVÁROS	1,381	166	12	1,415
FERENCVÁROS	529	19	4	828
TOTAL	4,252	1,146	27	4,932

Source: Károly Némethy, *A pest-budai árvíz 1838-ban* [The Flood in Pest-Buda in 1838] (Budapest, 1938), 149.

TABLE 9. HOUSING DAMAGE IN PEST
CAUSED BY THE FLOOD (%)

	SHATTERED	DAMAGED	LEFT STANDING
BELVÁROS	10.1	24.3	65.6
LIPÓTVÁROS	15.7	14.9	69.4
TERÉZVÁROS	57.5	28.7	13.8
JÓZSEFVÁROS	63.4	8.2	28.4
FERENCVÁROS	60.9	10.0	29.1
PEST (TOTAL)	48.7	17.7	33.6

Source: Károly Némethy, *A pest-budai árvíz 1838-ban* [The Flood in Pest-Buda in 1838] (Budapest, 1938), 126.

TABLE 10. TOTAL PROPERTY DAMAGE CAUSED BY
THE FLOOD IN PEST (FORINTS)

TERÉZVÁROS	3,686,334
JÓZSEFVÁROS	3,198,557
FERENCVÁROS	1,999,087
BELVÁROS	1,071,040
LIPÓTVÁROS	545,706
TOTAL	10,500,724

Source: Károly Némethy, *A pest-budai árvíz 1838-ban* [The Flood in Pest-Buda in 1838] (Budapest, 1938), 127.

Beyond the hardship and destruction, local correspondents also noted the beneficence of Jews and their willingness to help Jewish and non-Jewish victims alike. One noted that "no less respectable were those among the Jewish community who, between March 16 and 22, provided money, meat, and 3,500 loaves of bread to those in need regardless of religion."[22] Another Jewish wholesaler, József Kadisch, donated 860 pieces of clothing to the displaced residents of the Ludoviceum.[23] Another, who was also the factor of the court of the palatine, "immediately following these unfortunate events when the need was greatest, provided six hundred loaves of bread to those in distress and thirty pieces of gold to the misfortunate of the two towns. Isaac Rosenthal, in addition to an initial donation to victims, gave 25 forints apiece to the Nurses Institute in Buda, the Pest Public Hospital, the Orphanage Fund, the Synagogue Fund, the Institute for the Blind, and to Catholic, Lutheran, Calvinist, and Greek Orthodox churches in Pest."[24] Once the initial fear subsided, community president József Boskovitz called an emergency meeting to discuss what immediate actions could be taken: "This tragic event and its devastating deluge has caused many Jewish families to forfeit entirely their homes, their property, and their possessions. The situation demands that we allocate immediately without prior authorization 700 forints' worth of food and money to the victims of the flood." József Bach, preacher in the Pest Choral Synagogue, published an appeal in the Lipcse Jewish newspaper, asking for foreign assistance for the impoverished victims of the flood. These calls to action energized Jews, mainly affluent Jews in Pest and Vienna, to provide assistance.[25]

TABLE 11. MONETARY DONATIONS TO FLOOD VICTIMS
FROM PEST JEWISH NOTABLES, MARCH 1838

JAKAB KUNEWALD AND LIPÓT SCHULHOF	692 forints and 18 krajcár
SÁMUEL AUSTERLITZ AND MÁRKUS ABELSBERGER	807 forints
MÓZES GOLDNER	100 forints to the Cultusztempel
SIMON LAMED (ENNOBLED JEW IN VIENNA)	600 forints
JEWS OF VARASD	45 forints
JEWS OF ÚJVIDÉK	61 forints, 16 krajcár
VIENNA JEWS	34 forints, 12 krajcár

Source: *Hírnök* [Herald], May 10, 1838.

TABLE 12. MONETARY DONATIONS TO FLOOD VICTIMS
FROM PEST JEWISH NOTABLES, SUMMER 1838 (FORINTS)

MÓZES GOLDMANN	200
ENOCH KERN	100
HERTZ AND MÁRK POLLÁK	400
KUNEWALDER BROTHERS	200
FATHER AND SON KANITZ	600
TERÉZIA KANITZ	110
IZSÁK ROZENTHAL	300
GÁBOR ULLMANN	200
BIEDERMANN BROTHERS	500

Source: *Hazai és Külföldi Tudósítások* [Local and Foreign Dispatches] no. 4, Saint George, 1838; quoted in Jenő Erdődi, "A pesti nagy árvíz és a magyar zsidóság" [The Great Flood of Pest and Hungarian Jewry], *Egyenlőség*, Feb. 24, 1938, p. 10.

RECONSTRUCTION AND RECOVERY

Even before the floodwaters had fully receded, the residents and governments of Pest, Buda, and Óbuda were already facing the daunting task of repairing the damage, restoring a sense of normalcy, and determining how to prepare more effectively for future floods and other natural disasters. What became apparent almost immediately is that the damage and difficulties brought on by the Flood were not deterring immigrants from settling in the three towns, and above all, in Pest.

From the outset, it was clear that the damage was augmented by less than adequate construction, prompting a debate over how best to rebuild and repair damaged buildings: more resilient to future floodwaters or more aesthetically pleasing? This prompted city officials to revisit the construction regulation that, a decade earlier in 1827, Palatine Joseph had instructed the Pest City Council to implement based on construction regulations of the city of Vienna. To this end, the city council brought in an expert city planner from Vienna, Paul Strenger, who recommended a series of regulations for Buda and Pest based on the palatine's instructions, which became the first building code in either place: (1) every new building had to have a protective wall from the top of the cellar to the bottom of the roof; (2) no home could be more than three stories high; (3) no house could remain if it posed a threat to neighboring houses; (4) walls and pillars supporting a roof had to be built from stone or brick; (5) the masonry between pillars had to be at least as high as the highest water level during the flood, and could be built temporarily using clay and straw mortar. Eventually the city council fashioned two ordinances, a more detailed one for more densely inhabited areas, and a second for the "more peripheral outer boroughs of Pest." Each ordinance declared, additionally, that henceforth only regulated and licensed structures built by authorized master builders would be permitted, and no residential dwelling could be more than three stories high. (The Vienna regulation permitted residential buildings to be no higher than four stories.) The ordinances not only paid special attention to secure construction, but also provided greater possibility to shape the cityscape and enforce and carry out municipal regulations, both in areas that were already built and for those buildings that had yet to be constructed.[26]

These attempts to regulate construction brought out larger questions of jurisdiction—an incendiary question in 1838. Earlier in the decade, Buda and Pest had come under increased pressure to share administration with county and royal government—since county and royal institutions were housed there—beginning with the first bridge proposal submitted to the National Diet in 1836. The key issue was whether a bridge connecting Buda and Pest was part of one town or the other; or, alternatively, whether the Danube was part of neither town and hence under the jurisdiction of Pest County or the royal crown. Habsburg representatives asserted further that, since the Danube extended beyond the borders of Hungary, it should be administered by the Habsburg government in Vienna. Ultimately, the Diet of 1836 reached a compromise:

the bridge was to be built by an independent construction company and the royal crown, Pest County, and Buda and Pest would share the costs and jurisdiction over the bridge. This compromise became a template for subsequent reconstruction projects.

The debates over construction and jurisdiction unfolded against a surge of migration into Pest. Migrants from all over Hungary were streaming to Pest in growing numbers before the Flood, including several thousand Jews. By the end of 1838, undeterred by the Flood and its devastation, migration to Pest resumed apace and was already accelerating by 1840. This complicated the issue of reconstruction. In the short run, a growing population necessitated rapid repair of damaged buildings and construction of new housing. In the longer term, the arrival of thousands of people into Pest each year required a rethinking of the broader parameters for settlement in Pest. Jewish migrants epitomized this demographic surge and the challenges it created. During the Flood, Terézváros had lost more than nine thousand residents, more than one-third of its population. Once the situation began to return to normal, though, the population of Terézváros increased more rapidly than any other district of Pest or Buda, adding more than seven thousand residents between 1838 and 1840, more than 80 percent of the population lost during the Flood. Concurrently, the number of households in Terézváros nearly tripled.

TABLE 13. POPULATION NET CHANGE IN
THE THREE TOWNS, 1837–1840

	1837	1838	1839	1840	1837–1840	1838–1840
BELVÁROS	13,248	13,484	15,602	15,851	+2,603	+2,367
LIPÓTVÁROS	8,887	8,542	8,600	9,683	+796	+1,141
TERÉZVÁROS	24,896	15,640	18,017	22,761	-2,135	+7,121
JÓZSEFVÁROS	10,298	11,472	11,173	13,367	+3,069	+1,895
FERENCVÁROS	6,572	5,049	7,293	6,604	+32	+1,555
PEST (TOTAL)	64,531	54,587	60,685	68,266	+3,735	+13,639
ÓBUDA	7,712	7,530	7,529	7,570	-142	+40
CASTLE DISTRICT (VÁR)	3,743	3,792	3,812	3,821	+78	+29
KRISZTINAVÁROS	3,530	3,980	4,249	4,210	+680	+230
TABÁN	5,850	5,739	5,747	5,771	-79	+32
WATERTOWN (VÍZIVÁROS)	10,232	10,353	10,544	10,603	+371	+250
ORSZÁGÚT	3,490	3,471	3,477	3,432	-58	-39
ÚJLAK	3,267	2,882	3,199	3,227	-40	+345
BUDA (TOTAL)	30,112	30,217	31,028	31,064	+952	+847

Source: *Pest-Budai árvíz,* 57.

TABLE 14. INCREASE IN THE NUMBER OF
HOUSEHOLDS IN PEST, 1838–1849

	1838–1839	1848–1849
BELVÁROS	2,318	4,143
LIPÓTVÁROS	1,298	2,604
TERÉZVÁROS	3,216	8,987
JÓZSEFVÁROS	2,545	4,182
FERENCVÁROS	1,066	2,175
TOTAL	10,443	22,091

Source: *Pest-Budai árvíz*, 58.

Amid this increase in population and households was the concomitant growth of the number of Jews and Jewish households in Terézváros. Part of this increase was fueled by Jews who fled from a devastated Óbuda and, finding temporarary refuge in Pest, chose to remain. In this way, the Flood accelerated the gradual migration of Jews from Óbuda to Pest during the preceding two or three decades, and consummated the decline of Óbuda Jewry. Emblematic of this change was the decision by the Jews of Óbuda not to replace their chief rabbi, who had died in 1831. This office remained vacant until 1860.

The ability of the city of Pest to absorb this influx of newcomers so soon after the destructive events of 1838 was aided in no small part by a willingness to invest in the future of this rising boomtown. In 1839, the National Bank of Vienna lent Pest merchants two million pengő forints at the highly favorable 2 percent interest rate; the loan was guaranteed by Vienna merchants. The city also received a loan from Baron Rothschild of one million forints at 4 percent interest with no timetable for repayment.[27] This influx of capital was vital in restoring some sense of normalcy to Pest and its economy, as noted by one observer in October 1838: "Pest, once destroyed by the flood, is alive again. Construction is proceeding at lightning speed, and everywhere there are more beautiful, more orderly, and more durable houses. . . . The banks of the Danube are abustle with wagons loaded with sand, dirt, and stone for two uses: to deepen the Danube and to improve the streets." During the decade after the Flood, a series of new institutions appeared in Pest that reflected a stabilizing and growing commerce. These new institutions included the First Pest Local Savings Banks (Pesti Hazai Első Takarékpénztár), founded in 1839; the Hungarian Commercial Bank of Pest (Pest Magyar Kereskedelmi Bank), founded in 1842; the Pest Trade Association (Iparegylet), founded in 1840; the Industry Establishment Society, founded in 1844; and the Wholesalers Society (Kereskedő Egylet), founded in 1846.[28]

IMMEDIATE IMPACT

Once repair efforts were under way and the situation began to stabilize, the inefficiency and ineffectiveness of leaders in Pest and Buda became apparent, albeit for different reasons. In Buda, adherence to outmoded privileges prevented city government from acting swiftly. Initially, the town refused to allow the county or royal government to intercede, on grounds that such intervention would violate the town charter, and refused entry to and assistance from excluded individuals. For example, in the construction and fortification of dams, the city turned first to the bricklayers guild for assistance. Despite the urgency of the situation, local guilds clung to their self-imposed restriction on daily output of bricks per day and prevented nonguild bricklayers from providing assistance.[29] Within six weeks, however, most of these restrictions had been set aside. The town council turned flood control over to the county by the end of April. Because the flooding in Buda and Óbuda began several weeks prior to reaching Pest, residents of Pest—Jews among them—were able to provide assistance, at least for the moment. The Buda council eventually allowed Jews from Pest—who were still officially not even allowed to trade in Buda—to assist in building dams and Jewish boatmen to moor at docks in Buda. To be sure, Jews were still not allowed into Buda proper, but they were allowed to provide assistance in peripheral parts of the town, namely Víziváros and Újlak.

These ad hoc measures led incrementally to a broader rethinking of Jewish settlement in Buda. Prior to the 1830s, there had been virtually no Jewish presence in Buda and, in 1838, only a small unsanctioned, illegal Jewish presence. On the eve of the Flood, the number of legally residing Jews in Buda remained close to zero. During the 1830s, approximately five hundred Jews lived in Buda, for varying periods of time, without the acknowledgment of the city's government. This situation changed rapidly in the aftermath of the Flood. In a remarkable about-face, a few weeks after the Flood the Buda burghers proposed allowing Jews to settle legally in Buda. As one Jewish observer noted,

> Just as something good may follow in the aftermath of an unfortunate event, so we were affected by the lamentable deluge. Following the fateful days of March, the city council and judiciary of the royal free city of Buda announced the emancipation of Jews in their city, and the immediate decision that the Jews be allowed to settle in Buda, to acquire property, and to engage in all forms of trade. This proposed decree currently rests on the royal table.[30]

According to another (non-Jewish) observer:

> After the flood, citizens of Buda petitioned the Lieutenancy to grant Jews the right to settle and acquire property.... The petition initially came to nothing, but a year

later Simon Dubraviczky, who had lived through the flood, submitted a proposal to the National Assembly that "the Jewish religion should be acknowledged as a recognized faith and, through this pronouncement Jews should receive the same civil rights as other non-nobles."[31]

The upshot is that, in Buda, changes in the status of Jews resulted from a conclusion that the less than efficient and effective response to natural disaster reflected a backward polity and administration that was itself the result of a surplus of obstructive, antiquated regulations and restrictions, limits on freedom of movement, and reliance on guilds. As such, removing restrictions on Jewish settlement was part of a larger effort to overcome this backwardness born of outmoded privileges and restrictions.

In Pest, a similar debate was complicated by the differences in efficiency between the inner and outer city. The extensive damage in the outer city prompted discussion about improving the city of Pest beyond simply repairing and rebuilding homes and roads. On May 7, 1838, the Pest correspondent to *Hírnök* suggested that "the Pest community should do more toward realizing the beautification of our city.... The main streets should be paved, along with creating promenades on Váci Street and Üllői Boulevard and through the large Market Square [which today is Erzsébet Square]. For this we will have to remove the street booths."[32]

On October 11, 1838, the city council of Pest enacted a new Public Construction Ordinance (Közönséges Építési Rendszabályat), which reiterated a similar proposal that had been brought before the council in 1827 by the Pest Beautification Committee. The committee had divided its report into three parts: "Accomplished," "Partially Accomplished," and "Not Accomplished." According to the report, by 1827 the city had constructed a new theater, removed dilapidated arches and gates, relocated slaughterhouses, constructed a new royal nautical bureau, regulated the fish market, relocated the city's botanical garden from the city center to Ország Boulevard, constructed a salt bureau in the city's lower section, relocated the municipal execution house outside the city limits, removed the unsightly scaffolding from the farmer's market in Baross Square and the stocks from the fish market, regulated the purchasing and selling of lumber, cleared the "shambles and huts" from the coal market, planted more extensive gardens along Üllői Boulevard, filled in the milling and fisherman ponds, expanded and paved parks and streets (mainly in the *belváros*), expanded and extended canals leading to the Danube, and built new parish churches in Lipótváros and Ferencváros.

Partially accomplished tasks included removing blacksmith shops from more heavily populated and frequented streets, leasing barren city fields and lots "for the purpose of cultivation and profitability," designating new city streets beyond the city boundaries, regulating and insulating quays along the Danube River, regulating streets and houses in the inner city and outer city on a case-by-case basis, pruning and landscaping the City

Gardens, constructing various workhouses, and relocating the shooting range (*lövész-kert*) away from Lövész utca in the inner city. Tasks that had yet to be accomplished included widening the esplanades along the Danube, building a redoubt in Pest, converting the Piarist Abbey into a new town hall and razing the current town hall, relocating the Piarist priests and students to the Szervita Monastery, creating more space in front of the Invalide Palace by covering over the garden of the Szervita priests, and constructing a new accounting house (*mérlegház*).[33]

Those tasks that had been accomplished by the end of the 1820s had been brought to fruition more over the course of several decades with relatively little sense of urgency and were regarded as embellishments as much as necessities; these were now seen as non-negotiable, essential features of city life that had to be diligently maintained. Those tasks that had been partially accomplished or not at accomplished at all by 1828 were assigned a top priority in 1838 and given a renewed sense of urgency. Eventually, the individual goals laid out in the 1838 ordinance would crystallize into a broader reconceptualization of Buda and Pest as cities. Though the original reconceptualization of Buda and Pest did not mention Jews, the post-Flood ordinance would include improving the situation of Jews as a significant component of necessary improvements and transformation.

BROADER RECONCEPTUALIZATION

In a larger sense, the approval of the Public Construction Ordinance accelerated a broader discussion and debate, especially among three liberal-minded nobles who began to reexamine Hungarian politics and society: István Széchenyi, the aforementioned Miklós Wesselényi, and Bertalan Szemere. Széchenyi's new attitude toward the two cities peaked during the Flood but had begun to crystallize more than a decade earlier. During the late 1820s, as he spearheaded the revival of the Magyar language and Magyar culture, he grew increasingly frustrated even by like-minded colleagues who chauvinistically celebrated and justified the Magyar national revival in the name of cultural superiority, invoking the mantra *Extra Hungariam Non Est Vita si est vita non est ita*. Rather, Széchenyi argued, Hungarians should judge themselves more critically "as if we were seated at the bottom of a well, from which neither our spiritual nor physical products have achieved any fame.... I suggest instead that we search for the flaw in ourselves since, our patriotism notwithstanding, we cannot applaud the mud in Szeged, the countryside of Hortobágy, the pavement in Pest, and the shores of the River Danube with its dirty theaters, innumerable wayfarers, and disgusting beggars."[34]

Széchenyi concluded that, in order for the Magyar cultural revival to succeed, Hungarians had to look beyond a centuries-old Magyar superiority that, many believed, had

been smothered and undermined by Habsburg rule, German language, French literature, a sense of superiority that justified a narrow Magyar patrotism, and an uncondi-
tional, blind devotion to the Kingdom of Hungary. Rather, Széchenyi understood cultural revival to be one component of a sweeping set of reforms that would pare away
the backwardness and lack of vision that antiquated laws and privileges imposed on
Hungarian society, politics, and culture, and transform the Kingdom of Hungary and
the Magyar nation into truly vibrant entities.

For Széchenyi, overcoming prejudice against Jews was the final step in a trajectory
that began with a Magyar cultural revival and the unifying of Buda and Pest. He regarded the separation of Pest and Buda by the Danube, each with a restrictive charter
of privileges, as an obstruction preventing any attempt to improve commerce and administration in either city. Already in 1828, he called for the elimination of what he
saw as an antiquated divide: "The name of our capital must be changed to 'Budapest'
and, in this way, the two cities would be amalgamated, since currently the two do not
present one another in the best light. . . . Once we demonstrate the benefit of amalgamation, Hungary will have a burgeoning capital in no time."[35] In this way, he saw the
amalgamation of the two capital cities as integral to addressing the shotcomings of his
country: "Our sweet homeland would not be neglected and patriotism would attain
its true calling and destiny, if we could transform sandy plains into fertile fields, turn
the sickly swamps into flowering meadows, link our country to the sea, and connect
Buda with Pest."[36]

The underdeveloped character of Buda and Pest, in his estimation, epitomized the
backwardness of Hungary: "Our streets are for the most part unusable, our canals are
flawed, our waterways are in need of regulation." Any hope of transforming Hungary
into a country able to participate and compete in European commerce, he believed, had
to begin by improving basic infrastructure and reinventing Pest and Buda as more livable cities: "We must have stone streets that are amenable to wagons, and navigable canals. . . . Proper public transportation is a prerequisite to cultural revival." Ultimately,
he saw unifying Pest and Buda as a crucial first step toward achieving the larger aim
of placing Hungary on equal footing with more developed countries: "There are only
three ways to uplift Hungary: the nation, transportation, and commercial intercourse
with other nations."[37]

Emblematic of all of these shortcomings, he believed, was the fact that Buda and
Pest were still separated by the Danube. He understood this separation not only in actual terms but also metaphorically, as a chasm between progress-minded individuals
and those who clung to the antiquated traditions of a hallowed past. Eliminating the
actual separation, he suggested, would eliminate the figurative separation, too: "The
permanent bridge between Buda and Pest will not merely couple our country's twin
cities but will simultaneously put a stop to the situation in which a metaphorical river

divides our country in two." With this central aim in mind, in 1831 Széchenyi founded the Budapest Bridge Association (Budapesti Hídegyesület), whose aim was to raise money and awareness to help bring this goal to fruition.[38] Bridging the two banks of the Danube, moreover, would, in his view, bring immediate results, beginning with a surge of immigrants into Pest: "If Budapest would develop, there would certainly be twice, nay, many times more people living there than now." In his estimation, transforming and amalgamating Buda and Pest would not simply accomplish a commercial end but also be a step toward improving the quality of life for all people in Hungary, which he saw as a core aim in all the reforms he advocated: "In our country, every person (or at least the largest possible number) should not merely possess a stomach, head, or wallet, but should possess them with some security."[39]

To be sure, while critical of those who focused exclusively on a love of country, Széchényi did not regard the amalgamation of Pest and Buda, improving infrastructure there and elsewhere in Hungary, and improving the quality of life as mutually exclusive with a patriotism-driven pride in the Magyar nation and Magyar culture. On the contrary, he believed that Pest and Buda, transformed and amalgamated, would become exemplars of the greatness of *Magyarság* (Hungarianness) by seamlessly blending a love of country with the other changes he advocated. His vision of Pest, in particular, as a source of Hungarian pride was echoed by Hungarian laureate Mór Jókai: "Hungarians feel a particularly sweet pleasure when they think of Pest. We long to visit Pest. We want to see youthful, lovely Pest, that budding bride of the honored veteran [*hadastyán*] Buda, with its charming rows of houses, its renowned public buildings, and so many attractions that a newcomer's five senses would be overwhelmed if he wanted to savor them all."[40] Like Széchenyi, Jókai associated the transformation of Pest after the Flood as a pillar of the Magyar national awakening: "Only during the 1830s did an active vital Magyar life begin. The Flood of 1838 thwarted old Pest for the most part. The ensuing reconstruction had in large part a national spirit and, under this influence, Pest took on a Magyar character."[41]

Széchenyi's aim of transforming Pest remained more theoretical and aspirational than actual until 1838. The Great Flood added a more concrete and urgent dimension to the discussion about transforming Budapest. In the devastating aftermath of the Great Flood, the pressing need to repair and rebuild much of the city translated the theoretical musings of Széchenyi and like-minded thinkers about a new Pest-Buda into actual, concrete plans to recreate "Budapest" as a fundamentally new and different city. At the forefront of this newfound urgent practicality was Miklós Wesselényi.

Wesselényi, a prominent member of a leading Transylvanian magnate family, had emerged during the 1830s as a controversial figure in the Hungarian liberal opposition and an early proponent of Magyar cultural awakening and national solidarity. In his seminal treatise, *Balítéletekről* (On Prejudice), he articulated his liberal and national aims and, like other reform-minded nobles, regarded the two largely inseparable and indispensable in overcoming Hungarian backwardness: "Imagine what we could do in Hungary if the multitude of different national groups and religions would overcome all of these conflicting viewpoints and petty prejudices so that all of the nation's citizens, regardless of nationality, could join hands to bring about unity and a single national state by sacrificing their mutual animosities and suspicions upon the nation's altar?" [42] After several years of recurring entanglements with the Habsburg government in Vienna and its arch-conservative leader Clemens von Metternich, he insisted that all people in distress equally merited assistance, regardless of social class, nationality, or religious affiliation. As he noted in his diary, during the flood he grew angry at other nobles who were only interested in saving prominent flood victims in the inner city, and less interested in helping commoners in the outer boroughs where the situation was much more dire and lethal. As such, his actions were not only heroic but also a hands-on, lived demonstration of the patriotic liberalism he had advocated for nearly a decade. As one historian aptly noted:

> Wesselényi's actions during the flood made a hero out of the very man Metternich wanted to paint as a major state enemy. The hounded baron emerged as a national icon, while the Austrian government and its Hungarian representatives appeared peevish and short-sighted, if not incompetent.... Perhaps the most enduring influence of the 1838 flood is symbolic. In a time of crisis, a member of Hungary's titled nobility made a visible decision to physically rescue needy souls, regardless of their social status. A prominent, though embattled, national figure manned a boat to save imperiled lives rather than simply occupy space on the national stage. Wesselényi's conduct during the flooding reflects the congruence between his thoughts and actions. Without attempting to apotheosize him, we may note that Wesselényi's nineteenth-century liberal principles were not mere abstractions, but guiding forces of action, which directed him in a time of trouble. When lives were in peril he did not put his personal convenience above public concerns, but rather implemented his political beliefs to help others. At a time when his own life was on the line and when he was racked with bodily pains, he opted not to focus on his own personal woes, but repeatedly rowed out into the watery darkness to rescue his fellow men. [43]

Energized by Wesselényi, Széchenyi intensified his efforts to fund and construct a bridge that would connect Pest and Buda. Ever the pragmatist, Széchenyi reached out separately for sources of funding and for someone to begin the project itself. On March 21, 1838, he wrote to Baron George Sina, a leading figure in the finance and banking world of nineteenth-century Vienna and one of the richest men in Europe: "I hope the matter of the bridge will not fail to be permitted. At this moment there is nothing to say about the matter. God willing, it will soon come into play victoriously."[44] A week later he wrote to William Tierney Clark, a leading English architect who designed the first suspension bridge spanning the Thames River in London, and the eventual designer of the Lánchíd (Chain Bridge), the first bridge that connected Pest and Buda:

> You have recently been a great benefactor of the two cities. During the initial days following the awful catastrophe, you donated four thousand sterling forints to the poor and helped raise more money, and lent money so the government could begin reconstruction. Now if you can help connect the banks of the Danube with a bridge that will exalt the life of our entire country you will be immortalized as a great son of our motherland.[45]

Though the bridge that Tierney Clark later designed would not be completed for more than a decade, Széchenyi's exchanges with Sina and Tierney Clark in 1838 in the aftermath of the Flood were crucial first steps toward this eventual accomplishment.

Wesselényi's heroism was equally inspiring to other nobles, notably Bertalan Szemere. Szemere was not a native of Pest or Buda but hailed from Miskolc in northeastern Hungary, a frontier nobleman who wanted to see Pest transformed into an impressive national capital city. In late 1838 and 1839, Szemere had recently concluded an excursion across Europe in search of urban archetypes upon which to model the reconstruction of Pest in the aftermath of the Great Flood of 1838. He had traveled extensively in Europe and based on his experiences in London, Paris, Vienna, Berlin, and Amsterdam, he wanted Pest to be rebuilt in a way that would give it "a national image"; that is, he wanted Pest to become the city that represented a new Hungary: "We want nothing to remain from what we inherited from our forefathers. Rather, we should create something here that our progeny will inherit from us.... Like a family, a capital city should have its own pleasures and delights, its own gardens and parks.... The city council should have no regrets giving up a bunch of market squares and stalls. The city winds should breathe a well-ordered and spiritually uplifting atmosphere."[46]

Writing upon his return to Hungary, he contrasted Pest and Vienna with the more developed cities of Western Europe. After lauding the innovative, well-constructed grandeur of London and Paris, he lamented that Vienna was a city that, though pristine, was a haphazardly constructed town: "Vienna evinces no distinct character whatsoever, as least none that one can or must note.... Because of the expansive glacis, open fields and open air are distributed unevenly among the population of the city."[47] He described his beloved Pest even more disparagingly: "Seeing Pest with her decrepit stone walls, it often occurs to me, and I ask myself again and again: why don't we build cheerful, seamed streets? Why don't we allow more space for breezy squares?"[48] This perspective was not only a response to the more developed character of Western European cities, but to the failure of less developed cities like Vienna and Pest-Buda to withstand and respond effectively to the flooding of Vienna in 1830 and Pest-Buda in 1838.[49]

Like Széchenyi, Szemere advocated an array of reforms similar to that of Széchenyi, including the importance of remaking Buda and Pest and emancipating Hungarian Jews. With regard to the latter, Szemere was not only an advocate but one of the architects of Jewish emancipation. Even more so than Széchenyi, Szemere saw the emancipation of Jews and the inclusion of Jews in mainstream Magyar society as part of the same larger project that included the amalgamation of Buda and Pest and the revival and eventual dominance of Magyar language and culture over its rival national movements. "The capital should give our own nation its own face. . . . This principle rather than building individual houses, will create enclaves of houses and entire streets in a grand plan that will make Pest into a city of all sorts of regal residents."[50]

Given their predilection with English economic and social development, it is not surprising that Széchenyi and Szemere articulated a vision of the Hungarian capital that drew on comparisons with London. Széchenyi's use of England as a frame of reference is not surprising, given that reform-minded Hungarian nobles regarded England as an exemplar of moderate, gradual, incremental change that did not pose a threat to noble privilege. The complementary relationship between commercial expansion and social liberalism—a combination of Edmund Burke's moderate (i.e., nonreactionary) conservatism and John Stewart Mill's moderate (i.e., antidemocratic) liberalism provided a useful frame of reference for reform-minded nobles, many of whom discovered in English pragmatism a preferred path forward through which they could undertake necessary economic and political reforms without causing the upheavals that beset France.[51] This was no less true of Széchenyi's evolving attitude toward Hungarian Jews and the feasibility of Jewish emancipation in Hungary. In 1844, Széchenyi, addressing the National Assembly in the midst of a debate over the benefits and dangers of emancipating Hungarian Jews, contrasted Hungary with more advanced Western European countries: "The English nation can emancipate the Jews, since if I, for example, add a bottle of ink to a large lake, the water would not be ruined and all could drink from the lake without harm; thus the large English body can absorb the Jews. The same is true for France. However, if one were to add a bottle of ink to the Hungarian soup, the soup would be inedible."[52]

In a sense, their vision of a future Budapest as a thriving metropolis driven by thriving commerce and a diverse population recalled the vision of London that Voltaire had articulated more than a century earlier. Reflecting on his time in England during the second half of the 1720s, Voltaire noted the relationship between a diverse society and thriving urban commerce:

> Take a view of the Royal Exchange in London, a place more venerable than many
> courts of justice, where the representatives of all nations meet for the benefit of

mankind. There the Jew, the Mahometan, and the Christian transact together, as though they all professed the same religion, and give the name of infidel to none but bankrupts. There the Presbyterian confides in the Anabaptist, and the Churchman depends on the Quaker's word. If one religion only were allowed in England, the Government would very possibly become arbitrary; if there were but two, the people would cut one another's throats; but as there are such a multitude, they all live happy and in peace.[53]

Szemere, like Voltaire, saw Hungarian Jews as part of a grand vision of the Hungarian capital as a center of commerce and urban society:

I imagine Hungary as its peoples assembled around a large banquet table. Spread out on the table are the nation's property, life, peace, freedom, honor, glory, fortune, hope for the future, and blessing for the rest. All the peoples of Hungary are at the table and guard it to the last drop of blood, to the death. Off to the side, however, stands one nation, which rises in defense of the treasure-laden table; although it has no freedom on the table, no honor, no rights among those rights whose defense it takes part in . . . it sheds as much blood as the other peoples. This people is the Jewish people![54]

CONSOLIDATING CHANGE, 1840–1868

This first step toward realizing the broader visions that Széchenyi, Wesselényi, and Szemere articulated before and after the Flood came to fruition in 1840, when the National Assembly enacted a series of political, social, and economic reforms. Already in June 1839, the Pest County Assembly acknowledged the sense of solidarity between Jews and Christians in Pest and Buda who had weathered the Flood together: "Since the Hungarian people see the Jews not as a separate people but as a distinct part of its *Burghertum*, we confer on them the rights of the Hungarian townsfolk . . . with the understanding that they shall be expected to Magyarize their particular rituals and henceforth shall be obligated to follow the same laws." These reforms were, at once, a signature moment in the trajectory of Hungarian liberalism, in the development of Pest and Buda, and for Hungarian Jews. With regard to the latter, these laws elevated Jews to the level of other non-nobles in Hungary by eliminating most restrictions on residence and occupation—heretofore the two main legal distinctions between Jews and non-Jews.[55]

Two laws in particular, Law 15 and Law 29, were especially impactful. Law 15 defined the right of individuals not to be persecuted or disadvantaged because of their religious affiliation or observance—a crucial modification, especially for observant Jews who refrained from working on the Sabbath—and was an important step toward placing

Jewish merchants on equal footing with their Christian counterparts: "Christians on Christian holidays and Sundays, Israelites on Saturdays and on their holidays enumerated in the following paragraph, are not obliged to respond on these days to a complaint or to acknowledge being served; if therefore the last day of the time limit falls on such a day, the presentation or the declaration about its acceptance can be postponed to the next day." The law subsequently revealed a remarkable familiarity with and sensitivity to the Jewish observance of the Sabbath and festivals by acknowledging that these days begin the evening before: "On the days preceding Saturday or the festival days enumerated in the preceding paragraph, the Israelite is obliged to declare concerning acceptance only until three o'clock in the afternoon."[56] Law 29 complemented this new occupational liberty by removing the principal restriction on Jewish residence—exclusion from royal free cities, which hitherto included Buda and Pest—and by allowing Jews to engage in artisanal crafts and manufacture goods rather than only buying and selling them:

> All Jews who were born in the country or in the adjacent territories, as well as those who have legally obtained permission to live here, unless there is a proven well-founded objection impugning their moral conduct, can live anywhere in the country and adjacent territories—except the mining towns.... Under the existing conditions the Jews can found factories and practice trades, whether by themselves or with the help of journeymen of their own religion, and can instruct their young people in them—and can hereafter also practice those sciences and skilled crafts that they have practiced until now.[57]

These laws marked a significant change in the legal status of Hungarian Jews that culminated in the incremental changes set in motion during the 1830s and especially in the aftermath of the Great Flood. In effect, the leaders of Pest and Buda learned opposite lessons from the uneven damage caused by the Flood. In Buda, the problem was deemed to be a surplus of outdated regulation. In Pest, the poor response to the Flood, particularly in the outer city, was attributed to the lack of regulation. These contrary conclusions were crystallized into Law 29 of 1840. In addition, drawing on the experience of Pest during the Flood, a caveat was added to the new law, which distinguished native-born and long-time Jewish residents from recent arrivals and new immigrants. Unimpeded residence was granted only to those who had lived there for ten years or more. New immigrants were still obligated to petition for the right to settle.[58]

Law 29 impacted Jewish settlement in Buda and Pest differently. The new law permitted unobstructed Jewish settlement in Buda for the first time and the emergence, for the first time in a century and a half, of an actual Jewish community. In Pest, the impact was more mixed. While introducing the possibility for more Jews to reside in Pest legally, the law also subjected more Jews, especially less affluent Jews who had been living in Pest off the radar, to be denied legal residence officially, and required all would-be Jewish migrants to Pest to clear this new administrative hurdle. The mixed effect of these laws is most apparent in terms of subsequent Jewish settlement. After 1840, an increasing number of Jews settled in Buda but only affluent, connected, low-profile Jews. In this sense, the new post-1840 Jewish community recalled Jewish communities in medieval cities, with one difference. During the Middle Ages, the Jews needed special permission from a powerful authority figure to settle. In post-1840 Buda, the conditions were laid out by the Diet, and any Jews who met these conditions were allowed in.

1848: FROM GRADUAL TO RADICAL CHANGE

That neither Law 29 nor Law 15 elicited any significant backlash, moreover, suggests that neither introduced or advocated a situation that was novel in 1840. Rather, both laws crystallized changes that had taken place gradually over the course of the last several decades. The Jewish presence in Pest, though largely illegal, had become a routine social reality by the end of the 1840s. Indeed, there was a certain continuity between the status of Jews in Pest before and after the enactment of these laws. Heretofore, Jews lived in Pest under the protection of individual noble families, the Zichys and the Orczys. After 1840, Jews lived in Pest under the aegis of a noble institution—the National Assembly. In both cases, the right of Jews to live and trade in Pest was an integral part of a commercial and political alliance between Jewry and nobility.

By contrast, in 1848 the status of Jews in Pest veered sharply in a more radical direction with the outbreak of revolution, demands for the elimination of hereditary privilege, and full Jewish civic equality that included Jews joining the ranks of the Hungarian National Guard (Honvédség)—a radical departure from the status quo. Not surprisingly, this proposed change prompted an immediate backlash in the form of rising tensions that led to the outbreak of riots in Pressburg/Pozsony and Pest. On April 19, 1848, the public revolutionary assembly passed a resolution evicting all Jews from Pest who had settled there after 1838—effectively undoing the new view of the city after the Flood—and expelling Jews from the National Guard; 224 Jews were evicted from Pest immediately.[59] On March 15, a city captain in Pest reported "tensions with the Jews" caused by rumors that Jews would be called en masse to serve in the National Guard. Local burghers—mainly merchants, master craftsmen, and journeymen—feared that the acceptance of Jews as equal citizens was imminent. When Jews were admitted to the National Guard, these fears intensified.

Yet it is useful to note that the riots were not caused only by the announcement per se, but also by proximity and timing. The Jewish neighborhood was adjacent to

the heart of revolutionary activity in Pest. Most of the revolutionaries turned riot-
ers gathered barely half a mile from Terézváros and the Orczy House. Moreover, revolutionary tensions peaked in April during Holy Week, which happened to fall that
year right before Passover, thus fusing the conventional anti-Jewish animus associated
with the Crucifixion and the blood libel. On April 18, rousing speeches at the National
Museum demanded that city hall expel Jews from the National Guard. Members of the
crowd attacked Jewish national guardsmen stationed in front of the museum, and a
hunt began for others. Responding to (false) rumors that Jews were being sheltered in
the church in Barátok Square (today Ferenciek Square), a mob tried to tear down the
gates of the church. When this failed, the crowd made its way to the Jewish market on
Károly utca adjacent to the Orczy House, rammed the doors of the houses, smashed the
signs in the display windows, and looted and destroyed Jewish stores and small shops
there. Additional rumors that Jews on Király utca were throwing stones at passersby
incited further violence. In fact, the opposite was true: drunkards were carrying sticks
with the engraving "Jewish passports." A local newspaper, the *Pesti Divatlap*, reported
that "many stores were destroyed, and more Jews were pursued and beaten and shot."[60]
Finally, after several days of violence, gendarmes were called in from Buda to quell the
rioting and protect Terézváros and Király utca.[61] Sándor Petőfi and Mihály Vörömarty,
two of the main leaders of the revolution, protested the riots and were instrumental in
preventing the evictions from Pest from proceeding further, as Vörömarty declared:
"All at once, we heard that in Pest Jews are being attacked. Is this revolution, in which
we won freedom, not able to respect order?"[62]

In retrospect, the riots measured the limit of Jewish acceptance into the Pest mainstream, delineating between Jews living in Pest legally and as equal citizens. Yet within
six months, as the revolution morphed from a liberal struggle against tyranny into a
Magyar struggle against Habsburg imperialism, Jews were welcomed back in the revolutionary camp. Jews in Pest took the lead in this regard, donating money and even selling holy objects to help fund the war effort, even reducing the number of Jews employed
by the Pest Gemeinde. More tellingly, not only were Jews allowed to volunteer to serve
in the Honvédség, but large number of Jews were conscripted. Jews in Hungary flocked
to the Honvédség in droves. The largest single contingent of Jewish volunteers came
from Pest and included 5 majors, 11 captains, 14 first lieutenants, 34 second lieutenants,
44 master sergeants, 43 corporals, 186 privates, and one field chaplain (see appendix 1).

This was an important moment of solidarity between Hungary and Hungarian
Jews generally and between Pest and Pest Jewry, culminating in August 1849 with
an edict of Jewish emancipation. This edict was short-lived, abrogated following the
defeat of the Hungarians in the fall of 1849; yet its symbolic importance and impact
resonated thereafter. Doubts regarding the loyalty of Hungarian Jews to their country were largely laid to rest by the service of hundreds of Jews in the Honvédség, and

then reinforced by the number of Jews who were among the ranks of those arrested and punished after the war by the Habsburg government for participating in the revolution and in the War of Independence (see appendix 2). Most conspicuous perhaps was Löw Schwab, chief rabbi of Pest, who was sentenced to six weeks' imprisonment after the war ended.[63]

On reexamination, the revoking of the emancipation edict did not leave Hungarian Jewry worse off, in Pest and Buda no less than anywhere else. Here again it is instructive to compare the situation with that of Jews in England, and especially in London, a century earlier. In 1753, the English Parliament passed the Jew Bill, naturalizing all Jews living in England and elsewhere under British rule. A year later the law was revoked. Yet Anglo-Jewry was not really worse off after the law was revoked. The gradual gains made by Jews in England during the preceding decades were left intact; in particular, Jews in London continued to participate in and contribute to the commercial life of the city of London. Apart from a few restrictions, notably the right to run for Parliament and earn degrees from the universities of Oxford and Cambridge, Anglo-Jewry was de facto a community of naturalized subjects.[64] So, too, for Jews in Pest. Neither legal emancipation in 1849 nor its abrogation shortly thereafter significantly altered the day-to-day situation of Jews in Pest. Jews in Pest were already becoming part of the city's commercial and urban fabric by the end of the 1840s.

As in London, economic and urban development resumed after the revolution, with little or no significant interruption caused by eighteen months of revolution and war. In this regard, the completion of the Lánchíd (Chain Bridge) in 1849 on the heels of revolution and war, the first land link between Pest and Buda and the culmination of a project that Széchenyi had imagined two decades earlier, reflected the continuity between the pre- and post-path toward the amalgamation of Pest and Buda, as did railroad construction. The first railways in Hungary—the Pest-Vác and Pest-Szolnok lines, completed respectively in 1846 and 1847—were designed to enhance the status of Pest as an important economic and commercial hub. During the 1850s, the Habsburg government in Vienna tried unsuccessfully to undercut the commercial prominence and industrial influence of Pest through the routing of railway lines elsewhere, with limited success. The Székesfehérvár-Győr-Vienna line, completed in 1854, bypassed Pest completely and redirected train traffic from these important regional centers directly to Vienna. The other main lines, though, notably the Pest-Vác-Galánta-Poszony-Vienna and the Buda-Nagykanizsa-Trieste lines kept Pest at the heart of the railway network. After 1860, the Hungarian government reoriented railway construction so as to ensure even more that Pest retained its position of commercial and economic prominence.[65]

Construction and renovation in Pest, often organized and funded by the Habsburg dynasty, complemented these efforts to transform Pest further into a major commercial center. The wall around the inner city was replaced by a boulevard that became the heart of the city's commerce and transportation.[66] For the first time, the city invested more money in developing the districts of the outer city than on those of the inner city. By 1872, the city had spent 2.3 million forints on construction in the Belváros, and the balance on the outer city with the largest amounts allotted to construction in Terézváros and Józsefváros (3.5 million forints each) and Lipótváros (2.5 million forints). Belváros, though still regarded as the elite area of the city, was increasingly challenged in this respect beginning in the 1850s and 1860s by Lipótváros, where the newly emerging commercial and industrial elite of Pest increasingly lived. Jewish settlement in Pest proceeded along similar lines. As Jews in Pest rose in the ranks of the city's commercial elite, the number of Jews living in Lipótváros increased accordingly. The Jewish community of Pest, though now overwhelmingly comprised of legally residing Jews, still divided into a Jewish elite—living in Lipótváros as part of the commercial elite—adjacent to a growing mass of less affluent Jews residing in Terézváros.[67]

The most significant change in the relationship between Jews and the city of Pest, though, took place beginning at the end of the 1850s: the construction of a new great synagogue on Dohány Street. First conceived in the mid-1850s, the construction of this synagogue embodied the nexus between the new development of the city and its burgeoning Jewish community's expanding institutional network. The new synagogue quickly became part of the skyline of a new Pest, a clear indication that Jews were no longer merely a tolerated minority but part of the urban landscape. Indicative of this change was the contrast between an 1854 travel guide whose "must see" places in Pest-Buda made no mention of Jews, and the crowds of residents and tourists, Jewish and otherwise, who visited the Dohány Street Synagogue a decade later. Though not yet full citizens, Jews in Pest were no longer the marginal urban enclave they had been a generation earlier, and the Jewish population was not only larger but also embedded into the architectural fabric of the city.[68] The emergence of Pest signaled the triumph of the inclusive, diverse, and Magyarizing Pest over the hallowed, exclusive privileges of Buda and its still-German *burghertum*.

Even as the three towns moved closer to amalgamation under the leadership of Pest, there was still one last step for the city and its Jewish community to take: a full embrace of Magyar culture and Magyar nationalism. Still in the midst of a culture war, the residents of Pest needed to resolve where they stood vis-à-vis the contest for hegemony between *Deutschtum* and *Magyarság*. The dominant vernacular language and culture of major cities in East Central Europe at this point was German; and there was, as yet, no major city with a dominant Magyar culture. In this sense, Széchenyi understood correctly that the barrier to full acceptance of Jews had as much to do with the vitality of Magyar culture as the foreignness of Jews. This pointed to a crucial difference between London at the time of the Jew Bill and Pest a century later that haunted Széchenyi when he contemplated giving Hungarian Jews complete access to mainstream Hungarian society: was Magyar culture well developed enough to absorb an element still as foreign as Jews? There was no immediate threat in England to the primacy of English language and culture—Shakespeare, Milton, and Donne were unparalleled cultural icons. In Hungary, by contrast, in the mid-nineteenth century Magyar language and culture was still in the midst of a *Kulturkampf* with German language and Viennese culture; during the 1850s, the political efforts of the Habsburgs to subordinate the Kingdom of Hungary to the status of other Habsburg possessions elevated the latter over Magyar language and culture. In this environment, Széchenyi's reservations about Magyar culture resonated widely. By the end of the 1860s, as Pest emerged not only as a focal point of this struggle but as the bastion of an emerging liberal Magyar culture, the emancipation of Hungarian Jews would proceed naturally. Jews, no less than anyone else, would need to choose a path at a cultural crossroads between the German and Magyar cultures before attaining full citizenship and full acceptance into the mainstream of Pest society. The challenge for the Jewish community of Pest would be to create a Jewish identity that remained rooted in the world of Judaism and Jewish life while striking a usable and stable balance between two competing vernacular cultures.

5

A Model Neolog Community:
From Nordau's Pest to
Herzl's Budapest

*I was born in 1860 in Budapest in a house next to the synagogue.
... I first saw the light of this world on the front door of our house on
Dohány utca.*[1]

— *Theodore Herzl*

THIS BRIEF REMINISCENCE BY THEODORE (TIVADAR) HERZL EPITOMIZED NOT
only what it meant to come of age in Pest during the second half of the nineteenth
century, but how rapidly Pest and its Jewish community were changing at that time.
Herzl and Max Nordau, his sidekick in the Zionist movement, were born in Pest
barely a decade apart. Yet they lived in two very different cities. Nordau, born in
1849, grew up in Pest when the city of Pest and its Jewish community were only beginning to come of age and Pest was still very much a city dominated by German culture. Herzl, though growing up only a decade later, lived in a city that was reaching
full maturity by the time he was a teenager and was more a Magyar-dominated city.
Herzl lived next to the most prominent Jewish institution in Pest—the Dohány
Street Synagogue—which did not exist until Nordau was a teenager. Nordau's family regularly attended a small but still prominent synagogue near the Orczy House;
Herzl, though he lived only a stone's throw away from the newly completed Dohány
Synagogue, rarely attended services. Both grew up in the area that later came to be
known as the "Pest Jewish Triangle" (*pesti zsidó háromszög*), an area bounded by three
leading synagogues—the Dohány Street Synagogue, Rombach Street Synagogue, and,
later, Kazinczy Street Synagogue—and was densely populated by Jews. Yet Nordau
grew up surrounded by only a handful of communal institutions; Herzl grew up in
the midst of many more communal institutions, yet he was involved only sparingly
with the Jewish community.

In this regard, the childhood experiences of Herzl and Nordau embody the variety and scope of Pest Jewry at the midpoint of the nineteenth century. Both lived through seminal moments in the history of the city and its Jewish community. Nordau was born at the tail end of the Hungarian Revolution of 1848–1849 and the Hungarian War of Independence, and lived through the Neo-Absolutism of the 1850s, when the Habsburgs attempted to Germanize the city. Herzl was born in 1860, the year that marked the first step toward Hungarian rejection of Habsburg Neo-Absolutism and the first step toward Hungarian political autonomy within the Habsburg monarchy and cultural dominance within the Hungarian part of the monarchy. When Herzl was eight—the same year the monarchy was re-monikered Austria-Hungary—he lived through a high point of liberalism and the emancipation of Hungarian Jewry. When he was thirteen, his hometown Pest amalgamated with Buda and Óbuda to form Budapest. These were important capstone moments for Herzl, Nordau, and Hungarian Jews in Budapest and elsewhere in Hungary.

No less defining and varied was their connection to and involvement in Jewish communal life and the life of the city, and to the emerging Neolog movement. Nordau grew up in an observant family before eventually abandoning traditional Judaism as an adult; his childhood connection to Pest Jewry was the conventional nexus that revolved around synagogue and Jewish schools. Herzl, though largely nonobservant, remained connected to the Jewish community, partly because all Jews were required to affiliate but also to avail himself of the benefits of membership in this growing community. All in all, Herzl's experience in Pest was perhaps epitomized by the schools he attended: he attended a Jewish school for several years, and later he attended a leading Lutheran school whose student body was overwhelmingly Jewish.[2]

In tandem, Nordau's and Herzl's experiences represented the main stratum of a multilayered Pest Jewry: the Neolog community of Pest, which was the largest Neolog community in Hungary and the largest religiously progressive Jewish community in the world. Neolog Jewish identity, in Pest and elsewhere, came to represent two distinct but overlapping Jewish outlooks. For some Jews, Neolog meant an approach to religious observance that seamlessly incorporated tradition and innovation in Judaism. For religiously indifferent Jews, Neolog meant affiliation with the Jewish community through the payment of annual dues and a more vague, abstract sense of belonging. Both notions of Neolog encouraged Jews to live simultaneously and seamlessly in the world of the Jewish community and mainstream Pest culture and society. Though gravitating toward the notion of Neolog as affiliation rather than observance, both Herzl's and Nordau's lives in Pest pointed to a dual identity that combined Jewish and Magyar elements, a microcosm of a developing Jewish community with an expanding array of institutions and constituencies that was immersing more deeply in the broader urban life and culture of a city that was en route to becoming a major cosmopolitan European metropolis.[3]

To be sure, Herzl's and Nordau's dual identities were two of multiple possibilities. Reflecting on the intellectual and ideological diversity of Jewish intellectuals in early twentieth-century Budapest, Ferenc Laczó distinguished multiple varieties: "parallel" identities that apposed Jewish and Magyar dimensions, "combination" identities that integrated the two dimensions, "assimilating but self-preserving" that emphasized the Jewish over the Magyar, "assimilated but emphatically Jewish" that presupposed the Jewish and Magyar to be perfectly compatible, and "internally conflicted." These various dual identities manifest most clearly within the Jewish intelligentsia — rabbis and Jewish writers, social critics, and political thinkers — that matured during the second half of the nineteenth century and were heavily concentrated in Pest.[4]

Yet they can also be understood as strategies employed by Jewish communal institutions to help Jews in Pest, regardless of their outlook, live comfortably in both the Jewish community and the broader social mainstream. The use of one or more of these strategies is illustrated by the array of communal organizations that, seen together, measured the maturing of Budapest Jewry during the second half of the nineteenth century into both a vibrantly Jewish and actively Magyarizing community. Notable among these institutions are the Jewish hospital, which was founded for Jews but eventually served a broader clientele; the Pest *Realschule*, which epitomized the broadening educational horizons opened to Budapest Jews by the 1870s; the Dohány Synagogue, whose completion in 1863 marked the maturing of Budapest into a major European metropolis and Budapest Jewry into a leading European Jewry; the Magyarization Society, which steered all Jews in Pest toward the Magyar language and culture; the Pest Jewish Women's Association, which expanded Jewish philanthropy and charity into a template for the city's nascent social services network; the Magyar Israelite Crafts and Agricultural Society (MIKÉFE), which cultivated Jewish artisans with a strong sense of Jewishness; and Jewish intellectual cohorts such as the Israelite Hungarian Literary Society (Izraelita Magyar Irodalmi Társaság). Together these organizations molded a rapidly expanding Jewish community from a loosely connected array of communal institutions during the 1830s into a complex institutional network that facilitated the Neolog aim of living simultaneously in two worlds.

It was no mere coincidence that the completion of the Dohány Synagogue, in particular, coincided with the opening of the mainstreams of Pest society and culture; both developments reflected a similar expansion of Jewish space in Pest. The great synagogue became the first prominent Jewish element of the city's urban landscape when Jews like the young Herzl made their first inroads into the mainstream culture of the city. By the 1860s, Jews like Herzl faced little or no difficulty in participating in the institutional and cultural infrastructures of the Jewish community and the city. From the 1840s through the 1870s Pest Jewry expanded into a multilayered Jewish community whose members lived with one foot in a world defined by communal institutions and the other in an urban society that increasingly welcomed Jews.

Amid the growing opportunities that presented themselves after midcentury, Herzl and his Jewish contemporaries faced the challenge of navigating a fork in the cultural path of Pest Jewry that the bifurcated character of urban culture in Pest presented to the Jewish community. As the door to mainstream society opened more and more widely to Jews in Pest after midcentury, Jews that entered the mainstream found two vernacular cultures vying for dominance, each driven by its own revered language: the Magyar language and culture, and the German-language-driven Viennese culture. Within the Jewish community, the navigation of this *Kulturkampf* would play out, above all, in synagogues and community schools: in the former, over the language of the sermon and rabbinic discourse; in the latter, in the language of instruction and the relative primacy of Magyar and Viennese culture.

NUMERICAL INCREASE

The growth and development of Jewish communal institutions after midcentury was facilitated by the rapid numerical increase of the Jewish community. At the end of the 1830s Pest Jewry was crossing the tipping point from a smaller, more intimate community in which, to paraphrase Mack Walker, Jews "knew their neighbors and needed their neighbors" into a larger community in which Jews not only did not know one another directly or intimately but perhaps had never met or seen one another.[5] The number of Jews residing in Pest, which had barely exceeded five thousand in 1833, exceeded sixteen thousand by 1848. By the end of the 1860s, the Jewish population of Pest approached fifty thousand. When Pest was amalgamated with Óbuda and Buda in 1873, the total

TABLE 15. POPULATION OF BUDA,
ÓBUDA, AND PEST, 1836–1870

YEAR	BUDA/ÓBUDA	PEST	MILITARY	TOTAL
1836	37,439	64,313	—	101,752
1841	38,974	68,266	—	107,240
1845	42,124	79,777	—	121,901
1851	50,127	127,935	—	178,062
1857	55,240	132,651	—	187,081
1870	70,000	200,476	—	280,439

Source: Gusztáv Thirring, *Budapest székesfőváros a millennium idejében* (Budapest: Pesti könyvnyomda, 1898), 5.

TABLE 16. POPULATION OF BUDA AND PEST, 1851

	MAGYAR	GERMANS	SLAVS	SERBS	JEWS	ITALIANS	ROMANIANS	ROMA	TOTAL
BUDA	6,182	22,122	1,124	1,145	1,538	—	8	—	38,301
PEST	31,965	33,884	97	570	12,642	130	198	84	79,570
ÓBUDA	1,373	5,817	183	35	3,438	46	8	—	10,900
3 TOWNS	39,520	61,823	1,404	1,750	17,618	176	214	84	128,771

Source: Joseph Vincenz Haufler, *Topographische Skizzen und Wegweiser von Ofen und Pest* (Pest, 1854), 87–88.

population of the newly amalgamated Budapest approached sixty thousand. This numerical increase was not unique to Jews but reflected a broader increase in the overall
population of the three towns. Yet the increase in the Jewish population, especially in
Pest, outpaced the population of every other group.

This numerical increase resulted from several converging developments, first and
foremost being the legalizing and regularizing of the right of Jews to reside in Pest.
Additionally, the growth of the Jewish community was further fed by the proximity of
many smaller Jewish communities to Pest. The city of Pest was surrounded by numerous small and mid-size Jewish communities in Pest County and neighboring counties,
in addition to the more than three thousand Jews who lived in Óbuda. For thousands
of Jews living in one of these locales who chose to relocate to Pest after 1840, the journey was often less than 50 or 100 miles.[6] For many would-be Jewish migrants, moreover, travel to Pest was facilitated by improved transportation. For Jews living in one of
the towns situated along the Danube, improvements in the river after the Great Flood
of 1838 facilitated travel to and from Pest. For others, the expansion of the railroad further facilitated traveling to Pest. This was instrumental not only in encouraging Jews
to relocate to Pest, but also making it easier for Jews who had moved to Pest to visit and
send part of their earnings to the family they left behind.[7]

There was also a demographic shift in the profile of Jews migrating to and living in
Pest. Until the 1830s, the boomtown character of Pest appealed mostly to young entrepreneurs who often came to Pest alone in search of adventure and to earn a better living.
For Pest Jews who had hitherto lived in Pest illegally, legal residence meant no longer
fretting about legal entanglements—with Jews or non-Jews—that could potentially expose the lack of a residence permit and the possibility of eviction. This brought a greater
sense of stability that was particularly important to Jews with families and children. As
the institutional network of Pest Jewry expanded beginning in the 1830s, the town became more attractive to families looking for a suitable place to raise Jewish children.
By the 1860s, the demographic profile of Pest Jewry reflected this shift. Whereas previously most Jews living in Pest were single men without families, the 1848 census divided the sixteen thousand–plus Jews in Pest into just over three thousand households.
The average size of household was just over five individuals.[8]

This rapid numerical increase diversified the Jewish community in terms of occupation and wealth. As the community grew larger, the range of occupations broadened
concurrently. By 1848, just over half of Jewish householders in Pest were involved in
some form of commerce; many others, though, were engaged as artisans, in the food
service industry, and as salaried employees.[9]

The number of Jewish artisans, in particular, increased both in size and diversity.
One in seven Jews in Pest engaged in some form of artisanal craft by 1848. Collectively
Jewish artisans were engaged in twenty-seven different trades.

TABLE 17. PEST JEWS BY OCCUPATION, 1848

OCCUPATION	%	OCCUPATION	%
Merchant	26	Factory workers	2
Artisan	13	Cow herders	2
Shop clerk	9	Pawnbrokers	2
Peddler	9	Clergy	1
Broker/middleman	7	Musicians	1
Book dealers	3	Grocer	1
Caretakers	3	Innkeepers	1
Medical/health workers	2	Other	7
Teachers	2	Unknown	9

Source: *Első magyar zsidó naptár és évkönyv 1848-ik szökőévre* [The First Hungarian Jewish Almanac and Yearbook for the Leap Year 1848, hereinafter *Első magyar zsidó naptár és évkönyv*] (Pest: Landerer and Heckenastnál, 1848), 137.

TABLE 18. JEWISH ARTISANS IN PEST, 1848

ARTISANAL TRADE	MASTER CRAFTSMEN	JOURNEYMEN	APPRENTICES
Gold/silver smith	13	—	—
Table maker	2	5	2
Tinsmith	4	7	4
Umbrella maker	7	—	—
Button maker	12	50	8
Cotton maker	1	5	3
Upholsterer	4	5	3
Lithographer	2	15	—
Bookbinder	3	8	3
Locksmith	1	3	2
Butcher	4	—	—
Watch—case maker	1	—	—
Watchmaker	7	7	3
Haberdasher/furrier	5	50	8
Jeweler	15	—	—
Pipe makers	19	—	—
Cosmetologist	28	—	—
Hatmaker	17	—	—

Continued

TABLE 18. Continued

ARTISANAL TRADE	MASTER CRAFTSMEN	JOURNEYMAN	APPRENTICES
Tailor	204	410	—
Soapmaker	1	—	—
Toolsmith	1	—	—
House painter/decorator	42	—	—
Wallpaperer	3	—	—
Wallet maker	2	—	—
Tanner	3	—	—
Glazier	8	16	3
Cobbler	13	26	15
Total	422	607	54

Source: *Első magyar zsidó naptár és évkönyv 1848—ik szökőévre* [The First Hungarian Jewish Almanac and Yearbook for the Leap Year 1848, hereinafter *Első magyar zsidó naptár és évkönyv*] (Pest: Landerer and Heckenastnál, 1848), 138.

This occupational diversity continued unabated. As in other cities and towns, certain occupations were increasingly populated by Jews in disproportionate numbers. According to the 1869 census, one of every thirteen men in Pest (7.7 percent) was Jewish. Yet Jewish men comprised more than half of those engaged in commerce, seven out of ten bookkeepers and accountants, nearly one-third of all tailors and *pálinka* brewers, one-quarter of all furriers, nearly one-fifth of innkeepers and coffeehouse proprietors, and one in every nine jewelers.

TABLE 19. JEWISH OCCUPATIONS IN PEST, 1869

OCCUPATION	% JEWISH
Bookkeepers and accountants	70.2
Commerce	60.1
Tailors	36.9
Pálinka brewers	35.1
Furriers	25.0
Innkeepers/coffeehouse proprietors	18.4
Jewelers	12.5

Source: Károly Vörös, "A budapesti zsidóság két forradalom között, 1848–1918," *Zsidóság a dualizmus kori Magyarországon*, ed. Varga László (Budapest: Pannonia Kiadó, 2005), 42.

A larger community membership also diversified the Jewish community in terms of place of origin. Four strata emerged within the Jewish community by the end of the 1860s based on four areas of origin: (1) native-born Jews from Pest and Óbuda, (2) n-migrants from elsewhere in Hungary,[10] (3) immigrants from Central Europe, and (4) a much smaller enclave of immigrants from Galicia and Ukraine. These categories eventually crystallized into a pecking order based on country of origin and proximity to Pest-Buda, mainly because Law 29 of 1840 granted legal residency to Jews born in Hungary but not explicitly to Jews who were born elsewhere.

Beyond legal status, moreover, the closer one's place of origin was to Pest, the higher one's status. Jews from Galicia and Ukraine were at the bottom of the social scale, followed by Jews from the northeastern counties in and around the Carpathian Mountains, specifically Máramaros, Bereg, Ugocsa, Zemplén, Sáros, and Ung Counties; and then Jews from central and western Hungarian counties. Jews from Central Europe—specifically the Czech Lands, the Austrian *Erblande*, and the German states—were higher up. Jews born in Pest stood at the top of the pecking order.[11] By 1869, occupational tendencies had emerged within the various strata of the Jewish community. Jews born in Pest and second-generation Jews tended to work in more lucrative forms of commerce and the free professions. Recent Jewish arrivals from Central Europe trafficked in agricultural products, as the twin cities became a hub for the agriculture trade. Jews from Galicia, Ukraine, and the northeastern counties of Hungary tended to be petty merchants, peddlers, tailors, grocers, shopkeepers, brokers, porters, and—in a few cases—part of the intelligentsia or clergy. For Jewish women, the most common occupation was domestic servant (234 in 1848), while a few were hired as nannies (10 in 1848). In addition, the many women who worked in or helped run the family business with a father, brother, husband, or son were not listed in the census.

LIPÓTVÁROS

The growth of the Jewish community, coupled with the elimination of residential barriers, encouraged Jews to move beyond the confines of Terézváros, which had hitherto been a relatively compact Jewish neighborhood, to Lipótváros and Józsefváros; and eventually contributed to the subordination of the hitherto independent Óbuda Jewish community and the nascent Buda Jewry to the now largest and dominant Pest Jewry. By the 1860s Jews were settling in growing numbers in more parts of Pest and beyond. One-third of Jews still lived in Terézváros at the end of the 1860s; more than 20,000 Jews in the densely populated area bounded by Szerencsen, Király, Dob, and Dohány Streets; yet fully one-third of Pest had relocated to Lipótváros and Józsefváros by the end of the 1860s. The nascent Jewish community in Buda is also instructive in this regard. Jews had been effectively excluded from Buda until the 1830s; Jews in Buda were denied even a cemetery until 1830, and hitherto had to bury their dead in Pest or Óbuda. After Law 29 opened Buda to Jewish settlement, a small community developed there, a mixture of peddlers, who comprised half of Jewish households there in 1848, and upwardly mobile merchants and shopkeepers. By 1848, more than 200 Jewish children attended school in Buda.[12]

The move to Lipótváros, in particular, reflected not only an attempt by Jews to escape the crowded conditions of the old neighborhood, but also a measure of upward mobility.[13] Already by the late eighteenth century Lipótváros was an area reserved for families of means. Whereas Terézváros was inhabited largely by artisans and lower-income day laborers before the influx of Jews, Lipótváros was populated by leading magnate families. The Orczy family had built upscale homes on Károly utca and Országút, and later a warren on Marokkói Court. Though rents in Lipótváros were briefly devalued during the Napoleonic Wars and then again after the Great Flood of 1838, they otherwise rose consistently.[14] Jews began to settle gradually in Lipótváros during the 1830s. The area was one-sixth Jewish by 1840, one-quarter Jewish by 1850, nearly one-third Jewish by 1857, more than one-third Jewish from 1869 until the turn of the twentieth century, 30 percent Jewish from 1900 to 1914, and then again one-third Jewish from 1920 until 1930.[15]

As the Jewish community spread out of the old neighborhoods of Terézváros and Óbuda, the task of maintaining communal integrity intensified. It was not clear initially whether the rapidly increasing Jewish enclave in Lipótváros, for example, would become a separate community, especially given the ample resources of Jews there. For Jewish communal leaders, the first step toward taking on this challenge was creating a more formalized and less amorphous Jewish community. Demographic expansion challenged the Jewish community in Pest and its leadership to address emerging complexities in Jewish communal life, three in particular: administrative chaos, institutional redundancy, and demographic diffusion. A larger, rapidly increasing, more diverse, and more spread out Jewish community demanded a clearer definition of the obligations and benefits of membership and a more well-coordinated leadership structure. Hitherto, communal affiliation was a hybrid of older and newer communal practices. Like a classic Gemeinde and even a *Kultusgemeinde,* affiliation was required. Unlike the classic Gemeinde, once individuals joined and as long as they paid their dues, participation was largely voluntary. This larger, less intimate community retained some of the basic structure and function of its smaller, earlier counterpart; but it also required a more elaborate leadership structure to manage a much larger pool of communal revenue from a more varied system of taxation and charitable donations, as well as a membership that was more diverse in terms of origin, religious outlook, and occupation.

The occupational and economic diversity of the community, moreover, led to a wider distribution of income levels. During the 1830s, all but a handful of Jewish families were middle class or below, and many lived at subsistence level or below. The enrollment in the three levels of membership defined by the 1832 Statutes reflected this uneven distribution. From 1833 through the end of 1847, the number of *wohlhabende* Jews rose slightly from 5 to 10 percent of the membership during the 1830s to 10 to 15 percent by the end of the 1840s. The number of *bemittelt* members remained constant, fluctuating slightly between 50 percent and 60 percent. The number of poor Jews declined from about one-third in the mid-1830s to around 30 percent by the end of the 1840s. A generation later, the 1865 Statutes divided membership into five categories according to annual membership dues, with each new member assigned a tier by the community executive council. Annual dues ranged from Level 1 members, who paid annual dues of 15 forints, to Level 5 members, who paid 100 forints.[16]

The first step toward improving the leadership structure was the introduction of a greater sense of order and formality. Hitherto communal administration and decision-making had consisted largely of a small coterie of families attempting to manage a few thousand local Jews and a small group of loosely connected organizations. Typical of smaller towns and Jewish communities, community meetings frequently had been loud and contentious affairs, in which leadership redressed (or at least attempted to redress) a series of grievances. Individual members presented their grievances ad hoc, with no set order of prioritizing of issues. Grievances involving money—particularly disputes over commercial contracts and inheritance—and status, which often meant a dispute over a seat in the synagogue or a plot in the cemetery, not infrequently devolved into accusations of defamation of character, which at times were revisited as separate disputes in subsequent meetings.[17]

The leadership of the community had begun as early as 1832 to address this lack of order and decorum. The 1832 Statutes defined one of the raisons d'être of the Jewish community to be regulating settlement and residence. The introductory section of the 1832 Statutes noted that one of the effects of communal reorganization during the 1830s was "to escape from the chaos of every person having access to community meetings and a voice in deliberations."[18] This meant replacing the communal management as an open, often chaotic town hall format, which functioned almost like an extended family gathering, with a more systematic and orderly protocol. With this aim in mind, the 1832 Statutes instructed that each membership tier designate thirty members for an election committee, and this ninety-member committee would elect a thirty-member community council that would, in turn, appoint a five-member executive committee. The Statutes instructed further that each tier would elect four members of a twelve-member executive board to work with and advise the executive committee. By 1846, this selection was expanded, each tier nominating three candidates for each position and then choosing one.

TABLE 20. COUNCIL ELECTION OF 1846

SEAT	NOMINEES	ELECTEE
1	Herman Lőwy, Leopold Portzen, Sholem Englander	Herman Lőwy
2	J. H. Kassovitz, D. M. Koppél, Gerson Spitzer	J. H. Kassovitz
3	Jónás Kunewalder, Leon Hirschler, B. Sakenbacher	Jónás Kunewalder
4	Adolph Pinhas, Mór Schulhof, Mór Szinger	Adolph Pinhas
5	Joseph Stern, S. M. Sachst, Eli Katzburger	Joseph Stern
6	Leopold Portzen, Jonas Kramer, Mór Schlesinger	Joseph Stern
7	M. Singer, Gabriel Frankl, Carl Hürsch	M. Singer

Source: *Szefer Zichronot* [Gemeinde Protocol], PIH- I-2-4, *Zsidó Levéltár* [hereinafter PIH] #31 (1846).

The thirty-member council would also annually nominate a slate of officers to be approved first by a majority of the thirty-member committee and then by a majority of the membership at large. This slate included community president and vice president, two orphanage directors and hospital administrators, notary and vice notary, treasurer and comptroller, beadle for the synagogue, and, as needed, rabbi, preacher, and *hazzan (Vorsanger)*.[19]

Increasingly from the 1840s on, leadership positions, and especially the upper tiers, were held by members of a small coterie of elite families. The same six or seven families were consistently represented on the executive committee and the inner council of the Gemeinde. The same families were also the main donors and officers of the Hevra Kadisha, the Jewish hospital, and the community school, all three of which still operated independently at this point.[20] Reminiscent of the court Jews of the preceding century, these Jewish families had more access to mainstream society than most Jews, while remaining connected to the Jewish community. Occasionally a member of the Jewish elite would abandon the Jewish community—especially in moments of heightened political and social tensions, such as the revolutionary events of 1848–1849. For the most part, though, the Jewish elite in Pest remained largely intact and continued to preside over a growing Jewish constituency.

The families that formed this communal elite did not see themselves as a closed caste within the Jewish community. Instead, this coterie was at once open and exclusive: open to all families with the proper *yikhes*, the gateway to the communal elite.[21] The status of the elite families in the community underscored how the Jewish community was both egalitarian and hierarchical: egalitarian in the limited sense that all propertied men were equal members of the community in terms of the benefits of membership; yet access to the leadership elite—especially the executive committee and the inner council—depended largely on *yikhes* and was thus reserved for a small select group.

In a sense, the notion of *yikhes* as defining the relationship of the communal elite and the rank-and-file membership of the Jewish community mirrored the relationship between nobles and non-nobles in Hungarian society and, within the nobility, between its upper tier and the rest of the nobles. Like the Jewish community elite within the Jewish community, nobles had exceptional status within Hungarian society that entitled them, above all, to an exclusive right of political participation in the form of voting for delegates to the county and national diets and standing for election themselves. Like the Jewish communal elite, the nobility was a privileged but not a closed caste; non-noble families with the proper credentials could be ennobled. The nobility, like the Jewish communal elite, apposed egalitarianism and hierarchy. Legally, all nobles were equal, regardless of wealth and family connections; in reality, there were sharp inequalities within the nobility, particularly between its elite of magnate families and everyone else. So, too, members of the small coterie of the wealthiest Jewish families exerted influence beyond that of their communal leadership position. As with noble status, the concretely defined prerequisite for elite Jewish status created a natural sense of solidarity and commonality between elite Jewish families, and facilitated efforts by the leadership of the Gemeinde and other Jewish organizations to cooperate and eventually merge.

The obligations and responsibilities of communal leaders reflected the needs of rank-and-file members and were adapted as these needs expanded. Initially, responsibilities and obligations were limited mainly to monetary and financial matters. Board members were required "to participate in weekly meetings, and meet as needed to help deal with issues as they arose," approve ad hoc disbursements of communal funds of less than 100 forints, and "expand, modify, apportion, and recover communal debts, impositions, payments, and grants." The executive committee was required to present the annual budget to the general membership at the beginning of each fiscal year, at which point the outer council would elect a seven-member steering committee to advise the executive council regarding the budget.[22]

From the late 1840s the leadership structure of the community had increased both in number and complexity. The community leadership in 1865 consisted of 120 members: an eighty-four member outer council, nominated by the election committee, approved by the inner council, and elected by the general membership; a thirty-member inner council, nominated by the election committee, approved by the outgoing inner council, and elected by the outer council; and a six-member executive committee consisting of a presiding officer and five subcommittee chairs, nominated by the election committee and elected by the inner council. Theoretically, at least, all dues-paying members were eligible to vote in communal elections and serve as part of the community leadership. In practice, those holding leadership positions and, in particular, members of the executive and inner councils were older and more affluent members of the community—and among the highest taxpayers.

For rank-and-file members, obligations and benefits of membership expanded steadily. The 1865 Statutes defined membership more clearly than the 1832 Statutes: "In order for all members to have access, every Jew residing in Pest is obligated to affiliate with the *Religionsgemeinde*, and membership will include the wife and children of all affiliated members.... Each member, aside from those who are manifestly poor, are obligated to maintain the communal institutions and to pay the annual statutory dues assessed by the community council."[23] The 1865 Statutes formalized the prerequisites to vote in communal elections and hold a communal leadership position, first by distinguishing between voting (i.e., "active") and nonvoting ("passive") members. Voting members had to be at least twenty-four years old and contribute at least 5 forints annually to community charities, apart from annual dues. Salaried employees and servants of the community were disqualified from both active and passive membership. Those vying for a council position had to be at least thirty years old, have been voting members for at least five years, have a secure source of income, and donate at least 20 forints annually to the community. In addition, no blood relatives and in-laws of current members were allowed to join the inner council or executive committee.[24]

These prerequisites reflected the crystallizing of a hierarchy superimposed on an official egalitarianism in membership. Theoretically all members' dues were determined based on annual income using the same graduated scale; and all members received the same benefits of membership. The prerequisites for voting and holding a leadership position suggest an Aristotelian preference for leaders who were older, propertied, and philanthropic—an important hallmark of Jewish leadership generally. At the same time, the restriction on blood relatives and in-laws represented a pushback against nepotism and an attempt to limit, however broadly, the voice of elite families in communal affairs. This concern was well founded, given that the path toward a more formal organization did not displace but rather reinforced and then expanded an existing communal oligarchy.

GROWTH AND EXPANSION
OF INSTITUTIONS

The formalizing and stabilizing of membership and administration allowed the leadership to move beyond the relatively limited mandate of regulating settlement and focus on institutional development: "The leadership council has the duty of preserving and developing existing and future legal, social, religious, ritual, educational, and charitable institutions by appointing the wisest individuals to maintain and advance these institutions and to ensure that all members participate in these institutions."[25] This meant, among other things, expanding existing institutions and integrating them into a more well-coordinated institutional network. As long as the number of autonomous or semi-autonomous Jewish organizations remained constant, the situation worked reasonably. At the end of the 1830s, the Hevra Kadisha was one of only three benevolent societies in Pest. Thereafter, as the size of the Jewish community increased, the number of benevolent societies providing similar services increased geometrically. Amid the growth of the 1840s, a host of Jewish organizations appeared in Pest, mainly schools, synagogues, and benevolent societies that modeled themselves after extant, more conventional Jewish organizations in Pest and Óbuda. The Pest Gemeinde acted at this point only nominally as an umbrella, loosely connecting these organizations and only minimally supervising them; the Pest Hevra Kadisha, in particular, operated largely independently of the Gemeinde, aside from occasionally asking for financial assistance or free loans, despite an overlap between the leadership of the Gemeinde and the Hevra Kadisha.

Beginning in the 1840s, moreover, communal organizations expanded to service a larger constituency. In particular, the health and medical services provided heretofore by the Hevra Kadisha expanded to include an enlarged and renovated Jewish hospital. Jewish educational opportunities, once limited to a few small-scale Jewish schools, expanded in two directions: updating and upgrading existing Jewish community schools into more cutting-edge schools such as the Pest *Realschule* (later renamed the Pest *Népiskola*); and creating new Jewish educational organizations whose curricular aims were not specifically Jewish, that is, artisanal training and immersion in Magyar language and culture. Most dramatically, perhaps, smaller congregations and synagogues were absorbed by larger ones, above all by the Dohány Street Synagogue but also by the Rombach Street Synagogue, completed in 1872.

The proliferation of new Jewish organizations paralleled a broader emergence of voluntary associations in the three towns, particularly in Pest.[26] As with Jewish communal organizations, Christian organizations were formed and operated along confessional lines: Catholic, Calvinist, Lutheran, and Greek Orthodox. These communities formed voluntary societies that performed functions parallel to those in the Jewish community—philanthropy, benevolence, religious ritual, and a women's association. Like their Jewish counterparts, Christian voluntary societies in the capital cities had often operated under the radar of Habsburg censorship, albeit for different reasons. They had avoided the censors because, in Metternich's Europe, voluntary associations were often suspected of being cells of insurrection and revolution, and they were harassed by imperial and royal officials. Jewish organizations avoided the censors before 1840 because most Jews were not supposed to be there. For both Jewish and Christian communities in Pest, the development of a network of voluntary organizations formed the backbone of "civic society," a stratum between government and the individual in the case of Christian communities, and, in the Jewish case, between the Jewish community and individual Jews.[27]

Until the end of the 1840s, moreover, the limited array of Jewish institutions in Pest and Óbuda were still comparable. At the beginning of the 1830s, Óbuda Jews had organized, in addition to a Kehilla, a Hevra Kadisha and a Free Loan Society. The Hevra Kadisha, in addition to the standard responsibilities of a Jewish burial society—preparing and standing vigil over the deceased and preparing the body for burial—was also the main provider of medical care to Jews.[28] In addition to medical care, the Hevra Kadisha provided an annual stipend to its members. The Hevra Kadisha also operated a hospice with twenty-four beds and provided free medical care for the local Jewish poor (2,360 forints' worth of care in 1848).[29] The Free Loan Society, founded in 1832 in the aftermath of the cholera pandemic, grew rapidly beginning in 1838 in the aftermath of the Great Flood. Even though its building was destroyed in the flood, it continued to provide loans for more than two decades.

By 1848, there were fifteen Jewish voluntary associations in Óbuda, all under the jurisdiction of the Kehilla: a Talmud Torah Society, a Dvar Torah Society, a Hevra Kadisha, nine other benevolent societies, and three charitable organizations. The Dvar Torah Society provided stipends for clergy and, after the death of the community rabbi in 1832, hired itinerant preachers to deliver a weekly sermon in the synagogue. The Talmud Torah Society supported the local *Heder* and the local *Normalschul*, and made sure all poor and orphaned children had the means to attend. Annual membership dues and donations that members raised in the synagogue allowed this organization to donate an average of 6,000 forints annually, 2,300 to cover the tuition of poor children and the remainder to help cover teachers' salaries and clothe an average of thirty children each year.

More extensive was the array of complementary benevolent societies. Nine of the ten benevolent societies supplemented the services and assistance provided by the Hevra Kadisha,[30] which remained the most prominent in community affairs. All members of the Óbuda Jewish community were automatically members of the Hevra Kadisha, including lower-status individuals such as servants, apprentices, and journeymen. Until the mid-1830s, the Hevra Kadisha was supported primarily by annual dues from its members and personal donations. By 1848, it was also supported by an annual 200-forint contribution from the Pest Jewish community. The other benevolent societies supplemented the spiritual, medical, and eleemosynary support provided by the Hevra Kadisha. These organizations were smaller, and most were able to operate supported only by individual donation. The Menucha Nechona (lit. proper rest) Society helped "ensure smooth transition to the afterlife ... by praying for deceased at the funeral and, thereafter, at memorial occasions." Six other benevolent societies provided additional coverage for medical care. Two organizations—the Anshei Makom Society and the Sandak'ut Society—provided supplemental care for all who were infirm (the latter was supported, in addition to fees, by an annual gift from the Esterhazy family). In addition, the Családapa egylet provided hospice care for unmarried men; the Mish'enet Dalim Society provided 2 forints weekly for sick children; Nőegylet (Women's Society) provided supplemental medical care for women.[31] The Havit Yetomim Society provided orphans with a weekly stipend of 54 forints; by 1848, this organization was aiding sixty to seventy orphans each month, during which time no orphan received less than 648 forints annually. The Kenyér egylet (Bread Society) allotted three loaves of bread to every family; by 1846, this organization was doling out 3,148 loaves of bread annually.

Other organizations complemented the financial support provided by the Hevra Kadisha and other benevolent societies. The Kemach 'Aniyim (Flour for the Poor) Society provided indigent Jews with Passover matzo. The Zedakah Society disbursed 100–120 forints each month to widows. The Kupat Orchim (Sheltering Guests) Society arranged for each communal officer to provide a small stipend to help the local homeless find proper accommodations; this took on particular importance when the town banned local beggars.[32]

Parallels notwithstanding, there were two key differences between the role of the Kehilla in Óbuda and Pest and each one's relationship with other Jewish organizations. Óbuda Jewry was a relatively small and more compact Jewish community that was never able to sustain more than a single network of communal institutions. Pest Jewry was much larger, with a constituency large enough to sustain more than one of a particular institution and diverse enough to require more than one. The Kehilla in Óbuda, moreover, was created when the community was first recognized by the Zichy family, and thus predated the formation of other Jewish communal organizations there. There was an established Jewish communal elite by the time other organizations began to appear. These other organizations immediately came under the jurisdiction of the Kehilla; in some cases, Kehilla leaders were among the founders of these newer organizations. By contrast, in Pest the earliest communal organizations—the Hevra Kadisha, two synagogues, and a Jewish school—predated the official creation of a Pest Gemeinde that, even after it was established, had limited jurisdiction.

These two differences influenced the trajectory of institutional expansion in the two Jewish communities. In Óbuda, the Jewish community increased steadily but comparatively slowly during the middle third of the nineteenth century, from around three thousand Jews to just under seven thousand. The array of institutions in Óbuda, though already beginning to pale next to the burgeoning Jewish organizations in Pest, provided the latter a template to emulate. In addition, the new institutions that Pest Jews created during the 1830s and 1840s were often transplanted by Jews from Óbuda relocating to Pest. The Jewish organizations in Pest that were modeled after those in Óbuda quickly outgrew their older antecedents and surpassed them in complexity.

THE JEWISH HOSPITAL

The Jewish Hospital in Pest began as an extension of the Hevra Kadisha and the hospice it operated, much like the Hevra Kadisha and hospice in Óbuda. Until 1838, the hospital in Pest was small with limited patient capacity; at the outbreak of the Flood, the hospital had served an almost exclusively Jewish clientele. During the Flood, the Jewish Hospital began its transformation into a municipal institution. When the Flood made the building of the Jewish Hospital inaccessible in March 1838, the patients were transferred to the Jewish school, a larger space, on Könyök Street (which later became Andrássy Boulevard). This larger space made it possible for the hospital to open its doors and provide medical care to a number of Jewish and non-Jewish flood victims that exceeded the number of patients the hospital had treated previously.

This, in effect, demonstrated the hospital's as yet unrealized capacity. Once the Flood subsided, the Jews of Pest resubmitted a petition to purchase a plot of land in Pest for a newer, larger Jewish Hospital. In 1840, the Jews of Pest received permission from the city to purchase land on Gyár utca (later the corner of Aradi and Jókai utca) and build a new, larger, state-of-the-art hospital. The cornerstone laying ceremony took place on September 21, 1841, and was attended by local dignitaries, including Palatine Archduke Joseph, who laid the cornerstone himself.[33] Dr. Phillip (Fülöp) Jakobovics was hired as hospital director, a position he would hold for thirty-eight years. This new hospital was situated in a one-story building 1,025 fathoms long, with a spacious court, a garden, a seven-room infirmary, and three recovery rooms, each with twelve beds.[34] One local observer described the new hospital as "a handsome building with practical interior design, first rate medical and financial administration, fantastic doctors and scholars including Drs. Stahly, Wattmann, Balassa, Appert, and other local and imported scholars and doctors."[35]

The hospital was managed by a commission, which directed day-to-day affairs, and a board of trustees that oversaw financial matters. The former consisted of three physicians, Hospital Director Dr. Phillip Jakobovics, Chief of Medicine Dr. Anton Jakobovics, and Deputy Chief of Medicine Dr. Ignácz Glück. The latter consisted initially of three members of the Pest Gemeinde's executive council. By the 1860s, this oversight committee increased to seven members—three from the Gemeinde's commerce division and four from the health care division. For the most part, the hospital commission and oversight committee divided responsibilities and jurisdiction with relatively little fanfare. The commission submitted to the Gemeinde annually a report about hospital operations, budget, and requests for the coming year regarding personnel, equipment, and infrastructure. The oversight committee recommended how much the Gemeinde should allocate for the coming year.

All Jews who were legal residents of Pest were eligible for medical care from the hospital and its personnel. In determining how to pay for universal care, the oversight committee presumed financial assistance from the Hevra Kadisha, particularly in cases of more costly health care and economic hardship for patients suffering a more protracted illness that required a longer hospital stay. In addition, meeting annual costs depended on bequests and contributions from more affluent members of the Pest Jewish community, which were consistently a line item in the annual budget. In 1842, for example, these totaled 18,000 forints, including bequests of 4,000 forints from J. Schak, 3,000 forints from Elias Kohn, and 2,500 forints from the Jewish Traders Association.

The expansion and improvement of the Jewish Hospital, it should be noted, not only reflected the growth of the Jewish community but also the growing influence of Pest's leading hospital—Saint Rókus Hospital. Like the Jewish Hospital, Saint Rókus began as a hospice at the end of the eighteenth century funded, operated by, and serving a particular religious community. Completed in 1798, Saint Rókus started out with 237 beds, 100 of which were reserved for indigent patients. Regular patients paid a daily fee of 12 krajcárs; indigent patients were treated for free. More affluent patients could rent one of twelve private rooms for 50 krajcárs per day. In 1851, noted physician Ignatz Semmelweis accepted a position as chief of obstetrics. Semmelweis was in the process of revolutionizing hospital care through the introduction of basic sanitary practices such as requiring doctors and other medical professionals to wash their hands with chlorinated water before examining patients and keeping examination and operating rooms clean and hygienic. These novel ideas were radical enough at the end of the 1840s for Semmelweis to be dismissed from his position at a leading Vienna hospital whose starkly conservative board equated radical medical practices with radical politics. At the Saint Rókus in Pest, by contrast, these practices became standard during the 1850s, not least of all because they reduced the frequency of patients developing fevers during treatment below 1 percent. The medical practices at Saint Rókus became a model for other hospitals in Pest, including the Jewish Hospital.[36]

By the beginning of the 1860s, though, certain problems began to arise that brought the medical and financial leaders of the Jewish Hospital into conflict. As the number of patients increased, the challenge of providing quality medical care to all deepened. The number of patients admitted to the hospital increased steadily, from the annual range of 200–300 patients during the 1840s, to 300–500 annually by the end of the 1860s, before exceeding 900 annually by the 1880s.[37] While the patients treated in the hospital represented a diverse cross section of the Jewish community, most had limited financial means. The bulk of the patients were younger people; more than half were under twenty years old and came from low-income families. Half of the patients overall were lower-income individuals, including tailors (91), household servants (37), and

TABLE 21. THE PEST JEWISH HOSPITAL, 1849–1851

YEAR	PATIENTS	FEEDING DAYS	EXPENSES (FORINTS, INCLUDING MEDICINE)	NET REVENUE (FORINTS)
1849	365	6,388	6,004	1,341
1850	321	7,482	6,182	1,732
1851	353	6,482	5,863	2,342

Source: Henrik Hollán, *A Rókus kórház története: adatok és személynevek a Szent Rókus közkórház és fiókjai alapításának és fejlődésének történetéből* [The History of the Saint Rókus Hospital: Documents and Personalities from the History of the Saint Rókus Public Hospital and the Establishment and Development of Its Progeny], 28–29.

shoemakers (26), and they almost automatically needed not only medical care but assistance for their families, especially in the case of shoemakers and tailors.[38]

In addition, the medical staff began lobbying in 1858 to add medical specialists to the hospital staff. The increased cost initially elicited resistance from the oversight committee, but the doctors eventually prevailed, particular after Fülöp Gross replaced Antal Jakobovics as chief of medicine. Gross argued that the cost of adding specialists to the staff would be offset by raising the profile of the hospital and attracting a more upscale clientele from Pest and elsewhere. Accordingly, four specialists were hired in 1865: the surgeon Dr. Balassa, professor of medicine at the University of Pest; aural surgeon Dr. Bőke; odontologist Dr. Kohn; and shock therapist Dr. Wilhelm. In addition, the hospital was able to engage the services of Ignatz Semmelweis several times in 1864 and 1865.[39]

By 1860, moreover, the hospital building and facilities began to deteriorate. Initially, the executive committee of the Gemeinde voted to effect "incremental repairs and improvements" including "new hospital linens, furniture, and other household needs" in order to avoid the massive cost of full renovation—not surprising given that the construction of the Dohány Synagogue was still ongoing and costs still consuming a sizable portion of communal revenue. In November 1863, once construction of the great synagogue was completed, the committee voted for full renovation of the hospital. The new building was completed in 1866. In addition to new furnishings and equipment, the hospital included a large garden modeled after the city gardens.[40] The hope that investing in a renovation would improve the image of the hospital was soon realized. The new facility, combined with the addition of Semmelweis as an attending physician, improved the image of the hospital considerably. Upon completion, Habsburg empress (queen) Elizabeth, a beloved figure in the Hungarian capital, visited and took part in the dedication ceremony.

Eventually non-Jews in Budapest, too, began to seek medical care at the Jewish Hospital. During the cholera epidemic of 1872–1873, the hospital staff admitted and treated dozens of cholera victims. In turn, the city's Cholera Commission thanked the Jewish community for having its hospital "open its gates to all people regardless of religious difference," which, the commission noted, "attested to its noble and altruistic character acting in the interests of suffering people" who "for the duration of the cholera epidemic, regardless of religion, received the best possible treatment and medication." Several years later, during the Austro-Hungarian war against Bosnia-Herzogovina of 1878, the hospital treated fifteen soldiers at the joint expense of the Jewish community and the Hevra Kadisha.[41] The culmination of these encomiums came on December 29, 1885, when the Budapest city council announced: "The hospital founded . . . by the Pest Jewish Community, per the account of its respected chief of medicine, treats patients not of a specific denomination, but all who are sick. In this way, the hospital plays an important part in helping the authorities in the district care for those in need."[42]

Yet for all the renovation and expansion of medical services and clientele, the Jewish Hospital never abandoned its original mission: providing first-rate health care to the Jewish community. Two of the physicians employed by the hospital were designated "poor doctors" and were paid by the Hevra Kadisha to make house calls to indigent Jewish families. This became a source of tension between the physicians and the leaders of the Jewish community, especially those among the latter who saw the hospital, in part, as a vehicle for Jewish acceptance into mainstream Budapest society. While there was general agreement that Jews be given the best possible treatment as needed, there was not always consensus about Jewish patients receiving priority over non-Jewish patients, especially in more high-profile situations and dramatic moments. During the epidemic of 1872, amid the enthusiasm of the recently emancipated Jewish community joining fellow citizens in the city-wide response, Jewish and non-Jewish cholera victims were admitted without regard for religious affiliation. Treatment for Jews with nonurgent, non-cholera-related problems was deferred. Complaints from the latter to the executive council of the Jewish community went unheeded.[43] In the end, the significance of the hospital was summed up by Zsigmond Groszmann a half-century later: "Once designed for the needs of poor Jews, the hospital became in a short time a place that did not acknowledge religious differences, and thus one of the great creations of the Jewish community."[44]

EXPANDING JEWISH EDUCATION

As with the Jewish Hospital, the expansion of Jewish education began during the 1830s as a response to the numerical growth of the Jewish community. In this case, though, there were two added dimensions that reflected broader trends and debates regarding education in the city of Pest: the emerging opportunity for Jews in Pest to attend non-Jewish schools, and the growing *Kulturkampf* over whether German or Magyar language and culture should predominate in Pest. Until the end of the 1820s, educational opportunities for Jewish children in Pest resembled their limited, largely traditional counterparts in Óbuda: schools that were supported by the Gemeinde but set up and run by private individuals, who charged parents tuition; a *Heder* for boys ages three through ten, and a Talmud Torah for boys wishing to continue; assistance from the community for parents who lacked the funds; and the children of affluent Jewish families being tutored at home. [45]

In Pest, some Jews opted to attend non-Jewish schools when these schools accepted them. Already by 1830, 148 Jewish boys and 18 Jewish girls attended the German School. This number nearly doubled during the 1840s. [46] This added a novel element to debates over improving education. Previously, the only alternative to Jewish community schools had been homeschooling—an option available only to a handful of affluent Jewish families. The possibility of attending a non-Jewish school challenged the Jewish School Commission to maintain a quality of education that could compete with the education Jews could now receive at non-Jewish schools. This meant ensuring teachers were competent and properly trained and that the school building was suitably upgraded as necessary. To this end, amid a growing demand for early education, Farkas Weisz established in 1840 a new free nursery school for indigent children, which he funded from private donations and an annual stipend from the Gemeinde. The school employed two teachers and two nurses. By 1848, Weisz had 145 students. In 1850, the main Jewish elementary school relocated to a larger building on 12 Síp utca (where the community center and Dohány Synagogue would later stand). [47]

More impactful was the broader debate over how best to incorporate Magyar and German into the curriculum. From the mid-1830s, the linguistic and cultural struggle between proponents of a Magyar national revival and a Germanocentric Habsburg officialdom wove its way into debates over Jewish education in Pest. Jews in mid-nineteenth-century Pest, and more generally in Hungary, lived amid the two vernaculars vying to dominate the culture of the mainstream; at this point, it was not yet clear what the vernacular was or would be. For Jewish educators and communal leaders alike, the need to wind up on the winning side of this *Kulturkampf* posed a challenge that was at once practical and ideological: practical because of the benefit of helping Jews immerse themselves in the vernacular language and culture of the mainstream; ideological in the sense that the mother tongue of an individual or a community was a crucial marker of the loyalty and patriotism of that individual or community. Faced with this dual challenge, Jewish educators and communal leaders split the difference by including both German and Magyar in the school curriculum, while prioritizing one over the other according to their latest reading of the culture war.

Until the end of the 1830s, the linguistic and cultural balance in Jewish schools favored German, though Magyar was ascendant. The leading Jewish community school,
Öffentliche Israelitische Ungarische Deutsche Normalhauptschule, chose a German
name but listed Ungarische before Deutsche. This was in sync with the fact that, at the
time, even the most ardent advocates of replacing German with Magyar as the language
of government and culture in Hungary were still themselves German speakers. The curriculum of the school reflected a similar dichotomy. The preschool (*Vorbereitungsklasse*)
and first half of the first-grade curriculum included Hebrew and German language instruction; Hungarian language instruction did not begin until the second half of first
grade. In addition, the language of instruction in the school for general studies apart
from languages was German, although the curriculum allotted weekly time for teaching the Hungarian and Hebrew languages (which shared a single lump sum allotment).
This allotment diminished in the third and fourth grades to make room for a broader
range of general subjects.[48]

During the 1840s, as proponents of Magyar culture asserted its primacy more vehe-
mently, the situation was less clear and a debate emerged within the leadership of Pest
Jewry. Some wanted to maintain German as the first language of the community schools
and Magyar as a second first language. In April 1843, the School Commission adopted
two textbooks for language study: the Hungarian primer *Stancsics* and the German
primer and geography textbook used by the St. Anna Normalschule in Vienna.[49] As
a growing number of Pest Jews inclined toward the Magyar language and Magyar nationalism, the Jews who ran the Pest Normalschule increased the number of hours of
weekly Magyar language instruction from three in 1834, to nine by 1843, and twelve by
1847.[50] In 1846, these Jews founded the Magyarization Society. While not exclusively
an education program for children, a primary aim of this society was disseminating the
Magyar language among Hungarian Jews, in Pest and elsewhere in Hungary, particularly among young Jews. One of its first projects was a new "Magyar-Spirit Nursery"
where Jewish children could begin learning to read and speak Magyar from a formative age while learning about Magyar history and culture. Situated in a building on
Kétsas Street, in the heart of Terézváros, the preschool's board of twenty-four mostly
women enrolled more than ninety children. Most of the children paid a small annual
fee; the Jewish community paid for the dozen children who could not afford the fee.[51]

In the aftermath of the Hungarian Revolution of 1848 and the ensuing Hungarian
War of Independence, the Habsburg government spent much of the 1850s attempting to anesthetize Magyar nationalism—part of an effort to replace Hungary's constitutional relationship with the Habsburg dynasty into a direct Neo-Absolutist relationship—by obstructing the further cultivation of the Magyar language and culture.
They regarded education and curriculum as crucial in this endeavor, and attempted to
subordinate Magyar to German, beginning in the schoolhouse. Education reform and

expansion in Hungary during the 1850s, for Jews and non-Jews alike, was in no small part weaponized by a Habsburg regime.[52]

To this end, in November 1849 Karl Geringer, newly appointed provisional governor of Hungary, issued a series of strategic educational reforms that required all children ages six to twelve to attend school (and penalized parents who did not comply); and distinguished between elementary schools founded in smaller towns and villages (*alelemi iskolák*/subsidiary elementary schools) and those founded in Pest and other cities (*főelemi iskolák*/main elementary schools).[53] A follow-up decree from 1855 required children to attend four years of "higher elementary school" for a minimum of twenty hours per week and elementary schools to employ a minimum of four teachers. Geringer also mandated more thorough vetting and training of teachers. Previously, teachers were examined only in elementary school subjects; in 1854, Geringer required teachers to complete a two-year course at an accredited teacher training institute. In order to subordinate all educational endeavors to Habsburg policy, Geringer consolidated the various school systems—Catholic, Lutheran, Calvinist, Jewish—under a single state agency; he was supported by Minister Count Thun, who recommended that the Jewish School Commission in Pest be joined with the various Christian school commissions.[54]

While the initial goal of these reforms was to raise the level of education, a second main aim was Germanizing the Hungarian population by the use of German as the primary language of instruction in all schools.[55] This aim was reiterated periodically by teachers and other school officials in Pest-Buda. Michael Haas, a school counselor in the Pest-Buda District, predicted that "they will see, in five or six years that even the cowboy of the Alföld will learn the alphabet in German in the farm school. . . . If I am a school counselor for another three years, the shepherds of the Puszta also will be singing German songs."[56]

Applying Geringer's educational goals to Jews was aided by the National Educational Fund Act of 1851. This act converted the large tax arrears that Hungarian Jewry had owed to the Habsburg Crown since the abolition of this tax in 1846, and the large penalty imposed on Hungarian Jewry after the latter's role in the Hungarian Revolution of 1848, into a large endowment that would fund a network of state-sponsored Jewish schools in Hungary. The act also required all Hungarian Jewish children to attend these schools. Despite the originally punitive nature of the act, it allowed the Hungarian Jewish community to devote more than one million forints in tax arrears and punitive fines toward improving Jewish education under the aegis of the Habsburg dynasty. During the 1850s, this shifted the balance in the vernacular curriculum of Jewish schools back toward German language and culture, symptomatic of the broader Habsburg Neo-Absolutist limitations on Magyar language and culture.

Emblematic in this respect was the Pest Jewish Secondary and Middle School (*Pester isr. haupt-u. Unterrealschul*), a new Jewish school set up in 1856 for Pest Jews that was supported by the fund. This school was, from the outset, supported by a group of principal benefactors that included representatives of the Jewish community and local government officials. Representing the Jewish community were J. H. Kassowitz (head of the executive council) and Wolfgang Hollitscher (benefactor of the Jewish community and head of the Clothe the Orphan (*malbishe yetomim*) Society. Representing the government were Archduke Albrecht (civil and military governor of Hungary), the minister of religion and education, and Stefan Majer, priest of Graner Diocese and director of Pest Municipal Main- Elementary- and Private schools. Kassowitz and the executive council quickly earned the respect of the government officials, who noted how the "*Kultusgemeindevorstand* of Pest demonstrated an ongoing tireless commitment to preserving and invigorating Jewish education."[57] One of the first tasks of the group was to select a school inspection committee to make sure the school continued to adhere to its aims. This committee included local official Karl Jerenak (a local advocate for *Realschule* education) and six members of the Jewish community: Schwab, Joseph Bach (*Praediger*), Moritz Zilz (theology teacher and *Praediger*), Joseph Hausler, David Gans, and Jacob Kern.[58]

The new school consisted of a coed preschool with two grades (*Kinderbewehranstalt* and *Vorbereitungsklasse*), a boys-only *Hauptschule* with four grades and *Unterrealschule* with two grades, a girls' school with two grades, and a Sunday school program for children attending non-Jewish schools. The most novel element of the school was its inclusion of Jewish girls, particularly in the lower grades. During the summer of 1856, the school's first semester of classes, girls made up 40 percent of kindergartners and the *Vorbereitungsklasse* (where boys and girls were taught together). Thereafter, the girls' school enrolled around one-eighth of the total student population (106/804 students).[59]

The curriculum of the school followed the typical curriculum of a *Normalschule*: an expanded program of Jewish subjects that included Hebrew language and grammar, the Bible (i.e., "biblical history"), rabbinics, theology; and general subjects including mathematics, natural science, civics, penmanship, and German and Magyar language and literature. The latter favored the German language, though time was allotted in each school day for the Hungarian language. The language of instruction of all subjects but Hebrew language and grammar was German.

In order to ensure the availability of qualified teachers for new schools such as this one, the Jewish community, in cooperation with the state, used a portion of the National Education Fund to found the State Israelite Teacher Training Institute in 1859. The institute was based on the Teachers Training Institute founded a decade earlier in Miskolc, with one difference. The one in Miskolc, founded when Magyar cultural influence was ascending in Hungary, emphasized and trained its instructors to teach Magyar language and culture as primary subjects and German language and culture as secondary subjects. The new institute in Pest, founded when Habsburg influence in Hungary

TABLE 22. ENROLLMENT IN THE PEST JEWISH SCHOOLS, 1856

KINDERGARTEN	
Boys	98
Girls	72
Subtotal	*170*
VORBEREITUNGSKLASSE	
Boys	65
Girls	58
Subtotal	*123*
HAUPTSCHULE	
I. Grade	103
II. Grade	123
III. Grade	85
IV. Grade	50
Subtotal	*361*
UNTERREALSCHULE	
I. Grade	29
II. Grade	15
Subtotal	*44*
MADCHENSCHULE	
I. Grade	58
II. Grade	48
Subtotal	*106*
Subtotal (full time): 804	
SONNTAGSCHULE	
I. Grade	28
II. Grade	29
III. Grade	12
Subtotal	*69*
Total	893

Source: *Erstes Programm der Pester isr. haupt-u. Unterrealschul für Schuljahr 1856* (Pest, 1856), 45.

was still at its height, aimed at solidifying the primacy of German language and culture in state-sponsored schools in Pest and elsewhere in Hungary.[60]

In the end, though, the Habsburgs' Germanizing goals were realized only temporarily, above all in nonstate schools that were often beyond the reach of Habsburg policy and penalty. In the Catholic and Protestant schools of Pest-Buda and Nagyvárad Districts, for example, Hungarian continued to prevail undisturbed as the language of instruction.[61] The defiance of leading Hungarian statesmen such as Ferenc Deák, moreover, furthered the cause of Magyar as the primary language of instruction. Addressing a dance organized by Pest University law students in 1858, Deák championed the primacy of Magyar over German: "We here in Pest in no way want to become Germans, and the more we are pressed to do so, the more reluctant we are to part with our nationality. It is a natural instinct, in an individual as much as in an entire nation, that one does not want to die."[62] Deák's words, and others like them, resonated deeply among Jews in Pest, who organized, in 1860, the first Jewish-Magyar Brotherhood Festival.[63]

At this point, a shift in the balance of power between Hungary and the Habsburg dynasty facilitated a resurgence of Magyar language and culture in Hungarian schools; Jewish schools were no exception. The institutions that the Habsburg state had established in cooperation with the Jewish community continued to operate, but with a renewed orientation toward Magyar language and culture. In retrospect, the Habsburgs unwittingly aided this effort by creating an educational infrastructure that, after 1860, helped Magyarize the Jews of Pest. The school they helped established during the 1850s became the template for Magyarizing Jewish schools thereafter. In 1865, the name of the *Normalschule* was changed to *Népiskola*. Enrollment in the Pest *Normalschule/Népiskola* reflected the ebb and flow of German and Magyar culture in Pest. Enrollment reached a high point of 553 in the mid-1850s, a reflection of the influence of the Habsburgs' Germanizing policy. It then dipped to 349 toward the end of the decade as this influence began to wane. Once the school transitioned to Magyar culture in 1860, the enrollment rose steadily, from 408 in 1860 to 706 in 1870.[64] In 1868, the school, along with the Jewish community, affiliated with the Neolog movement, reinforcing the school's commitment to Jewish identity and Magyarization. The Pest *Népiskola* emerged as a fixture of the Jewish community, a mediator for Jews between German and Magyar culture, and a vehicle for an accelerating process of Magyarization.

THE DOHÁNY SYNAGOGUE

The most dramatic indicator of the growth and expansion of Pest Jewry and its immersion into the fabric of Pest urban society was the Dohány Street Synagogue. Since its completion in 1863, this great synagogue has been not only the defining landmark of Budapest Jewry but also a fixture of the city of Budapest's skyline. Yet it was not only

the architectural and aesthetic achievement that defines the importance of this massive edifice, but also the timing and location of its construction and the Neolog service
that took place inside.

The leaders of the Jewish community began discussing the construction of a new,
larger synagogue in the spring of 1852. Hitherto the existing synagogues had been large
enough to accommodate more traditional and more progressive Jews who attended services on a daily and weekly basis. The two main synagogues, known as the synagogue
and the chor-temple, differed somewhat. The synagogue preserved the traditional service largely unchanged, while the chor-temple, modeled after the Seitenstattengasse
Synagogue in Vienna, used the *Wiener Minhag*, a combination of traditional practices
and aesthetic innovations: a sermon in the vernacular and a professionally trained cantor and choir. Those who attended the two houses of worship coexisted amicably and
saw themselves as part of a single community. Löb Schwab and David Brody-Steeliczky,
who were rabbi and cantor of the synagogue, and Jacob Bach and Ede Károly Denhof,
who were *prediger* and cantor of the temple, maintained a close, collegial relationship
despite their different outlooks.[65]

The situation became more volatile with the founding of the Pest Israelite Reform
Society in 1848. This prayer group, modeled after the congregation of radical religious
reformer Ignác Einhorn, introduced changes that were far more radical than in any
other synagogue in Pest: more extensive use of the vernacular, elimination of parts of
the liturgy, and changes in the text of the liturgy for ideological purposes.[66] Though it
lasted four years, this radical group was largely an outlier with respect to Pest Jewry for
two reasons. First, the Reform Society "seceded from the Pest Gemeinde and formed
an independent community after attaining government recognition as an official community." Its embrace of ideological rather than exclusively aesthetic changes was largely
unprecedented in Hungary.[67]

As a result, though relatively short-lived, its erstwhile presence in Pest impacted
communal discussions over synagogue innovations, even after it disbanded. This was
due, not least of all, to the decision by the chor-temple in 1851 to begin using an organ during the Sabbath service. The members of the chor-temple regarded the soon to
be disbanded Reform Society to be overly radical in its practice, and they differenti-
ated their decision to adopt the use of an organ on purely aesthetic grounds from the
Reform Society's ideologically driven innovations. For the more traditional Jews who
prayed at the synagogue, though, there was a lingering concern lest the chor-temple or
any future house of worship become another radical reform society. This concern came
to the forefront in 1852, when a proposal for a new, larger synagogue came before the
Gemeinde. The proposal was prompted by a concern over space. The Jewish community
numbered more than twelve thousand, and the existing synagogues were no longer able
to accommodate the crowd. There was also a concern that, absent a large central synagogue that would attract and house the bulk of the Jewish community, there would be

a proliferation of *shtiblach*—smaller synagogues and prayer groups haphazardly strewn all over the area of Jewish settlement. These, it was believed, would project a less impressive and far less orderly image than a single, prominent, magnificent synagogue.[68]

From the outset there was a broad consensus about investing the money and resources into the new synagogue, but far less consensus as to whether the service in the new synagogue would be modeled after the service in the existing main synagogue or the chor-temple. Ultimately the advocates of a chor-temple-style synagogue won, partly because this group included the affluent, influential families who dominated the ranks of the executive council, but also because of broader willingness to follow the lead of the Vienna Jewish community. A minority would continue to dissent and would eventually found a separate synagogue on Rombach Street.

Once the decision to build the new synagogue as a chor-temple was reached, the Gemeinde hired the noted architect Ludwig Forster to design the synagogue, the same architect who had designed the new Leopoldstadt Synagogue in Vienna. The choice of location was largely a matter of expedience—proximity to the largest number of Jews, many of whom still did not use animal or mechanized transportation on the Sabbath or Jewish holidays. The location of the new synagogue was Dohány Street, near the boundary of Terézváros and neighboring Józsefváros and in the direction of Lipótváros, which reflected the trajectory of secondary Jewish settlement movement out of Terézváros that was already underway by the time the synagogue was completed.

The original cost of building the Dohány Temple was projected to be 200,000 forints, but it quickly spiraled above 500,000 because of unexpected costs of materials and labor.[69] The bulk of the construction costs were covered by the sale of seats to community members. The four thousand seats on the ground floor and women's gallery were divided into three categories according to sale price; families could purchase seats for 500, 300, or 200 forints apiece. The revenue from these sales helped amortize the construction costs, which were projected at the end of 1858 to exceed 500,000 forints.[70] Sale of seats in the Dohány Temple began in November 1853 and continued through the decade and into the 1860s. By January 1854, the committee had pledges for 604 seats totaling 184,200 forints. Typically, community members purchased sets of seats from the men's section and proximate seats in the women's section. All told, the communal protocol of Pest Jewry reported more than seventeen hundred sales of seats in the new synagogue between late 1853 and 1859 when the synagogue was completed.[71] That Pest Jewry was able to bear this expense attests to the economic growth, accumulated wealth, and upward mobility of this community. As one historian noted: "The synagogue in Pest, the largest in Europe, attested to the prosperity of the Jewish community, a central player in the commercial development of Hungary's economic center."[72]

Yet the decision to undertake this enormous venture reflected more than wealth. A willingness to invest money and resources on such a grand scale reflected an expectation of a long-term connection to the city and a powerful sense of security and self-confidence. A Jewish community that regarded its presence in its host city as temporary or ephemeral, and aimed at living there inconspicuously so as to avoid antagonizing Christian neighbors, would not have constructed a synagogue as large and conspicuous as the Dohány Street Synagogue. Remarkably, nearly a decade prior to legal emancipation, Jews in Pest felt a strong sense of civic equality even though *de jure* they were still second-class citizens. They were not the only Jews who evinced this sort of confidence. The Jews of Vienna, too, began construction on a great synagogue, the Leopoldstadt Temple, a decade before full emancipation.[73]

This outlook was buoyed by the fact that, by the 1850s, Jews had been placed on equal footing with other non-nobles over a decade earlier by Law 29 of 1840. Legal and commercial accomplishments undergirded the Neolog aim of being Jewish and part of the city. As Julia Richers noted: "The new feeling of self-assurance and the pride in economic achievement allowed the Jewish community to develop an attendant self-confidence in open use of public space.... Dohány was the hallmark of Neolog Jews understanding their presence as a permanent component of the city."[74] Jews in Pest believed wholeheartedly that their residence would be long-term if not permanent and that they had no reason to fret over an overly conspicuous Jewish house of worship. In retrospect, prior to the First World War, there was no reason to believe otherwise.[75]

The eclectic design and layout of the new synagogue combined, as one historian recently noted, "the layout of a church, the ornamentation of a mosque, and the function of a synagogue."[76] The decision to construct a Moorish-style synagogue, moreover, reinforced Pest Jewry's sense of kinship with the Magyar nation born of a shared non-European heritage. This architectural style celebrated the "Oriental" or "Asiatic" roots that Jews and Magyars shared in common. For Hungarian Jews aspiring to be accepted as Magyars, the celebration of the eastern, non-European origins of the Magyars preempted the outlook that elsewhere in Europe, and especially in Central Europe, saw Jews' Asiatic roots as insurmountably foreign. This aspect of Jewish identity was inverted in Hungary, where the Asiatic roots of Jews and Magyars became a source of kinship, not exclusion. The Moorish style of the Dohány Street Synagogue boldly underlined and celebrated this kinship.[77] All of this contributed to the grandeur of the new synagogue for Jews and non-Jews alike.

The opening of the synagogue on May 6, 1863, was greeted with great festivity. Local journalists noted the who's who of Pest society in attendance, in addition to a large crowd:

On the morning of May 6, the newly built Jewish house of worship [*Izraelit Gotteshaus*] was dedicated in a festive and dignified ceremony. The events, which included our Jewish fellow citizens and which did not pass without arousing the lively interest of broader circles, were witnessed also by her ladyship, wife of the imperial and royal vice-lieutenant Sir Ede Cseh of the General Staff, and many leading figures from civic, spiritual, and military life. Already by eight a.m. the courtyard of the synagogue was filled with a crowd in a reverential mood.[78]

Another observer noted that local dignitaries included representatives from the noble and ecclesiastical hierarchy:

> The celebration began at nine, but already by eight the immense synagogue was completely full, the balcony occupied by a ring of festively clad ladies, while the ground floor was filled with invited gentlemen, among whom were numerous Catholic, Orthodox, and Protestant clergy, many high-ranking soldiers and honoratiores, who sat in seats by the sanctuary. In the area in front of the sanctuary, which was blocked by a gilded iron grate, were high-ranking civic and military authorities with pews, who made an official appearance for the ceremony.[79]

The large crowd that filled the four thousand–seat capacity of the Dohány Synagogue for Friday night and Saturday morning services was comprised of a mishmash of traditional and progressive Jews, and of observant and nonobservant Jews. The melange of outlooks and practices that assembled in the Dohány Synagogue mirrored the service that took place there, a mixture of traditional and innovative customs modeled after the *Wiener Minhag*. The sanctuary faced east in accordance with custom (despite the fact that this meant resolving a serious design problem due to the spatial orientation of the sanctuary vis-à-vis the street). The congregation used a traditional prayer book and liturgy, and followed the traditional course of the prayer service and the traditional cycle for the reading of the Torah.

Typical of a chor-temple, the Dohány Synagogue was saturated with pomp and grandeur, the service being conducted by a professionally trained operatic cantor who was accompanied by a professional choir. The cantorial repertoire drew from a nearly identical musical canon and featured the leading cantors of Europe, for whom the synagogue was an important stop on the Central European tour of great synagogues. As in the Vienna synagogue, moreover, the sermon was delivered weekly rather than the traditional semi-annually; addressed contemporary political and social issues rather than merely explicating rabbinic texts; and, above all, was delivered in the vernacular. At Dohány, though, the language of the sermon pointed to the cultural orientation of the rabbis and, more broadly, to the Jews of Pest. For the first two or three decades after the synagogue opened, the sermon was, more often than not, in German and not Hungarian; likewise, the original name of the synagogue was the Pester Israelitischer

Kultustempel.[80] Thereafter, the pendulum swung in the opposite direction until, by the turn of the twentieth century, the sermon was a Magyar sermon the vast majority of the time. For the diverse array of Jews in attendance—rich and poor, immigrant and native, acculturated and unacculturated—the sermon represented an overarching goal of Jews in both communities: acculturating without abandoning a sense of Jewish identity and a sense of belonging to the Jewish community.

The most salient feature of the Dohány Synagogue and the point where it diverged from its Viennese counterpart was the use of an organ on the Sabbath and festivals. Elsewhere in Central Europe, the organ was a shibboleth that distinguished traditional from Reform congregations. Yet a key difference between the use of the organ at Dohány Synagogue versus the use of the organ in Reform temples was the manner in which this innovation was justified. In Reform temples, the use of the organ was justified by the zeitgeist, that is, the use of the organ in other contemporary houses of worship, such as a Lutheran church. At Dohány, the use of the organ was justified in terms of the halachic precedent, emblematic of the Neolog outlook. Accordingly, the Dohány Synagogue was constructed such that the organ was situated outside the frame of the synagogue; technically, then, the organ music came from outside, and, strictly speaking, did not violate Jewish law or custom. The person who played the organ on Shabbat was non-Jewish, therefore permissible within the rules of a gentile performing work for Jews on the Shabbat (*Goy shel Shabbat*).[81]

Not all the Jews who attended services on Friday evening or Saturday morning were there for reasons of ritual observance. For Jews in Budapest who had long since abandoned prayer and the rest of traditional Judaism, the new synagogue was still a place to congregate and a central hub for social intercourse. Many Jews came to services at the synagogue not to pray or reflect, but for purposes of commercial and social networking and, for upper-class Jews and social climbers, to enhance their standing in the Jewish community. For nonobservant young Jewish adults, this was also a place to meet a future husband or wife. It is noteworthy in this regard that the hybrid Moorish style of the synagogue paralleled that of other public buildings in Pest: railroad stations, cafés, public baths, and zoos.[82] The appeal of the Dohány Synagogue to observant and nonobservant Jews alike exemplified an important aspect of its impact on Jewish communal life: an incentive for Jews who were indifferent to Judaism to remain connected to the Jewish community in some fashion. Elite Jews, in particular, saw the synagogue as a source of status. Obtaining a preferred seat or even a minor role in the service was a source not only of religious honor but social standing—much like a seat on the board of the hospital or the School Commission. A connection to the great synagogue was, in this sense, the ultimate benefit of membership in the Jewish community. At a time when the community had long since lost its coercive authority, the allure of the Dohány

Synagogue, like the advantages of being able to receive care from the Jewish Hospital or a first-rate education from the Pest *Népiskola*, compensated for the loss of coercion with a powerful incentive to participate voluntarily.

By the end of the 1860s, the Dohány Synagogue had replaced the Orczy House as the center of the Jewish community and the most visible Jewish landmark in Pest. Whereas the Orczy House was a safe haven, in a sense, for Jews who lacked the legal right to reside anywhere in Pest, the Dohány Synagogue was a focal point for Jews living legally all over Pest, Óbuda, and Buda. The synagogue acted as a centripetal force connecting Jews who were spreading out across the three cities. In this way, the founding of the Dohány Synagogue was a powerful step toward the eventual joining of the three cities and their Jewish communities. This was especially important given how spread out the Jewish community had become by the 1860s. From a community concentrated largely in few square blocks in Terézváros, Jews now lived not only all over Pest, but in Óbuda and in Buda, where one out of eight Jews in the three towns lived on the eve of amalgamation in 1873. The prominence of the Jewish Hospital, Jewish schools, and especially the Dohány Synagogue even attracted Jews living across the Danube, albeit in different ways. In Buda, where mainly the most successful Jews from Pest were able to live, the Dohány Synagogue and other institutions in Pest kept these Jews connected. In Óbuda, younger Jews, in particular, were increasingly drawn to Pest, a more exciting place to live, work, and be Jewish. The array of communal institutions in Óbuda simply could not compete with their more impressive counterparts across the river.[83]

CONSOLIDATION

By the early 1870s, the main aspects of Jewish life—health care, ritual needs, education, and communal charity—were under the jurisdiction and direction of the Pest *Hitközség*, as the Jewish community was now known. This was a markedly different situation from a generation earlier, when the proliferation of independent Jewish organizations had challenged the communal leadership to coordinate between these organizations and eliminate redundancy in the services they provided. The leaders of the community expanded the benefits of membership to include Jewish organizations that had originated as independent or partially affiliated but were now fully part of the communal network of institutions. The success of the Jewish community in consolidating these organizations under a single, centralized Jewish administration was echoed in the opening section of the 1865 communal statutes. These statutes shifted the emphasis from the statutes of 1832 on well-ordered membership and leadership into a new focus of the Jewish community: ensuring that "the regularly residing Israelites in the area of the free city of Pest establish a unified indivisible religious community association that is not a political association"; and "the establishment and maintaining of all religious and Mosaic beliefs through the association's established institutions."[84]

Accordingly, the 1865 Statutes enumerated five main aspects of communal administration that, over the course of the previous generation, the Jewish elite had brought under the jurisdiction of the Pest *Hitközség*. In tandem, these areas of activity provided both the main source of community revenue through taxation and benefits of membership: (1) ritual—"everything related to synagogue services and other rituals, clergy and synagogue personnel, issues related to religious ritual, rabbi and his housing"; (2) education—"supervising all Jewish schools, educational institutions, religious instructions, and the rabbinate"; (3) philanthropy—"providing housing and education for orphans, overseeing the Jewish Hospital, and providing free medical care for the community poor"; (4) accounting—"managing revenue, expenses, and salaries"; and (5) budget—"preparing and presenting annual community budget, properties, proceeds, construction and repairs."[85] This more consolidated array of communal activity did not appear during the 1860s *ex nihilo*. Rather, it marked the crystallization of three decades of institutional development that had consolidated a group of semi-autonomous, loosely connected Jewish organizations under the umbrella leadership and regulation of a centralized Jewish community. Even the Hevra Kadisha, the oldest extant institution in Pest and the most resistant to being subordinated, was now a satellite organization of the main Jewish community, "one of several organizations operating in connection with the *hitközség*, under the auspices and guidance of the community's board."[86]

Indicative in this regard was the fate of the Jewish hospice in Óbuda, set up by the Óbuda Hevra Kadisha next to the synagogue in 1772. In 1852 the Óbuda community hired a doctor and nurse for the first time. In 1863, a second doctor was hired to make house calls to poor families. The same year, the building of the hospice turned hospital was expanded to accommodate forty beds. The Jewish community applied to the city for tax-exempt status for the hospital; the request was denied, but the city allotted a small sum from the municipal poor fund to support the hospital. In 1866, the small hospital admitted and treated wounded soldiers from the Austro-Italian war. In 1869, however, the hospital closed; its patients were transferred to the Jewish Hospital in Pest. From this point on, Óbuda Jews relied on the latter for hospital care.[87]

Of course, the consolidation of communal institutions under a centralized Jewish community did not preclude new institutions and organizations from forming as the situation warranted. From this point on, the central Jewish community would be directly involved from the outset and often dictate the terms of new organizations being created. In 1867, for example, a group of twenty-three Jews who had been praying at the Dohány Synagogue decided the service there—particularly the organ—was too progressive for their taste and decided to found a more traditional congregation, that is, sans organ, around the corner on Rombach Street. The group, several of whom were affluent members of the community, had sufficient funds and connections to purchase the land and secure building permits from the city. Yet they were blocked from proceeding by the leaders of the main Jewish community who were concerned lest the community take on another large debt before the costs of the Dohány Synagogue were paid in full. After a series of negotiations, the group committed to cover all costs and received permission from the main Jewish community to construct the Rombach Street Synagogue.[88]

The proliferation of synagogues and other Jewish institutions, however, did not displace the Neolog movement and its leadership as the heart and soul of Budapest Jewry. Emblematic in this regard was the founding of the Budapest Rabbinical Seminary in 1877. The founding of this soon to be venerated institution marked a culmination of communal expansion and the bridging of Jewish and Magyar cultures. Created in the image of the Breslau Seminary, the Budapest Seminary aimed at training rabbis who were not only first-rate Jewish scholars but also well versed in secular learning and Magyar language and culture. Initially the faculty and students of the seminary, amid the *Kulturkampf* between German and Magyar culture, embraced both. By the turn of the twentieth century, though, the seminary would be a mainstay of the community's efforts to Magyarize as many Jews as quickly as possible.[89]

In this sense, the emergence of the Pest Jewish community as the central administrative body for the erstwhile separate and independent communities of Jews in Pest, Óbuda, and Buda at the end of the 1860s paralleled and complemented the emergence of Pest as the center of a new amalgamation of the cities of Pest, Óbuda, and Buda into Budapest at the beginning of the 1870s. For Jews in Budapest like the young Theodore Herzl and Max Nordau, both Budapest and Budapest Jewry would present a broadening array of opportunities, opportunities that fortified and complemented the Neolog goal of living simultaneously as a Jew and as a citizen in Budapest.

Yet, like the newly amalgamated metropolis of Budapest, the newly created Budapest Jewry was not yet fully formed. During the decades from 1870s through World War I, a crucial dimension of Budapest Jewry would reach maturity, led by a subcommunity that had yet to make a significant impact: Jewish women in Budapest who would take control of and refashion Jewish philanthropy and social services. In doing so, these prominent women would play a key role not only in the further development of the Jewish community but also the city itself. They would help Budapest Jews navigate a central challenge of the late nineteenth century: embracing the new opportunities of urban life while remaining connected to the Jewish community.

6

The Pest Jewish Women's Association: A Cautious Path to the Mainstream

I N HIS 1947 NOVEL, *FEAR NOT MY SERVANT JACOB*, THE HUNGARIAN-JEWISH novelist Illès Kaczér contrasted the pious husband Scholem / Sholem, completely oblivious to worldly concerns such as providing for his children and charging the market price for his wares, with the industriousness and practicality of his wife Regina. While the husband thinks first of ways to spend time at the table of his spiritual and religious mentor, Regina, in addition to raising the children and keeping house, runs the business, finds customers, and even secures her husband a better job as a tavern keeper; Regina, in other words, manages the family's private and public affairs. The same year, essayist Mátyás Eisler impugned the right of women to participate in public life, not least of all because of their wanton sexuality: "Women eternally lust for sin, and because a man cannot resist them, he descends again and again into sin." For Eisler, Jewish women are like the primordial Eve, corrupting the otherwise moral men around them, in the coffeehouse no less than in the synagogue, and should therefore remain at home.[1]

These contrasting turn-of-the-twentieth-century appraisals of Jewish women point to a disjunction in the attitudes toward the role of Jewish women in the public sphere of late nineteenth-century Budapest. The status of Jewish women like Regina was determined in large part by a deeply entrenched presumed division of responsibility, within Jewish and Hungarian society, between the private and public spheres. Women like Regina were consigned to the home and only selectively admitted to the public sphere. In practice, this meant excluding women from positions of lay leadership and the rabbinate, and permitting them only limited access in the synagogue, all of which was reinforced by separate curricula and educational aims for Jewish boys and girls. Women were responsible for the proper transmission of traditional Jewish and Magyar values to the next generation—girls and boys alike—and expected to prepare children to participate in and contribute to public and Jewish communal life in Budapest. Women were thus taken to task for the imperfections and iniquities of the younger generation, even though women themselves were not allowed to participate fully in and contribute fully to the very Jewish life that they were expected to pass along to their children.

The dissonance between expectations and opportunities was especially pronounced with respect to elite Jewish women. Jewish women who were affluent enough to hire domestic servants and thus liberated from the time-consuming tasks of child-rearing and keeping house; who received a first-rate Jewish and general education, often alongside their brothers, by first-rate private tutors; who benefited from the same commercial and political connections as their fathers and brothers; and who were thus well suited for lay positions of leadership in the Jewish community and mainstream society, found that they were unable to use their abilities fully and to apply their talent where it was best suited. For Jewish women, limited participation in the synagogue was not that different from limited access to coffeehouses, theaters, reading clubs, and sports clubs. Innovative outlooks like Neolog diminished the dissonance somewhat, as will be discussed below, but did not eliminate it.

The triangular disjunction between what Jewish women were able to do, expected to do, and allowed to do was a central factor in the birth of the Jewish women's association in Budapest and in many Jewish communities. During the second half of the nineteenth century, the Pest Jewish Women's Association (Pesti Izraelita Nőegylet, hereinafter PIN) was formed by Jewish women searching for an acceptable entree into public life; they regarded their new organization as a medium through which to channel their skills and resources toward the improvement of the Jewish community and above all its philanthropic capabilities. By the beginning of the twentieth century, this aim expanded to include ameliorating not only Jewish communal philanthropy but the network of charitable assistance for all residents of Budapest.[2]

The founding and expansion of the PIN during the second half of the nineteenth century is thus not only a story about Jewish women and their accomplishments as they assumed the role of the philanthropic arm of Budapest Jewry. It is also an important variation on the interplay between Jews and the broadening social and cultural opportunities in Budapest, a variation that suggests a need to rethink the dynamics of Jewish assimilation in late nineteenth-century Budapest. From the outset, the central aim of the organization was to expand the philanthropic reach and impact of the Jewish community through an array of charitable activities. In the course of time, the existence of the PIN provided Jewish women with a way to pierce the boundary between the private and public spheres by providing socially acceptable ways for them to participate in and contribute to public life within in the Jewish community and beyond.[3]

The conventional venues through which the interplay between Jews and the city has been presented have typically been public spaces that were dominated by men—the workplace, leadership organizations such as the Jewish community council and the city council, and Jewish and non-Jewish public venues for the exchange of culture and ideas: the synagogue, the schoolhouse, the coffeehouse, and social clubs such as the casino and sports clubs. Yet Jewish women had limited access to these institutions, thus the dynamics of Jewish women entering the mainstream of Budapest society proceeded along a different trajectory, including participation in the social and charitable activities of the PIN. This was not the only venue for Jewish women to enter mainstream society; yet insofar as this organization straddled public and private life while conjoining aspects of Jewish and Magyar identity, it was an important dimension of the entry of Jewish women into the Budapest mainstream and their active role in the Jewish community.

A CHANGING LANDSCAPE

The founding of the Pest Jewish Women's Association unfolded amid a sharp increase in the number of Jewish women who wanted and were able to participate in and contribute to public Jewish and public city life. At that moment, they were greeted with an elaborately constructed insistence that they remain at home or, at best, participate in public life only when escorted by a husband, brother, or father. For these Jewish women, in particular, the PIN provided a way to enter public life in a way that did not explicitly reject the prevalent notion that they did not belong there. The growth of the organization was aided by the convergence of four developments in mid-nineteenth-century Pest and Hungary: the accelerating growth of Budapest at the end of the 1860s; new economic possibilities and the emergence of an upwardly mobile Jewish middle-class centered in Lipótváros; a surge in the number of Jews in need, that is, lower-income and indigent Jews; and a broadening of the role of women in public life.

From 1869 to 1910, the population of the three amalgamated cities increased from 270,000 to 880,000. The population density increased accordingly as multistoried residential buildings allowed more people to reside in a certain area. In 1869, three-fourths of houses were one-story; by 1914 nearly half were two stories or higher. Increasing population and density led to, among other things, the rezoning of the eastern part of Terézváros into the separate district of Erzébetváros.[4] The number of Jews in Budapest increased from just over 50,000 in 1873 to 71,000 by 1880, 103,000 by 1890, 166,000 by 1900, and 203,000 by 1910. This rapid increase outpaced the growth of the city itself. In 1869, one in six people in Budapest was Jewish; by 1910, nearly one in four.[5] Along with rapid growth was an increasingly varied occupational profile. As statistician József Kőrösi noted in 1891:

The Jews are still the most numerous in the area of commerce, they are disproportionately represented in just about every branch of commerce but especially in man-
ufactured goods and credit. Aside from that, they are also well represented in the
following areas: coffee dealers, pálinka brewing, dry goods, tailoring, seamstresses,
haberdashers, bottlemakers, buttonmakers, jewelers, and goldsmiths, tinkers, bar-
bers, upholsterers, porters, lawyers, and doctors.[6]

According to Kőrösi, the occupations with the heaviest Jewish concentration in 1891
were grain traders (838/946), grocers (839/2152), and lumber merchants (263/562).
Jews constituted more than two-thirds of all manufacturers (5,476/7,980).[7]

As with men, the occupational situation for Jewish women varied according to class
and wealth. Women who came from a family of means were more likely to marry into
another family of means—thus obviating any need to earn a living. More visible wom-
en's occupations were those of unmarried women, especially young women of lesser
means who immigrated or in-migrated to Budapest alone. These women had access neither to any commercial, industrial, or artisanal occupation, nor to any professions, nor
a family business to provide employment and livelihood. For these women, the most
common and readily occupations available were domestic servant or day labor jobs such
as washerwomen. Many women, too, worked in small commercial and industrial ventures, typically helping their father, brother, or husband run a store or business—such
was the case of the aforementioned fictional Regina. These women were often overlooked by statisticians such as József Kőrösi.

In general, the occupational profiles of Jewish men and women in Budapest changed
during the second half of the nineteenth century, typical for Jews in the major commercial and industrial centers of nineteenth-century Europe. Men and women experienced occupational change and upward mobility, often from one generation to the
next, but though different paths. For men, change in the occupational profile was two-
fold: a vertical move up the ladder of commerce from peddler to shopkeeper and, in a
few cases, to major industrialist financier; and a horizontal or lateral move from commerce into the liberal professions, notably medicine and law; and, particularly among
recent Jewish arrivals, a shift toward artisanal trades, especially those connected to the
clothing trade—tailors, seamstresses, and button makers. The son of a peddler might
wind up as a shopkeeper, whose son in turn grew up to be a doctor or lawyer. The son of
a bathkeeper expanded the family business into a steam works factory. In the remarkable—albeit atypical—case of Manfréd Weisz, the son of a small-time grain trader
could wind up running one of the largest canning factories on the continent.[8] Upward
mobility for women was more limited; a domestic servant might be "promoted" to
nanny; some washerwomen "graduated" to become seamstresses. The most common
path of upward mobility for women was through marriage.

Upward economic mobility for men and women, moreover, was accompanied by increased residential and social mobility. By the turn of the twentieth century there was no part of Budapest that did not have at least a small number of Jewish residents. Even the Belváros and highbrow neighborhoods of Buda such as the Rózsadomb, once bastions of the erstwhile privilege to exclude Jews, had small Jewish enclaves. Jews in growing numbers relocated from Terézváros to Lipótváros, which emerged by the second half of the nineteenth century as Pest's and Pest Jewry's upper-class neighborhood *par excellence*. For most Jews, the move to Lipótváros was made possible by upward mobility and was the gateway to social acceptance, not only into mainstream society but into the higher reaches of Jewish society. Indeed, perhaps the only mark of a higher status than a lavish home in Lipótváros was an even larger mansion in Rózsadomb. The high status and degree of acceptance were epitomized by the ennoblement of more than two hundred Jewish families in Budapest, most of whom lived in Lipótváros, the Belváros, or Buda. Ennoblement was not a necessary prerequisite to joining the Jewish elite or the Budapest elite, but it simplified the process. For the majority of upwardly mobile Jews who were not or were never ennobled, the very possibility of ennoblement signaled a degree of acceptance that was unparalleled in Europe, and perhaps anywhere in the world.[9]

The high level of acceptance was complemented by the limited presence of anti-Jewish or antisemitic agitation in Budapest prior to the First World War. There were antisemitic moments, of course: the Tiszaeszlár blood libel in 1882 and the ensuing riots, the harsh rhetoric of Győző Istóczy, and the debates in the Hungarian National Assembly about immigration and the *Ostjuden*. Yet these disturbing moments did not upend the broader sense of optimism among Hungarian Jews and, above all, among Jews in Budapest. If nothing else, one could reasonably conclude that, even in tandem, these events did not preclude the conclusion that, in dualist Hungary, antisemitism was more a marginal than a mainstream phenomenon, and that mainstream Hungarian society beckoned to Jews with arms wide open. Jews who lived in Budapest during the half century from emancipation in 1868 until the end of World War I saw themselves living in a golden age (*aranykor*).

In retrospect, the picture was less cut and dried. As Julia Richers argues, the belief in the *aranykor* was more a myth invented and perpetuated by Hungarian Jews following the Revolution of 1848 out of a desire for "acceptance into a broad social space." This hope for integration, she argues, remained for the most part unfulfilled, but the myth of Hungarian Jewish symbiosis and emphasis on acceptance remained in Hungarian Jewish historiography.[10] Similarly, Miklós Konrád has shown that even at the height of the putative golden age there were areas of society still not fully accessible to Jews, even to wealthy and ennobled Jews. The upper tier of the nobility, for example, rarely if ever invited Jewish nobles to their parties or other social gatherings, and ignored or declined similar invitations to attend the parties thrown by Jewish nobles. Even so, insofar as most Jews did not aspire to acceptance on such an elite level, such impediments did not mean very much. For upwardly mobile Jewish young men like Theodore Herzl and Max Nordau, the doors to mainstream Budapest society were flung wide open during the second half of the nineteenth century, with few impediments barring entry, immersion, and virtually full participation.[11]

In this regard, the role of the women's association offers an additional dimension in which to reconsider the relationship between the Jewish community and cities like Budapest with greater complexity. These organizations did not merely extend the bounds of private life but profoundly altered the range of possibilities for women. What one historian noted with respect to American Jewish women's associations was no less true of those in Budapest and elsewhere in Europe: "Behind the myth of self-sacrificing female benevolence existed a quietly radical redefinition of behavioral norms for Jewish women. Without overtly challenging inveterate notions of Jewish womanhood, Jewish club women assumed new roles and responsibilities within the Jewish community."[12] Women's organizations, according to this view, were part of "an interactive social process that involved a complex reworking of gender ideals and the division between private and public space within the Jewish community."[13] Because they were typically composed of and run by wives of the commercial elite, women's associations highlighted not only the disparities between Jewish men and women but also between elite and rank-and-file Jews. As one historian pointed out, "It would be as foolish to assert that all women share an identity of interest irrespective of class and ethnic culture as it has been to claim that all members of an ethnic group or class share an identity of interest irrespective of gender."[14]

In this regard, the PIN was part of the broader emergence of women's associations in a Jewish, Hungarian, and urban context. In Hungary, women's associations were a typical part of communal life in all but the smallest Jewish communities. Founded as voluntary societies, these associations collected and distributed, provided education for poor girls and dowries for poor brides.[15] The organizational models for the PIN were both the *Judenfrauenverein* in Vienna and the Pesti Jótékony Nőegyesület (the Pest Women's Philanthropic Association). Like the former, the PIN began as a natural extension of the existing array of Jewish communal institutions, and it quickly became the philanthropic arm of the Jewish community. As in Vienna and many other Jewish communities, charitable activities and acts of loving kindness (*tzedakah* and *gemilut hasadim*), though often public, were regarded as natural and acceptable activities for women; it was the women's responsibility to care for those in need, at home and beyond.[16]

The Pest Women's Philanthropic Association, founded in 1817, was also a model for the PIN. This organization began locally by providing medical care and medical assistance, finding employment for several thousand women as handworkers, and spearheading efforts to improve conditions for women in the workplace. It also helped with larger municipal efforts to clear beggars and panhandlers from the street by providing meals and temporary housing, medical care for the disabled and the poor, and stipends for poor families to purchase food, clothing, and firewood.[17] The PIN, too, began as a response to specific local problems and addressed challenges facing Jewish women that were specific to Budapest.[18] The immediate origin of the PIN was a growing concern for war widows and orphans, Jewish and otherwise, of the Battle of Königgratz.[19] In response, ten women who were wives of leading Pest Jews founded the PIN in 1866 with 230 members and laid out two initial aims beyond assistance to families of war victims: supporting the poor, especially sick or disabled widows and poor orphans, and helping to raise orphaned girls. A month later, the new organization was recognized officially by the royal governor.[20] With this recognition in hand, the founders raised and allocated money to help the wounded from the recently ended Battle of Königsburg, and paid 16 forints to allow sick people to use therapeutic baths. They also allocated 93 forints for linen and undergarments, and arranged for a local pharmacist to distribute free medicine to the poor. In addition, they arranged for the Ullmann and Goldstein bakeries to provide two pounds of flour each week to each poor woman who requested it. Within three months, they had distributed more than three thousand breakfast coupons.[21]

The leadership of the PIN elected officers who met regularly at the organization's headquarters at 41 Dessewffy Street and annually with the general membership. Initially, the leading members of the women's association came almost exclusively from leading, well-connected, well-established, acculturated Jewish families, to the exclusion of less affluent women and those who were recent immigrants.[22] Accordingly, the group elected Johanna Fischer Bischitz as their first president. Bischitz was the daughter of Mór Fischer, an upper-middle-class industrialist who had founded the Herendi Porcelain Factory. Her siblings had fought in the Revolution of 1848 War of Independence, while she had served as a nurse tending to the wounded in that struggle. In 1878, Bischitz volunteered as a nurse during the Bosnian War and received the Golden Cross from Habsburg monarch Franz Joseph. As the wife of a rich wholesaler, she devoted her life and used her financial resources to do good works.[23] In 1879, Bischitz founded the Budapest Poor Children's Association (Fővárosi Szegény Gyermekkert Egylet) at 32 Akácfa utca. In 1882, she contributed to the legal defense fund for the Jews who were accused during the Tiszaeszlár blood libel. In 1895, her family was ennobled and received a coat of arms partly in recognition of her philanthropic efforts. She served as the president of the PIN until her death in 1898. According to a report in *Egyenlőség*, her funeral that year drew "innumerable crowds." Chief Rabbi Sándor Kohn officiated, and she was eulogized by the great Hungarian novelist and social critic Mór Jókai.

In 1867, Bischitz presided over the acquisition and renovation of a building at 36 Kertész Street to house a new orphanage for Jewish girls. She personally raised the funding, soliciting an endowment from Baron Mór Hirsch and assistance from Chief

Rabbi Farkas Alajos Meisel. The orphanage was completed in May 1867 and became filled to capacity within a month. In October, the Pest Jewish community sponsored a dedication ceremony. As a reporter from the *Pester Lloyd* noted, the most moving part of the ceremony was when "the shawl-covered Borbála Herz Pollák, who had donated 10,000 forints to purchase the building, joined similarly garbed orphans in a moving processional."[24] In 1870, Bischitz helped found a soup kitchen; initially founded for the Jewish poor, it eventually provided free meals to all. By the end of 1869, the organization was thriving. The membership exceeded one hundred, and the treasury had over 17,000 forints invested at two banks and in securities and bonds.[25] When the women's society sponsored a lottery in honor of Katalin Fleischl to raise charitable donations, they sold more than 50,000 tickets in a few weeks and raised more than 16,000 forints. In 1869, the PIN founded a second orphanage for 100 girls with an adjacent public kitchen that served more than 300 meals daily. The kitchen continued to operate even after the orphanage moved in 1900.

A series of successful ventures earned the organization wide acclaim beyond the Jewish community. In 1869, the National Diet enlisted the women's association to help encourage Jewish girls to learn a craft. In 1871, Empress Elizabeth visited the girls' orphanage. Jewish communities from as far away as Switzerland and East Prussia petitioned the PIN for financial support. The organization was invited by city literati to plan the city-wide celebration of Róza Laborfalvi's (Mór Jókai's wife) jubilee as a stage actor. Most impressive, perhaps, was when Franz Liszt performed at the organization's annual ball, and then offered to play again the following year.[26]

Despite these early successes, the PIN faced external resistance and internal growing pains. The city council of Pest expressed doubt that the new organization could function autonomously, and recommended that the PIN operate under the supervision of either the Pest Jewish community or a more established Christian charitable association. Bischitz resisted this pressure, insisting that the PIN had the resources to function as an independent organization, and its leaders had the knowhow and savvy.[27] In addition, since most members came from elite households and expected some sort of leadership voice, the leadership grew disproportionately to the membership. The executive committee, which initially had eight members, increased to thirty by 1873 and

TABLE 23. PESTI IZRAELITA NŐEGYLET FINANCIAL PORTFOLIO, 1869 (FORINTS)

MAGYAR KERESKEDELMI BANK	4,700
ÁLTALÁNOS BANK	1,800
SECURITIES	11,900

Source: Katalin *Gerő, A Szeretet munkásai: A Pesti Izraelita Nőegylet története* (Budapest, 1937), 32.

forty-five by 1890. Tensions reached fever pitch during the election of new officers in 1870, particularly between older members who favored expanding the existing operations and younger members who wanted to extend into new areas such as crime prevention. In the end, a compromise was reached. The younger members agreed to table their request to address crime prevention and in exchange received leadership positions in the organization. The officers accommodated the increased demand for positions by dividing the organization into four subsections: outpatient care, long-term care, orphanages, and fundraising, each with its own executive officer and six-woman advisory board.[28]

Each of these divisions defined a concrete set of goals. The orphanage division, for example, laid out a six-part plan in 1875 that included arranging for Sabbath and holiday services at the orphanage, afternoon tea accompanied by edifying lectures for the residents, better lighting for the orphanage to enhance evening programs and socializing, and a 200-forint annual stipend for any resident who got engaged. The other divisions articulated equally well-defined plans.[29]

The immediate impact of the PIN was not simply its aid to the poor but its systematic organization. In the mid-1870s, assistance for the poor in Budapest was still carried out haphazardly, mainly by religious organizations; there was as yet no systematic state assistance for the poor.[30] Shrewd individuals found ways to get food and clothing from

TABLE 24. SECTIONAL LEADERSHIP, 1875

I. SHORT-TERM CARE

Executive Officer: Mária Herzl
Advisory Board: Sarolta Barnay, Julia Deutsch, Róza Goldstein, Kornélia Heidlberg, Babette Hirsch, Mária Holitscher

II. LONG-TERM CARE

Executive Officer: Róza Goldberger
Advisory Board: Paula Deutsch, Katalin Kahn, Antónia Keppich, Hermina Oppenheim, Rozália Popper, Rebekka Rechnitz

III. ORPHANAGES

Executive Officer: Fanny Stein
Advisory Board: Zsófia Egger, Róza Ellenberger, Nina Ehrlich, Jozefin Ganz, Ida Kohner, Róza Munk

IV. FINANCIAL MATTERS

Executive Officer: Mrs. Emil Ullmann
Advisory Board: Fery Brüll, Matild Fleischl, Henriette Holitscher, Johanna Pollák, Róza Schlesinger, Lina Schwarz

Source: Katalin Gerő, *A Szeretet munkásai: A Pesti Izraelita Nőegylet története* (Budapest, 1937), 62.

multiple places, depleting the available provisions before less resourceful individuals could get anything. As new agencies for assisting the poor appeared during the 1880s, they merely added to an already disjointed and skewed state of affairs. Part of the problem was that, until 1914, there was no legal standard for regulating such agencies. The state defined such agencies as privately run charitable enterprises, and presumed that improvements in assistance for the poor would originate in the private sector.[31]

The Pest Jewish Women's Society's organizational structure validated this expectation. When cholera struck the city in 1873, the short-term division distributed food and medicine. The long-term division helped quarantine victims of the epidemic. The orphanage division set up a series of soup kitchens at strategically located points in the city to feed the afflicted.[32] In the wake of the epidemic, the women's association added divisions to aid victims of natural disasters—epidemic, fire, and flood—to help improve existing hospitals and hospices and to build new ones, and to create and run a food bank, the first in Budapest. The Budapest Food Bank, opened in 1875, was based largely on that of the Women's Association. Special committees were also added as circumstances dictated.[33] In 1883, a special committee was created to channel relief funds for victims of Russian pogroms.[34] During the mid-1870s, the PIN addressed a growing concern for religious laxity by organizing an annual Chanukah party at the orphanage that became a major communal event, and by organizing smaller-scale cultural and social events at local synagogues. These events typically included a speech by the chief rabbi and a performance by the cantor and choir,[35] and were instrumental in expanding the parameters of synagogue life from purely religious to include a broader array of cultural and social events.

Beyond these initial accomplishments, the PIN enhanced the ability of elite Jewish women to raise the next generation of Jews with a dual commitment to Jewish life and an ability to contribute to mainstream society and culture. The emergence of the Jewish women's association in Budapest was thus more than an addition to an existing array of Jewish communal institutions; it was also the solution to an inherent contradiction between the abilities of women and what a male-dominated society was willing to let them do.

REDEFINING AND REINFORCING THE BOUNDARY BETWEEN PUBLIC AND PRIVATE

The PIN, like other Jewish women's associations in Hungary, allowed women to navigate this contradiction within the peculiarities of Hungarian society, particularly the way in which traditional Jewish society and the Hungarian world of nobility and chivalry selectively absorbed novel aspects of liberal, middle-class views of women. While liberal ideas and policies generally improved the lot of Jewish men—at least proper-tied, educated Jewish men—for Jewish women these changes produced mixed results. For Jewish women, liberal notions of individual rights to property, careers open to tal-ent, and civic equality were unable to uproot fully from Jewish and Hungarian society a lingering, socially conservative view of women and laws and customs regarding the sta-tus of women. Traditional Jewish laws and customs excluded women from three central aspects of communal life: communal leadership positions, leading the synagogue ser-vice, and full access to Jewish education. Medieval scholars such as Rabbi Solomon ben Isaac (aka Rashi), puzzled as to why Moses instructed in Deuteronomy 1:13 to "choose from your tribes men who are wise, discerning, and experienced," queried whether "it would even occur to you to appoint a woman?" This became the basis for excluding women from positions of Jewish communal leadership. Moreover, a combination of two early rabbinic apodictic statements—the exemption of women from the obliga-tion to observe positive, time-bound commandments coupled with personal obliga-tion as a prerequisite to lead the synagogue service—combined to exclude women from public roles in the synagogue, culminating in a statute in a sixteenth-century code of Jewish law (*Shulchan 'Aruch*) concluding that calling women up to the Torah would dishonor the community. Finally, the rabbinic interpretation of the biblical instruction to "teach your children" was interpreted to refer to sons and not daughters. In tandem, these three rabbinic positions combined to exclude Jewish women from positions of prominence in Jewish communal life.[36]

The truncated role of women in Hungarian public life was rooted in a different set of traditions: noble chivalry and a medieval Hungarian corpus of law and privilege. The impact of the former on women was summarized by István Deák: "The concept of masculine honor relegated women to the role of helpless, weak, and easily seduced victims whom it was the absolute obligation of husbands, fathers, and brothers to pro-tect. By their supposedly capricious, irrational, and often lascivious behavior, women were perceived as constantly endangering the honor and therefore the very lives of the men charged with their protection. It followed clearly that women should be held un-der strict control."[37] This chivalric notion complemented the legal status of women in Hungarian society that originated in a diverse corpus of medieval privileges, many of which were systematized in the *Tripartitum* of 1517. A Hungarian woman was defined legally as an extension of the primary male figure in her life—her father or brother un-til marriage, and then her husband. Husbands were required to provide their wives with sustenance, clothing, and a suitable domicile, and to meet her "spiritual needs."[38] In marriages between a noble and non-noble, a woman attained her husband's name, rank, and status regardless of her own; a woman from a non-noble family who mar-ried a nobleman obtained the rights of nobility.[39] If a couple divorced and the divorce was ruled the wife's fault, she forfeited her ex-husband's name, rank, and status; if the husband was ruled responsible, the wife had the option of retaining his name and rank; thus an uncensured divorcée might land in a most favorable position.[40]

At the same time, in cases when a noble included his daughters as heirs of his estate, daughters were legally entitled to the same portion of commercial and hereditary property as male heirs.[41] Male and female heirs also had the same burden of proof when it came to establishing that they were legitimate heirs.[42] In addition, Christian women, as well as Christian men, were permitted to change their religion from the age of eighteen onward; this law was renewed in 1844 and again in 1868. Finally, whereas a man had to wait until age twenty to obtain a crafts or industry permit, a woman could obtain one at the age of sixteen.[43] These "dents in the patriarchal hierarchy," appearing several generations before nineteenth-century liberal and democratic activists began to champion the cause of women, laid a foundation for the first public discussions of the status of women in Hungary. In 1780, a series of pamphlets by the French Encyclopedists appeared in Hungary asking whether or not the universal brotherhood of man included women.[44] In 1787, a more self-consciously feminist study appeared entitled "On Scholarly Women." This anonymous essay introduced a crucial element into the debate over women in Hungary: the tendency to distinguish between upper-class and rank-and-file women: "If [female members of noble families] would receive decent training in honorable sciences through diligent, careful, good education . . . there would be the greatest hopes to find among them Lockes, Newtons, and other such scientific spirits."[45] This class-oriented approach to the issue appeared again in a 1790 pamphlet submitted by Péter Bárány to the National Diet entitled "A Humble Invitation to Hungarian Mothers Presented before the Assembled Magnates and Hungarian Fathers." In this essay Bárány asked that women be admitted to hear debates in the National Diet, although they could not vote.[46] A full generation would pass, however, before even a minor improvement in the status of women was seriously entertained. In 1812, a German-language pamphlet asserted that inequality between the sexes was not only unnatural but contrary to divine will:

> Where does the subordination of women come from? Does God know anything about it? When, how, and in what way did God, who has no gender, declare that men should command while women should be submissive? It is not permissible that gender, the last surviving difference between the classes, should cause the frustration of civic equality. Bitter is the fate of women, who have access neither to legislation nor to the execution of the law.[47]

Ascribing a political ulterior motive to the subjugation of women, the author explained that "the weaker physical demeanor of women is taken advantage of for the purpose of enacting strict laws. Weaker individuals should be burdened no more than

stronger individuals."[48] By the end of the Napoleonic wars, two distinct and potentially conflicting impulses had appeared within the debate over the status of women in
Hungary. Those in enlightened circles agreed that improving the status of women to
some degree—at the very least, expanding their education—was essential. The extent
of such changes was the point of contention: should enlightened women abandon their
primary roles as wives and mothers in favor of other economic or intellectual pursuits,
or aspire simply to become enlightened wives and mothers?

By the second half of the nineteenth century, the rising influence of liberalism had
begun to erode both Jewish and Hungarian traditional views of society. For women,
these changes produced a deleterious by-product, despite increased opportunities. A
nascent bourgeois notion of domesticity paradoxically resubordinated women by excluding them from public life and confining them to the same traditional roles of wife
and mother—effectively replacing older traditional rationales with a liberal one. This
disparity between the impact of nineteenth-century changes on men and women was
noted more than three decades ago by the late Joan Kelly:

> If we apply Fourier's dictum—that the emancipation of women is an index of the
> general emancipation of an age—our notions of so-called progressive developments
> ... undergo a startling re-evaluation. ... In Renaissance Europe [progress] meant
> domestication of the bourgeois wife and the escalation of witchcraft persecution
> which crossed class lines. And the [French] Revolution expressly excluded women
> from its liberty, equality, and "fraternity." Suddenly we see these ages with a new
> double vision.[49]

In other words, enlightened liberal male intellectuals defined the importance of
women, first as wives and daughters acting in concert with their husbands, fathers, and
brothers; and also as women nurturing and preserving the soul of the Hungarian people. Increasingly women were seen as embodying the Magyar national cause, creating
a duality within Hungarian politics between the powerful male state and the nurturing female nation, an image captured poignantly by Lajos Kossuth in his description
of women in the Revolutions of 1848:

> It is no arbitrary praise—it is a fact—that, in the struggle for our rights and freedom,
> we had no more powerful auxiliaries, and no more faithful executors of the will of the
> nation, than the women of Hungary. ... I never met a single mother who withheld
> her son from sharing in the battle; but I have met many who commanded their chil-
> dren to fight for their fatherland. I saw many and many brides who urged the bride-
> grooms to delay the day of happiness till they should come back victorious. ... The
> heart of a man is as soft wax in your tender hands. Mold it ladies.[50]

This duality between liberals' notions of civic equality and the less than equal status of women was mirrored in the Neolog mentality. Progressive Jewish movements such as Reform Judaism in Germany and Neolog in Hungary advocated greater access for women to education and the synagogue service. Aaron Chorin, the original progressive rabbi in Hungary and a pioneer of the Neolog mentality, articulated this aim clearly:

> Gone are the barbaric ages when the stronger half of mankind thought to elevate it-self over the nobler half, when it was thought sinful to put women on the level with men.... We owe to our women the larger portion of the moral training of our youth, as well as our mores, our esthetic sense, and all that which is good and beautiful, and true. Therefore, women must not be excluded from the soul-satisfying experiences which come to us through a solemn worship service.[51]

Yet the public role of women in the service at Neolog synagogues and Reform temples remained largely unchanged. Budapest Jewry, like most Jewish communities in Europe, continued to assign exclusively to men the responsibilities of leadership in Jewish communal life and honors in the synagogue, while prioritizing the time and energy of Jewish women to run the home and raise the children. While more prevalent perhaps in Orthodox and Hassidic circles, these beliefs remained a part of progressive Jewish communities, too, into the twentieth century. Budapest Jewry's progressive majority community was no exception. Apart from the PIN, the entire communal leadership and the leadership of every Jewish organization was comprised exclusively of men. This was evident, too, in Neolog houses of worship such as the Dohány Street Synagogue. In the Dohány Synagogue, women were permitted to sit only in the women's gallery. They were excluded from leading the service, reading the Torah, being counted as part of a prayer quorum (minyan), and being called up to the Torah. Above all, prior to the twentieth century the idea of a woman being ordained as a Neolog rabbi was no less unimaginable than a woman being ordained an Orthodox or Hassidic rabbi. This social conservatism within Jewish society was complemented by a parallel conservatism within liberal Hungarian society that reinforced the socially conservative outlook of chivalric notions with an emerging bourgeois notion of female domesticity that stigmatized women working outside the home. Together, these notions defined the status of Jewish women in Budapest and placed formidable impediments between them and full participation in a burgeoning urban life and culture.[52]

Indicative of the lingering bifurcation of Jewish communal life and Budapest public society was the general attitude toward the participation of women in two cornerstones of public life: the casino and the café. The casino, an integral part of an emerging civic society in mid-nineteenth-century Pest, was a place where men of means and status gathered to play cards, read books and newspapers, discuss and debate the affairs of the day, and socialize in a leisurely setting. Initially for high-ranking nobles, most of these clubs were located in Lipótváros. Eventually there were casinos for men of other ranks, too—middle and lower nobility, and upper-middle-class merchants and industrialists. Membership in a leading casino was an indispensable means of social advancement and networking. Jewish men, though largely excluded from the National (*nemzeti*) Casino, were eventually admitted to others, including the State (*országos*) Casino and others. For upwardly mobile, acculturating Jews in Budapest, membership in a casino was an important marker of acceptance not only into mainstream Budapest society but into mainstream Budapest high society.[53]

Women were largely excluded from these casinos and allowed to attend only when chaperoned by their husbands. While some were paid members of the Országos Casino, they were not part of the board or listed in membership rolls. As higher education became more available to women from upper-class families, more were interested in participating, especially in the intellectual activities of the casinos. This eventually brought into clearer relief the growing disjunction between the intellectual capabilities of educated, affluent women from proper families, and the lingering disapproval among casino members regarding women joining the casinos as members or coming to the casino unaccompanied. Yet since women were not the only people excluded from the casinos—most men, too, did not have access—their exclusion was less egregious, and the discrepancy between their education and access to the casinos less problematic.[54] This discrepancy became more problematic with the growing popularity of the other new focal point of public life in Budapest, the café. Unlike the casino, the café was a more democratic institution; a more diverse cross section of the population frequented the dozens of cafés that opened in Budapest. As Ödön Gerő (aka Viharos) noted in 1891: "No place in the world maintains the culture of the café like Budapest; and, in Budapest, nowhere like in Terézváros. There are many clubs in Lipótváros, churches in the Inner City, breweries in Erzsebétváros, taverns in Ferencváros, and cafés in Terézváros."[55]

For many Jews in Budapest, too, the café became a place where Jews met to socialize and to discuss a variety of topics—some Jewish, some not—and a central gateway to mainstream Budapest society. Chief among the cafés was the Abbázia, a textbook example of what sociologist Milton Gordon termed "acculturation without integration."[56] The Abbázia Café was a place that Jews frequented to interact with other Jews and with non-Jews. Vilmos Vázsonyi, one of the first Jews elected to the National Assembly and the representative of Teréz- and Erzsébetváros, recalled fondly the hours he spent at Abbázia. Not only did he engage in conversation and debate there; he also met leading Budapest intellectuals such as Károly Eötvös, who cultivated Vázsonyi's interest in pursuing a career in politics. Yet it was also a place where Jews—and, Jewish intellectuals, in particular—talked to and argued with other Jews and Jewish intellectuals. There was nothing specifically Jewish about the café or the conversations that took place there, but the clientele was overwhelmingly Jewish and the Jewishness of the place was undeniable. More than a few Budapest Jews recalled that the conversation at Abbázia often revolved around articles and essays in the Jewish press. For Neolog Jewish intellectuals, Abbázia was a place to discuss Jewish matters in a neutral, nonsacred space. Other than the fact that the primary language of this café was Hungarian and not Yiddish, it would have been difficult to distinguish this café from cafés frequented by Jews in Warsaw, or a generation later in Tel Aviv.[57]

Yet the Abbázia Café, like other cafés, was predominantly a world of men. Jewish women, like their non-Jewish counterparts, increasingly pressed for a way to gain unchaperoned access, not only to the Abbázia but to cafés and casinos generally. This growing interest among women prompted contrary reactions among Hungarian intellectuals, beginning with an exchange in the Hungarian weekly *Új Idők* (Modern Times) between Kőris (aka Károly Lyka) and Igric (aka Róbert Tábori). Lyka regarded the presence of women in clubs and cafés as detrimental to society: "We have accepted into our social life a new figure: the coffeehouse-attending and cycling 'club-women,' the casino-going lady. . . . It is a simple fact that there is a need to suppress the whimsy of this so-called women's emancipation." Tábori disagreed, arguing that women "who would otherwise have no opportunity to leave the four walls of their home" need an outlet to leave the home and participate in public life. Yet he distinguished between the club and the café. The casino was preferable to a café, he argued: although the café was more democratic and more accessible, it lacked proper decorum for women. In addition, he argued that the weekly tea parties that were hosted in the casinos were essential for middle-class women to be socially accepted in civilized Hungarian society.[58]

This exchange of views prompted two responses that appeared in the following issue of *Új Idők*. Countess Mrs. Sándor Teleki agreed that the casino was more exclusive, and thus attracted only members of the middle nobility and aristocracy, while "poorer members of the middle class fled to the café." Her solution, however, was not to discourage women from visiting cafés. Rather, she suggested that "in order to connect women properly with these institutions, there is clearly a need for libraries for women so that the women going to the cafés would become ladies [*asszonyak*]." Emil Szontágh carried this argument a step further, claiming:

> Women are not modern enough, and need to be dislodged from the home. Women becoming more worldly and engaging the culture of the café would make them less likely to impede men from engaging in aspects of the modern world. As long as the child learns from his mother, the young man from his governess, and the husband from his wife only philistine lessons, he will never contribute to public life and his individual talent will not exceed the limits of birth and privilege.[59]

Yet Szontágh believed that the casino and not the café was better suited to raise the cultural level of women by "creating for women the possibility to get to know members of other classes, without obscuring social distinctions." Making periodicals and books available for women to read and lectures to hear in casinos, he argued, would enable the aristocracy, gentry, and middle class to draw nearer to one another. The main impact of the activities of the women's club would be that uneducated women would no longer impede the amalgamation of social life.[60]

The pervading ambivalence even about women and casinos culminated in a failed attempt in 1898 to create a special casino for women in Budapest. This casino was the brainchild of the all-male leadership of the State Casino. Once opened, the Women's Casino invited women to become members, yet the entire board was comprised of men and dominated by three men: Baron Béla Atzél, Oszkár Vojnich, and Béla Bálasz. Women had little or no influence in the larger decisions or in the day-to-day operation of the casino. The men who founded the casino shut it down in 1908. As one historian concluded: "The first women's casino was sacrificed for the convenience and cultural needs of men. What did women get as compensation? One or two annual casino balls, smaller dances, and concerts. The men's casino never even reported the closing of the women's casino in its annual report, only noting that the building needs to be enlarged."[61]

Jewish observers, echoing Tábori, agreed that women visiting cafés was a bigger problem than women in clubs. An anonymous contributor to *Magyar Zsidó Nő*, a weekly publication published by men for Jewish women that appeared in 1900 and 1901, expressed concerns about Jewish women in the café, specifically that women frequenting cafés was symptomatic of a larger degradation of society:

> Amongst the evermore prevalent flippancy of modern society, nothing is more distasteful and frowned upon than the café-going vagary of big-city women.... Even the most enthusiastic advocates of the emancipation of women acknowledge that the atmosphere of the café is not suitable for ladies; not because men should have more of a right to go wherever they please; not out of an egoism in which the stronger sex wants to monopolize pleasure at the café. The café is not suitable because stepping into the café, first of all, robs women of the precious time they would otherwise be able to spend more wholesome time at home.... second, even if the café atmosphere maintains a standard of elegance, it is actually not amenable for the more delicate sex to be able [to] feel comfortable among the non-respectable elements.[62]

The writer emphasizes further that the time a woman spends in a café is time away from the place she is most needed and for which she is best suited—the home:

It is yet to be seen whether a respectable, devoted wife and good mother can feel better in the atmosphere of the café than at home with her husband and in the circle of her family. Her majestic calling binds her to her home and to the possibility that she finds it more agreeable to be amongst her husband and children. The task of raising children is so lofty and beautiful that it constitutes the highest ambition for a woman; happy is the woman whom fate does not deprive of the wondrousness of raising her children.

Even women without children, the writer suggests, should stay home: "But if destiny smites her with none to caress with motherly love, many pleasant duties remain.... In the first place, aiding her bread-winning husband with honor and love, looking after their house naturally would not be suitable for one who goes to the café. Second, she is bound to the standard of religion whose conscientious observance entirely excludes all but that which an observant, religious, pious woman should uncontrollably maintain the family hearth." Ultimately, the writer echoes the aforementioned argument by Mátyás Eisler, that women in public lead men astray:

The present writer—who happens to belong to the stronger sex—very often finds it amazing that café women and men are seen and the intercourse between them is narrowly noted. And if any among our readers do the same, make sure that they do not act as defiantly and boldly as the unknown women. The moment a woman sets down her petite enamel-shod foot in the café, it is possible to discern symptoms of a disease in the white-vested men. The sickness' scientific name: Leering disease (*fix-írkór*). Its symptoms surely include the young man beginning to cough, a plum pit getting stuck in his throat. Soon his fashionably upturned mustache starts to twitch such that he begins twirling it; he asks the waiter for the latest vintage of Figaro—all this only to impress a woman.

Ultimately, the writer concludes that women simply should not visit the café at all:

Is it not justifiable, after taking all of this into account, to pose the question whether a respectable woman should expose herself to this sort of unpleasantness? And if, after all this, it appears that our ladies for the most part feel good in the café, does it not imply a feebleness of character? It is not possible that a good wife, caring mother, a woman eminently performing her calling and function could enjoy the bodily and spiritually noxious atmosphere of the café. Our women are more noble, the champions of more sublime ideas who will soon be reconciled with their calling that they should not expose themselves to insipidness.

For Jews, though, the attitude toward women in public was further animated by a broader challenge at the turn of the twentieth century to the authenticity of the Hungarianness of Hungarian Jews. One of the loudest voices in this chorus of criticism was Miklós Bartha, a member of and publicist for the hypernationalist Independence Party. In his treatise *Kazár földön* (In the Land of the Khazars), Bartha refuted the claim by Budapest chief rabbi Sándor Kohn and others that Hungarian Jews were descendants of Khazars who had settled in Hungary along with Árpád and the original Magyar settlers—a claim that, for Kohn and other Jews, authenticated the connection of Jews to the Kingdom of Hungary. Bartha claimed instead that the Jewish descendants of the Khazars were Polish Jews who had immigrated to Hungary only beginning in the 1870s. This claim was part of Bartha's larger claim that Jews were inherently foreign and incapable of becoming Magyars.[63] What's more, he singled out Jewish women as the weak link in any effort to fuse Jewish and Magyar identity: "Jews are the dikes of the barricade of Magyarization, yet Jewish women, in particular, fill this role as grievously as the upper ranks of the royal and imperial officer corps."[64]

In response, a woman writing to the *Magyar Zsidó Nő* rejected Bartha's claim: "We who name Hungarian Jewish women as the caretakers of patriotism in spirit, we cannot dumbly remain silent [and] refrain in the face of Bartha Miklós's unjust claim.... Jewish women are not only not unpatriotic—on the contrary! Their hearts and spirits go out for their homeland. Hungarian Jewish women are indeed Hungarian, who love their motherland as much as this distinguished gentleman."[65] A follow-up letter to Bartha addressed this thinly veiled criticism more directly by contrasting modern Hungarian Jewish women with their lesser precursors: "We are hurt by the worthless and undeserved accusation that you made with respect against Hungarian Jews, particularly against Hungarian Jewish women. If in the past Hungarian Jewish women fit this accusation, in no case is the claim justified today, when Hungarian Jewish women cultivate these vital ideas with complete ardor.... The Jewish mother teaches her babbling child to pray in Hungarian and to love our country."[66]

Bartha not only impugned the patriotism of Jewish women but also their ability to raise children properly, that is, as proper Jews and Magyars. In this he was not alone. Some Budapest Jews, concerned regarding the lack of universal embrace of the Magyar language among Jews, raised concerns about the way Jewish mothers reared their children, specifically that they still preferred German to Magyar language and culture:

One of the more consistent complaints is that Jewish women are lax in Magyarizing, turning instead toward a German spirit ... we hear endlessly the claim that Jewish family life is foreign and the Jews' language of intercourse is not at all Magyar.... We do not want Jewish women to speak German and raise children in the German

spirit.... Jewish women! Cast out the weeds, so that they do not infect the rosebuds.
Raise your children in a Magyar spirit, teaching them to love our dear mother tongue.
Let us be Magyars in heart and spirit, no less in fashion, language, social intercourse,
and in the most intimate family life ... a nation lives in its language.... Let us speak
Magyar! Magyar everywhere and at all times.[67]

In the face of these exchanges, the activities of the PIN declawed at once the criticism of Jewish women participating in public life and their lack of Magyar patriotism, and demonstrated the ability of Jewish women in Budapest to venture out in public without compromising their abilities as mothers to raise children who were good Jews and good Magyars. By expanding their philanthropic efforts beyond the Jewish community to other residents of Budapest in need of assistance, moreover, the women of the PIN transformed the nature of philanthropic activities from ad hoc acts of kindness into a systematic social safety net that heretofore had existed neither in Budapest nor in its Jewish community.

Indeed, the PIN set a tone that city leaders in Budapest soon followed.[68] When the Józsefvárosi Liberals Club organized a conference to discuss founding a municipal shelter, the leaders of the PIN were invited to participate. By the end of the 1890s, city leaders began debating a series of reform initiatives that included the creation of a city-sponsored communal child welfare network. It was no coincidence that this debate began in the aftermath of the cholera epidemic of 1895, during which the women's society played a major role in providing aid to victims and helping to contain the spread of infection. A decade later this was a central campaign issue in the 1906 mayoral election. There was a certain irony in a women's association pioneering the realm of public health. Excluded from government and public life, and confined to private endeavors like charity, the leaders of the Pest Jewish Women's Association expanded and developed their private realm into an increasingly integral part of municipal government. By the beginning of the twentieth century, what had once been a specifically Jewish program of philanthropic acts had expanded into an integral part of a broader system of civic welfare.[69]

This synergy between the PIN and the shift in municipal policy pointed to the path that Jewish women followed from the Jewish community to mainstream society. The women who founded and participated in women's associations found common ground with noblewomen, who faced a similar sort of exclusion despite their abilities. In both cases, affluent, educated, well-connected women who were freed from household responsibilities by domestic servants found a crucial outlet in the eleemosynary and educational activities of women's societies, Jewish and Christian. This common experience, as Susan Zimmermann recently noted, laid the foundation for the Hungarian feminist movement. It is not surprising that the founders and leaders of this movement came from a similar background. Rózsa Schwimmer and Mária Gárdos, two leading figures of the movement's first generation, were born in Budapest (Schwimmer later lived in Temesvár) into affluent families. Both were educated in elite schools, entered the family business, and benefited from their family name. Both found a political voice as leaders of a women's association, working to erode the male-dominated hierarchy of Hungarian and Jewish society.[70]

In a sense, the challenge of expanding Jewish philanthropy beyond the parameters of the Jewish community without compromising its integrity was mirrored by an increasingly complex relationship between Jewish and Magyar identity within the Jewish home. For the growing number of nonobservant, self-consciously Magyarizing Jewish families in Budapest, Jewish identity and their connection to the Jewish community was defined less by religious standards than by an impetus to associate with other Jews. The challenge, both for contemporary observers and subsequent historians, has been describing and assessing the Jewishness of these Jews and the extent to which the epithet "assimilated" applies to them. That is, how do we determine, based on social rather than religious behavior, whether or not Jews who abandoned traditional Jewish behavior patterns in favor of the culture and mores of the mainstream still evinced a strong sense of Jewishness?

A useful measure in this regard is the practice among some Neolog Jews in turn-of-the-twentieth-century Budapest Jewry to display a Christmas tree in their homes during the Christmas holiday. This debate was set in motion by a poem that was published in the Liberal Jewish weekly *Egyenlőség* (the main publication of the Neolog community) during the 1890s:

> *I arrive at home when Christmas is dawning*
> *There the Christmas tree already stands with gaudy finery all around it . . .*
> *Whither, whither bright little pine tree—As I depart to the big world I wonder*
> *Whether you are going or returning*
> *Says the little tree, I am not going anywhere*
>
> *No holy water, no holy host—why is the tree there?*
> *Christians celebrate Christmas with one another*
> *but Jews have nothing of this old heritage*
> *Yet year in year out there is great concern*
> *as to what kind of Christmas tree there will be*
> *another holiday to imitate*
>
> *In a Mosaic house there is a little Jesus*
> *they do not fit beside one another*

Christians light and Israelites
Father, Son and Holy Spirit
Cannot mesh with a Jewish house
The belief in three has no place where God is only one[71]

Critics of this practice assumed that a Jew celebrating any aspect of Christmas had crossed over into the realm of radical or total assimilation. One Neolog rabbi lamented in 1886: "Jews, too, illuminate a Christmas tree. Their children are no longer familiar with the Chanukah lamp, the menorah.... They are not familiar with Shabbat candles. Alas ... in their stead is the cult of the Christmas tree." Another rabbi lamented that the real impact of emancipation and the placing of Judaism and Christianity on equal footing was not civic equality but "our predilection to celebrate Christmas."[72]

Yet many Jews in the desacralized atmosphere of turn-of-the-twentieth-century Budapest regarded Christmas more as a national or civic holiday than as a religious holiday (i.e., more like Thanksgiving, a day that had religious roots but was eventually redefined as a civic holiday). These Jews regarded a desacralized Christmas as being in the same secular category of attending a synagogue or church for nonreligious purposes or congregating in a café. Budapest Jews celebrated Christmas to demonstrate their Magyarness rather than their Christianness. One Budapest Jew observed that "we are the most boisterous, the most clamorous, the most sentimental, the most festive. Jewish ladies buy the largest Christmas trees, and Jews write the most Christian spirit in the holiday papers." Another noted that "these days the Hungarian Israelite families among us are first in line on Christmas eve."[73] The notion of Christmas as something other than a religious holiday was not only embraced by Jews. One observer noted the general lack of religious affinity for the holiday: "Common people do not know from Christmas trees, but only the display cases where bakeries display their pastries, which they gaze at for an hour at a time beside the radiant lights. If they did not know what it was for, they would probably have assumed it was for only fine stuff for gentlemen."[74]

Yet although the celebration of Christmas was purged of religious significance, there was a limit as to how deeply Jews were willing to immerse themselves in this holiday. One contributor to *Egyenlőség*, whose family exchanged gifts but did not have a tree, regarded the celebration of Christmas by Jews as a sort of no-man's-land between the Christian and Jewish communities: "Orthodox Jews," he noted, "shook their heads at us because we received Christmas presents; Christian friends shook their heads because we had no Christmas tree." Yet this same contributor was not terribly bothered: "We are Neolog Jews; we have presents but no tree." For this family, even though the Christmas tree was beyond the pale, Christmas presents were not.[75]

In retrospect, the Christmas tree became a shibboleth for two different attitudes regarding the relationship between one's Jewishness and one's Hungarianness. This is evidenced in an exchange between an Orthodox and a Neolog rabbi. The former claimed that putting up a Christmas tree could only lead Jews away from Judaism, toward complete abandonment of tradition and total assimilation. In response, the Neolog rabbi replied that the real issue is "whether Jews practice beneficence beside the Christmas tree; whether the Christmas tree helps them to do good for the poor and orphans, for the hungry and the destitute." He added: "As long as they do not compromise their Judaism . . . in my opinion, putting up a Christmas tree is not more Christian than attending a Christian carnival."[76]

This exchange points to a larger challenge for Jews in an increasingly open and desacralized Budapest society: how to define the boundary between engagement with the non-Jewish world that enhances a sense of Jewishness, and an engagement that ultimately deludes it. Nonreligious behavior in the synagogue and Jews gathering in a nonreligious space such as the café were deemed acceptable. Jews incorporating an aspect of Christmas in their homes, even in a desacralized fashion for national reasons, was more difficult for some Jews to swallow and thus was more often seen as a form of assimilation and disaffection.

In this sense, the Christmas tree debate and the success of the PIN were mirror images of each other. The Christmas tree debate revolved around the possibility of desacralizing something non-Jewish in order to import it into a Jewish home that was enthusiastically blending things Jewish with things Magyar. The Christmas tree, redefined as a nonreligious symbol by nonobservant Jews, became a useful tool in this endeavor. The PIN, too, helped define and clarify the boundary between the Jewish and the Magyar, albeit in the opposite direction; exporting something specifically Jewish and desacralizing it to make it adaptable to a broader mainstream program of social welfare. The varied aims and activities of the PIN reflected more broadly the way that the Neolog outlook championed flexibility and fluidity in Jewish life, allowing individual Jewish families to pick and choose from among the myriad of Jewish laws and customs and to fashion their own particular blend of tradition and innovation, observance and nonobservance.

The way the PIN facilitated the entry of Jewish women into mainstream urban society points to a broader dimension of this process. Not all Jews followed a single path from the world of the traditional Jewish community to mainstream society. Just as social class and economic standing affected this path, so, too, did the particular set of possibilities available to Jewish women and the impediments they faced as they undertook this journey.[77] Just as the story of Budapest Jewry's entry into the mainstream cannot be told without including the experiences of Jewish women, so, too, it cannot be told without considering the particular situation of two other groups within Budapest Jewry: Orthodox Jews and lower-income, working-class Jews.

7

The Other Side of Budapest Jewry: Orthodox and Lower-Income Jews

WRITING IN 1911, NOVELIST AND ESSAYIST TAMÁS KÓBOR RECALLED his childhood home in Budapest, juxtaposing a nostalgic and often humorous longing for his childhood with a not-so-subtle critique of traditional and working-class lifestyles and the harshness of life in the neighborhood of his youth. Indeed, Kóbor used his childhood stories as a point of departure in which he described his journey out of the old neighborhood into the more materially satisfying life of the acculturated, upper-middle-class, Jewish intellectual elite who had left Terézváros:

> My father was a poor tinsmith on Szerecsen Street.... I remember his shop, which was separated from our flat by a blue paper divider.... My dear father worked and worked, from daybreak to midnight but was never able to earn a living. The builders did not pay him, vendors would not accept his credit. One Friday evening he came home from the synagogue with a guest. My mother raised her eyebrows uncomfortably—there was not a lot for dinner, and the portions of meat were already allotted. The guest, a stranger whom my father met at the synagogue, was invited for Shabbat, according to Jewish custom regarding visitors. He was more panhandler than guest, but he made himself at home.[1]

As one reads further through Kóbor's autobiography, one cannot but notice an uneven mixture of revulsion and nostalgia. While occasionally lamenting how the world of his childhood was rapidly fading and disappearing, Kóbor also expressed a sense of relief and liberation for having escaped the dreary world of the old neighbor-hood—hence the title of this memoiristic work, *Ki a gettóból* (Out of the Ghetto). In no small part, Kóbor was describing what he regarded not only as a change in his own life but a broader movement of Budapest Jewry away from that traditional world.

In fact, the situation is more complex. It is true that, beginning in the latter half of the nineteenth century, a significant portion of Budapest Jewry ascended up the economic ladder to the upper middle class and embraced the religiously progressive ideas of Neolog in one fashion or another. Yet other elements of Budapest Jewry not only remained a significant minority of Budapest Jewry into the twentieth century but thrived. Specifically, Budapest Jewry's Orthodox community increased from barely 150 at the end of the 1860s to more than 20,000 by the end of the 1930s; Budapest Jewry's lower-middle and working-class Jews numbered more than 13,000 at the turn of the twentieth century. Recent Jewish arrivals to Budapest, immigrants and in-migrants, accounted for a considerable portion of both Orthodox and working-class Jews. The size and vibrance of these segments of the Jewish population suggests a Budapest Jewry more eclectic and diverse than is often portrayed.[2]

This points to a crucial, often overlooked feature of Budapest Jewry: the coexistence, especially from the 1860s onward, of disparate Jewish constituencies—Orthodox and Neolog, middle class and lower income, native-born and newcomer—living in rel-atively close proximity on a scale unmatched by other Hungarian Jewish communi-ties. In relative terms, the Orthodox, lower-income, and immigrant subcommunities were always a minority within the larger Budapest Jewish community that, during the decades leading up to 1914, became increasingly Neolog, upwardly mobile, and Budapest-born. In absolute terms, however, these minority subcommunities were con-siderably larger than any Orthodox community or lower-income Jewish enclave any-where else in Hungary.

In this regard, Kóbor's description reflects not only a personal appraisal, but a broader "Whiggish" historiographical tendency to present Budapest Jewry largely as a religiously progressive, upwardly mobile community, while focusing far less on the thousands of lower-income, religiously traditional Jews, many of whom had only recently relocated to Budapest. As Anikó Prepuk noted: "In contrast to the rapidly Magyarizing and modernizing Neolog, Orthodoxy has not hitherto received due at-tention; rather it has been understood as the survival of a massive anachronism, as a de-ficiency in assimilation, or as unfilled expectations with regard to liberal doctrine."[3] In a similar vein, Miklós Konrád recently noted: "When Jewish (or non-Jewish) middle-class journalists, publicists, and writers [in Budapest] referred to 'Jews' they meant the cultivated, (upper) middle-class. As a result, hardly anything was written about lower-middle-class Jews; and when they were mentioned, the emphasis tended to be on the area in which they lived." This, Konrád noted, led to overlooking the thousands of Jewish retailers, craftsmen, minor public officials, tailors, grocers, brokers, and porters who comprised the bulk of the Jewish and overall population of the city's sixth and seventh districts.[4]

Several reasons can be adduced to explain the historiographical lacuna that has marginalized these groups. For contemporary observers like Kóbor, Jewish and non-Jewish alike, a religiously progressive demeanor and outlook were regarded as more conducive and amenable to Magyarization. Jewish communal leaders and ideologues rarely missed an opportunity to link examples of their community's progressive outlook with an affinity for Magyarization. Non-Jewish observers, too, regarded a Budapest Jewry that was more upwardly mobile, native-born, and professional as more productive and moderate and thus preferable to working-class Jews who were seen as more prone to radicalism and social upheaval. The perception that recent arrivals from Galicia, Ukraine, Russia, and northeastern Hungary tended to be lower-income, working-class, unacculturated Jews impelled Hungarian Jewish leaders and ideologues to downplay the foreignness and radicalism that voices critical of the Jewish community associated with these foreign Jews.[5]

For historians, the task of more fully incorporating Orthodox and less affluent Jews into the broader narrative of Budapest Jewry requires navigating through certain complexities. The two groups overlapped substantially, but not entirely. Many Orthodox Jews and recent arrivals from northeastern Hungary and Galicia were petty merchants and artisans, and vice versa. Yet there were also upwardly mobile Orthodox Jews and acculturated, nonobservant lower-income Jews. Orthodox and lower-income Jewish subcommunities in Budapest, moreover, were themselves far from monolithic but part of a more amorphous array of observant Jews whom historians describe using multiple epithets: traditional, Modern Orthodox, Orthodox, Ultra-Orthodox, and Hasidic. In particular, there was no consensus among this mishmash of observant Jews between those who saw themselves—and, in 1870, were defined by the state—as a denomination and community separate from the Neolog Jewish community of Budapest, and those who saw themselves as still part of the main Jewish community.[6] No less challenging has been defining the boundaries of the mass of lower-income Jews, who have been described alternatively as lower-middle-class and working-class elements of the Jewish community. Elsewhere, the emergence of an industrial labor force was preceded by and facilitated by the decline of a preexisting artisanal population. In Hungary, though, the emergence of a population of working-class Jews in the classical sense of the term coincided with the continued presence of a considerable number of Jewish artisans, who remained a conspicuous part of the Budapest Jewish community into the twentieth century. The distinction between skilled factory workers and artisans, for example, was not always obvious.[7]

Given these complexities, a useful first step toward incorporating lower-income and Orthodox Jews into the larger narrative of Budapest Jewry is to focus on a core institution related to each group: for Orthodox Jews, this was the Budapest Hevra Shas (aka *Talmudverein* or *Talmudegylet*); for lower-income, working-class Jews this was the Magyar Israelite Crafts and Agriculture Association (*Magyar Izraelita Kézmű- és Földművelési Egylet*, hereinafter MIKÉFE). Both organizations were established originally as part of the network of voluntary associations that formed the matrix of Jewish communal life in Budapest. While the aims and main concerns of the two organizations focused on different things—living a fully observant Jewish life, in one case; engaging in occupations more productive than petty merchants and pawnbrokers, on the other—there were parallels in their relationship to the main Jewish community. Both groups had a constituency centered in Terézváros and Erzebétváros that was fed primarily by a steady influx of in-migrants from northeastern Hungary, the Slovakian Highlands, and immigrants from Galicia.

Both organizations, moreover, were also aided by the support of prominent local rabbis, who first endorsed and then actively participated in the development of each organization. For MIKÉFE, this leader was Rabbi Löw Schwab. For the Hevra Shas, transformational leaders were the first prominent Orthodox rabbis who settled in Budapest, Chaim Sofer and Viktor Sussman. Neither organization's constituency shared the high social aspirations of their more progressive and upwardly mobile coreligionists. Orthodox and lower-income Jews rarely imagined that they might gain entree into Budapest high society, let alone be accepted into the ranks of the nobility; even relocating to the more affluent parts of Terézváros near Andrássy Boulevard—let alone to Lipótváros or Buda—was a pipe-dream. Rather, these Jews had more modest day-to-day goals: earning a living, putting food on the table, owning or renting a comfortable home in a safe neighborhood, and providing a decent education for their children; they wanted little more than a sense of material and spiritual stability amid the increasingly tumultuous atmosphere of the big city.

Accordingly, there were parallels and differences between the aims and programs of the Hevra Shas and MIKÉFE. Both organizations wanted to improve the lot of Jews, younger and older, who they believed were not optimally served by the broadening economic and social opportunities of the 1860s. For young Jews, this meant providing an educational alternative for lower-income Jewish families who lacked the financial means or connections to send their children to an elite community or state school, and for Orthodox families for whom the community schools lacked sufficient religious content. For Jewish adults, this meant designing activities that offered an alternate use of leisure time than sitting in a café—the progressive upper middle ideal form of leisure. On this point, though, the two organizations proposed diametrically opposed alternatives. The central aim of Orthodox organizations like the Hevra Shas was maximizing the time that Jewish men could devote daily and weekly to the study of rabbinic texts. The leaders of MIKÉFÉ lumped the study of rabbinic texts together with sitting in a café as nonproductive and unhealthy uses of leisure time; instead, they advocated physical activity and productive work.

Furthermore, the two groups regarded their members' involvement with the overall Jewish community differently. The overall mentality of each organization reflected a different ideal. In the case of the Hevra Shas, this was the traditional Jewish ideal of the *batlan* as a defining feature of a fully developed Jewish community. Like other Orthodox organizations, the Hevra Shas aimed at limiting its members' involvement with mainstream society and especially with non-Orthodox Jews—hence the drive to provide alternate education and leisure time. They aimed at ensuring that the children of Orthodox Jews remained Orthodox Jews; when they did not, their families were scandalized. By contrast, the broader ideal pursued by MIKÉFE was productivity as a central aim of enlightenment and citizenship. MIKÉFE provided a way for children from low-income families to engage with communal institutions more productively and as a means to ascend the economic and social ladder; when the children ascended, the parents proudly rejoiced.[8] Thus it is not surprising that, while both organizations started out as communal organizations supported by and under the jusrisdiction of the main Budapest Jewish community, by the twentieth century MIKÉFE remained a semiautonomous subsidiary, supporting a separate set of economic and educational opportunities but heavily dependent on the financial support and annual fundraising campaign of the main Jewish community; while the Hevra Shas emerged by the beginning of the 1890s as the cornerstone of an Orthodox community that moved steadily toward full autonomy from the main community. This last aim was realized when the Hevra Shas became fully financially independent thanks to substantial endowments that produced enough annual income to cover the organization's costs more or less in perpetuity.

MIKÉFE: PRODUCTIVITY AND IDENTITY

The notion of a Jewish crafts association originated in the broader discussion of ways to productivize young Jews by steering them clear of petty commerce and small-scale moneylending (i.e., pawnbroking). This meant improving existing Jewish schools by keeping up with new developments and innovations in education and vocational training, a core aim of Jewish emancipation in Hungary as understood by Kossuth and Baron József Eötvös. Drawing on the ideas of English liberals such as John Stewart Mill and French liberals such as Alexis de Toqueville, Kossuth and Eötvös believed that liberty had to be rooted in a vibrant civil society with a citizenry willing to form and maintain voluntary associations and autonomous social and economic groups. To this end, in 1842 Kossuth founded the National Crafts Association to provide vocational training and new occupational opportunities to the children of indigent and nonproductive families. In Eötvös's view, contrary to a popular stereotype at the time, the disproportionate number of Jews engaged in "nonproductive" occupations such as petty commerce and moneylending resulted neither from a Jewish affinity for these occupations nor a self-conscious Jewish desire to avoid manual labor. He believed that the dearth of Jewish farmers and artisans resulted from restrictions placed on Jews by a Christian state and society. He believed that some Jews, at least, would willingly exchange commerce for crafts and agriculture. The reforms of 1840 made this possible by requiring master craftsmen to take on apprentices regardless of religion.

For Kossuth and Eötvös, Jews in cities like Pest were an important litmus test of the possibility of making Hungarian Jews more productive.[9] Accordingly, Kossuth invited Jews to participate in this endeavor. Communal leaders, too, enthralled by Law 29 requiring Christian guilds to accept Jewish artisans and to train Jewish apprentices, hoped that Jewish artisans and aspiring artisans would join Kossuth's new organization.[10] Jews, however, were reluctant to join due, first, to a concern that the restrictions removed by Law 29 might well be reinstated by a less liberal government; and, second, because joining Kossuth's organization or a Christian guild would lead young Jews away from the Jewish community. In addition, German-dominated guilds were often epicenters of anti-Jewish rhetoric.[11] Instead, Jewish communal leaders in Pest pursued an alternative that in their minds would be more palatable to Jews: vocational training combined with a proper Jewish education. Thus was born the Magyar Israelite Crafts and Agriculture Association (Magyar Izraelita Kézmű és Földművelési Egylet, MIKÉFE), founded on April 3, 1842, and recognized by the state in 1847.[12]

From the outset, the leadership of MIKÉFE reflected its close connection to the main Jewish community. At the inaugural meeting, the community's chief rabbi, Löw Schwab, was elected the first president and Fülöp Jakobovics, superintendent of the Jewish Hospital, was chosen as director of the new program. Ignác Barnai, secretary of the Jewish community, was selected to be vice president.[13] Like the main Jewish community, the association divided membership into three tiers: rank-and-file members who paid annual dues of 2 forints; "founding members" who paid minimum annual dues of 100 forints; and "honorary members" who paid minimum annual dues of 500 forints. To cover the costs of the association, Schwab requested financial assistance from the Gemeinde. Two years later, Gemeinde president Hermann Löwy proposed allotting a portion of revenue from annual dues to the support and expansion of the new association. After several years of debate, due mainly to recurring disagreements about the need for vocational training among Jews, the resolution passed in 1847. By 1851, the association had more than five hundred members, who paid more than 1,600 forints in annual dues, and was receiving 1,100 forints from donations collected in the synagogue, 600 forints for clothing and 500 for shoes.[14]

THE HEVRA SHAS: ORTHODOXY IN
A COSMOPOLITAN METROPOLIS

The Hevra Shas was founded as a voluntary organization in 1842 by Ede Fleischmann and Gusztáv Taub to serve the specific needs of the small complement of observant Jews living in Pest. It encouraged its members to devote as much time as possible to the study of rabbinic texts, the latest in a series of communal initiatives to encourage and support a coterie of full-time scholars. Like the nascent Kollel movement in Lithuanian Jewish communities, the Hevra Shas provided space, resources, instruction, a stipend, and camaraderie. In this way, the Hevra Shas created a viable traditional option for the leisure time of observant Jews in Budapest.[15] This operating principle was rooted in a centuries-old notion that venerated at once the study of sacred texts, individuals who devoted themselves maximally to this endeavor, and Jewish communities that supported them. The Mishnaic tractate Megilla 3:1 opens with a programmatic statement that defined a mature Jewish community (*'ir gedolah*) as one with at least ten *batlanim* (*Kol she-yesh ba 'asara batlanim*). The designation *batlan*, understood literally as an idler, was interpreted in rabbinic literature as men who had been freed by communal support from the burden of earning a living and were thus able to devote themselves entirely to serving the community (*b'teilin mi'melachtan v'oskin b'tzorchei tzibbur*). Describing the Jewish community of eleventh-century Baghdad, Benjamin of Tudela noted "the ten *batlanim* who do not engage in any other work than communal administration; and all the days of the week they judge their countrymen, except on the second day of the week, when they sit with the chief Rabbi Samuel, the Gaon, who in conjunction with the other *batlanim* judges all those that appear before him."[16]

The notion of *batlan* soon evolved from being a communal servant to being a full-time rabbinic scholar. The Jerusalem Talmud described *batlanim* as "ten men that refrain from doing any work, so they should be present in the synagogue"; to which Rabbi Judah clarified, "for example, we who are not dependent on our learning to earn our livelihood."[17] Along similar lines, Moses Isserles iterated the obligation of each community to support *Lomdei Torah*, men who studied full time. This instruction was fortified by eighteenth-century Jonathan Eybeshütz, who rooted it retroactively in antiquity: "Ezra the Scribe ordained that on Mondays and Thursdays ten verses should be read in the synagogue corresponding to the *batlanim* who refrain from engaging in work and instead engage in the study of Torah." By the end of the sixteenth century, such an obligation had often been woven into the fabric of Jewish communal life. The statutes of the Jewish community of Gai, Moravia, required "every small community that has a *melamed* or that has one or two members or, better yet, more who are learned, and all the more so communities who have a rabbi but not a yeshiva, are obligated to establish times for communal learning to study together daily. The head of the community is obligated to enforce this directly with a large fine so that the Torah will not be forgotten." [18]

This notion of Jewish leisure remained entrenched, even amid the increasingly complex Ashkenazic world of the late nineteenth century. Historian Jacob Katz characterized leisure as "a plane on which conflicts were resolved and the demands of aesthetic life were satisfied, the consolidation of society took place, social hierarchies put into place, the rising generation was educated, and ethnic self-awareness was developed." The importance of this notion to the traditional Jewish world lay in the fact that "as long as it was obligatory for every Jewish male to continuously study the Torah and Talmud, the most important aspect of leisure time in the traditional Jewish world was the reading of religious texts." [19] Thus, as one scholar noted, "any time, however brief, that remained after the performance of the obligatory commandments, earning one's livelihood, and taking care of the other necessities of life was to be devoted to the study of Torah." [20]

Accordingly, the Hevra Shas facilitated an intensive devotion of nonworking hours to Jewish communal service and, above all, to text study. To this end, the Hevra Shas maintained a prayer service and a house of study (a *minyan* and a *bet midrash*) in a synagogue in Pest's Sixth District, first on Két Szerecsen Street and then on Vasváry Street. The organization also set up a kosher slaughterhouse (*kosherbank*) and a butcher under strict halachic supervision, opportunities for Torah study during the week and on Shabbat, and later a library. All of this was designed to provide for the spiritual needs of traditional Jews. By the early 1860s, the members of this small organization were pooling their efforts and meager resources toward "supporting Biblical and Talmudic discourse and assuring that all deceased members have someone to recite the *Kaddish*." [21] Such associations formed frequently in Jewish communities of varying sizes, in small towns and large cities alike; a Hevra Shas was an integral part of the backbone of traditional—and, later, Orthodox—Jewish communal life that bridged the gap between the individual and the community. [22]

Eventually the Hevra Shas became a cornerstone of a nascent Orthodox community in Budapest. The rapid growth of the Hevra Shas at the end of the nineteenth century was an important vehicle through which traditional Jews maintained a strong commitment to an observant lifestyle amid the pressures and allures of urban life. In Pest, this meant creating a space for Jews outside a community dominated increasingly by the mentality and aims of Neolog Judaism. What Andreas Reinke noted with respect to Jewish voluntary associations in Breslau applies no less saliently to the relationship between the Hevra Shas and the Jews of Pest:

In the highly conflicting course of exchange between orthodox [*altglaubigen*] and progressive [*neolog*] streams, associations provided, on the one hand, an alternative to what had hitherto been the social and religious life . . . that allowed various religious currents to merge in an ever-united union; and, on the other hand, in lieu of the traditional compulsory-structured Gemeinde, the *Verein* guaranteed an underlying cohesion that was oriented to new forms of social organization.[23]

The Hevra Shas, in this sense, is a useful venue through which to examine the rise and expansion of an upstart Orthodox community in a "hostile territory" such as Budapest from a tactical and organizational vantage point; and the success of a marginal handful of observant Jewish families during the 1870s in expanding into one of Europe's largest and most dynamic enclaves of Orthodox Jews by the beginning of the twentieth century.

In retrospect, this accomplishment was made possible by the Hevra Shas accomplishing three tasks. First, the Hevra Shas expanded the traditional rabbinic notion of the *batlan* from a pietistic ideal into a more standard, male requirement that defined the proper use of leisure time and regulated the contact between members of the Hevra Shas and the non-Orthodox Jewish community. Second, the Hevra Shas created new rabbinic and teaching posts that soon attracted first-rate Orthodox rabbis and scholars to Budapest for the first time, who eventually formed the leadership core of the nascent Orthodox community. The presence of much-revered rabbis fortified the Hevra Shas and the small Orthodox subcommunity around it with a sense of pride and self-confidence, and attracted not only observant Jews but sympathetic nonobservant donors to the ranks of the organization. Third, and perhaps most importantly, the Hevra Shas cultivated independent sources of funding to support its primary emphasis on the study of religious texts, and eventually attained financial independence from the main Jewish community. This allowed the organization to expand its range of operation and influence. Financial independence, in turn, expanded the importance of affluent, nonscholarly, and even nonobservant laity in the organization's leadership as donors and fundraisers, above all affluent Orthodox and non-Orthodox Jewish women. Including these affluent individuals, even if only for financial and other pragmatic reasons, required a willingness to set aside an ideologically driven reluctance to have excessive contact with non-Orthodox Jews. Such reluctance was diffused by the financial benefits: financial independence from the mainstream Neolog-dominated Jewish community was worth the price of honoring non-Orthodox Jews and giving them a voice.[24]

Like MIKÉFE, the Hevra Shas drew from the large concentration of Jews in Budapest, and especially more traditional, newly arriving Jews from northeastern Hungary and Galicia, and provided them with a refuge from the challenges of urban life. As the (unabashedly pro-Orthodox) Aron Fürst noted in his history of Budapest Jewry: "Budapest itself, the great bustling metropolis, never appeared to be a place suitable for a *yeshivah*. However, there were many *Talmidei Chahamim* among the householders who set aside time to study Torah and spent time in places like the Hevra Shas."[25] The rise and development of the Budapest Hevra Shas, in this light, provides an alternative perspective that integrates Orthodox Jews more comprehensively into the larger narrative of Hungarian Jewish history. In general, studies of the rise of Orthodoxy in Hungary have heretofore tended to focus on Orthodox communities whose members had overwhelmingly embraced Orthodoxy. This has allowed historians to presume—quite accurately with regard to Poszony, Munkács, Ungvár, and similar cases—the religious outlook and practice of rank-and-file Jews in such cases to be consistent with some form of Orthodox ideology, and to focus instead on global rather than local and individual tendencies. This, in turn, led to a greater focus on Orthodoxy's ideologues and its most radical and zealous part such as the *Hevra Shomre ha-Dat* (Hitőr magyar zsidó egylet/ Society of the Guardians of the Faith).[26]

Given the predominance of this approach, it is not surprising that the Orthodox community of Budapest—although numerically the largest concentration of Orthodox Jews in Hungary by the end of the First World War—is included in this narrative only selectively. Typically, Budapest's Orthodoxy community draws scholarly attention either with respect to the struggle between Orthodox and Neolog around the time of the Hungarian Jewish Congress of 1868–1869 or the career of prominent rabbis such as Benjamin Sofer who served in Budapest for a short time; or as part of a broader scholarly tendency to underline Budapest Jewry's polarized, extreme tendencies as paradigmatic of Hungarian Jewry as a whole. *Shomre ha-Dat* and the ideology it championed, no less than the schism between Orthodoxy and Neolog, were powerful and indispensable elements in the development of Hungarian Orthodoxy, and especially its Ultra-Orthodox wing. Yet the rapid expansion and entrenchment of Hungarian Orthodoxy stemmed not only from what Michael Silber termed "the invention of a tradition," but also by the successes of rabbinic and lay leaders at the level of communal organization, institutional expansion, and an ongoing recruitment of new members.[27]

The Hevra Shas was not driven by ideological concerns. Its activities were rooted largely in day-to-day Jewish communal life: charity, taxes, buying books, supporting teachers and students, and, above all, creating opportunities for the study of rabbinic texts. The statutes of the organization, published in 1852 and then reissued in 1875 and 1898, spelled out this mission:

> Since knowledge and study of the Holy Teachings and fundamentals [*Torah ha-Kedosha und Grundlagen*] of the Jewish religion has been and still is a sacred obligation of every Israelite, we are required to maintain the study of Talmud in order to support and affirm this spiritual awakening in every possible way. Thus one finds in every great Jewish community public institutions of study [*offentliche Lehranstalt/*

Batei Midrash] where every opportunity is made possible to be able to devote time every day to the Holy Torah through daily public lectures.[28]

Appended to this general objective was one specific to the particular situation of Jews in Budapest: "It is all the more a sacred obligation to situate such an institution in the capital of Hungary where there are so many fellow-believers [*Glaubensgenossen*], whose needs will be met thoroughly only by these aims." The statutes emphasized the importance of helping indigent pious Jews by offering "to subsidize those destitute Talmudic scholars who regularly come to hear the daily Talmudic discourses; even those who are here only temporarily are still worthy Talmudic scholars [*Bnai Tora*]"; and to make sure that "industrious children of less well-off parents who want to acquire a superior Hebraic education, can participate free of charge." To this end, the statutes of the Hevra Shas required its members

> to maintain study halls, to worship together in a permanent synagogue [*Bethaus/Imaház*], to acquire a suitable library . . . and to employ two permanent first-rate Talmudic scholars: one, a so-called Shasz [*sic*] Rabbi who, in addition to being the spiritual head of the association, is obligated to deliver discourses with suitable commentaries daily in the morning and the evening; the other to deliver a discourse each evening on the Bible using Rashi's commentary, and every Saturday morning a discourse on the weekly Haftorah.[29]

From the outset, membership in the organization was open to "any upstanding Israelite" (*tiszta jellemű izraelita*, per the 1898 statutes) whose admission earned membership benefits for himself and his parents. Women could join, too, but "without active and passive electoral privileges." Each new member was expected to pay an admission fee, determined on a case-by-case basis by the council based largely on the new member's financial situation, and annual dues of six forints. Failure to pay the annual dues for three consecutive years required the council to decide within thirty days whether or not to revoke membership status. Beyond the payment of dues, the principal obligation of membership was "*yahrzeit*-related duties." Each member was required to attend a scheduled series of weekday prayer services and to be available upon request to attend additional prayer services, when necessary, to ensure that there was a prayer quorum.

In its day-to-day routine, the Hevra Shas operated much like a traditional Jewish version of a reading club, that is, studying texts instead of reading literature. The main concern of the Hevra Shas was creating and supporting opportunities for Torah study; the *lamdanim* (Torah scholars) that it supported were its focal point. The weekly schedule of learning was largely an extension of the conventional times when traditional Jews

TABLE 25. STUDENT/SCHOLAR (*LAMDANIM*) STIPENDS, 1875–1876

	1875	1876
RABBI WOLF SUSZMAN	1,450	1,450
NATHAN FELDMAN	936	936
PÁL FISCHER	180	180
PHILIP ESKELES	150	150
G. L. SCHILL	100	100
JOSEF MAI	60	60
LOEFFLER	50	50
ARON LUEGER	50	50
JACOB MANDL	150	150
M. SCHLESINGER	200	200
FREUNDE/BNAI TORA	50	50
TOTAL	3,376	3,376

Source: *Budapesti Talmudegylet jegyzőkönye* #151 (1875), #19 (1876).

came to the synagogue: after the morning service, and prior to and after the afternoon and evening services. The total time that an individual devoted to learning depended on whether or not they could afford to forego other sources of income. In 1875, the earliest year for which records are extant, stipends for ten scholars accounted for nearly half of the organization's annual expenses. These stipends varied. The largest were awarded to two full-time scholars, Rabbi Wolf Sussman and Nathan Feldman. Smaller stipends were given to seven other scholars who were expected to spend several hours daily engaged in Torah study. The smallest stipends were available to *bnai torah* (*Freunde*), individuals who dropped in to learn on an ad hoc basis.

In theory, revenue to cover operating costs was raised primarily from the payment of annual dues and, when necessary, secondarily by individual gifts and endowments, excises on endowments and organizational assets, and selling or renting out pews in the *bet midrash* (*tanterem*). The main source of revenue, though, came initially from the annual interest accrued by the initial endowment of 20,000 forints and subsidies from the main Pest Jewish community, supplemented by smaller donations. Typical in this regard was the 100 forints that Samuel Herzfeld donated for two seats in the *bet midrash* and to arrange to have a special rabbinical kaddish prayer recited for the benefit of his soul (*le-to'elet nishmato*) following learning sessions.[30] Initially this was more than enough to cover the limited expenses of what was as yet a small-time organization, whose entire annual budget hovered around 700 forints until the end of the 1870s. Annual expenses included stipends for indigent students, the salaries of the two rabbis, six instructors, and a custodian, and an array of lesser operating expenses. Even in those years when annual revenue fell short of annual expenses, the deficit was never more than around 300 forints, which would subsequently be covered either through a special donation from an individual donor or by drawing on the principal of the original endowment. Until the end of the 1880s, these sources of revenue sustained the association, mainly because the number of Orthodox Jews in Budapest numbered only a few hundred.

TABLE 26. BALANCE SHEET,
MAY 1875 (FORINTS)

EXPENDITURES	
SALARIES FOR RABBIS	
Leon Reiner	300
S. Loffler	500
Stipends for teachers 6 @ 420	2,520
Stipends for scholars	3,376
BASIC EXPENSES	
Gas	125
Synagogue implements	50
Yahrzeit donations	75
Bet midrash maintenance	45
Candles	15
Wood	70
Housecleaning	50
Etrogim and Lulavim	25
Repairs	25
Learning for deceased	125
New books	340
REVENUE	
Subventions 22 @120	2,640
Admission dues	550
Mikveh fees	240

Source: *Budapesti Talmudegylet jegyzőkönye* (August 23, 1874–May 17, 1885), Mic #9805, JTSA Library #136 (May 24, 1875).

BUDAPEST ORTHODOXY COMES OF AGE

The slow growth of the Orthodox community was not surprising given that Budapest Jewry was quickly growing into the largest progressive Jewish community in the world by the end of the nineteenth century. The triumph of Neolog in Budapest discouraged Orthodox Jews from relocating there. For much of the mid-nineteenth century, traditionalists in Hungary derided Pest Jewry. One contemporary observer noted during the 1860s that "there is not yet an Orthodox community in Pest and the Hevra Shas is the lone institution of the conservatives."[31] Along similar lines, Meir Eisenstadter, rabbi of Ungvár, delineated between Pest and more traditional Jewish communities. Ignoring the existence of several synagogues in Pest, he concluded that Pest Jewry was so devoid of real religious commitment or organization that Jewish law had no impact there: "So, too, in the holy community of Pest, where there is no communal synagogue, and they only lease one from the landlord . . . laws pertaining to synagogues do not apply. . . . One cannot infer [regarding Pest] from a city that actually elevates the honor of the Torah [*Ma'ala kvod torato*]."[32] Similarly, Mordehaj Winkler, a leading Orthodox rabbi from Mád, looked askance on divorce proceedings conducted by rabbis in Pest, not least of all because he suspected that all rabbis in Pest were either themselves Neolog rabbis or, at least, sympathetic to and influenced by Neolog Judaism.[33] Such strident condemnations of Pest continued into the 1870s. Writing in 1878, leading Orthodox rabbi Moses Schick noted:

> It has been twenty years or more that the men of the Pest Kehilla intervened with state officialdom to give them authority over educational matters and other matters everywhere in Hungary and Transylvania. And when this became known, the God-fearing and Torah observing Jews stood against them as much as was possible, because the level of learning among and education of the youth in Pest became known, that they do not put on *tefillin* or even know what *tefillin* are, and the same is true of other commandments . . . and if, heaven forbid, they have control and leadership on all aspects of education of all the Jews in Hungary, and schools and learning will be according to what they want under their guidance, Torah and piety will be forgotten by our children like in Pest.[34]

The upshot is that, in the mind of Orthodox Jews, until the 1870s the absence of a charismatic Orthodox rabbi or lay leader comparable to the Neolog leadership preempted conditions conducive to the growth of the Orthodox enclave in Budapest.[35] The Hevra Shas was less part of a besieged Orthodox community with a particular ideology or movement than a traditional organization operating under the aegis of a Neolog-dominated Jewish community as part of the network of semiautonomous voluntary associations that operated with limited independence. Like other voluntary associations in Pest, the Hevra Shas assessed and collected its own membership dues and solicited its own endowments and voluntary donations; and its statutes and by-laws were subject to approval by the main Jewish community (and by the Hungarian minister of religion). More importantly, like other Jewish communal institutions, the Hevra Shas relied on an annual stipend from the main Jewish community in order to meet its financial obligations. In this regard, the Hevra Shas and its relationship to the main community resembled that of the Hevra Kadisha a generation earlier. The latter, too, provided those Jews who needed a haven from the confusion and sense of dislocation in the burgeoning city with a meeting point and social circle encapsulated with familiar trappings of Jewish tradition: reciting prayers, studying religious texts, and providing support to their neighbors in time of need. Indeed, this aim was woven into the fabric of the Hevra Kadisha.[36]

Yet there was a crucial difference between the two communal organizations. The traditional outlook and aims of the Hevra Kadisha did not affect in any significant way its relationship with the main Jewish community; prior to the public debate and eventual schism between Orthodox and non-Orthodox Jews, the Hevra Kadisha remained part of a Jewish community that was still, for the most part, amorphously traditional in its outlook. The Hevra Shas began this way until it eventually came under pressure to identify and affiliate with a crystallizing Orthodox community. Hitherto the Hevra Shas's nonideological demeanor, amid an increasingly boisterous intra-communal polemic, left it in limbo between Budapest Jewry's more traditional and more progressive elements. The leadership of the Hevra Shas, and what little other Orthodox leadership there was in Pest during the 1870s, divided over whether to remain connected to the main Jewish community or to secede; and, if remaining, what level of accommodation was acceptable. At the heart of these conflicting views was a tension between religious and financial concerns: could an Orthodox subcommunity that was largely subordinate to a non-Orthodox main Jewish community require Orthodox Jews to defer to the preferences and practices of non-Orthodox Jews and a non-Orthodox leadership? On the other hand, would the lack of independent sources of funding preclude the survival of an autonomous Orthodox community without the support of the main Jewish community, despite the autonomy granted to Orthodox Jews by the state?[37]

For their part, the non-Orthodox leadership of Budapest Jewry along with city officials continued to regard the Hevra Shas as part of the main Jewish community even after 1868, when the schism between Neolog and Orthodox Jews became a matter of public debate. Nearly two decades after the state recognized Orthodox Judaism in 1870 as a legally recognized denomination, the liberal Jewish weekly *Egyenlőség* relayed to its readers the comments of Hungarian minister of education Ágoston Trefort, noting:

Among the arguments by Trefort Ágoston ... is that all of the Jewish groups constitute a single religious denomination; domestic law recognizes only one Israelite denomination. Likewise, in the entire world, the Jews themselves do not regard themselves as multifarious denominations, and one community or another joining with
one party or another has not changed anything in their substance, customs, or institutions, and does not denote a distinguishing criterium.... The Progressive Party's
Dohány Street Temple, the Orthodoxy-leaning Rombach Street Synagogue, the entirely Orthodox Sasz Chevra [*sic*], the Hassidic Polish Temple, and the Sephardic
Synagogue *are all under the aegis of the Pest main community*.[38]

For a time, this issue remained largely academic. The Hevra Shas was consistently
overshadowed by two much larger Jewish voluntary associations: the Hevra Kadisha,
which paid out more than 70,000 forints in annual benefits in 1870 at a time when
no other Jewish association in Pest paid more than 5,000 forints; and the Zion Verein,
founded in 1851, which allocated virtually endless interest-free loans to aid the needs
of the sick.[39]

This situation began to change during the 1870s with the rapid growth of the Pest
Orthodox community, facilitated by four developments. First, like MIKÉFE, the
Hevra Shas drew from the large concentration of less acculturated recent Jewish arriv-
als who settled largely in the Sixth and Seventh Districts, that is, in the older part of
Terézvaros and in neighboring Erszébetváros (the erstwhile eastern part of Terézváros).
As upwardly mobile Jews left these neighborhoods for Lipótváros, the concentration
of un- or less-acculturated newcomers became even more pronounced.[40]

Second, the opening of a new traditional synagogue on Rombach Street further
raised the image of Pest as a place suitable for observant Jews. The impetus to build the
Rombach Street Synagogue originated among a handful of affluent, more traditional
Jews during the 1860s when construction of the Dohány Street Synagogue was in its
final stages. These Jews were not comfortable praying at the new great synagogue that
used an organ on the Sabbath; neither did they want to continue praying at the older,
more rundown synagogue in the Orczy House.[41] As an alternative, in the summer of
1867 they purchased the Kehrn-Tomola lot on Rombach Street, where the Jewish nursery had once been, and then formed the Synagogue Construction Committee, which
applied for a building a permit and hired the Vienna architect Otto Wagner and local architect Mór Kallina to design a new synagogue. Construction began in May 1870
and was completed in October 1872. Services were held there sporadically during the
winter of 1872–1873 until the synagogue began operating full time beginning on Rosh
Hashana in the fall of 1873. Though Wagner and Kallina did not design the synagogue
in the basilica style of the Dohány Synagogue, they nonetheless included other ro-
mantic and Oriental features, including the twin towers at the entrance. Moreover,

the layout of the sanctuary was more conservative than the Dohány's, with the *bima* in the center rather than at the front and a detached balcony for the women's galleries. The sanctuary was also designed such that master lighting would not necessarily be needed.[42]

The Rombach Synagogue, though much smaller, was architecturally and stylistically impressive like the Dohány. This appealed especially to affluent traditional Jews who wanted to display the economic success and Magyarization of the Jewish community without compromising their traditional synagogue practices. When faced with the choice of affiliating with the Orthodox and Neolog movements—a choice every congregation and community within Hungarian Jewry was required to make following the Jewish Congress of 1868–1869 and the subsequent state recognition of Orthodoxy in 1870—the members of the Rombach congregation chose a alternative to Neolog and Orthodoxy—a third Jewish denomination eventually recognized by the state as the *Status Quo Ante*. Nonetheless, the presence of the Rombach Synagogue as a traditional alternative to the smaller, unimpressive synagogues raised the image of Orthodoxy in Budapest.[43]

Third, the downplaying of religious reform as a prerequisite to Jewish citizenship, embedded in the political outlook of Baron József Eötvös, made the notion of a Magyarized Orthodoxy plausible. Hitherto, Lajos Kossuth and other outspoken advocates of Jewish emancipation had premised the extension of civic equality to Jews on the latter paring away the particularist aspects of Judaism and Jewish life. Kossuth's vision of an emancipated Hungarian Jewry in a liberal Hungary included only acculturated religiously progressive Jews.[44] This quid pro quo was hard-wired into the mentality of Neolog Judaism, but meant that an Orthodox Jewish outlook and way of life appeared inherently incompatible with citizenship and admission to the ranks of the Magyar nation.

By contrast, Eötvös emphasized the embrace of the Magyar language and culture as the main prerequisite to citizenship and becoming Magyar, without an expectation of religious innovation. His understanding of the religious freedom embedded in liberalism, moreover, precluded impeding an individual's or community's right to observe their own religious dictates. Thus, when Orthodox Jews complained that affiliating with and subordinating to Neolog communities would violate their right to practice their religion freely, he recognized Orthodox Judaism as a separate denomination at the end of the 1860s. Eötvös's view precluded Orthodox Jews in Hungary from having to choose between a commitment to an Orthodox way of life and reaping the material benefits of citizenship. This vision resonated broadly in Hungarian society during the second half of the nineteenth century. Mór Jókai, Hungary's leading novelist and social critic, wove this attitude toward Orthodox Jews into his positive and sympathetic depictions of Jewish characters in his novels. For Jókai, like Eötvös, an observant or Orthodox demeanor and lifestyle did not preclude a Jew from being seen as heroic, virtuous, and patriotic.[45] Eötvös's admiration for the French system of *consistoires*, moreover, led him to create a similar system in Hungary as minister of education as a way to help religious communities administer their communities effectively. Unlike in Paris, where a single Jewish consistory was empowered by the state to regulate French Jewry, the conflict between Orthodox and Neolog precluded the realistic possibility of a single consistory for Hungarian Jewry. Instead, Eötvös authorized the creation of the Orthodox Bureau as the head of Hungarian Orthodoxy, thus affirming that Magyarized Orthodox Jews, no less than Magyarized Neolog Jews, were an officially recognized part of Hungarian society. Situating this institution in Budapest further mollified the view among Orthodox Jews that Budapest was inhospitable to Orthodox Judaism.

Finally, the Hevra Shas benefited from the endorsement and active involvement of prominent rabbinic figures. Much like Schwab's role in the expansion of MIKÉFE, the emergence of a formidable Orthodox rabbinate and lay leadership in the 1870s consolidated the growing Orthodox population into a coherent Orthodox community. The Hevra Shas attracted leading Orthodox rabbis to Budapest who became the guiding force of the Hevra Shas and Orthodox Jews in Budapest generally. This new leadership brought to Budapest the scholarly prestige and social connections of leading Orthodox rabbinic dynasties from Pressburg, and defined Budapest Orthodoxy more or less from this point on. The first two of these rabbis were Chaim Sofer and Viktor (Wolf) Sussman. Born in Pressburg, Sofer (1821–1886) studied at Pressburg and Ungvár under the tutelage of Moses Sofer (no relation) and Meïr Eisenstädter. Before coming to Pest, he served as the rabbi of Nagymárton (Mattersdorf), Gyömöre, Sajó-Szent-Péter, and Munkács. He served as the rabbi of the Orthodox congregation in Pest from 1879 until his death in 1886. The presence of a nascent Hevra Shas was one of the factors that led him to accept this offer.[46]

A periodic lecturer and teacher for the Hevra Shas, Sofer saw in the Hevra Shas a way to manage the bifurcated interaction between the richness of an observant Jewish lifestyle and the ongoing demands and possibilities of urban life, in favor of the former. He insisted that all members of his congregation in Budapest observe the Sabbath and the dietary laws, and periodically made surprise visits to homes of followers whom he suspected of violating the Sabbath. At the same time, though, he conceptualized mainstream society in a way that allowed Orthodox Jews in Budapest to participate as necessary in the life of the city. In his commentary on Psalms 19:11, Sofer alluded to the importance of engagement with the outside world:

> The Holy one, blessed is he created man to eat and to sate his soul from that which
> is permitted to him and to strengthen his body strong and bold in the service of the

creator; but he need not be an ascetic [*nazir 'olam*] and separate himself from the pleasures of the world by fashioning wings of separation and subsisting only on the joys of looking upon the countenance of the living king, for he will become empty and lost from the world … because he cannot tolerate the burden of abstinence and asceticism.[47]

In this way, Sofer also made it possible for the Hevra Shas to recruit non-Orthodox Jews as members and students, amid other secessionist and seclusionist impulses emanating from other Orthodox rabbinic circles.

Sussman translated Sofer's implicit willingness to engage the non-Orthodox world into a more concrete series of tactics and programs aimed at recruiting new members from the mass of non-Orthodox Jews in Budapest. Born in Pressburg/Pozsony, Sussman, too, studied in the yeshiva of Moses Sofer and, after Sofer's death, with the Ketav Sofer and then with Moses Schick. After serving as the rabbi for two small Orthodox communities, Vázsony and Szentgrót, he was appointed rabbi of the Pest Hevra Shas in 1869. He was the chief rabbi of the Hevra Shas from 1869 until his death in 1895. His appointment as rabbi of the Hevra Shas suggests that initially the organization existed in the gray area between mutually antagonistic Orthodox and Neolog camps. Just as the Hevra Shas began as part of a network of communal institutions, Sussman's family had strong ties to both Orthodox and Neolog Judaism. His brother was the president of the Hevra Shas, while his nephew, Sándor Eppler (1890–1942), was a leading figure in the Neolog movement and the Neolog community of Budapest.[48]

Sussman evinced the outlook of what Haim Gertner recently termed a "reactive rabbi" (*rav megiv*),

who was aware of the options put forth by modernity and of the new images of the future that presented various factors in the community and chose to contend with them. Reacting rabbis cannot be characterized based on their moderate or conservative outlook nor based on their tendency to be stringent or lenient in their activity as adjudicators of Jewish law. The uniqueness of a reactive rabbi is, in essence, his decision to act from an awareness of his borderline status. "Contending" included first and foremost an updated defining of the boundaries between different options.[49]

This notion of an Orthodox rabbi, actively engaging the modern city though ideologically opposed to or uncomfortable with much of it, reflects a common feature of what sociologist Samuel Heilman characterized as a "tolerator" type of Orthodox Jew, that is, one who is "personally entrenched in the traditional Orthodox world, but does not altogether deny the surrounding situation of modernity," and who believes "he can undermine modernity and via his tolerance bring back those on the outside to a more genuine Jewish life as he understands it." Thus Sussman's willingness to look beyond a still small Orthodox enclave, not only for potential new members but for ways to reach out to potential new members, did not constitute approbation of the non-Orthodox trappings of urban life, but rather the usefulness of such trappings to enhance their own community.[50]

Indicative of this approach to the non-Orthodox world of Budapest is the Hevra Shas's use of the liberal Jewish weekly *Egyenlőség*. In 1899, during a search for an additional instructor, the Hevra Shas placed the following ad in *Egyenlőség*: "*Ba'al tefila* and *ba'al kore*, 800 forints/year. Applicants are requested to provide copies of documents that attest to family status, Hungarian citizenship, and a strict religious lifestyle [*szigorúan vallásos életmód*]."[51] It is noteworthy that this advertisement used a non-Orthodox publication to further its aim of restricting its teaching faculty to Orthodox Jews exclusively.

EDUCATION AND LEISURE: TWO APPROACHES

Their differences notwithstanding, the overarching goal of both the Hevra Shas and MIKÉFE was to regulate their members' leisure time. Leisure time in this context did not connote nonworking hours per se, but rather was more akin to leisure as defined by Louis Brandeis: "In order that men may live and not merely exist, in order that men may develop their faculties, they must have a reasonable income; they must have health and leisure. . . . But leisure does not imply idleness. It means the ability to work not less but more, to work at something besides bread winning, to work harder while working at bread winning, and to work more years at bread winning."[52] Accordingly, the leaders of the Hevra Shas and MIKÉFE saw in their respective organizations a duty to fill a lacuna in the lives of their constituents. MIKÉFE in this respect focused more on giving young people an alternative to commerce and trade. They targeted boys from middle-class families who would likely wind up in a family business, and especially the children of lower-income families who would likely wind up as peddlers, hawkers, or pawnbrokers, or—the least productive of occupations—idlers with no real occupation. For all of them, MIKÉFE created a school whose curriculum combined vocational training with the standard Jewish and general studies.

This was not a new idea, but dated back a century to the educational musings of Moses Mendelssohn, Naftali Herz Weisl, and other late eighteenth-century *Maskillim*, and made its way to Hungary through the works of educational reformers such as Abraham Hochmuth.[53] Prior to the founding of MIKÉFE, though, there had been no significant, concerted attempt to implement such a program on a communal scale in

Budapest. At MIKÉFE's inaugural meeting, Löw Schwab laid this out as a main goal of the association: "to cultivate competence among poor and orphaned boys in crafts-manship, manufacturing, industrial labor and agriculture through training, above all, in practice of robust crafts and industry . . . and encouraging the practice of agriculture."[54] In addition, the association also aimed to "nurture the Magyar language among its members and trainees" and "to spread morality and practical knowledge . . . by impart-ing skills in crafts and agriculture in a traditional setting." The association was to "pay special attention to the students' development and to fortifying the students' Magyar spirit and religious mindset . . . by maintaining a religious school, furnishing students with religious texts, and arranging to observe and honor major holidays."[55]

Schwab also announced the founding of a school to impart these skills to Jewish boys age twelve to seventeen. In general, the cost of attending school would be deter-mined based on a case-by-case basis. Children of propertied parents, and orphans with some means, were invited to attend the school and expected to cover their own ex-penses. Priority, however, was given to local orphans without means, especially those at the Jewish orphanage in Pest, who would be the first children admitted to the new training program. Accordingly, the organization would help these children by "improv-ing their material and spiritual situation." This meant waiving all tuition and fees and "providing novices with clothing, underwear and outerwear, and a stipend for necessary supplies." Beginning in the 1870s, when state vocational schools began accepting Jewish students, the organization encouraged young Jews to attend these schools by provid-ing them with subsidies to cover tuition and, when necessary, room and board. The as-sociation also encouraged students to excel by offering an additional stipend for stu-dents "who excel and demonstrate an outstanding disposition." Students who wanted to pursue training beyond the minimum could apply for additional support. Aid to students did not end with vocational education. Once students completed the train-ing program, the association helped them find employment.[56]

The Hevra Shas, too, wanted to redirect their members away from leisure activities that its leaders regarded as less than ideal for observant Jews, particularly idling in beer halls, sports clubs, and coffee bars. Its learning programs, though, were designed largely for adults.[57] For indigent adults, in particular, the offer of financial assistance and sub-sidized learning allowed the Hevra Shas to compete with the other Jewish communal initiative that aimed at improving the lives of Jews in Pest, and especially of indigent Jews, not least of all by programming their leisure time. The central goal of the Hevra Shas in this respect contradicted that of MIKÉFE. The latter regarded sedentary activ-ity such as sitting inside studying antiquated texts as a paradigmatically poor use of time and as the antithesis to the much-needed increase in Jewish productivity and physical activity. The leaders of MIKÉFE often attributed the backward, unenlightened, non-productive character of Jews to the hours devoted to the study of Jewish texts in the *bet midrash* and yeshiva; and, consequently, regarded their progressive aims of cultural enlightenment and learning a trade as a way to liberate Jews—and especially young and indigent Jews—from the stultifying world of classical text study.

In sharp contrast, from the 1870s on the Hevra Shas expanded these notions of leisure and the *batlan* by actively seeking new members to join the Hevra Shas and devote as much time as possible to Torah study. A first step in this direction was the Hevra Shas appending Torah study onto the weekly Saturday morning service. Since all members were expected to attend Sabbath and festival services regularly, the Hevra Shas added a study session immediately following the service. As one member recalled:

> Shabbat-morning *musaf* at that time still ended promptly at 11:50 a.m., unless one or more *Bar Mitzvahs* were interspersed in the service. Ten minutes later everyone moved over to the *Sasz Chevra* [*sic*] where at 12:05 p.m. a suitably chosen weekly appointed rabbi or *dayan* commenced with the Shabbat *drash* in the great synagogue on Kazinczy Street, where the *Dayanim* all had Orthodox rabbinic certification. The *drash* ended precisely at 12:30. The orations were delivered in Yiddish or German. (Most of us understood Yiddish well, even the children.) The orations included lovely Hebrew quotations and sayings. The speeches concluded in every case in the same way regardless of which rabbi or dayan gave it . . . at which point a giant chorus of "*Skejach*" came from those in attendance.[58]

In addition, the organization operated an ongoing drop-in *Bet ha-Midrash* in the synagogue of the Hevra Shas, where any male over thirteen could participate in text study. The Hevra Shas's library of rabbinic texts was available for anyone to study on a noncirculating basis. Aside from instructors, members were permitted to remove the texts from the premises only with special permission and under extenuating circumstances. The latter included using texts to teach or preach at the homes of the infirm (who were not able to come to the synagogue) or a house of mourning (while mourners were not permitted to attend the synagogue). Individuals who borrowed a book without permission were fined; repeated offenders faced the possibility of having their membership and benefits suspended. The Hevra Shas never stipulated a minimum required number of hours devoted to weekly study, but relied instead on the piety of its members and the quality of instruction that it could provide. This proved to be a fruitful dual strategy. Individuals drawn to the Hevra Shas for the learning it provided were generally either favorably predisposed to devote leisure time to text study, or indigent individuals more than willing to participate in exchange for food and financial support.

In addition to drop-in learning, the Hevra Shas provided daily and weekly lectures, typically appended to morning and evening services on weekdays, Sabbaths, and festivals. The allure of these lectures was enhanced by the quality of instruction the Hevra

Shas provided. In contrast to comparable organizations elsewhere, whose scholars were often "preachers rather than halakhic scholars of the first order," the lecturers engaged by the Budapest Hevra Shas from the 1870s on were generally well-established, illustrious scholars, among whom were Wolf Suszmann, Lázár Szoffer, Mihály Herskovits, and Mór Eppler. By the 1880s, these lecturers averaged a daily attendance of 100, and the number of students rose steadily thereafter.[59]

TOWARD INSTITUTIONAL AUTONOMY

Under the leadership of Sofer and Sussman the more fluid relationship between the Hevra Shas and the main Jewish community gravitated toward a more autonomous relationship that was typical of an Orthodox minority in a non-Orthodox Jewish community. Several differences between the statutes of 1875 and 1898 attest to this shift in mentality. The earlier statutes did not regulate the relationship between the rabbis of the Hevra Shas and the main Jewish community; often its rabbis supplemented their income by working concurrently for other communal organizations. Reiner and Loeffler, the Hevra Shas's two main instructors during the 1870s and early 1880s, were also teachers for the (non-Orthodox) community primary school.[60] This practice was abolished, at least formally, by the Hevra Shas's 1898 statutes, which noted: "The revered chief rabbi may act only as rabbi of the Budapest Hevra Shas and may not assume any function for the community or for any other association; the revered chief rabbi may not perform his functions under the auspices of the *Izraelita hitközség*."[61]

This shift toward institutional autonomy was facilitated in no small part by the success and growth of the Hevra Shas by the end of the 1880s. The amount of money collected in annual dues increased from 277 forints in 1878 to 2,461 forints by 1883, and to 5,276 forints by 1890—this with little or no increase in membership dues. Additionally, the number of full-time scholars supported by the Hevra Shas increased from twelve to thirty-one, and the number of indigent students from fifteen to fifty-three.[62] The growth of the Hevra Shas after 1890 was noted by a visitor from Trencsen: "On Monday, the local *Sasz Chevra* [sic] held their Siyyum banquet for completing Tractate Ketuboth, which took place from 4 in the afternoon until midnight. The feast began with a flood of toasts, by the rabbi and the president of the organization. The membership of this organization is multiplying steadily and rapidly."[63] Beginning with Sussman's tenure as rabbi of the Hevra Shas, moreover, the classes and the public lectures of the Hevra Shas drew an increasing number of students and participants. In 1880, the typical audience at a Shabbat morning lecture ranged from twenty to thirty-five. By 1895, the audience typically exceeded 100 and often more than 200 people. The number of students provided with a stipend increased threefold, and the number of teachers doubled.[64] The expansion of the Hevra Shas spearheaded the expansion of the Orthodox community in Budapest. The number of Jews in Budapest registered as Orthodox increased steadily from the 1880s on. In addition, Orthodox institutions began to appear. In 1873 the Orthodox community founded its first school, and in 1883 a separate burial society and home for the aged.[65]

A measure of the Hevra Shas's growing prominence was the role it played in resolving a conflict that threatened to divide the still small nascent Orthodox community at the end of the 1880s. Following Chaim Sofer's death in 1886, two factions fought over who should succeed him. One, led by Moses Freudinger, named Moses Katz, chief rabbi of Nagymagyar, as Sofer's replacement. The other, led by Hermann Frankl, named Koppel Reich of Verbó. The central issue dividing these two groups was the relationship between the Orthodox community and the rest of Budapest Jewry. Freudinger and Katz advocated a more ideologically driven secessionist approach; Frankl and Reich advocated a more pragmatic, cooperative approach. Here the success of the Hevra Shas and Sussman in reaching out beyond the confines of the small Orthodox enclave helped tip the balance of the conflict in favor of Koppel Reich. When Jacob Schachter, a member and important benefactor of the Hevra Shas, supported Reich's election in 1890, the conflict was largely over. Sussman and Reich, sharing a vision of the future of the Orthodox community, were natural partners in bringing it to fruition.[66]

Reich accelerated the development of the Orthodox community and mended the rift within it. Within a generation, he fashioned "a whole array of new institutions such that the community became the most unified, well-organized, and affluent in the world."[67] He transformed the Budapest Orthodox community from a small enclave into the largest Orthodox enclave in Hungary and Central Europe. The Hevra Shas, no longer the lone institution serving the needs of observant Jews, became a pillar of the Orthodox community, whose overall demeanor exemplified the relationship between the Orthodox community and the main Jewish community.[68]

This demeanor and, more specifically, the Hevra Shas's ability to walk a fine line between Orthodox distinction and communal engagement, is reflected in several of the statutes that were added to the organization's bylaws by 1898. For example, the bylaws stipulated that "only association scholars are permitted to hold a class," thus excluding all other scholars. On the other hand, the bylaws encouraged public disagreement, within reason. When addressing the matter of public disagreement between members or factions, the bylaws required the rabbi "to answer comprehensively whatever questions may arise, on matters pertaining to his lecture or otherwise; extensive debates, however, can be avoided." On the other hand, the bylaws also instructed all rabbis "to answer question pertaining to the lesson clearly; meaningless, rambling disputes can remain unresolved."[69] In order to preempt the political clashes that had nearly divided the Orthodox community, moreover, the bylaws drew a sharp line between the appointed rabbis of the organization and scholars supported by the organization, even if the latter were rabbis, and created a sort of checks and balances between the rabbi and the lay leadership: "All rabbinic functions are forbidden to scholars supported by the Hevra Shas (i.e., but are not rabbis of the Hevra Shas); however, with the approval of the president, they can deliver the eulogy in the cemetery for an association member."[70]

By the beginning of the twentieth century, MIKÉFE and the Hevra Shas had widely different relationships with the Jewish community. The former was still very much connected to the main Jewish community and beholden to it for support. MIKÉFE consistently operated at a substantial annual deficit that, in 1914, approached 30,000 forints. This chronic financial situation prompted one of the leaders of the association to ask rather dismayingly: "What is the future of this 72-year-old organization?"[71] By contrast, the growth of the Hevra Shas brought not only new opportunities but new challenges. The growing number of participants required additional lectures and longer hours of operation for the *bet midrash*. This meant additional costs of maintaining the building and, even more costly, hiring additional teachers. As the quality and prestige of rabbis and teachers rose—beginning with Sussman—so did salaries and expenses such as housing and health care. Sussman's salary, initially 450 forints, increased to 1,000 by 1877 and to 1,400 by 1880. A decade later it had more than doubled, and three other rabbis were being paid more than 750 forints annually. Revenue from membership dues could not keep pace. Like the Orthodox community generally, the Hevra Shas naturally oriented itself from Terézváros toward Erzsébetváros, where most *Ostjuden* and in-migrants from northeastern Hungary resided. As upwardly mobile, acculturated Jews relocated to Lipótváros and Józsefváros, a growing portion of the Hevra Shas's membership and potential new members were low-income or indigent Jews who paid only reduced dues or none at all. The Hevra Shas had operated during the 1870s with an average annual deficit of 250 forints out of a budget of around 2,500 forints. By 1907, the budget was more than ten times the size (26,607) with a deficit of more than 1,500 forints.

Annual donations, though substantially larger by 1907 than they had been a decade or two earlier, diminished the debt somewhat but not enough to alleviate concerns over the financial viability of the organization. Repeated efforts to solicit new members from among the more affluent Jewish families in Budapest were frustrated by the religious and ritual requirements of membership. The correlation between the level of observance and affluence, in other words, impeded the ability of the Hevra Shas to cover its expanding costs and serve a growing constituency. What's more, the original solution to this budgetary imbalance—relying on an annual endowment from the main Jewish community—was no longer a viable solution. To be sure, this option was still available, since the leaders of the Jewish community continued to regard the Hevra Shas as a constituent association. Yet there was a growing reluctance among the leaders of the Hevra Shas to depend on the main community for support.

Instead, the leaders of the Hevra Shas resorted to a different preexisting strategy that other Jewish communal organizations had used in this situation: a bifurcated membership. Initially, membership in the Hevra Shas entailed not only the payment of dues but a religious commitment as well. In the face of growing financial difficulties, the organization created a new type of membership, incorporated by 1898 into the bylaws: "The board can nominate as honorary members those men who merit this distinction either through pious actions alongside exceptional Talmudic learning or through setting forth actions to help the revival of the association."[72] In theory, this seemed to connote the same ritual obligation as previously; in its application, this statute allowed honorary members to contribute monetarily and receive the same benefits, without any religious obligations.

This had an almost immediate, dual effect on membership and revenue. It simplified the task of soliciting nonobservant Jews as members. Revenue increased steadily after 1898, and the annual deficit was less than 250 by 1910.[73] More importantly, the new type of membership allowed women to participate in the organization for the first time. Hitherto, the participation of women in any fashion had been sharply curtailed by the legal and customary taboos on women studying classical texts. In contrast to a traditional communal organization like the burial society, where women had for centuries played a key role in the preparation of women's bodies for burial, there was no comparable role for women in an organization that revolved primarily around communal study and public prayer. Honorary membership, with no requirement for study or communal prayer, was entirely available to women, and especially women of means. Indeed, once this form of membership was in place, affluent women donors appear more regularly, frequently, and prominently as annual donors and honorary members. In 1875, Sali Schlesinger was the lone woman donor. In 1905, sixteen women made donations totaling more than 4,000 forints or more.[74]

The expanding role of women as donors culminated in 1907 with a major endowment to the organization by Rozália Blasz.[75] This endowment was large enough for the annual income to cover more than half of the organization's annual costs. In effect, it replaced the original endowment from the main Jewish community that had supported the Hevra Shas initially, with a private endowment that allowed the organization to exist, from this point, not only nominally but actually independent of the main Jewish community. The growth of the Hevra Shas continued unabatedly. By 1929, the organization had nearly 3,000 members and an annual budget of 30,000 forints, of which more than half went to charitable donations and to support indigent Talmudic scholars. Once women of means like Blasz emerged as substantial contributors, within three years they formed a separate Jewish women's association for Orthodox women, apart from the larger, more established Pest Jewish Women's Association.

In the end, the emergence and development of the Hevra Shas, amid the external pressures of urban life and the internal pressures of a schism between Orthodoxy and Neolog, helped committed, observant Jews remain observant while navigating the complexities of urban life. As such, the Hevra Shas reflects the extent to which Orthodox communities, congregations, and communal organizations were built and joined by members who had—in the face of real alternatives—voluntarily embraced not only a particular sense of piety and religious observance, but also the rules of their community and the virtually absolute right of their leaders to enforce these rules as though endowed with the coercive communal authority of previous centuries. This was a crucial element in the success of the Budapest Hevra Shas. Jews in Budapest who joined Orthodox congregations lent their support and allegiance to Orthodox synagogues and other institutions in the face of available alternatives that were only a few blocks or even a few steps from their home. In this way, the Hevra Shas provided a source of communal coherence that had been eroded by the transition from premodern traditionalism to the Orthodoxy of the nineteenth century, and the ensuing intracommunal conflicts between the Orthodox and non-Orthodox elements of the Jewish community.

The mounting success and eventual autonomy of the Hevra Shas alongside the more tepid situation of MIKÉFE reflected several key differences between the two organizations that, among other things, helped one to become independent while assuring the other remained wholly subsidiary to the main Jewish community. MIKÉFE faced challenges that the Hevra Shas did not. As mechanized factories displaced artisans and their handcrafted wares, the allure of vocational training diminished. Jews who pursued an artisanal trade found themselves competing more intensely with other artisans for jobs. Moreover, some of the Jews who received assistance from MIKÉFE to find their livelihood and stability as artisans eventually aimed higher either for themselves or, at the very least, for their children. In the fluid economic hierarchy of Budapest, some Jewish artisans who earned and saved enough money eventually acquired the means to open their own shop—effectively transforming themselves from artisan to shopkeeper and moving into a different echelon of the middle class. Moreover, the children of artisans who attained enough education attended university and entered the free professions. The boundary between working-class artisans and mid-level merchants and shopkeepers was generally permeable, not only economically but also socially. As the once inaccessible upwardly mobile, upper-middle-class, higher-income lifestyle became available, MIKÉFE members and beneficiaries took advantage of the opportunity.

By contrast, the members of the Orthodox community that grew up around the Hevra Shas were far less tempted by their more progressive rival religious community. As the Orthodox community of Budapest grew in size, wealth, and prestige it was able to retain its members more effectively. Indeed, the community would weather difficult times such as years of war and revolution and emerge intact during the 1920s.[76] In this sense, gestating in the compact urban space of Budapest acted as an incubator for a nascent Orthodox community amid the external pressures of urban life and the internal pressures of a schism between Orthodoxy and Neolog. The neighborhood around the Hevra Shas became a place where observant Jews, learned scholars, and wealthy donors clustered together to form an Orthodox alternative to the Neolog-dominated Jewish community of Budapest.

This was a crucial element in the success of the Budapest Hevra Shas. By providing a means through which to, at once, enhance and regulate the leisure time of its members the Hevra Shas, itself a voluntary organization, became a cornerstone in the construction of a larger voluntary organization: the Orthodox community of Budapest that became, to borrow the words of Menachem Friedman, "a small, well-defined, discrete minority, organized in contiguous voluntary communities, set within a modern, open society with competition, confrontation, dependency, and interrelations within this surrounding society."[77] Ultimately, though lower-income and Orthodox Jews comprised, even in tandem, a minority of Budapest Jewry, they nonetheless represented a significant and, at times, conspicuous minority and an integral part of the diverse tapestry that was Budapest Jewry at the turn of the twentieth century.

More broadly, communal organizations like MIKÉFE, the PIN, and, to a lesser extent, the Hevra Shas maintained connections within a Budapest Jewry that had become geographically more spread out and socioeconomically and culturally more diverse. As Julia Richers pointed out, these organizations furthered regular contact between Jews in different parts of the city and the social hierarchy: "Here Jewish men and women from two entirely different socioeconomic neighborhoods discussed and debated questions of Jewish existence in the city. They did this—especially examining their statutes, organization, and the transformation of their various activities—with an extraordinarily high level of awareness, professionalism, and efficiency."[78] As such, these organizations were the connective tissue in the emergence in Budapest of the more fluid and integrated framework of an ethnoburb.[79] The Jewish neighborhood of Terézváros was a physical and cultural nexus between the lower-income, less acculturated, first- and second-generation immigrant Orthodox Jews who lived mostly in Erzsébetváros and the upwardly mobile, more acculturated, Budapest-born Neolog Jews who lived in Lipótváros. These neighborhoods, though geographically distinct on a map, in reality were far more fluid in day-to-day Jewish communal life. On the eve of World War I, this area was still a mishmash of these different sorts of Jews. Jews who lived in Lipótváros or the nicer parts of Terézváros often worked in Erzsébetváros. Most importantly, perhaps, the Dohány Synagogue and, to a lesser extent, the Rombach Synagogue, along with communal organizations such as the PIN and MIKÉFE, reinforced this fluidity by remaining focal points that attracted Jews of all ilks to weekly Sabbath and holiday services. A measure of this fluidity and connection between these neighborhoods was the debate by Jews in Lipótváros over whether to build a second great synagogue there. They had the means and permission from the city. Yet their connection to the Dohány Synagogue and the "old neighborhood" where it stood precluded this project from ever taking place.

In retrospect, the diversity and fluidity of Budapest Jewry reached a high point in 1914. Thereafter, a series of hardships would upend decades of stability and growth for the city of Budapest and its Jewish community. In particular, the influx of Jewish refugees from Galicia during the First World War would test the limits of an inclusive, cosmopolitan city and raise the question: are unacculturated *Ostjuden* welcome? This would be the first in a series of difficult challenges and setbacks that Budapest Jewry would have to weather during the ensuing years of war, revolution, and counterrevolution; and then in the harsher reality of a new post-Trianon Hungary.

By 1914, the city of Budapest was regarded with surging pride by the overwhelming majority of Hungarians, not least of all in the way that the grandeur of Budapest equaled that of virtually every other European metropolis—most importantly Vienna, the empire's other capital. Budapest was the Magyar nation's great *világváros* (cosmopolitan city),[80] the capital of the Kingdom of Hungary, itself the largest constituent part of the Austro-Hungarian Empire. As in the Kingdom of Hungary generally, Magyars in Budapest were hegemonically perched over a dozen ethnic minorities. The diversity of Budapest and the preeminent position of Magyar language and culture there in 1914, even over German language and Viennese, epitomized everything great about Budapest and the Hungarian kingdom around it.

Budapest Jewry's relationship with Hungarian Jewry in 1914 paralleled the relationship between the city of Budapest and the Kingdom of Hungary. Jews played a central and pivotal role in the development and success of the economy and culture of the city. According to the census figures from 1910, Jewish industrialists in Budapest owned most Hungarian mines and heavy industries, and a majority of Hungarian banks and retail firms; Jews also published the vast majority of newspapers in the capital; one half of all doctors and lawyers, and 70 percent of university students were Jews.[81] The sweeping embrace of Magyar language and culture by Budapest Jewry by 1914, the widespread entry of Budapest Jews into mainstream Budapest society, and the emergence of Budapest Jewry as the heart and soul of commerce and industry in Budapest exemplified the realization of what Viktor Karády and other historians called "the liberal contract" between Hungarian Jewry and the Kingdom of Hungary. This contract, and the grandeur of Budapest and Budapest Jewry, would face its greatest test beginning with the outbreak of war in 1914.

Part III

After Trianon

8

Paradise Waning: War, Revolution, and the New Budapest, 1914–1938

THE OUTBREAK OF WORLD WAR I CHALLENGED THE STEADY RISE OF BUDA-pest and its Jewish community that had reached an apogee during Hungary's dualist period, the half-century between the 1860s and the outbreak of World War I. The difficulties of the Great War, for those in the field and on the home front, strained the resources and morale of the city of Budapest and its Jewish community. The challenges of the war left the city weakened and less able to lead the country through the difficult terrain of the immediate postwar years, thus leaving Hungary vulnerable to revolution, counterrevolution, upheaval, and a surge in antisemitism, xenophobia, and violence. Looking back from 1992, historian Péter Hanák noted that

> the people, substance, value, and self-confidence of Budapest suffered a great loss during the first world war. The Aster Revolution [Őszirózsás forradalom] in 1918 at-tempted to revive the exhausted city and raise it from the ravages of war; but, like all unarmed apostles, was doomed to fail. Then came the Red Revolution [Vörös for-radalom] that, apart from its provisions of populism and social equality, ushered in Bolshevik dictatorship and terror.[1]

The difficult aftermath of the war notwithstanding, Hanák's bleak appraisal reflects a view that, in hindsight, has presented the events of World War I as a prelude to a chain of difficult events through much of the twentieth century: the White Terror that fol-lowed the collapse of democratic and Communist revolutions, the economic collapse at the end of the 1920s, the rise of fascism, the impact of Hitler and Nazism, another world war, and decades of Stalinist repression from which Budapest began to recover only after 1990.

Historians of Hungarian Jewry have similarly dealt with the impact of the First World War on Budapest Jewry largely as a segue between the remarkable success of Jews in the capital during Hungary's Golden Age and the deteriorating conditions of the interwar years. Nathaniel Katzburg, for example, noted that "the resurgence of the Jewish Question during the war came as a great disappointment to Jews, since it had appeared during the second half of the nineteenth century that Antisemitism was diminishing and the full rapprochement between Jews and Magyars was on the verge of being fully realized. . . . Current circumstances infused the old Antisemitism with new life."[2] The merits of Hanák's and Katzburg's views notwithstanding, it is important not to pigeonhole these years merely as a prelude or first step to the more difficult times that followed. The period of the war was more than a transition for Budapest Jews from a more favorable to a less favorable situation.[3]

The more elusive question, lacking the twenty-twenty hindsight of later generations, is how Jews in Budapest understood the events spiraling around them during the war years and the significance of these events immediately thereafter. While it is reasonable, in retrospect, to see the impact of World War I on Budapest Jewry as a prelude to the challenges that Budapest Jews would confront during the ensuing two decades, it is equally important to stress that, however obvious this connection appears in hindsight, there was nothing inevitable about this course of events, and no reason for Jews in Budapest to presume that the difficulties of the war would lead directly to the surge of antisemitism henceforth.

A useful alternative to understanding this connection would be to understand the war years less as a prelude and more as a template that Jews in Budapest adapted to the more protracted and eventually more difficult challenges of the interwar years. Jews who lived through the First World War and its aftermath recognized that difficulties and challenges lay ahead, and they were determined to help preserve and recover the greatness of their city. The war years and the political upheaval that followed in the aftermath of defeat tested the viability of Jewish communal institutions in Budapest to deal with an abruptly changing and, in some ways, a deteriorating cultural and political landscape.

Jewish communal institutions in Budapest, steeled by the hardships of the war years, implemented the coping strategies they devised during the war to weather the eroding situation of the 1920s and especially the 1930s. The war years tested the vitality and dedication of Budapest Jewry by forcing upon individual Jews and Jewish institutions alike a mentality of crisis that demanded swift action and a willingness to rethink conventional strategies and ideologies in the face of changing circumstances. The travails of this period infused the Jewish community with a sense of urgency hitherto largely absent in the day-to-day operation of its institutions. Speaking at the inaugural ceremony of the Hungarian Jewish Museum in Budapest in 1916, Jewish community president Ferenc Mezey acknowledged the urgency of the moment while striking a determined and cautiously optimistic tone:

> We Jews, feeling the pressure of the times, not only grieve for universal human suffering and the dark horrors that our co-religionists suffer, but also, in our patriotic heartache, we are becoming painfully aware of claims of our lack of gratitude and spitefulness during the War.... Yet none of this will alienate us, neither our idealistic sense of duty nor the love of country that springs forth from all of our actions.[4]

This new mentality, born in the chaos and uncertainty of war and revolution, would guide Budapest Jews through the lingering hardships of the 1920s and 1930s. It is this newfound sense of urgency that distinguishes the war years from the preceding decades and underscores the continuity between the war years and the decades that followed. Prior to 1914, Jews in Budapest had faced comparatively few and relatively brief moments of urgency—the Tiszaeszlár blood libel and its aftermath during the 1880s and the *Recepció* debate of the 1890s, for example. On the whole, though, Budapest Jewry maintained an even keel in the face of largely favorable and improving conditions for Jews in Budapest and elsewhere in Hungary; situations that would later be addressed with great urgency during the war and thereafter elicited a hitherto more casual albeit deliberate response from the Jewish community.

The mentality of Budapest Jewry was not exceptional in this regard, but reflected a broader view emanating from the city that, even after years of war and liberal and Communist revolutions, Budapest remained Budapest. As Alexander Vari recently noted: "In spite of these mass retaliations, interwar Budapest continued to be a city which was cosmopolitan, liberal and left-wing in spirit. This spirit was especially manifested in Budapest's inner core districts as well as in the capital's industrial districts."[5] There was much to this outlook. Budapest was still the largest, wealthiest, and most populous city in Hungary, and one of the largest, wealthiest, and most populous in Europe; it was still the center of the Hungarian economy and Hungarian politics, society, and culture. Likewise, Budapest Jewry remained the center of Hungarian Jewry—political, economic, demographic, cultural—not only after the war but for decades afterward. Prior to the war the population of Budapest was 4.8 percent of the total population of Hungary. After the truncation of Hungary by the Treaty of Trianon, the percentage would increase to 11.63 percent. Similarly, Budapest Jewry made up between one-fifth and one-quarter of Hungarian Jewry prior to the truncation of Hungary; thereafter, nearly half of Hungarian Jewry (45 percent) lived in the capital.[6]

TABLE 27. JEWISH POPULATION OF BUDAPEST, 1910–1935

YEAR	POPULATION	% OF OVERALL POPULATION
1910	203,687	23.1
1920	215,512	23.2
1925	207,563	21.6
1930	204,371	20.3
1935	201,069	18.9

Source: *Statisztikai osztályának közlemények* 2 (1947).

The most significant change was not to the layers that comprised the city and its Jewish community but how the image of Budapest and Budapest Jewry in the eyes of Hungarians outside of the capital inverted after the war. Like the earlier rise of Budapest and Budapest Jewry, the decline of the city and its Jewish community were linked. The erosion of the civic status of Budapest Jewry, along with that of Hungarian Jewry as a whole, paralleled the erosion of the city of Budapest amid efforts by an increasingly right-wing government to centralize power and authority in the hands of an autocratic ruler and his bureaucracy. Despite the surge of antisemitism after the Great War, the continued presence and influence of Budapest Jews in the economy, culture, and politics of the capital paralleled the continued prominence of the capital itself, even in a changing political and cultural landscape.[7]

The outbreak of war in 1914 was a natural opportunity for Jews to demonstrate their solidarity with their city and their country, and for their non-Jewish compatriots to demonstrate a willingness to embrace this solidarity.[8] As the war lingered on, the hardship and chaos of these years threw into flux the image of Budapest among Hungarians elsewhere, who increasingly felt alienated from their metropolitan capital. As Vari noted:

> The concentration in Budapest of financial capital and factories, the spread of liberalism, democratic ideas, socialism, anarchism, trade unionism, modern technologies such as electric lighting, the use of telegraph and telephone, transportation by tramways, subway and steamboats, the embrace of modern arts and literature and other Western trends by a growing Hungarian and Jewish middle class, in tandem with the emergence of urban mass culture, made conservatives and nationalists feel estranged in the modern metropolis. To make up for it they idealized the countryside and the Magyar peasants, while berating the cosmopolitan decadence of the capital.[9]

After the war, Hungarians outside of Budapest looked increasingly askance at the capital. As one social critic noted at the time, "I searched for Magyar character in Budapest but did not find it, neither externally nor internally; there is no virtue there."[10] Another contemporary observer noted this change even more poignantly:

> The city was like a huge stomach that for years had swallowed all the immigrants from Galicia and now was suffering from heartburn. It was a terrible heartburn. Syrian faces and bodies, red placards and red hammers, were whirling in it. The freemasons, feminists, members of the editorial boards [of the progressive journals], members of the Galileo circle, customers of shady coffeehouses, and the rabble of the stock exchange all floated on its surface, while the inhabitants of the Dob Street ghetto had all attached national cockades and white daisies to their lapels.[11]

From contemporary observations such as these, one historian recently concluded that "in the rhetoric of the exponents of the Christian path, the capital and its leaders were held accountable for the war and the cataclysmic revolution that followed. Budapest was not only the 'guilty city,' but also filled the role of scapegoat . . . and reckoned to be an international Sodom." Another noted that "the propagandists of the counter-revolution insisted on identifying the revolutions with Budapest, with alien influence in this city and, generally, with urban culture. They contrasted an image of urban degeneration with that of an idyllic, racially pure, rural Hungary."[12]

This change of heart was not unique to Budapest, but part of a broader criticism of urban life in interwar Europe. As Vari noted, "The epithet of the 'Guilty City' (bűnös város) that Magyar nationalists used to describe Budapest was . . . the product both of local (the revolutionary context of 1918 and 1919) and European-wide historical developments that in the wake of the nineteenth-century processes of industrialization, urbanization, modernization and globalization invested the city and the countryside with opposite meanings."[13] Symptomatic of this changing attitude was the diminishing extent to which mainstream Hungarian society accepted Jews into its midst, even in Budapest. The mainstreaming of racial attitudes toward Jews, coupled with the re-mainstreaming of an older, early nineteenth-century contempt for Jews—both of which had been marginalized by the triumph of Hungarian liberalism—upended what many regarded as a natural symbiotic relationship between Jewry and the various incarnations of Magyar identity as championed by the Hungarian nobility, Magyar nationalism, and the Magyar-dominated and -led Hungarian state. The synergy of the prewar years would emerge intact but battered and more tenuous, and would make the search for normalcy thereafter more difficult amid the rising antisemitism and economic hardships of the 1920s and 1930s.

In turn, Jewish communal responses to the difficulties of the war years laid the foundation for more expansive communal responses to urgent conditions later on. During the war individual Jewish philanthropists such as Manfréd Weisz and Jewish organizations such as PIN and MIKÉFE responded to shortages in food and growing impoverishment by expanding their network of public kitchens that they had created before the war, while MIKÉFE found renewed support during the war for its vocational training program as a shortage of manual labor gripped the capital. Additionally, in response to the surge of negative popular sentiment during the war against immigrants and, above all, Jewish immigrants, the leaders of Budapest Jewry began more self-consciously and tactically to devise ways to respond to this rising xenophobia.

As the more specifically directed xenophobia of the war years expanded into a broader xenophobically driven antisemitism directed against most or all Jews in Budapest and Hungary—native-born and immigrant alike—Budapest Jewry had a field-tested set of responses at their disposal. Jews and Jewish organizations would build on the efforts during the war years to help Jews who were economically displaced and harmed by the *Numerus Clausus* of 1920, who faced disruptions to commerce and trade caused by the truncation of Hungary in the Treaty of Trianon, the growing social discrimination against Jews in the workplace, and the economic depression at the end of the 1920s. Along similar lines, disruptions to communal education caused by the war, for Jews and for Budapest generally, eventually prompted Jewish communal leaders to found, for the first time, a Jewish high school in Budapest in 1919. Though initially seen as a short-term, stopgap solution, it laid the foundation for the Jewish community to respond to a much larger crisis in education during the ensuing decade: the impact of the *Numerus Clausus* on the educational aspirations of Budapest Jews. All of these endeavors reflected the overarching efforts of Jews in Budapest to preserve some sense of normalcy during and after the war, as a way of coping with the disruptive changes in the situation of Jews in Budapest that began in 1914 and continued through the 1920s and 1930s.

ON THE BATTLEFIELD

When war broke out in September 1914, Hungarian Jews almost immediately sprang into action in support of their beloved country. Hundreds of Jews enlisted both in the Austro-Hungarian K.u.K. Army and in the Hungarian National Guard (Honvédség). Budapest Jewry spearheaded the efforts by Hungarian Jewry to immerse themselves in the war effort and the efforts on the home front.[14] Budapest Jewry expressed great pride in those who had enlisted. The liberal Jewish weekly *Egyenlőség*, in addition to publishing weekly reports about the course of the war, printed short biographical sketches of soldiers who were fighting and, in some cases, had died in battle.[15] One of the first to be profiled, in October 1914, was Armand Berényi, a metal works factory owner in Budapest. Berényi enlisted as a private in the 17th infantry regiment, quickly rose to the rank of second lieutenant, and was killed in action at Mount Dugo near Krupanje. Another was Andor Fentl, a Budapest shopkeeper at the beginning of the war who joined the 32nd infantry. He was decorated during the Serbian campaign near Szabács [today Sabac] for unparalleled valor and self-sacrifice for his regiment. Though a commoner, he was promoted to sergeant and awarded [the] First Class Order of Merit from Archduke Joseph. Fantl sustained more than one hundred war injuries. His father, Mór Fantl, was also a soldier, during the Bosnian Occupation.[16]

These weekly reports continued through much of the war, and took on greater importance amid the ever more strident attacks on the patriotism of Hungarian Jews.

By the beginning of 1915, it became clear that the willingness of Jews to serve was not deemed sufficient evidence of Jewish patriotism; only active frontline contributions by Jews to the war effort provided the evidence necessary to countermand these accusations. Such was the case of Lipót Lázár, royal technical advisor and son-in-law of the late Jozsef Scheyer. As the Budapest correspondent of the *Allgemeine Zeitung des Judentums* reported in March 1915: "Lázár served for 18 months in the field in charge of field communications. Two weeks ago he received the distinguished service cross from Emperor Franz Jozef. He was celebrated not only as a Jew who volunteered for active combat, but as an innovative thinker whose technological savvy was aiding all soldiers in the field."[17] Jewish frontline soldiers came from all strata of Budapest Jewry. Ludwig Lichtenstein, the grandson of Koppel Reich, the leader and chief rabbi of Budapest's Orthodox community, received a medal of valor and was praised by his field commander for his actions at the front.[18] To underline the significance of these personal stories, the editor of *Egyenlőség* elicited from Archduke Joseph an appraisal of Jewish soldiers generally, and printed the archduke's reply:

I have had many opportunities to observe our soldiers of the Jewish faith and I saw no difference between them and other soldiers. Their valor, their dedication to the cause is at all times praiseworthy.... Many Hungarian Jews are among the most outstanding Hungarian soldiers. Not once did I see even one shy away from conflict, even in the most bitter conditions. Jews proved that they are true patriots and brave soldiers just like all other.[19]

No less important in refuting claims of Jewish disloyalty were Jewish efforts to help the war financially. Hungarian Jews regarded such efforts with the same fervor and pride as active duty. One leader of Budapest Jewry, soliciting funds for the war efforts, articulated this passionate view:

The much-needed mobilization of capital for the national defense continues. One is easily moved by what even common folk and school children are doing and what the

middle classes of society and all representatives of all tiers of economic life are under-
taking. And the churches, all of whom see the efforts of *magyarság* as the highest example, animate the patriotic devotion that galvanizes our material strength so that
we can help fight for all of our lives, welfare, future, and happiness. Let us demonstrate the noblest characteristics of Hungarian Jewry's denominational structure and
national disposition, as we put forth an unbreakable commitment to the aspirations
of our nation, to its future, and to its glory.[20]

His efforts resonated deeply and elicited massive contributions from individual Jews
and from Jewish communities and organizations in Pest and elsewhere in Hungary. In
July 1916, for example, the Jewish-owned Budapest firm Julius Wolfner & Co. endowed
a fund of 500,000 koronas for wives and widows of soldiers serving in the Honvédség.[21]
To honor fallen Jewish soldiers, the Pest Hevra Kadisha dedicated a portion of the
Jewish cemetery for the burial of Jewish soldiers killed in the war, and fashioned a memorial for the soldiers.[22]

TABLE 28. JEWISH SUBSCRIBERS TO HUNGARIAN
WAR FUND, NOVEMBER 1914

DONOR	SUBSCRIPTIONS (IN KORONAS)
Pest Chevra Kadisha	500,000
Pest Jewish Community	250,000
Buda Jewish Community	100,000
Buda Chevra Kadisha	100,000
Menház	50,000
PIN	
General fund	10,000
Orphanage fund	15,000
Buda clerical pension society	50,000
Hungarian ITO Establishment	25,000
Pest Education Fund	2,000
Szeged Women's Association	15,000
BAJA	
Jewish Community	15,000
Chevra Kadisha	15,000
Samuel Fischer Fund	40,000
Nőegylet	15,000

Continued

TABLE 28. Continued

DONOR	SUBSCRIPTION (IN KORONAS)
BAJA (continued)	
Girls' school	2,000
Benevolent fund	5,000
Nagyvárad Kongressi Community	20,000
Nőegylesület	25,000
Arad Jewish Community	300,000
Zagreb Jewish Community	124,000

Source: "A magyar zsidóság és a hadikölcsön," *Egyenlőség,* November 22, 1914, p. 9.

ON THE HOME FRONT

The difficulties created by the war, while not diminishing concern for the plight of orphaned and indigent children, raised a new challenge to the welfare and stability of Jewish families in which the father, older sons, or both were away at the front for an extended period of time: the impact of family members being absent on mothers struggling on the home front to provide basic needs for their families. Donations once directed to a variety of Jewish causes and institutions were now more frequently reserved for families and children in need. Ferenc Székely was one of many prominent individuals who specifically helped Jewish children orphaned by the war. The Budapest Orthodox community collected and disbursed more than 200,000 forints for families in need.[23] PIN president Katalin Gerő described this emerging problem especially poignantly. The impact of absent fathers, she noted, was more straightforward: "Many of our young men have fallen on the battlefield. The endless conscriptions again and again cast another throng onto the battlefield.... So many families have both father and son out at the front." The difficulties at home were perhaps less obvious. Gerő underlined how women, though not facing imminent death and danger on the battlefield, were also engaged in a difficult struggle, in this case, against hunger and the looming collapse of the family:

> And the ladies? They "stand on line." This is a new term that we have learned only recently. The grocery stores are depleted, there is less and less to buy and sell. The central authorities, languishing under the blockade, are beset from all sides. Supplies are rationed so that everyone gets at least something. Families and organizations receive food coupons so as to be able to buy a prescribed quantity of flour, meat, lard, sugar, bread, legumes, and other foods. Sellers submit the food coupons in order to

receive more food. Whatever they receive runs out right away. Whoever comes late to obtain food, receives nothing. Thus began standing on line. Ladies arrive to purchase food even before the store opens, or race to a store when a rumor spreads that a new shipment has arrived, only to get there and discover that the store is not even open.... At times, the line is long enough to extend to the next cross street. In winter cold, under the hot summer sun, and in the chilling rain the ladies stand on line with their small baskets, often with small children in their arms, to wait for hours to get a handful of food.... From time to time an ambulance arrives to take away someone who has collapsed from the cold or fainted from the burning sun.... Fathers lie dead on the battlefield, mothers are exhausted on the line, and the children wind up in an orphanage.[24]

In response, Jewish philanthropic organizations reoriented their efforts to help the underprivileged. Prior to the war, the PIN and other charitable organizations had focused their family-oriented philanthropic efforts primarily on underprivileged children, that is, on housing, clothing, feeding, and educating orphans; and on helping low-income or indigent young Jewish women get married by providing them with dowries. These efforts expanded during the war to include helping adults in need as well. During the first Passover of the war, the PIN provided Passover meals for all eight days of the holiday to soldiers stationed in Budapest, students at the university and the teacher-training institute, and refugees. All told, during the holiday the PIN served 15,000 koronas' worth of food to 342 soldiers, 85 students, 22 teachers in training, and hundreds of refugees.[25]

In a similar vein, Jewish communal leaders encouraged the more affluent members to endow money in support of less fortunate Jews.[26] These donations were highly individualized, allowing donors to direct their contribution as generally or specifically as they wanted, and to direct the funds to help the situation they deemed most pressing. Thus Rozália and Jákob Reik endowed 1,900 koronas to the Pest Jewish community to start a fund for poor single girls, regardless of religion. Ernesztine Hertzka donated 380 koronas to provide dowries for "lower-income unmarried Jewish girls who live in the iv–ix districts." Ármin Reich and Fanny Blau donated 470 koronas for Jewish brides from poor families. In the aggregate, the individual donations listed in the weekly press amounted to tens of thousands of koronas during the war years, continuing years of generosity by an increasingly affluent Budapest Jewry.[27]

By the end of 1915, as Budapest was beginning to feel the disruptions caused by the war, the general problem of poverty was aggravated by limitations in the area of food production and distribution. As more food was redirected to supply frontline soldiers, the open markets of Budapest that relied heavily on food transported in from neighboring towns and villages experienced chronic shortages and delays in receiving daily and weekly shipments of basic foodstuffs, including bread and fresh produce. In addition, in the summer of 1916 the City of Budapest reduced the number of public market days from two down to one, to the detriment of petty Jewish merchants who relied on these semiweekly public markets to sell their wares. Shortly thereafter the remaining market was moved to Saturday, which placed an added burden on observant Jews who preferred not to work on that day. [28]

In response, philanthropic Jewish individuals and communal organizations, beginning with the PIN, shifted their focus from peacetime concerns to more pressing wartime concerns. The PIN turned its attention toward aiding women not only as war widows and the wives, sisters, and daughters of heroic soldiers sacrificing at the front, but as "soldiers" struggling against the increasingly difficult conditions of daily life on the home front. Acordingly, the PIN's erstwhile emphasis on aiding children directly shifted toward easing the burden of mothers raising their children in unduly harsh conditions. In this way, they prevented children from becoming orphans. The PIN also expanded its prewar network of public kitchens. By 1910 the organization was operating a kitchen on Dob utca in the VII District for anyone, regardless of religious affiliation. While the proprietors charged a nominal price of 20 fillers for a meal, those who could not afford even this were fed at no charge; and the indigent could also receive vouchers from the PIN that were redeemable at any public kitchen in the city. In 1914, the PIN provided breakfast and lunch to more than three thousand individuals each month. This number would increase steadily during the war as the number in need increased. This did not mean curtailing or reducing assistance to orphans and poor brides, but expanding operations to tackle other problems as well. [29]

Expansion required additional funding. In February 1915, Gerő and other executive committee members solicited a major contribution from Alice Weiss, the wife of Manfréd Weiss, the most affluent Jew in Budapest. Heretofore Alice Weiss had remained aloof from direct involvement or extensive contributions to the PIN. As with the members of other leading and ennobled Jewish families, her philanthropic efforts had been directed more toward the charitable needs of the general populace rather than specifically toward the needs of the Jewish community. Given this predilection, the PIN approached her initially to help fund a new maternity hospital that was not to serve Jewish women exclusively, but "wives of soldiers of all persuasions." Weiss endowed the new hospital with enough money for eight beds and nightstands, and "a large quantity of bedsheets, kitchen utensils, and carpets," and was rewarded with a lifetime honorary membership. Three months later, as conditions in Budapest worsened, the PIN elicited from Alice Weiss an additional donation of 10,000 koronas to PIN, which she did not earmark for a particular project but invited the PIN to use as necessary. This sum became the seed money to increase the number of public kitchens in Budapest, not least of all as an alternative way for a mother to procure enough food to feed her family without standing on line all day. Subsequently, the number of public kitchens run by the PIN in Budapest increased more than tenfold by the end of the war, serving daily between 1,000 and 1,200 meals throughout the war.[30]

The impact of the PIN's public kitchen network set a philanthropic example that others emulated on a larger scale, above all Manfréd Weiss himself. Weiss founded the largest privately owned public kitchen on Váci Street 89 in the Sixth District and donated 25,000 koronas as startup funds. This kitchen began operating in the fall of 1914, and by the summer of 1915 it was outproducing the kitchens run by PIN. Initially the Weiss Kitchen distributed between 1,000 and 1,400 daily meals; eventually their output reached 2,000 daily meals. Moreover, the Weiss Kitchen was a state-of-the-art facility, with a 200-square-foot cooking area that could accommodate food preparation simultaneously in ten 300-liter cauldrons. Whereas, like the PIN kitchens, the Weiss Kitchen embraced the laudable aim of providing every hungry person with food, its added operating principle was "bountiful portions, everyone going away satisfied."[31] Not surprisingly, the Weiss Kitchen attracted the largest clientele, serving 1,000–1,200 lunches daily during the war years. This prompted other family members to set up satellite kitchens elsewhere in the city. Manfréd's daughter, Elsa Weiss, founded one on Izabella u. in the Seventh District that served 300–400 meals daily throughout the war. Weiss's nephews Baron Adolf Kohner and Ede Spitzer ran the second largest kitchen, serving 700–750 daily meals on Aréna Street. Weiss's son-in-law Alfréd Mauthner and his father, Ödön, sponsored another public kitchen in the Seventh District at 33 Rottenbiller utca.[32]

The efforts by Jews and Jewish organizations in Budapest to provide food for the indigent were complemented by a MIKÉFE program to aid in the production and distribution of food for the city generally. The shortage of workers that resulted from more and more men being conscripted into the army eventually led to an inadequate number of people growing food in and around Budapest and helping to distribute the food to the markets around the city. The rising demand for gardeners prompted MIKÉFE to reinvigorate and reorient its training program accordingly. On the eve of the war, MIKÉFE had entered a period of decline, attracting fewer members annually and deeply in debt. The surge in the demand for gardeners gave the organization a chance for renewed life by focusing primarily on the training of gardeners:

> Currently most gardening assistants are serving at the front. However, in the midst of this devastating war, as we feel the spring breeze approaching, we can discuss the future of Jewish gardeners who have been called upon to augment the productivity of our country and who can increase the quantity and quality of foodstuffs, especially in cities. . . . This is the challenge of the MIKÉFE gardener training camp program: to develop their expertise, and to bring more new enrollees to this program. One or

two trained gardening assistants will be needed for each private garden. We know the importance of gardeners. We know well that even a smaller garden can help with the dwindling food supply caused by the war. This will be especially helpful to Jews, not only because of added income but will also be a way to encourage more young Jews to pursue the avocation of gardening. MIKÉFE's beneficent gardener training mission has developed considerably. We hope that with further development from year to year, Hungarian Jewish gardeners will reach a position of prominence among gardeners in Europe.[33]

The new training program, in addition to easing the shortage of agricultural workers, provided much-needed employment for out-of-work young Jewish men and women. By the end of 1916, a city official noted the organization's efforts to address these problems: "MIKÉFE deserves the greatest recognition. It plays a serious role in public nutrition in Budapest. It brings food to the city and connects crops with the vegetable markets."[34]

PATRIOTISM AND XENOPHOBIA

The war years marked a high point of solidarity and camaraderie between Budapest Jews and their beloved city and the ability of Jews in Budapest to live seamlessly in mainstream and Jewish society. This was epitomized by the election of Ferenc Déri as deputy mayor of Budapest in 1916, the same year he became an honorary member of the Hevra Kadisha. Hitherto no Hungarian Jew had risen that high in the hierarchy of local or national politics.[35] At the same time, the difficulties of the war stirred a backlash against Budapest Jewry. Despite Jewish contributions to the war effort, at the battlefront and on the home front, antisemitic newspapers accused Jews of various forms of disloyalty: lack of patriotism, evading military service and especially active combat duty, corruption in provisioning supplies to the troops, war profiteering, and orchestrating an "invasion" of Jews into Hungary from Galicia.[36] Some of these concerns crystallized into unsubstantiated conspiracy theories. The Hungarian correspondent for the *Weser Zeitung* in Bremen, for example, claimed that "each Jewish marriage in Budapest produces four children; figures for Magyars and Germans are not nearly so high. This means that, at this rate, Jews will eventually be a majority in Budapest—the result as much of influx of Jews from abroad as natural increase."[37]

These criticisms reflected decades-old concerns in more conservative circles about the growing Jewish presence and influence in Hungarian society and politics, especially in Budapest. These concerns had appeared already prior to the war in the form of growing xenophobia regarding the growing stream of newly arriving unacculturated Jews

from northeastern Hungary and Galicia. During the early 1880s, fear of an influx of
Jewish refugees from Russian-Poland following the pogroms in the spring of 1881 became a centerpiece in the rhetoric of antiliberal politicians, above all Viktor (Győző)
Istóczy. In a parliamentary address in 1883, Istóczy railed against the looming horde of
foreign, unacculturated *Ostjuden* that was preparing to swarm into Hungary and over-
whelm the more civilized Magyar culture and society; he called for an immediate ban
on immigration from Russia and Galicia.[38]

The manifesto of Istóczy's newly formed Independence Party articulated this concern in greater detail. The manifesto called for "the shattering of Jewish power and mod-
erating their influence in politics and society, economy, in the press, in finance, commerce, trade, industry, and transportation." More specifically, it advocated limiting
the right of Jews to sign legal documents for a transfer of the license to brew liquor to
village authorities in order to ban Jews from operating taverns; to table any discussion
of a new law permitting marriage between Jews and Christians; and, finally, a wholesale reform of immigration regulations that would halt the flow of Jewish immigration
into the country. At the time, this manifesto had limited impact on Hungarian politics;
Istóczy had limited following in the 1880s.[39] Yet the issue of *Ostjuden* in Budapest itself
lingered on for several decades. In 1904, the influx of Jewish immigrants from northeastern Hungary and Galicia raised concerns among Jewish communal leaders regarding the unacculturated character of these would-be Jewish settlers and the backlash it
might provoke in Budapest. By this point, Jewish communal leaders, too, were concerned about *Ostjuden* importing into Hungary and Budapest radical political ideas
such as socialism and Zionism. Jewish leaders responded effectively by deterring many
of these Jews from settling in Budapest or remaining long-term. The response, though
effective, never reached the level of public spectacle or scandal.[40]

A decade later, amid the more heated atmosphere of the war, the same issue would
rise to the level of public scandal along with other anti-Jewish claims and elicit a more
urgent response from Jewish leaders in Budapest. In response to the claim of Jews
shirking active combat duty, moreover, in 1915 the leaders of the Jewish community expanded the ad hoc weekly reports about Jewish patriotism and military service in the
weekly Jewish press into a more systematic and thoroughgoing catalogue, culminating
in the founding of the Hungarian Jewish Military Archive (Magyar Zsidó Hadi Ar-
chivum), whose archivists catalogued more than 40,000 listings about the actions of
Jewish soldiers. This, they hoped, would deflate the anti-Jewish accusations: "Only sta-
tistics will be an effective way to deny the accusations against us. In 1848 Jews volunteered in disproportionately large numbers; so, too, now there [is] no reason to think
that their participation will be any less."[41]

In response to the deleterious claims regarding the unnaturally rapid growth of Budapest Jewry through immigration, the Hungarian correspondent to the *Allgemeine
Zeitung des Judentums* retorted that "without Jews, Budapest would not be moving

so expeditiously toward modernity—this is a fact. Without Jews, Temesvár, Szeged, Grosswardein (Nagyvárad), and other provincial cities would in no time be reduced to swampland and unpaved villages, as they were for years with streets crowded with cattle and feces."[42] The most arduous Jewish response to complaints against Jews, though, was regarding the "invasion" of Jewish refugees from Galicia, Bukowina, and Russia. From the outset, as Galicia became a major arena of the eastern front between Austria-Hungary and Russia, thousands of Jews, dislocated by the war, crossed the border from Galicia into Hungary.

The immediate response of city officials was humanitarian assistance. In late September 1914 the interior minister issued a statement calling on the city of Budapest to "provide relief, in the form of money or sustenance, to all refugees who need it, regardless of whether or not they are victims of the war." The leaders of Budapest Jewry answered this call and spearheaded efforts to provide for the basic needs of the refugees by finding and securing temporary accommodations in city parks and schools and providing kosher food and food for the Sabbath. The cost of these measures was shared by the Jewish community and the city. The latter covered the first 78 fillers per person; the balance was covered, for the most part, by the main Jewish community, and in part by the Orthodox community.[43] The small Hungarian Zionist Organization set up the Jewish Public Aid Office (Zsidó népsegítő iroda) in Budapest to provide assistance for refugees from Galicia and Bukowina.[44]

The stream of Jewish immigrants from the east continued through much of the war, prompting one Jewish communal official to comment that "it seems as if there is no end to them."[45] Sándor Bródy, a leading Hungarian-Jewish writer and poet, expressed his initial discomfort as trainload after trainload of Jewish refugees arrived at the Keleti Train Station during the winter of 1914–1915:

> Swarthy foreigners are inundating the city. They advance rapidly from surrounding roads and are already in the suburbs chatting away peripatetically.... They are refugees who have arrived from the northernmost counties and from Galicia. Not only the need and the longing to wander but the scent of business brought them here, where they are determined to remain and put down roots. They are Jews; I, who am from this race ... look at them with a certain curiosity.... They are here. A thousand or ten thousand, I do not know. Yet I, who have made equal rights to all a necessity and an occupation, cannot worry about them but only stare at them.... They appear to me to be Arabs or Persians or Jews in their ancient homeland in Palestine. For now, I am amazed by their gloomy appearance, long-bearded faces, their biblical character, by their uniqueness.[46]

When Bródy finally deigns to approach one of the refugees on the train platform, gives him money, and asks him what he can do to help, the new arrival responds by asking for additional assistance, namely, that he send a letter to the mayor on the new arrival's behalf and a request for assistance to Manfréd Weiss.[47] Bródy's ambivalence reflected a growing concern in Budapest. The influx of often poor arrivals strained the resources of the city, especially the already strained supply of food and available housing. During the war, the construction industry, depleted by the conscription of many workers into military service, was now even less capable of addressing the deepening problem. In response, the city attempted to place a moratorium on rent payments and called for all space to be used—to no avail.[48]

Yet it was not only shortages that shifted Jewish public opinion in Budapest against immigrants and refugees, but also the unacculturated behavior and appearance that immigrants brought with them into a highly Magyarized Jewish community. Since the turn of the twentieth century, the majority of Jews in Budapest spoke Magyar at home and in the street; and many whose mother tongue was not Magyar still spoke the language in public. At a time when national pride was synonymous with and epitomized by one's mother tongue, the presence of thousands of Jews speaking another language—viewed, by many, as a less than European, uncivilized patois—was jarring; and, for acculturated Jews, unnerving. This changing mood left the leaders of Budapest Jewry in a quandary as to how to deal with Jewish refugees. Morally, they felt impelled to help their fellow Jews fleeing the difficulties of the war, but they could not ignore the risk of unacculturated *Ostjuden* undermining the political and social status of Budapest Jews. In the end, they settled on a middle-ground solution. They transported as many newly arriving Jews as possible out of the capital by train, mainly to Vienna, thereby deflecting the quandary of dealing with Jewish refugees amid a surge of popular xenophobia to the local Jewish community there. To mitigate the harshness of this decision, they ensured that the Jews would be transported out of Budapest by train rather than being left with no recourse other than walking the long distance to Vienna.[49]

As the war dragged on, the problems plaguing the city worsened. By the last year of the war, even those institutions that had weathered the difficulties of the war years began to deteriorate. This was especially evident in the realm of public education. The conscription of more and more schoolteachers into military service eventually drained the supply of educators. Nonetheless, many public schools continued to operate, often on a less than comprehensive or limited basis. For Jewish students in public schools, the shortage of schoolteachers was compounded by a less hospitable attitude among remaining teachers as antisemitic sentiments seeped into the schoolhouses of Budapest. This prompted a renewed debate among Jewish communal leaders over the hitherto passionate support for Jewish children to attend first-rate non-Jewish schools and the consensus that Jewish communal education be largely supplementary education programs for Jewish students in non-Jewish schools. The struggles of non-Jewish schools to maintain the prewar level of excellence, along with increasing antisemitism, prompted

Jewish communal leaders to doubt that public high schools still provided the optimal learning and social environment for Jewish students.

The solution to these problems was a renewed and increased support for Jewish community schools, not only for underprivileged but for all Jewish children. An important first step in this direction was taken by Roza Gomperz in the summer of 1917. Gomperz, mother in-law of former Rabbinical Seminary chancellor Dávid Kaufmann and a leading figure in Jewish philanthropy, bequeathed one million forints for the establishment of a Jewish women's teacher training institute. Per Gomperz's dying wish, the primary goal of the new institute was "not only to train new teachers for a girls' schools, but also to diminish the need to bring non-Jewish teachers who will lead the girls astray."[50] Gomperz's endowment reanimated the debate regarding the founding of a Jewish high school. This debate lasted more than two years until, at the end of 1919, the decision was reached to found two Jewish high schools, one for boys and the other for girls.[51] The pressing need to maintain Jewish education despite the difficulties caused by the war softened the attitude of some Budapest Jews toward the *Ostjuden* and led, in some cases, to a warmer attitude toward Zionism. Zionism had yet to garner much of a following in Hungary, least of all in Budapest.[52] During the first years of the war, at the height of solidarity between Budapest Jewry and the Magyar nation, Zionism seemed more foreign and out of place than ever before. The convergence of an influx of Jews with the surge of antisemitism, though, at times directed not only against the *Ostjuden* but Hungarian Jews generally, created a situation in Budapest that was more conducive—or, at least, less unconducive—to Zionism.

As it became clearer that many refugees would be remaining in Budapest, some communal leaders began to see them more as part of the Jewish community. In January 1916, the Jewish community approved a petition from Achdut (Unity), a local Zionist organization that had recently been founded by a group of Jewish refugees from Galicia, who asked for permission to set up a Hebrew language school and library. The community not only granted the request, but also leased them a house in the heart of Terézváros and provided them three rooms in local Jewish schools free of charge. This new learning program consisted of five simultaneous Hebrew language courses for children at different levels, and a twice weekly Hebrew course for adults. The organization's committee reflected the cooperative nature of this venture. Two out of five officers and four out of seven members of the advisory board were Magyarized Budapest Jews; the others were unacculturated recent arrivals. At the time, this one endeavor did not appear that significant. In retrospect, though, this marked an early move toward what would eventually become a larger following for Zionism in Budapest.[53]

The subtle shift in the attitude toward Zionism on the pragmatic, day-to-day level of communal administration was paralleled on the level of intellectual discourse. In 1917, the public debate over Jewish refugees and the mainstreaming of heretofore marginal antisemitic views prompted a broader debate over the "Jewish question" in Hungary, for the first time in decades. In 1917, the progressive publication *Huszadik Század* (Twentieth Century) solicited from leading Jewish intellectuals an answer to the question "Is there a Jewish Question in Hungary?" and devoted an entire issue to the responses they received. Some respondents reiterated the longstanding, entrenched belief—an article of faith among most Jews in Hungary, especially in Budapest—that, unlike in Germany and France, there was no such issue in Hungary, and that the travails of the war years were either an anomalous result of exigent circumstances or the last gasp of an older Jew hatred that was fading into oblivion, recent events notwithstanding. Others clung to the widely held notion that, left to their own devices, Magyars of the Jewish faith coexisted peacefully and fruitfully with their non-Jewish compatriots, and only the intrusion of foreign rulers and ideas—the Catholic Church, the Ottoman Turks, the Habsburgs; and Franco-German ideologies such as racism, antisemitism, and exclusionary chauvinistic nationalism—undermined this natural coexistence.[54]

Others, however, saw in current circumstances a new phase in the relationship between Hungarian Jews and the Hungarian state and nation. Among the more outspoken proponents of this point of view was Ármin Beregi, an engineer who was also one of the leaders of the small Zionist enclave in Budapest:

> The Jewish question in Hungary is no different from the Jewish question in Germany, Austria, or anywhere else; thus its solution cannot be any different than anywhere else. There is no impugning the loyalty of Hungarian Jews to their Hungarianness.... In every country and in Hungary, too, the Jewish question is an internal Jewish question, distinct from the economic status of the Jews.... The Jewish question cannot be solved with the help of social and legal reforms; these will perhaps alleviate certain internal problems, as the past has shown, but none that address the heart of the issue. The Jews are like a seed that errantly landed on a crag in a rock ... in certain places the seed can sprout and flourish without finding fertile soil, but only held by a crack on the periphery of the rock or by cracking the rock itself.[55]

For Beregi, the economic prosperity, social acceptance, and cultural immersion of the half-century leading up to World War I was as exceptional as it was remarkable; but, he believed, it was also situational and transactional and would ultimately be upended when circumstances changed and the needs of the host nation shifted away from needing Jews. In fact, Beregi was merely reciting a standard Zionist view of the diaspora. In this instance, his skepticism turned out to be correct as the end of the war and the ensuing events set in motion the very situational and transactional changes he posited.

POSTWAR CHAOS

The conclusion and immediate aftermath of the war worsened what were already difficult conditions. At the beginning of 1918, the daily newspaper *Pesti Napló* reported that "the capital is now living through its most desperate hour. . . . The most serious shortage looming is not the tragic lack of housing but starvation. Budapest's currently more than 600,000 people are consuming bread whose supply may not be replenished."[56] Mass strikes in January and June of 1918 reflected the growing despair that gripped the populace of the city. Hundreds of soldiers returning to Budapest from the front further exacerbated chronic shortages of food, medicine, and housing.[57] The housing situation had reached the point where, according to one observer, "in Budapest, the housing shortage is so widespread that entire families are living in carriages and train cars. Thousands and thousands of families are destitute."[58] Budapest Jewry languished along with the rest of the city. Jewish schools shut down or operated on a severely limited basis. The PIN was forced to close down its orphanage due to a lack of coal and firewood. Additional gifts from philanthropists such as Manfréd Weiss, who donated 500,000 koronas (in addition to the 125,000 koronas he gave previously) to help keep child care centers open helped, but only for a month or two.[59]

As the existing government teetered on the verge of collapse, an increasingly desperate populace placed its hope in a series of radical political movements: Mihály Károlyi's democratic revolution, Béla Kun's Communist revolution, and Miklós Horthy's proto-Fascist counterrevolution. Despite the very different politics and aims of these movements, Hungarian Jews, and especially Jews in Budapest, were targeted by supporters and opponents of all three movements. The Democratic government of Mihály Károlyi that came to power as a result of the Aster Revolution lasted only several months, largely because of its inability to address any problems with even partial success. As Romanian forces advanced into Hungary, Károlyi's government was unable to halt their advance. Moreover, the economic situation worsened, especially in the capital. In December 1918 Czech fighters took control of Nyitra and Eperjes—two important commercial way stations for goods heading to Budapest. The same month, the Czechs, Romanians, and Serbs blocked shipments of coal and gas to the capital.[60]

The Pest Jewish community attempted to help alleviate this situation. One month after the Aster Revolution the Jewish community assumed responsibility for the debt owed to the city by Jewish refugees. The community saw refugee rabbis as a useful tool to help organize and calm the growing mass of Jewish refugees, who were becoming more boisterous and conspicuous as they became more desperate. To this end, the community extended interest-free loans to refugee rabbis to help stabilize their situation and lead more effectively. At the end of November, community president Lajos Adler resigned from his position in frustration, advocating that the community embrace the radical changes proposed by the new government.[61]

The leaders of the Jewish community, moreover, alarmed by the increasingly stentorian claims that Jewish loyalty lay outside of Hungary, reiterated their commitment and connection to their country. In early 1919, the National Association of Hungarian Rabbis issued a declaration proudly announcing:

> The Jewish religion exists independent of state and land, of people [*Volk*] and nation. A Jew is a member of our religion who avows Jewish beliefs; his people is determined by where he was born or by which nation's son he is through political affiliation. This has been the concept of the Jewish religion for the last two thousand years and still is today. This belief affirms the irrefutable fact that Judaism has been a religion for two thousand years and neither nation nor nationality.... It has fulfilled this mission in the past and will continue to do so in the future.[62]

Ultimately, neither the measures taken by the Jewish community nor the declaration by the rabbis made much of the difference in the face of the overwhelming economic problems besetting the city. During the brief tenure of Károlyi's government, polemical and physical attacks against Jews resulted from the widening belief among opponents of the revolution that Jews were instrumental in carrying out the revolution and supporting the new government. Defenders of the traditional layers of Hungarian society and politics—nobles, townsfolk, artisan guilds, and churches—focused their fear that Jews would undermine or eliminate these time-honored institutions. In response, the Károlyi government helped Jews organize self-defense units that foiled some of these attacks and defended Jews against others.[63]

Ultimately, however, the Károlyi government was largely ineffective and too short-lived to improve the situation, for Jews or for anyone else in Budapest, and within a few months, it was overthrown and replaced by the Communist regime of Béla Kun.[64] This revolution, far more radical than Károlyi's, elicited even more strident support and opposition; this time, too, Jews bore the brunt of both. Like Károlyi's, Kun's revolution was regarded by its opponents as the brainchild of Jews qua Communists, a notion that, for those who believed it, was erroneously legitimized by the fact that Kun himself (like Trotsky in Russia) was of Jewish origin. The Communist regime prevented widespread systematic harassment of Jews, but supporters of the revolution regarded Jews as capitalist enemies, above all the large-scale Jewish capitalists among Budapest Jews.[65] The disdain for Jewish capitalists at times impacted Jews indirectly as well. The Kun government addressed the chronic shortage of housing by forming the Budapest Housing Commission. Theoretically, this agency was supposed to redistribute housing space so as to accommodate as many homeless people in Budapest as possible. In

fact, the commission seized ownership over private residences and then invited supporters of the revolution to live there. Often this meant evicting the "Jewish capitalist
residents" from these domiciles.[66]

Ultimately, the impact of these two relatively short-lived revolutions resonated beyond their specific policies and changes. In tandem, they eroded faith in government,
especially after the Communist Revolution was defeated, and especially outside the
capital. As Emily Gioielli aptly noted: "Prior to the revolutions, the state had been
a perceived source of stability and security for middle- and upper-class Hungarians.
Their privilege vis-à-vis the state had been naturalized rather than contested. The revolutionary government rapidly overturned these assumptions, and the sudden loss of
status, coupled with the constant threat of violence, exposed this population in ways
that were unfamiliar."[67] This erosion of trust in local and state government would become a decisive factor in the deterioration of the status of Jews, and especially Budapest
Jews during the 1920s and the 1930s. Previously, the synergy between Jewry and nobility
in Hungary had been a central pillar of stability and civic amelioration for Hungarian
Jews, epitomized by Jews in Budapest. The widespread notion that the two revolutions,
whose central aims included dislodging the nobility from its position of prominence,
were perpetrated by Jews upset this synergy.

This fraying of the noble-Jewish alliance was exacerbated by the Treaty of Trianon
in 1920 that forced the Hungarian state to cede two-thirds of its territory to heretofore
subordinate national minorities in the name of national self-determination. This truncated the multinational Kingdom of Hungary, the largest constituent part of the recently defunct Austro-Hungarian Empire and one of the largest states in Europe, into
a small, landlocked Hungarian state. The post-Trianon state was wistfully nicknamed
Csonka Magyarország ("Rump Hungary") by a devastated and traumatized Hungarian
nation.[68] The impact of Trianon was felt quickly in Budapest. The arrival into the capital of nearly 400,000 Hungarians from territories assigned to other countries further
strained the already less than adequate food supply and rapidly deteriorating housing
shortage, and stirred further anti-immigrant xenophobia. The truncating of Hungary
also eroded the status of Hungarian Jews. Hitherto the heart of the economy of the
Kingdom of Hungary had been an occupational division of responsibility between Jews
dominating commerce and industry and nobility comprising the bulk of the state bureaucracy. The much-reduced government of the truncated Hungarian state needed
far fewer bureaucrats, prompting many nobles to move horizontally from civil service
to commerce and industry and into direct competition, often for the first time, with
Jews for employment.[69]

No less important was a new attitude toward Jews as part of the Magyar nation.
Prior to the Treaty of Trianon, the Magyars made up only 45 percent of the total population and thus were an ethnic minority in the multiethnic Kingdom of Hungary, at

a time when national majority status was taking on greater political significance. Since Hungarian Jews made up 8 percent of the population, the Magyars saw in Magyarized Jews who identified as Magyars an opportunity for Magyars to become the majority of the population (45% + 8% = national majority). Thus Jews in Hungary were encouraged to embrace Magyar language and culture and to see themselves as Magyars by nationality and Jewish by religion. In addition, Jews, especially outside of Budapest, were seen by the Magyars as "Magyarizing agents" who would get members of other ethnic groups to embrace Magyar language and culture. In the newly formed post-Trianon Hungarian state, Magyars were the overwhelming majority and no longer needed Jews to become or to be counted as Magyars. Right-wing ultra-nationalists, in particular, increasingly regarded Hungarian Jews more as Jews in Hungary than as Magyars of the Jewish faith. Coupled with the animosity toward Jews in the wake of the two revolutions and the upending of the noble-Jewish symbiosis, these changes transformed the situation of Hungarian Jews from a highly favorable situation before the war into a much more difficult situation thereafter. This change was especially dramatic for Jews in Budapest, who were the most Magyarized and the most deeply invested in the Kingdom of Hungary.[70]

The first incarnation of this new reality appeared in Budapest with the counterrevolution and the ensuing White Terror. The hero and the face of the counterrevolution, Admiral Miklós Horthy, arrived in Budapest in November 1919, inaugurating more than two years of, at best, uncertainty, and, at worst, tragedy for Jews in Budapest. The Jewish community reached out to Horthy in the attempt to create some sort of working arrangement, but even a gift of 100,000 koronas did not alleviate the new regent's disdain for Jews. On the contrary, during the months after arriving in Budapest, he issued several ad hoc decrees to the detriment of the status of Jews in Budapest, and elsewhere in Hungary. He ordered the dismissal of Jewish government and military workers; he prohibited Jews from trading in tobacco and wine, and barred Jewish students from attending academic institutions. Outside of Budapest, these decrees took a greater toll on Jews, since smaller Jewish communities were less able to assist Jews who lost their jobs; this led to an influx of Jews from the hinterland into Budapest. The barring of Jewish students from academic institutions elicited the most pointed Jewish communal response. In December 1919, communal leaders accelerated plans to open a Jewish high school in Budapest for the first time. The goal of the school would be to accommodate Jewish students who no longer felt safe or welcome in their public high school; the faculty was made up of teachers who had lost their positions as a result of Horthy's decree, which soon after was expanded and codified into formal law, the *Numerus Clausus*.[71]

Legal disabilities, however, were not the worst problem that Jews faced. Jews were highly prone to experience violence, because of the widespread belief that they were Communists or, at least, had collaborated with Kun's Communist government.

Horthy's government did not officially condone the violence that came to be known as White Terror, but did little to rein it in. On December 15, 1919, the government passed a new law allowing for arrest without trial; many Jews were arrested and imprisoned. He ordered a raid on the first meeting of the Jewish community that took place after his arrival in the capital; Jews were taken to the basement of the Hotel Brittania and interrogated and, in some cases, imprisoned and even shot. Individual Jews would periodically disappear; their bodies would appear several days later in or along the Danube. Jewish communal leaders formed a new legal aid bureau to collect and litigate claims, with little success.[72]

A low point came in the fall of 1920 when acts and threats of anti-Jewish violence reached the point where only a small minority of Jews attended synagogue services on Rosh Hashana for fear of being assaulted. Jewish communal leaders tried to allay some of these concerns by meeting with local officials and law enforcement. A week later, larger crowds of Jews attended synagogue services on Yom Kippur. Perhaps the most apt summary of the difficulties that faced Budapest Jewry was expressed in the spring of 1920 by a parent writing to *Egyenlőség*, whose children eagerly awaited the end of winter and the arrival of spring: "In Budapest, thousands and thousands of anemic children living in crowded apartment houses await the burgeoning spring and the warming turn to summer. . . . these difficult years of war made them like little human seedlings desperately awaiting an opportunity to be in the sunshine."[73] After several years of chaos and upheaval, Jews in Budapest, like the city itself, were desperately in need of a return to normalcy.

By the end of 1920, anti-Jewish violence in the capital subsided as Horthy and his government became more entrenched atop Hungarian politics and society. Thereafter, Horthy's policies regarding Jews combined efforts to limit the presence of Jews in public life and institutions while allowing some Jews to contribute to economic growth. This dual aim was epitomized by Law 25 of 1920, the *Numerus Clausus*. The law stipulated that the percentage of students from a particular nationality or race who attended these schools could not exceed the particular nationality or race's percentage within the overall population. While not explicitly targeting Jews, it was clear that, because Jews more than any other group disproportionately attended higher schools, the newly imposed quota would affect them more adversely than it affected any other group.[74]

THE SEARCH FOR NORMALCY

As conditions stabilized, the Budapest Jewry community looked to establish a working relationship with the Horthy government and to jumpstart communal organizations, institutions, and activities as a way of reviving the routine of day-to-day life. In February

1920 Jewish leaders met with Horthy and requested that he move to curb anti-Jewish violence, compensate the community for the cost of repairing buildings damaged in anti-Jewish attacks, and refund the exit fee paid by Jewish apostates who now wanted to rejoin the Jewish community. That they submitted an "endowment" of 100,000 koronas with these requests suggests a return to the situation in Pest and Óbuda a century earlier when Jews had regularly provided their magnate benefactors and state officials with bribes and gifts as part of political and commercial negotiations. The government promised "to hold perpetrators of violence and abuse against Jews accountable," "to hinder such acts in the future," "to compensate the Jewish community for damage to the synagogue on Arena Street," and to refund the exit fee of Jews returning to the Jewish community.[75] The request to refund the exit fee was especially impactful. From January to August of 1921, 129 Jewish apostates in Budapest returned to Judaism and rejoined the Jewish community.[76] This coincided with an exodus of Jews out of the Jewish community in response to anti-Jewish violence and the *Numerus Clausus*.[77]

This simultaneous departure from and return to the Jewish community reflected the still porous boundary between the Jewish community and the broader Budapest community. At the same time, the return of Jewish apostates to the Jewish community reflected how the *Numerus Clausus* and the other growing difficulties of Jewish life forced Jews in Budapest to reorient themselves not only to a narrowing entrance into a once wide-open social mainstream, but also to a less optimistic future. For example, Jewish students displaced by the *Numerus Clausus* organized new industrial ventures that were operated almost exclusively by Jews, including a paper factory and electrical repair shop. Such Jewish ventures, though born of necessity, provided much needed encouragement for those in the Jewish community looking for an alternative source of employment. From the vantage of the communal leadership, the surest path toward optimism was to reinvigorate the Jewish community itself and the Jewishness of Budapest Jews. To this end, in January 1920, the Neolog community announced its renewed efforts to "reverse the trend of declining piety . . . and create stronger connections between individual community members and the overall community and a larger, stronger united Jewish society." The first step in this direction was a direct response to the *Numerus Clausus*: expanding and improving communal Jewish education. The main impediment created by the *Numerus Clausus* prevented Jewish teenagers from attending middle school, high school, and university. As one observer noted in the fall of 1920:

> 90% of Jewish students who took the entrance exam to Hungarian middle schools [*középiskola*] were denied entrance. Those schools that had 70–80 Jewish students now had two or three. This had caused panic and aggravation among parents who have asked the Jewish community schools to enroll their children. . . . The problem is that the entry level of the Jewish middle school can admit only forty new

students.... The Ministry has allowed Jewish schools to set up parallel classes to accommodate all Jewish students. The Jewish community will set up three or four additional classes as needed.[78]

In response, the community authorized Béla Fekély, superintendent of a local Jewish school and the chair of the community's committee on education, to lay out a plan to revamp communal education. Fekély's program of education reform fashioned a dual curriculum that had three central aims. First, he recognized that, prior to the *Numerus Clausus*, most Jewish children in Budapest had received a more than adequate and often first-rate general education in a local public school; Jewish community schools now had an obligation to fill this new lacuna and also an opportunity to attract the best and brightest Jewish students, who previously opted for the top state schools. In addition, Fekély recognized the importance of offering vocational training for students who were less academically oriented: "We will create an intermediate vocational school to train iron and metal workers. The plan is for this school to be in a factory.... With the aim of expanding the schools the community should lease the building on the corner of Munkácsi Street and Andrássy Boulevard, where the boys' orphanage and girls' gymnasium used to be. We also plan to set up a mercantile school for boys and girls."[79] Above all, Fekély recognized the vital importance of improving religious education. He regarded the lack of proper supervision and oversight as the main reason why Jewish schools had remained mired in mediocrity and was determined to avoid this pitfall:

> We must first focus on religious instruction. We must agree that for years now, the level of religious instruction has been abominable. Religious instruction suffered especially during the war and the rule of Károlyi and then the Bolsheviks. As a result of incessant interruptions and disorder in state and communal schools, as in the Jewish community as a whole, religious education became unattainable. For this reason, beginning with the next school year we are undertaking extensive reforms. The first order of business will be to make sure the religious instructors are able to exact from the students religious learning. The superintendent of the school will closely regulate the religious instructors. In addition, a committee that we will create from members of the community council will monitor continuously the instruction.[80]

Beginning in the fall of 1920, Fekély's vision became a template for the expansion of Jewish community education in Budapest, marked by the founding of seven new schools within eighteenth months. Communal leaders made sure that all Jewish children, regardless of their family's income level, could attend one of these schools.

More ambitious was the communal attempt to help Jewish college students who were expelled by the *Numerus Clausus*. In order to preempt antisemitic claims of Jewish particularism and that Jews were foreigners, the leaders of the Jewish community argued that Magyars of the Jewish persuasion had as much right to found a Jewish university as Magyars of a Christian persuasion had a right to found a Christian one: "There can be no doubt that we are entitled to establish a university. The Reception Law gave us this right by declaring the equality of our denomination. Other denominations, too, have their universities: Debrecen University is Calvinist and its theological wing is Calvinist. There can be no principled objection to the establishment of a Jewish university." Such efforts to improve communal education were part of a broader attempt to retrench and reinvigorate the Jewish community as a whole in the aftermath of years of chaos and adversity. As initial steps in this direction, the community focused on three aspects of Jewish communal life: the rabbi, the synagogue, and the availability and supervision of kosher meat. They reiterated the role of the community rabbi as having "a position of prominence not only in religious life but also in communal administration"; and "the honor of the synagogue is the religious, spiritual, and moral obligation of everyone who attends the service."[81]

The community's renewed focus on regulating kosher meat was the most challenging task of all. The destruction and dislocation caused by years of war, revolution, and terror had disrupted the infrastructure of Jewish communal life and its institutions, not least of all the licensing and meticulous supervision of local kosher butchers. By 1920, most kosher butchers were operating more or less independently, self-supervising and self-accrediting, and relying on reputation and word of mouth to attract customers. In response, the leaders of the community announced their renewed control over the supervision of all facets of *kashrut*: "The Pest Community has regulated the kosher poultry butchers by taking steps toward creating a consortium; they set up stands in Garay, Teleki and Klauzál Square provisionally; the rabbinate has provisionally agreed. The larger cuts will be 10 korona; the smaller pieces 5 k. smallest 3k."

In practical terms, this meant community supervision of ritual slaughters and the preparation and sale of kosher meat; factories producing smoked meat; slaughter and sale of kosher poultry, kosher for Passover mills and matzo bakeries, the kosher equipment of public kitchens, and "all other agencies that require religious supervision and oversight." A month later the Ritual Committee of the Jewish community approved eleven kosher butchers, including a smokehouse on Dob utca 18 and butcheries in Garay, Teleki, and Klauzál Squares.[82]

This renewed activity of the Jewish communal leadership spurred a growing popular interest in other communal organizations that one observer described as a "renewed religious momentum" of the Jewish community.[83] There was an increase in the number of Jews who joined the Hevra Kadisha, in part to attain access to decent health care that came with membership, and the founding or rehabilitating of twenty-three synagogues and seven new Talmud Torah schools in 1920 and 1921. There was also a steady increase in the number of community-organized public lectures and more public kitchens and other philanthropic and welfare programs. In February 1920 the Orthodox Community of Budapest founded a new hospital and sanitorium.[84] This increase in participation in religious activities and institutions took place mainly in Terézváros and Erzebétváros; those who participated tended to be more observant, less acculturated Jews who were either recent arrivals or the children of recent arrivals. Yet the revival of communal activity extended beyond these Jews and these neighborhoods. The more affluent Jews in Lipótváros, too, reinstated their own communal activities. In May 1920, for example, a Jewish cultural organization in Lipótváros resumed its monthly gathering after a hiatus of nearly three years. Rabbi Simon Hevesi introduced the event with a homily about the possibility of rebirth and renewal, after which noted opera singer M. Havas Gyöngyike performed a medley of arias, Hungarian songs, and Hungarian Jewish folk songs.[85]

The cumulative effect of all of these communal activities created a sense of stability for Budapest Jewry, although the Jewish community continued to face difficulties. Financially, the Jewish community struggled to keep pace with this surging interest and demand for social and cultural programs. In September 1923, for example, the community purchased sixty carloads of wheat to alleviate the growing problem of Jewish hunger, and then an equal amount the following spring to ensure all Jews in Budapest had matzo for Passover. The community's debt increased further as more and more Jews in Budapest applied for financial support and free loans, this at a time when steady inflation limited the actual value of these loans. Beginning in the spring of 1922, international Jewish philanthropic support, notably the Joint Distribution Committee, assisted Budapest Jewry with an influx of financial assistance and by providing sound economic advice. Antisemitic violence, too, continued to plague the Jewish community. Despite the promises of Horthy's government, antisemitic violence and hooliganism continued. In 1923, a bombing attack on the Liberal Club in Erzsébetváros, whose clientele was known to be mostly Jewish, killed nine people and wounded twenty-three others seriously. Such attacks, although they occurred with less frequency than during the White and Red Terrors, maintained a level of urgency within the Jewish community and among its leadership for much of the decade.[86]

THE BETHLEN ERA, 1922–1932

The appointment of István Bethlen as prime minister stabilized the relationship between Budapest and the rest of the country and improved the situation of Jews. As Jenő Lévai noted, looking back from 1944:

> His ten years of premiership managed to put a halt to the antisemitic reaction, which had seemed insurmountable.... He gradually eradicated the so-called counterrevolutionary spirit, slowly removing the regent's Szeged clique, thereby creating an

opportunity for more peaceful development.... The legal status of the Jews rapidly moved toward full equality before the law.... His government sought to quell with a strong hand the now rather sporadic atrocities and abuses.[87]

Though he himself had no love for Jews, pragmatic considerations of the mid-1920s impelled him to move the country away from the violence and disorder of the first years of the Horthy government by curbing street violence and restoring the rule of law. Bethlen recognized, first of all, that securing the foreign loans, without which full economic recovery would be difficult if not impossible, rested on his government honoring the minorities clause in the Treaty of Trianon. This meant, in effect, that the mistreating of Hungarian Jews put these loans in jeopardy. In addition, Bethlen recognized that top-tier Jewish industrialists were indispensable in efforts to rebuild and grow the Hungarian economy. To this end, he rehabilitated and reincorporated Jewish businessmen to their positions of prominence in industry and government. He rejected attempts by other politicians to exclude these Jews on racial grounds: "It is impermissible to proceed against honest businesses and banks using police means simply because they are run by Jews."[88] In 1924, Bethlen appointed Baron Frigyes Korányi to a cabinet post. A year later, in November 1925, Bethlen joined the Jewish community in celebrating its 125th anniversary at a ceremony attended by state and city officials; he congratulated Budapest Jewry on its successful integration into Hungarian society. In 1928 he appointed six Jewish industrialists to seats in the Upper House of the National Diet, and later appointed two rabbis as well.[89] One Jewish observer noted that Bethlen "was certainly not liberal, but maintained orderly conduct between the denominations and curbed religious violence."[90] When he left office in 1932, he validated this appraisal: "I wish now to regard that part of Jewry which acknowledges a community of fate with the nation in a fraternal fashion and in the same manner as my Hungarian brothers." In other words, Bethlen's cordiality toward Jews was pragmatically, not ideologically driven.[91]

Emblematic of the close working relationship between Jewish industrialists and Bethlen and the Horthy regime was Ferenc Chorin Jr., son-in-law of Manfréd Weiss. Chorin became the leading Jewish industrialist after his father-in-law's death in 1922. Chorin had a close working relationship with Bethlen and, more importantly, with Horthy. He established the Hungarian Employment Center in 1922 and was president until 1931. He was elected vice president of the Association of Hungarian Industrialists in 1928 before joining the Upper House two years later.[92]

On the whole, the Bethlen years were a mixed bag for Jews, in Budapest and elsewhere in Hungary. In 1927 a resurgence of antisemitism on university campuses led to many Jewish students being assaulted. In this instance, Bethlen's minister of justice responded, instructed the university rectors to expel attackers, and threatened to close the offending universities if order was not restored quickly. In 1928, Bethlen modified the *Numerus Clausus* law so as to soften its impact on Hungarian Jews by removing specific reference to Jews. Access to universities was still limited for Jews, but less so. Though the percentage of Jews in universities never returned to prewar levels, it more than doubled from 6 percent to 14 percent after 1928 and remained at 14 percent all the way through the 1930s.[93] On the other hand, a state-guided reestablishment of new health organizations for workers deprived several hundred Jewish doctors of their livelihood.[94] The same year, though, Jews as a religious group gained representation for the first time in the Upper House of parliament. Immánuel Löw, the rabbi of Szeged, was elected to represent the Neolog community; Koppel Reich, the rabbi of the Orthodox community in Budapest, represented the Orthodox. In 1927, the Zionist Alliance was permitted to renew its activities. In the mid-1930s, the movement had perhaps just 4,000–5,000 members; subsequently, this number grew to 10,000–12,000.

Bethlen's policies regarding Jews remained in effect for several years with only minor changes even after he resigned in 1931, withstanding the pressures of economic depression for much of the 1930s. For example, the Ministry of Trade and Transport introduced Law #45.268 in 1935, which established Sunday as the national day off and prohibited stores from opening on that day. This threatened the livelihood of the hundreds of observant Jews in the food industry who did not work on Saturday; when Jewish leaders appealed, the ministry exempted the food trade from the law, thus avoiding a "May Laws-esque" catastrophe from decimating the Jewish community.[95] The case of Jewish engineers is equally instructive. Even after the *Numerus Clausus* capped the number of Jews training to become engineers, those who completed the training were able to find employment in the field through much of the 1930s, despite the efforts of right-wing engineering groups such as Hungaria to exclude Jews from the field. Most found employment in private Jewish architectural and construction firms that had existed before World War I. By 1937, while the percentage of engineers who were Jewish dropped from 40 percent to 18 percent, the percentage of Jewish engineers employed by private firms was still 38 percent. This reinforced the stereotype of the Jewish engineer as capitalist, individualist, and competitive; but it also allowed scores of Jewish engineers to continue to earn a decent living.[96]

In general, life for Jews in Budapest combined elements of normalcy with a chronic wariness about rising antisemitism. Ágnes Adachi (née Ágnes Mandl) was born in Budapest in 1918 into a well-to-do assimilated family and was the only Jew who attended a first-rate Calvinist school where she learned French and English, in addition to Hungarian. She also learned German from her Austrian nanny. Her mother, a "happy housewife," and her father, who owned a textile factory, had a broad social circle of Jewish and Christian friends. She, too, had "lots of Jewish and Christian friends, some of whom were children of aristocrats." Annually her father threw a Christmas party for his employees. "We had a good life," she recalled, "because my parents had a very big social life of Jewish and Christians, and so I never knew the difference between people." This largely favorable situation began to unravel in 1935, when a classmate called her a dirty Jew, at which point she broke the classmate's nose. This setback, though difficult and shocking, did not leave her or her parents disillusioned about their future in Hungary: "By the time we got home, our parents knew about it and were quite upset because such things never happened. Within about a week or two, that young lady apologized to me, explaining that she only heard that word and that's why she used it." The family remained in Budapest until 1939, when they left for Switzerland with the help of her nanny.[97]

Iván Dévai, too, remembered Budapest as stable and livable for much of the 1930s. He was born in 1932 to a traditional family that observed the Sabbath and kept a kosher home ("We ate fish out but not meat"). His family lived in Erzsébetváros. "Before the war," he recalled, "Budapest for me was the trams and wide avenues and snow in winter and flowers and gardens in summertime. School, family, going out into the mountains over to Buda with my father, mother, and their friends and children. We lived a normal, civilized, middle-class life." In 1937, his father lost his license to operate his dairy factory and his suppliers refused to deliver goods to him. In 1938, there were still many Jews attending his Hungarian primary school, and relatively little antisemitism: "There were always a couple of big mouths, but generally it was frowned upon."[98]

Frank Gipps remembered the period differently. Born in 1923, he grew up in a middle-class liberal family in Buda, the son of a lawyer. He experienced antisemitism earlier and more harshly, and "could feel the disadvantages of being a Jew." At age six, he was assaulted on the way home from school by a group of boys who yelled "You killed Jesus. You killed our God, so that's what you deserve." In middle school and high school he was one of only thirteen Jews in a class of forty. When sending the Jewish students to a separate class on religious instruction, his teacher would announce, "All stinking Jews out from the class. Your rabbi is here." He was unable to attend university because of the *Numerus Clausus*.[99] Marianna Glazek, though, remembered positive and negative aspects of life in Budapest. She was born in 1922 into a nonobservant, upper-middle-class family. She grew up in a large apartment along the Körút (the boulevard that ringed the city) next door to the office where her father practiced medicine. She recalled as a young child playing in the park and strolling around the city with her German governess and swimming in a pool in the Danube during the summer. "There was antisemitism," she recalled, "but it was not so apparent. . . . Jews lived separate from gentiles in a subtle kind of way. . . . We were excluded from big balls and dances . . . and were not invited to any places reserved for gentiles."[100]

By the late 1930s, the situation of Jews in Budapest began to deteriorate further, beginning with the move away from Bethlen's policies. This move began in 1935 under the more right-wing prime ministers Gyula Gömbös and Kálmán Darányi. In 1935, a new policy enacted by the Gömbös government required private Jewish engineering firms to hire gentile engineers, significantly undermining the situation of Jewish engineers. More broadly, after 1935 the conditions that had shaped Bethlen's attitude toward Jews inverted during the second half of the 1930s. Increased social tensions caused by the deepening economic crisis called for broader economic reforms, including increased state control over industry and commerce. This diminished the need for the cooperation of Jewish industrialists. In addition, the retreat or withdrawal of the liberal democracies that had supplied or promised loans—Great Britain, France, and the United States—negated the importance of honoring the minorities clause. Finally, the rise of Nazi Germany as a military and economic power meant an alternative source of economic aid and the possibility of regaining lost territory. This pressured Hungarian statesman to treat Jews more harshly so as to appeal to Hitler and his regime.[101]

The upshot is that the changes that confronted Budapest Jewry after the First World War challenged the stability of Jewish life and the sense of security that Jews felt previously. Prior to the end of the 1930s, Jews in Budapest were able, in varying degrees, to adapt to these changes and recapture at least some of the sense of normalcy they had lost as a result of war, revolution, counterrevolution, and a surge in antisemitism. Aiding them in this endeavor was a network of Jewish communal institutions that, steeled by the difficulties of the war, were able to respond to the difficulties that followed thereafter. For Budapest Jewry, the ability to manage and cope with these changes attested to both their sense of connectedness to the city and the vitality of the Jewish community. Tasked by nearly a decade of upheaval, nonetheless Jews in Budapest—individually and communally—drew on their sense of belonging to weather the difficult conditions of the interwar years.

9

1938 and Beyond

I N LATE DECEMBER 1937, A DELEGATION OF BUDAPEST JEWS MET WITH MIKLÓS
Horthy to discuss the situation of Budapest Jewry. The delegation was a who's
who of prominent, well-connected Budapest Jews: Neolog community president
and Upper House member Samu Stern, leading Jewish industrialist and Upper House
member Leó Budai-Goldberger, commercial magnate Jenő Vida, and Lajos Láng, legal counsel of the Anglo-Hungarian Bank. The immediate impetus for the meeting was
the recent spate of arrests that, during the previous month, had landed more than five
hundred Budapest Jews in a nearby prison camp; the interior minister claimed that all
were Jews residing in Budapest illegally, and the roundup was not specifically aimed
at Jews. The delegation, apart from interceding on behalf of fellow Jews, believed that
the arrests not only targeted Jews specifically, but were also connected to rumors swirl-
ing about at the time about a new set of anti-Jewish discriminatory laws; the delegation hoped, at once, to preempt further arrests and to head off the laws by convincing
Admiral Horthy to intervene on behalf of Budapest Jewry. Horthy reassured the delegation by reiterating an earlier claim that neither individual attacks on Jews nor arrests
of Jews by law enforcement reflected state policy; he reassured them that he would protect them from subsequent incidents.[1]

In fact, subsequent events suggested otherwise. In April 1938, Horthy appointed
László Endre, an outspoken and strident proponent of racial antisemitic claims against
Budapest Jews, to the position of deputy sheriff of Pest County. This was interpreted by
Jews to be a direct strike not only against Jews but against the liberal values that, they
believed, defined the cosmopolitan city of Budapest. In response, newspaper editor
Lajos Szabolcsi lamented the appointment of László and called on his fellow Jews and

liberals in Budapest to contest the appointment of this controversial figure: "We must calmly but deliberately oppose this appointment. . . . There can be no doubt that this appointment marks a serious and grave defeat of the ideas of Liberalism. In the very same room where emancipation was once declared . . . this man is now enthusiastically chosen to be deputy sheriff of Pest County."[2]

These two events, Horthy's reassurance to leading Jews about the threat of antisemitism followed by an appointment shortly thereafter that validated antisemitism, reflected how 1938 was a point of inflection in the situation of Budapest Jewry. From this point on, the situation of Budapest Jewry would worsen steadily as the political and cultural space for Jews in Budapest diminished precipitously. By the summer of 1938, Jews in Budapest would find themselves enduring restrictions that neither they nor their forebears had encountered in nearly a century. In this sense, the meeting between the Jewish notables and Horthy recalled a different meeting that had taken place almost exactly two centuries earlier. This meeting, too, was between a delegation of leading Jews and a powerful Hungarian authority figure—Countess Zichy. Two centuries before the meeting with Horthy at the end of 1937 marked the beginning of a period of decline, the meeting with Countess Zichy had marked the beginning of a period of expansion.

Seen together as static moments, the two meetings appear parallel. In both cases, Jewish notables negotiated with an authoritative Hungarian political figure so that the latter could affirm the welcomed status of the former. In addition, Regent Horthy and Countess Zichy met with a delegation of elite Jews for a common purpose—to secure and benefit from the commercial alliance with and support of leading Jewish businessmen. Each was willing to overlook a broader ideological concern—Catholic piety in the case of Zichy, racially motivated antisemitism in the case of Horthy. Out of context, the two moments appear to be mirror images of each other. When seen as as part of a broader trajectory, the two ostensibly similar meetings reflect the relationship between Jews and their Hungarian benefactors moving in opposite directions. The meeting with Countess Zichy introduced the possibility of Jews living in Óbuda as legal residents under the protection of the Zichy family, the first step toward the rise of the Jewish community of Óbuda, then the Jewish community of Pest, then ultimately the Jewish community of Budapest. The meeting with Horthy signaled the beginning of the decline and eventual near demise of this Jewish community.

As such, these two events are bookends around the bicentennial rise of Budapest Jewry from marginal, humble beginnings during the eighteenth century to a major metropolitan Jewish community by the beginning of the twentieth century. Countess Zichy could scarcely have imagined that the privileges she gave to a few Jewish families would eventually blossom into a six-figure Jewish community living predominantly in Pest. Rather, she saw the tax revenue, gifts that a handful of Jewish merchants would deliver to her family's coffers, and increased commerce that they would help stimulate in the town her family was trying to develop. She rewarded in 1738 what she imagined as potential growth. Nor could she have imagined that a few dozen Jewish families would eventually multiply into one of the largest Jewish communities in the world, a community that, by 1900, had five times as many Jews as were in all of Hungary in her day. Horthy, by contrast, aimed at truncating the vibrant Jewish community of Budapest by paring it back down to the handful of elite Jews it had once been. He extended to the Jewish commercial elite in 1938 a promise of protection in exchange for economic contribution—much like the promise Countess Zichy had extended two centuries earlier—a promise that he kept for half a decade. Yet his promise ignored the presence of several hundred thousand Jews and left them highly vulnerable.

The differences between the two situations reflect the remarkable rise and development of Budapest Jewry in two centuries. In 1738, the very idea of Jews living in Buda and Pest was difficult to imagine, and even living in the adjacent market town required the machinations of a powerful magnate family. By 1938, not only was Budapest home to several hundred thousand Jews, but many of these Jews belonged to families that had lived there for multiple generations. Budapest was not only the city where they resided, but the beloved capital of their beloved homeland. The rise of this Jewish community was an important and defining element of the rise of the city of Budapest itself—a development equally unimaginable to Countess Zichy in 1738. Indeed, the rise of Budapest and Budapest Jewry were inexorably linked for two centuries. The deeply rooted connections between the city of Budapest and its Jewish community are well illustrated by the tenacity of Budapest Jewry to remain a part of the city despite the increasingly difficult conditions of the 1920s and 1930s.

An even more striking illustration, perhaps, was the fact that, after a half-century of languishing under the Nazi and Arrow Cross assault on Jewish survival followed by the Stalinist assault on the survival of Judaism and Jewish identity in Budapest, in 1990 the Jewish community sprang back to life almost immediately following the departure of the Communist regime. In 1989, on the eve of the collapse of the Communist government, an estimated thirty Jewish children in Budapest attended a Jewish school of one kind or another. Within three years, Budapest Jewry had established multiple Jewish day schools, one of which—the Anna Frank School—had more than eight hundred students. The ability of a Jewish community to bounce back so quickly and formidably after a half-century of struggle and dormancy attests to the vibrancy of what had been and the determination of the post-1990 community to recover it.[3]

This recovery did not only take the form of institutional development. Rather, it was driven by a renewed sense of pride, self-confidence, and a sense of belonging. When emigration to Israel or to America became a possibility for Hungarian Jews after 1989, many Jews in Western Europe and America assumed most would leave—why remain in a country that had suppressed your right to be Jewish? Instead, most remained and rebuilt not only their community and identity but their connection to their native city and country. A measure of this newfound confidence was the name that Jews in Budapest chose for a new annual festival that celebrated Jewish life and Jewish culture: the annual Judafest festival in Budapest. By naming a proudly Jewish festival as a variation on "Judapest"—the erstwhile quintessentially antisemitic epithet of the city and its Jews—Budapest Jewry reclaimed an epithet that once signaled the rejection of Jews as part of Budapest society. In this way Budapest Jewry reaffirmed their deep connection to the city and their rootedness in it.[4] This is a perspective absent from most other erstwhile great Jewish communities in Europe. Warsaw, Vienna, Berlin, Breslau, Vilnius, and others—their story ends more or less with destruction by the Nazi regime. The story of Budapest Jewry continues—Jews in Budapest continue to write it.

Notes

Chapter 1

1. On Buda and its Jews, see Ferenc Raj, *A History of Jews in Hungary under the Ottoman Domination, 1526–1686* (PhD diss., Brandeis University, 2004); Fülöp Grünvald, *A zsidók története Budán* (Budapest, 1938).

2. Antony Polonsky, "Warsaw," in *YIVO Encyclopedia of Jews in Eastern Europe*, https://yivoencyclopedia.org/article.aspx/Warsaw; François Guesnet and Glenn Dynner, eds., *Warsaw: The Jewish Metropolis: Essays in Honor of Antony Polonsky* (Leiden: Brill, 2017); Claudia-Anne Flumenbaum, "From the Beginnings until 1789," in *Jews in Berlin: A Comprehensive History*, ed. Andreas Nachama, Julius H. Schoeps, and Hermann Simon (Berlin: Berlinica Publishing, 2013), 9–52; Steven Zipperstein, *The Jews of Odessa: A Cultural History, 1794–1881* (Stanford: Stanford University Press, 1991); Leonid Praisman, "Moscow," in *YIVO Encyclopedia of Jews in Eastern Europe*, https://yivoencyclopedia.org/article.aspx/Moscow; Mikhail Beizer, *The Jews of St. Petersburg: Excursions through a Noble Past* (Philadelphia: Jewish Publication Society, 1989); Benjamin Nathans, "Saint Petersburg," in *YIVO Encyclopedia of Jews in Eastern Europe*, https://yivoencyclopedia.org/article.aspx/Saint_Petersburg; Till van Rahden and Marcus Brainard, eds., *Jews and Other Germans: Civil Society, Religious Diversity, and Urban Politics in Breslau, 1860–1925* (Madison: University of Wisconsin Press, 2008); Natan Meir, *Kiev, Jewish Metropolis: A History* (Bloomington: Indiana University Press, 2010).

3. Julia Richers, *Jüdisches Budapest: Kulturelle Topographien einer Stadtgemeinde im 19. Jahrhundert* (hereinafter Richers, *Jüdisches Budapest*) (Köln, Weiner, Vienna: Bohlau Verlag, 2009), 344.

4. Viktor Karády, "Les Communautés Juives: des Profiles Contrastes," in *Vienne-Budapest, 1867–1918: Deux Ages, Deux Visions, un Empire*, ed. Dieter Hornig and Endre Kiss (Paris, 1996), 63–64.

5. Ibid., 345.

6. On these two meanings of Neolog, see Howard Lupovitch, "Neolog: Reforming Judaism in a Hungarian Milieu," *Modern Judaism* 40, no. 3 (2020): 330–331. Neolog as a basis of synergy between Jews in the city is discussed in greater detail in chapter 5 in this volume.

7. Julia Richers, "Zeiten des Umbruchs und der Liminalität: Lebenswelten Budapester Juden im Vormärz," in *Konzeptionen des Jüdischen: Kollektive Entwürfe im Wandel. Schriften des Centrums für Jüdische Studien*, ed. Petra Ernst and Gerald Lamprecht, Vol. 11 (Innsbruck:

Studien Verlag, 2009), 106–131. The responses of the Jewish community of Budapest to the challenges of the 1920s and 1930s is the subject of chapter 9 in this volume.

8. Along with Budapest, the extensive list of "Parises" has included Baku, Beirut, Bucharest, Cairo, Esfahan, Hanoi, Irkutsk, Istanbul, Jaipur, Kabul, Lahore, Leipzig, Manila, Phnom Penh, Pondicherry, Prague, Riga, Ross Island, Saigon, Saint Petersburg, Shanghai, and Warsaw.

9. Lajos Hatvany, "Magyar irodalom a külföld előtt," Nyugat 5 (March 1, 1910): 286, quoted in Gwen Jones, *Chicago of the Balkans: Budapest in Hungarian Literature* (New York: Rout-ledge, 2013), 1; Mary Gluck, *The Invisible Jewish Budapest: Metropolitan Culture at the Fin de Siecle* (Madison: University of Wisconsin Press, 2016), 216. See Máté Tamáska, "The Industrialization of the Danube Cityscape: Danube Ports during the Concurrent Urban Development of Vienna and Budapest, 1829–1918," *Zeitschrift für Ostmitteleuropa Forschung* 67, no. 4 (2018): 553.

10. The most notable example is Thomas Bender and Carl E. Schorske, eds., *Budapest and New York: Studies in Metropolitan Transformation, 1870–1914* (Russell Sage Foundation, 1994).

11. See Richard Geehr, *Karl Lueger: Mayor of Fin de Siecle Vienna* (Detroit: Wayne State University Press, 1993), especially 105ff.

12. Alexander Mintz, "Die Lage der Juden in Osterreich," *Protokoll des I. Zionistenkongresses in Basel vom 29. Bis 31. August 1897* (Prague, 1911), 69; Theodore Herzl, "Der Baseler Kongress," in *Theodore Herzls Zionistische Schriften*, ed. Leon Keller (Berlin, 1920), 244. "Transleithania" was the official term for the Hungarian part of the Austro-Hungarian Empire. The Leithe River symbolically divided the empire between Cisleithania (the Erlande, the Czech Lands, and Galicia) and Transleithania.

13. Heinrich Mitteis, "Über den Rechtsgrund des Satzes 'Stadtluft macht frei,'" in *Festschrift Edmund Husserl: Zum 70. Geburtstag Gewidmet* (Halle, 1929), 342–358; also appeared in *Die Stadt des Mittelalters*, II, ed. C. Haase (Darmstadt, 1976), 182–202; Richard Sennett, *Flesh and Bone: The Body and the City in Western Civilization* (London: W. W. Norton, 1996), 151ff.

14. To be sure, this notion of the city has been around since antiquity. It could be applied with equal relevance to ancient Rome, Athens, Nineveh, or Jerusalem, as it could to New York, London, Paris, and Moscow. Even so, this kind of city has appeared most often and most vividly during the last two or three centuries.

15. On the Jews of Paris, see Paula Hyman, *The Jews of Modern France* (Berkeley: University of California Press, 1998), especially 1–17; on Vienna, see Marsha Rozenblit, *The Jews of Vienna, 1867–1914: Assimilation and Identity* (New York: SUNY Press, 1984), especially chap. 1; on Berlin, see Steve Loewenstein, *The Berlin Jewish Community: Enlightenment, Family, and Crisis, 1770–1820* (New York: Oxford University Press, 1994); on Breslau, see Hettlin Mandfred, Andras Reinke, and Norbert Conrads, eds., *In Breslau zu Hause: Juden in einer mitteleuropaischen Metropole der Neuzeit* (Hamburg: Dölling and Gratz, 2003); on Kiev, see Meir, *Kiev, Jewish Metropolis*, 23ff.

16. On the Port Jews, see David Sorkin, "Port Jews and the Three Regions of Emancipation," *Jewish Culture and History* 4, no. 2 (2001): 21–36; Lois Dubin, "Port Jews Revisited: Commerce and Culture in the Age of European Expansion," *Cambridge History of Judaism VII* (2018): 550–575.

17. See Heidemarie Peterson, "Kraków," in *YIVO Encyclopedia of Jews in Eastern Europe I*, https://yivoencyclopedia.org/article.aspx/Krakow/Krakow_before_1795, p. 2.

18. See the sources cited above in note 2.

19. Nathaniel Katzburg, *Pinkas ha-Kehillot: Hungariya* [Encyclopedia of Jewish Communities: Hungary] (Tel Aviv, 1978), 191.

20. Sándor Büchler, *A zsidók története Budapesten* (Budapest, 1901); Kinga Frojimovics, Géza Komoróczy, Viktória Pusztai, and Andrea Strbik, eds., *Jewish Budapest: Monuments, Rites, History* (Budapest and New York, 1999); Alfréd Moess, *Pest megye és Pest-Buda zsidóságának demográfiája, 1749–1846* (Budapest, 1968).

21. Katzburg, *Hungariya*, 188.

22. This is the main theme of chapters 2 and 3 in this volume.

23. On this tendency, see Kati Vörös, "How Jewish Is Jewish Budapest?" *Jewish Social Studies* 8, no. 1 (2001): 90–93.

24. Bettina Hitzer and Joachim Schlör, "Introduction to God in the City: Religious Topographies in the Age of Urbanization," *Journal of Urban History* 37, no. 6 (2011): 820.

25. Richers, *Jüdisches Budapest*.

26. The seminal work of Miklós Konrád is a recent example of the thoroughgoing exploration of the extent, depth, and nuance of Jewish assimilation in Budapest. See, for example, Konrád, *Zsidóságon innen és túl. Zsidók vallásváltása Magyarországon a reformkortól az első világháborúig* (Budapest: BTK TTI, 2014); "Asszimilációs elvárások és zsidó válaszok az emancipációig" [Assimilationist Expectations and Jewish Responses until Emancipation], *Századok* 154, no. 5 (2020): 903–934; "Mixing with Meshumads: Social Relations between Jews and Converted Jews in Modern Hungary," in *Jewish Studies at the Central European University IX, 2017–2019*, ed. András Kovács, Michael L. Miller, and Carsten L. Wilke (Budapest: Jewish Studies Project of the Central European University, 2020), 25–42.

27. After Budapest, the next largest Jewish community in Hungary was Nagyvárad (today Oradea, Romania), which numbered approximately 18,000.

28. Ferenc Erdei, *Magyar Város* (Budapest: Akadémiai Kiadó, 1974), 26. Erdei distinguished *városiasodás* from the other dimension of urbanization—*városodás*, the numerical increase in the urban population.

29. Árpád Tóth, *Önszervező polgárok: a pesti egyesületek társadalom-története a reformkorban* [Self-Organizing Citizens: A Social History of Associations in Pest during the Reform Era] (Budapest, 2005), 9–10. The city's atypically large population and diversity challenged not only Jews, but other urban minorities, too. Protestant societies in Budapest, living in a predominantly Catholic city, faced a similar challenge of preserving their religious identity in the face of an enticing urban mainstream that was preeminently Catholic. Like

NOTES TO CHAPTER 2

Jews, Protestants focused on sociability, self-help, philanthropy, and education. Thus it is not surprising that the community-building efforts of Pest Jewry coincided with the period when other groups, too, were forming communal institutions in Pest, amid what Robert Nemes has characterized as "a mania for associations." Robert Nemes, *The Once and Future Budapest* (DeKalb: Northern Illinois University Press, 2005), 61–65. An older but still useful detailed survey of voluntary associations in Hungary is Sándor Matlekovics, *Magyarország közgazdasági és közművelődési állapota ezeréves fennállásakor*, vol. IX (Budapest, 1898).

30. Donald R. Morrison, "The Utopian Character of Plato's Ideal City," in *The Cambridge Companion to Plato's Republic*, ed. G. R. F. Ferrari (Cambridge and New York: Cambridge University Press, 2006), 233ff.

31. This epithet was based on II Samuel 20:19. When David's general Joab laid siege to and threatened to destroy the city of Abel bet-maaca, a woman from the city rebuked him, saying: "In olden times people used to say 'Let them inquire of Abel' and that was the end of the matter. I am one of those who seek the welfare of the faithful of Israel. But you seek to destroy a mother-city in Israel. Why should you destroy the Lord's possession?"

32. *Bereshit Rabba* 23:2.

33. On these two Yiddish expressions, see Zipperstein, *The Jews of Odessa*, 1; Scott Ury, "Lost and Found?: Jewish Historians, Jewish History, and Narrativization of Order in East European Cities," *AJS Review* 41, no. 1 (2017): 10. As Ury notes: "The study of the city has passed from a field that focuses on neighborhoods, ethnic communities, and urban conflict, to one that emphasizes the experiences of liminal individuals as well as the elusive but alluring ideal of urban cosmopolitanism. No longer bound by ethnic communities of fate and hate, the city has been reconceived as the definitive laboratory for societies in which strangers are able to transform and embody the very essence of (post) modernity."

34. The Dohány Street Synagogue is discussed in greater detail in chapter 5 in this volume.

35. Richers, *Judisches Budapest*, 341. Richers notes further: "The topographical appropriation of space proceeded in two distinctly discernible phases. The first was allotment of the Orczy house which was followed by expansion and founding of a Jewish quarter and eventually, by the mid 19th century, construction projects like the Dohany synagogue, Jewish hospital, Jewish orphanage, kosher public kitchens, Rombach synagogue and the rabbinical seminary. Second phase was organizations that had less common activities between Jews and non-Jews."

Chapter 2

1. J. Lipót Berger, "Az óbudai izraelita hitközség iskolájának monográfiája" [A Study of the Obuda Jewish Community School], in *A Magyar-Zsidó felekezet elemi és polgári iskoláinak monográfiája* [Monographs on the Elementary and High Schools of the Hungarian Jewish Denomination, hereinafter Barna and Csukási] I, ed. Jónás Barna and Fülöp Csukási (Buda-

pest: 1896), 245; Bernát Mandl, *Das Jüdische Schulwesen in Ungarn unter Kaiser Josef II (1780–1790)* (Posen: Merzbach Buchdrakerei, 1903), 15.

2. According to Nathaniel Katzburg, the Jewish population of Óbuda was 2,635 in 1803, 3,289 in 1828, 3,530 in 1840, 3,000 in 1848, 2,700 in 1850, 2,400 in 1869, 2,500 in 1880, 2,900 in 1890, 3,200 in 1900, and 3,700 in 1910. This meant a net increase of 1,065 and 40 percent in the span of 107 years. Katzburg, *Pinkas he-Kehilla: Hungariya* (Jerusalem: Yad Vashem, 1976), 132.

3. This was much like the situation on the estates of the great Latifundia in eastern Poland, where, since 1539, magnates had ruled with no intrusion from the royal crown. Adam Teller, "Radziwill, Rabinowicz, and the Rabbi of Swierz: The Magnates' Attitude to Jewish Regional Autonomy in the 18th Century," *Scripta Hierosolymitana* 38 (1998): 247.

4. R. J. W. Evans, *Austria, Hungary, and the Habsburgs: Central Europe c. 1683–1867* (Oxford: Oxford University Press, 2006), 179.

5. For the text of the royal patent from 1766, see Sámuel Kohn, "Az óbudai zsidó hitközség a múlt század közép felé," *MZsSz* VIII: 255–259. On the minimal differences between this patent and the Zichys' 1765 patent, see Gyula Klein, "Az Óbuda Izr. hitközség történetéhez," MZsSz (1891), 349, in which Klein notes: "1766 document is a word for word copy of a letter to the Jews dated January 1, 1765 and signed by Erzsébet Zichy. The two documents differ in that the Countess required 1260 for annual protection, and further, that the Jews had to pay 200 forints for the lord's birthday and name day, and for Easter and Szent Márton's day."

6. *Óbudai iratok* [Writings about Óbuda] I #86 (1788). Cited with permission of the Central Archive for the History of the Jewish People in Jerusalem.

7. See, for example, ibid., #93 and #234.

8. On Jews and the Zichy Estate during the first half of the eighteenth century, see Éva Gál, "Az Óbudai uradalom zsidósága a 18. században" [The Jews of the Óbuda Estate during the eighteenth century], *Századok* 126, no. 1 (1992): 3–28, especially 7–18.

9. Rebecca Gates-Coon, "18th Century Schutzherren: Esterhazy Patronage of the Jews," *Jewish Social Studies* 47, no. 3/4 (1985): 208.

10. Éva H. Balázs, *Hungary and the Habsburgs, 1765–1800: An Experiment in Enlightened Absolutism* (Tacoma: University of Washington, 1997); George Barany, *Stephen Széchenyi and the Awakening of Hungarian Nationalism, 1791–1841* (Princeton: Princeton University Press, 1968).

11. Historians of eighteenth-century Hungarian Jewry, by focusing almost exclusively on these more established Jewish communities of Transdanubia, concluded that Joseph II's Patent of Toleration introduced a singular moment of heretofore unprecedented opportunity for Hungarian Jews. See Gates-Coon, "18th Century *Schutzherren*," 189–208.

12. On the history of the Zichy family, see Iván Nagy, *Magyarország családai czimerekkel és nemzékrendi táblákkal* [The Families of Hungary with Coats of Arms and Genealogical Tables], vol. XII (Pest: Ráth Mór, 1868), 371–384, especially 379–381.

13. The text of Zichy's letter is in *Magyar Zsidó Oklevéltár* [hereinafter MZsO], VIII #364, 286–288.

14. On magnate-Jewish relations in Poland, see Adam Teller, *Money, Power, and Influence in Eighteenth Century Lithuania: The Jews of the Radziwill Estates* (Palo Alto, CA: Stanford University Press, 2016); Moshe J. Rosman, *The Lords' Jews: Magnate-Jewish Relations in the Polish-Lithuanian Commonwealth during the Eighteenth Century* (Cambridge, MA: Harvard University Press, 1990); and Gershon Hundert, *The Jews in a Polish Private Town: The Jews of Opatów* (Baltimore, MD: Johns Hopkins University Press, 2019); on Bohemia and Moravia, see Ruth Kesztenburg-Glatstein, *Neuere Geschichte der Juden in Böhmischen Landern, vol. I, 1780–1830* (Tubingen: Mohr Sieback, 1969); on Hungary, see Rebecca Gates-Coon, *The Landed Estates of the Eszterhazy Princes: Hungary during the Reforms of Maria Theresa and Joseph II* (Baltimore, MD: Johns Hopkins University Press, 1994); Éva Gál, *Az Óbudai uradalom a Zichyek földesurasága alatt, 1657–1766* (Budapest: Akadémiai Kiadó, 1998); Howard Lupovitch, *Jews at the Crossroads: Tradition and Accommodation during the Golden Age of the Hungarian Nobility, 1728–1878* (Budapest: CEU Press, 2007).

15. Gershon Hundert, *Jews in Poland-Lithuania in the Eighteenth Century: A Genealogy of Modernity* (Berkeley: University of California Press, 2004), 40.

16. MZsO VIII #364, p. 288.

17. MZsO VI/2 #429 (1716).

18. MZsO VIII #418, pp. 331–332 (1728).

19. MZsO III #34, pp. 59–62 (1714). Charles VI/III refers to the dual nature of the Habsburg monarchy, in which he was Charles VI as the Habsburg emperor and Charles III as the king of Hungary.

20. MZsO VIII #428, p. 347.

21. MZsO #1065, pp. 157/158 (1717).

22. MZsL VIII #1055, 147.

23. MZsO XII #171, pp. 200–201 (1728).

24. Éva Gál, "Zsidók Zsámbékon a 18. Században," *Évkönyv* (Magyar Izraeliták Országos Képviselete) [Yearbook of the Hungarian Israelite State Bureau] (Budapest, 1984), 7.

25. On Edelény, see Lupovitch, *Jews at the Crossroads*, 66.

26. MZsO VIII #456/7, pp. 382–383.

27. MZsL XI #1059, p. 107 (1741).

28. Gál, "Zsidók Zsámbékon," 149.

29. Lajos Nagy, *Budapest története III: a Török kiűzésétől a márciusi forradalomig* [The History of Budapest from the Expulsion of the Turks to the March Revolution] (Budapest: Akadémiai Kiadó, 1975), 87.

30. Ibid., 110.

31. Ibid., 103.

32. "Óbuda mezőváros földesura gr. Zichy Miklós által kiadott szabályzata" [The Statutes

Issued by Count Miklós Zichy, Lord of the Market Town of Óbuda], in *Források Buda, Pest, és Óbuda történetéhez* [Sources for the History of Buda, Pest, and Óbuda] *I, 1683–1873*, ed. Vera Bácskai (Budapest, 1971), 134–136.

33. MZsO V/2 #1050, p. 142 (1715).

34. Katzburg, *Pinkas ha-Kehillot*, 132.

35. Sándor Büchler, *A zsidók története Budapesten a legrégibb időktől 1867-ig* [The History of the Jews of Budapest Pest from Ancient Times until 1867] (Budapest, 1901), 269.

36. Büchler, *A zsidók története Budapesten a legrégibb időktől 1867-ig*, 273.

37. MZsO V/2 #462 Óbuda, pp. 753–755 (Sept. 29, 1737). This patent, though issued in the autumn of 1737, took effect on January 1, 1738.

38. Kohn, "Az óbudai zsidó hitközség a múlt század közép felé," MZsSz 8 (1891), pp. 255–259; the patent is discussed by Büchler on 281ff.

39. MZsO V/2 #462, p. 754.

40. Ibid., 755.

41. Katzburg, *Pinkas Ha-Kehilla*, 133.

42. The Kehilla leadership consisted of a presiding officer, three deputies, and three trustees (*Gabbaim*), who were elected annually by the membership of the community. Beyond the officer core, a council of elders met with the officers six times per year. When the first Kehilla board was elected is not entirely clear. One possibility can be inferred from a petition submitted by council member Majer Hazan in 1787, who petitioned the board for financial assistance due to "blindness and other physical difficulties," and asked the council to forgive his annual dues for three years, provide assistance to his daughter, and allocate funds to renovate his home. In response, the council awarded him 30 forints of assistance "in recognition of 35 years of faithful service," which suggests that the council had existed at least since 1752. *Pinkas Kehilat Kodesh Oben Yashan* (JTSA MS 8336, hereinafter *Pinkas Oben Yashan,*) folio 2, #30–31, cited with permission of the Jewish Theological Seminary of America; *Óbudai irtoki* [Writings about Óbuda] *I* #12 (1794); #167 (1787); II #27 (1809); *Óbuda iratok* II #99 (1787) (italics added). Cited with permission of the Jewish National Archive in Jerusalem.

43. MZsO V/2 #462 Óbuda, pp. 754–755 (Sept. 29, 1737).

44. *Pinkas Oben Yashan* folio 1 #3–4.

45. *Óbudai iratok* II #29 (1787).

46. *Óbudai iratok* VI #15 (1783).

47. Ibid., III #208 (1791).

48. Ibid., II #172 (1789).

49. Ibid., II #186 (1790).

50. Ibid., VI #9.

51. MZsO V/2 #462, p. 754.

52. *Óbudai iratok* II #209 (1791).

53. Büchler, *Budapest*, 281ff.
54. *Pinkas Oben Yashan*, folio 9 (1769).
55. Ibid., folio 10.
56. *Óbudai iratok* II #226 (1790).
57. Büchler, *Budapest*, 283–284. The *Schulklopfer* (lit. synagogue knocker) was the beadle/town crier who, in addition to reminding Jews to attend synagogue services, informed community members of the decisions of the Kehilla.
58. *Óbudai iratok* VI #21/4 (1788).
59. Ibid., IV #268 (1789).
60. *Óbudai iratok* III #13 (1783–1786).
61. Ibid., III #212 (Óbuda 1791).
62. Ibid., VI #29 (1784).
63. Ibid., VI #30 (Óbuda 1784).
64. Ibid., III #241 (1790).
65. *Pinkas Oben Yashan*, folio 10 #11.
66. *Óbudai iratok* III #21 (1784).
67. Katzburg, *Pinkas Ha-Kehilla*, 134; *Óbudai iratok* II #190.
68. Katzburg, *Pinkas Ha-Kehilla,* 134.
69. Mandl, *Jüdische Schulwesen*, 25. The Jewish communities that supported the school were in Vörösvár, Zsámbék, Tétény, Tinnye, Abony, Irsa, Chón, Dabas, Szele, Apostag, Aszód, Peczel, and Domony.
70. Berger, "Az óbudai izraelita hitközség iskolájának monográfiája," 248.
71. Mandl, *Jüdische Schulwesen,* 26–27.
72. *Óbudai iratok* II #191 (1790).
73. Ibid., II #194 (1790).
74. Ibid., #192 (1790).
75. Ibid., II #206 (1791), #4.
76. Berger, "Az óbudai izraelita hitközség iskolájának," 251.
77. *Óbuda iratok* II #232 (1791).
78. 1737 Patent #8; 1765 Patent #11.
79. 1737 Patent #7.
80. *Óbuda iratok* II #207 (1791).
81. See, for example, Gil S. Epstein, "The Political Economy of Kosher Wars," in *Jewish Society and Culture: An Economic Perspective*, ed. Carmel U. Chiswick, Tikvah Lecker, and Nava Kahana (Bar Ilan University Press, 2007), 158–160.
82. See, for example, BT *Pesachim* 101:a–b.
83. *Óbuda iratok* III #5 (1789).
84. Ibid., III #3 (1779).
85. Ibid., IV #292 (1786). In 1786, for example, the three licensees were Jacob Bineter, Manes

Watzon, and Mojses Lobl, who were the son or brother of a member of the Kehilla board.

86. See, for example, *Shulchan 'Aruch Yore De'a* 341:7.

87. The centrality of meat on the Sabbath as a well-established measure of Jewish status in East Central Europe was prevalent enough to be the main target of one of Judah Leib Gordon's scathing parodies of traditional Jewish society in his short story, *Kaf regel 'egel* [Leg of a Calf].

88. *Óbudai iratok* VI #10 (1790).

89. See, for example, *Óbudai iratok* III, #169 (1787), #182 (1781), #193 (1790).

90. Ibid., I #19 Óbuda (1776).

91. Ibid., II #278 (1789).

92. Pest Jews asserting their independence from the Jews of Óbuda is a subject of the next chapter.

93. *Óbudai iratok* #31 (1773).

94. Ibid., V/33 (1772) (italics mine).

95. *Óbudai iratok* V #39 (1768).

96. Ibid., II #190 (1790).

97. Ibid., III #213 (1791).

98. Ibid., II #213 (1791).

99. Ibid., II #203 (1790).

100. Ibid., II #234 (1790).

101. Ibid., II #185 (1790).

102. The specifics of Jewish access to Pest will be discussed in greater detail in the next chapter.

103. *Óbudai iratok* VI #26 (1784).

104. Ibid., II #165 (1787).

105. Ibid., III #290 (1790).

106. Ibid., III #247 (1788).

107. *Pinkas Oben Yashan*, Folio 12, #11.

108. John Anshel and Theodore Lavie, eds., *Pinkas ha-Kehillot: Romania* II (Jerusalem, 1980), 223.

109. The following discussion is based on correspondence between the Jews of Óbuda and Csenger, *Óbudai iratok* VI, #214–220 (1791).

Chapter 3

1. On Jews and market towns, see the sources cited in chapter 2.

2. Jacob Katz, *Tradition and Crisis: Jewish Society at the End of the Middle Ages*, rev. ed. (Syracuse: Syracuse University Press, 2000), 37–42. *Kehilla* (lit. community or congregation) and *Gemeinde* refer to the officially recognized Jewish community in a given locale, which was defined by the state as an autonomous corporation with juridical authority over its members; *Kultusgemeinde* (*hitközség* in Hungarian) refers to a Jewish community whose authority was truncated to cover ritual, education, and charity.

3. Stefanie Siegmund, "Communal Leaders (*rashei qahal*) and the Representation of Medieval and Early Modern Jews as Communities," in *Jewish Religious Leadership: Image and Reality*, vol. 1, ed. Jack Wertheimer (New York: Jewish Theological Seminary, 2004), 334.

4. *Monumenta Hungariae Judaica (Magyar Zsidó Oklevéltár)* XVI, p. 167.

5. Zsigmond Groszmann, "A pesti zsinagóga" [Synagogues of Pest], *Egyenlőség* (December 12, 1915), 13.

6. Nathaniel Katzburg, *Pinkas ha-Kehillot: Hungariya* (Tel Aviv, 1978), 191; Vera Bácskai, "A pesti zsidóság a 19. század első felében" [Pest Jewry during the first half of the nineteenth century], *Budapesti Negyed* 8, no. 2 (1995): 1. Note: Citations from this article are from the online version.

7. Vera Bácskai, "Budapest and Its Hinterland: The Development of Twin Cities, 1720–1850," in *Capital Cities and Their Hinterlands in Early Modern Europe, ed.* Peter Clark and Bernard Lepett (Aldershot, 1996), 185–187.

8. Béla Király, *Hungary in the Late Eighteenth Century: The Decline of Enlightened Absolutism* (New York: Columbia University Press, 1969), 45.

9. Other Jewish communities that increased this rapidly during the second half of the nineteenth century included Lodz and Warsaw. See, for example, François Guesnet, "Lodzer Juden im 19. Jahrhundert: Ihr Ort in einer multikulturellen Stadtgesellschaft," in *Annäherungen; Beiträge zur jüdischen Geschichte und Kultur in Mittel und Osteuropa*, ed. Stefi JerschWenzel and Günther Wartenberg (Leipzig, 2002), 3–4.

10. Albert Moess, *Pest Megye és Pest-Buda Zsidóságának Demográfiája, 1749–1846* (Budapest: 1968), 64. In 1787, 22,442 people lived in Pest; 75,520 lived there in 1840.

11. Moess, *Pest Megye és Pest-Buda*, 64–65. In 1799, 1,075 Jews lived in Pest; 3,987 lived there in 1823.

12. Vera Bácskai, "A pesti zsidóság a 19. század első felében" [Pest Jewry during the first half of the nineteenth century], *Budapesti Negyed* 8, no. 2 (1995): 1.

13. "Census of 1797," BFL Miscellenia #7105, Budapest Főváros Levéltára [Budapest Municipal Archive, hereinafter BFL] Intimata #6061. Cited with permission of the Budapest Főváros Levéltára.

14. Bácskai, "Budapest and Its Hinterland," 184–190.

15. Ibid., 188.

16. David Sorkin, "The Port Jews: Notes toward a New Social Type," *Journal of Jewish Studies* 50, no. 1 (1999): 88–95; Peter von Kessel and Elisja Schulte, eds., *Rome and Amsterdam: Two Growing Cities in Seventeenth Century Europe* (Ann Arbor, 1998), 5—6.

17. Lajos Nagy, *Budapest története a török kiűzésétől a márciusi forradalomig* [A History of Budapest from the Expulsion of the Turks to the March Revolution, hereinafter Nagy, *Budapest története*] (Budapest, 1975), 343–344.

18. For a brief overview of the checkered history of this institution, see Kinga Frojimovics et al., eds., *Jewish Budapest: Monuments, Rites, History* (Budapest, 1994), 70ff.

19. Bácskai, "A pesti zsidóság," 14; Moess, *Pest Megye*, 60.

20. Boüena Wyrozumski, "New Sources for the History of Cracow during the Middle Ages," in *Kroke-Kazimierz-Cracow: Studies in the History of Cracow Jewry*, ed. Elhanan Reiner (Tel Aviv, 2001), 30–31; Moshe Elijahu Gonda, *A debreceni zsidók száz éve* (Haifa, 1970), 47.

21. Lajos Nagy, "A Terézváros kialakulása" [The Establishment of Terézváros], *Tanulmányok Budapest Múltjából* (1956), 103.

22. Lajos Nagy, *Budapest története*, 60; Catherine Horel, *Histoire de Budapest* (Paris: Fayard, 1999), 70.

23. Nagy, *Budapest története*, 61.

24. Sándor Büchler, *A Zsidók története Budapesten a legrégibb időktől 1867-ig jelentkorig* [The History of the Jews of Budapest Pest from Ancient Times until 1867] (Budapest, 1901), 175.

25. Nagy, *Budapest története*, 435–438.

26. Géza Komoróczy, "Városképen, héber betűkből: bevezetés" [On City Images, Hebrew Characters], *Ami látható és ami láthatatlan: Erzsébetváros zsidó öröksége* [The Visible and the Invisible] (Budapest, 2018), 19.

27. "Die Hegemonie der Judische Gemeinde in Ungarn," *Ben Chananja* 18 (1861): 161.

28. Ibid., 177; Nagy, *Budapest története*, 439.

29. *Budapest története,* ibid., 397.

30. Ibid., 398.

31. Erica Lee, *At America's Gates: Chinese Immigration during the Exclusion Era, 1882–1943* (Chapel Hill and London, 2003), 192.

32. Paul Mendes-Flohr and Yehuda Reinharz, *The Jew in the Modern World* (Oxford, 1995), 18.

33. Benjamin Nathans, *Beyond the Pale: The Jewish Encounter with Late Imperial Russia* (Berkeley/Los Angeles/London: University of California Press, 2002), 114.

34. On the role of Podiacheskii as a hub of Jewish immigration, see Nathans, ibid., 117–118.

35. "City of Pest's 1703 Letter of Privilege," in *Források Buda, Pest, és Óbuda Történetéhez, 1686–1873* [Sources on the History of Buda, Pest, and Óbuda, 1686–1873], ed. Vera Bácskai (hereinafter Bácskai, *Források*), 32.

36. Ignácz Peisner, *Budapest a XVIII. században* [Budapest in the Eighteenth Century] (Budapest, 1900), 31.

37. Ibid., 31–32.

38. Komoróczy, "Városképen, héber betűkből: bevezetés," 21.

39. This incident is described in detail in Büchler, *A zsidók története Budapesten*, 337 passim, and is recapitulated in English in Frojimovics, *Jewish Budapest*, 69.

40. Nagy, *Budapest Története*, 116; Marta Bur, "A balkáni kereskedők és a magyar borkivitel a XVIII. században" [Balkan Merchants and the Hungarian Wine-Export in the Eighteenth Century], *Törtenelmi Szemle* 21, no. 2 (1978): 288ff. In eighteenth-century parlance, merchants from the Balkans were referred to colloquially, and imprecisely, as "Greek" in reference to the fact that they were Greek Orthodox Christians. "Greek" merchants included Serbs and Armenians. For this reason, I refer to them as Balkan merchants.

41. Lajos Nagy, *Budapest története* III, 120–121.

42. Ibid., 122.

43. Ibid., 123.

44. Peisner, *Budapest a XVIII században*, 123.

45. Bur, "A balkáni kereskedők," 293.

46. The Latin text of this patent was reprinted in *Magyar Zsidó Szemle* XIII (1896), 367–274, with an abridged translation in Hungarian on pp. 323–324.

47. Lajos Nagy, *Budapest története*, 396.

48. Lajos Nagy, *Budapest története*, 397.

49. Quoted in Büchler, *A Zsidók története Budapesten*, 346.

50. Bácskai, "A pesti zsidóság," 2.

51. Ibid., 3.

52. "Letter from Alexander Leopold to Francis I, November 13, 1792," in *Sándor Lipót főherceg Nádor iratai, 1790–95* [The Papers of Crown-Prince Palatine Alexander Leopold], ed. Elemér Mályusz (Budapest, 1926), 865.

53. Bácskai, "A pesti zsidóság," 4.

54. "Instruction from Palatine Joseph regarding the Military Exchequer's Oat-Exception" [zabkivétel], in *József Nádor élete és iratai* [The Life and Papers of Palatine Joseph], ed. Sándor Domanovszky, vol. II, 240: "Any impediments possible must be placed before the so-called *Kornjuden*, even stemming the flow of Jews." In 1805, Joseph would note in his diary that "Jews are among those who pass false bank notes while promising to bring more suitable coins into circulation," ibid., vol. III, 309. The initial complaints regarding forgery are in ibid., vol. II, 477–478.

55. On the history of the Zichy family, see Iván Nagy, *Magyarország családai czimerekkel és nemzékrendi táblákkal* [The Families of Hungary with Coats of Arms and Genealogical Tables], vol. XII (Pest: Ráth Mór, 1868), 371–384, especially 379–381; on the Orczy family, see ibid., vol. VIII, 291.

56. "Udvari konferencia jegyzőkönyv" (December 24, 1792), in Mályusz, *Sándor Lipót főherceg nádor iratai*, 299; ibid., 490.

57. Budapest Főváros Levéltára [Budapest Metropolitan Archive, hereinafter BFL], Intimata #6061; "Census of 1797," BFL Miscellenia #7105.

58. *Óbuda Lajsztromozatlan iratok (1801) #5.* The Jewish National and University Library, Jerusalem.

59. *Óbuda iratai* [Óbuda Documents], JUNL VI #43 (1784), and VII #99 (1788).

60. Ibid., VII #134 (1787).

61. Ibid., IX #261 (1792).

62. Ibid., IX #389 (1794).

63. Mályusz, *Sándor Lipót főherceg nádoriratai* [Documents of Palatine Alexander Leopold], 440 and 445.

64. Frojimovics, *Jewish Budapest*, 71–72.

65. *Óbudai Iratok* I #69 (1786).

66. Ibid., I #203 and #234 (1790).

67. Büchler, *Zsidók Budapesten*, 351.

68. Ibid., 348.

69. Bácskai, "A pesti zsidóság," 8.

70. Büchler, *Zsidók Budapesten*, 354.

71. "Pest *Burgerschaft* to Pest Magistrate" (August 17, 1814), BFL Intimata #6314.

72. "Pest *Burgerschaft* to Pest Magistrate" (June 16, 1817), BFL Intimata #6336.

73. "Census of 1799," BFL.

74. *Óbudai Iratok* XV #251 (1799).

75. Büchler, *Zsidók Budapesten*, 360.

76. Bácskai, "A pesti zsidóság," 9. Ironically, Ullmann's son Moses would spearhead the opposition of Pest Jews to a similar claim from a Vienna merchant.

77. BFL Intimata #6112 (1793); Moess, *Pest Megye*, 65.

78. Groszmann, "A Pesti zsinagóga," 13; Rudolf Klein, *The Great Synagogue of Budapest* (Budapest: TERC, 2008), 24–26.

79. *Pinkas de-Hevra Kadisha* [Minute Book of the Pest Hevra Kadisha], Pest Izraelita Hitközség [hereinafter PIH] I-Z-I Összeirátok, 1825–1869, 71/168. This source is cited with permission of the Hungarian Jewish Museum and Archive [Zsidó Levéltár] in Budapest.

80. István Csillag, "A régi pesti zsidókórhaz" [The Old Jewish Hospital in Pest], *Évkönyv: kiadja a Magyar Izraeliták Országos Képviselete* 78 (1977): 96.

81. Groszmann, "A pesti zsinagóga," 16.

82. "*Pinkas de-Hevra Kadisha*" [Minute Book of the Burial Society], Magyar Zsidó Levéltár HU PIH I-Z-2, second day of Hol ha-mo'ed pesach, 5564 (April 16, 1805). The Hebrew text: "פנקס דח"ק דק"ק פעסט נעשה ע"י אוביר גבאים דח"ק: ה"ה הקצין הר"ר יעקב בערלין, והתורני מוה"ר יוסף גלוגא נ"י וע"י אונטר גבאים ה"ה הר"ר אייזיק פעציל והר"ר אברם פאלאק והר"ר וואלף קן, בשנת תקס"ה לפ"ק"

83. Ibid., folio 3a.

84. Ibid., folio 5b.

85. Typical examples can be found in *Pinkas ha-Hevra Kadisha* (Pest, 1805), folio 6b, 9b; and in *Óbuda iratok* II #38 and IV #17.

86. J. David Bleich, "The *bet din*: An Institution Whose Time Had Returned," *Tradition: A Journal of Orthodox Jewish Thought* 27, no. 1 (1992): 58–59.

87. The following discussion draws from Büchler, *Zsidók Budapesten*, 371–391.

88. Büchler, *Zsidók Budapesten*, 376.

89. Ibid., 379.

90. Bernát Mandl, "A Pesti Izraelita hitközségi fiu-iskola monográfiája" [Monograph of the Pest Jewish Community's Boys School], in *A Magyar-Zsidó felekezet elemi és polgári iskoláinak monográfiája* [Monographs on the Elementary and High Schools of the Hungarian Jewish Denomination] I, ed. Jónás Barna and Fülöp Csukási (Budapest, 1896), 4–5.

91. Groszmann, "A pesti zsinagóga," 15.

92. Ibid., 16.

93. Quoted in Mandl, "A Pesti Izraelita hitközségi fiu-iskola monográfiája," 6–7.

94. Ibid., 9.

95. Ibid., 10. The members of the committee were Isaac Preisach, Lipót Rosenfeld, Abraham Koppel, Lipót Funk, Elkan Schindler, Gabriel Baruch, and Jacob Keppich.

96. Ibid., 11–12. "בית חנוך נעורים לתועלת ילדי בני ישראל"

97. Ibid., 15. These costs included 800 forints to lease the space, 300 for remodeling, 800 for head teacher Heller, 250 for assistant teacher Grunnagel, 125 for second assistant teacher Jacob, 120 for the Hungarian instructor, and 800 for three Hebrew teachers.

98. Ibid., 18–19.

99. Ibid., 16n1. The description is quoted in Solomon Judah Loeb Rapoport, *Bikkure Ha-'Ittim* (Prague, 1828).

100. There were ninety-nine first-graders, thirty-seven second-graders, twenty-one third-graders, and twenty-five fourth-graders.

101. Magyar Zsidó Levéltár *Szefer Zichronot* [*Gemeinde* Protocol] PIH-I-2-4 (1828); "A Kórus melyben Vázsonyi Vilmos énekelt," *Egyenlőség* (August 15, 1925): 7.

102. Most fatalities from cholera result from extreme dehydration. Eventually, physicians and other health care providers learned to treat cholera victims with rehydration solution with a combination of salt and sugar that would treat the disease effectively and minimize fatalities even where the number of afflicted was high.

103. Ágnes B. Lukács, *Az 1831–32. Évi Magyarországi kolerajárvány néhány jellegzetessége* [Some Characteristics of the 1831–32 Cholera Epidemic in Hungary], 99.

104. Ibid., 114–115.

105. Pest *Gemeinde* Protocols PIH-I-2-5 #32–34.

106. Komoróczy, "Városképen, héber betűkből: Bevezetés," 29.

107. *Reglement für die Pester Israeliten yur Werwaltung ihrer religosen und ökönomishcen, sie allein betreffenden Gegenstande un Geschafte* (Pest, 1832), "Introduction" #1, reprinted in *Ben Chananja* no. 22 (May 31, 1865): 362.

108. Ibid., "Introduction" #2.

109. Ibid., 364.

110. Ibid., Section IX #1.

111. Ibid., Section IX #3.

112. Ibid., Section II #3.

113. This will be discussed in greater detail in chapter 5 of this volume.

114. Mandl, "A Pesti Izraelita hitközségi fiu-iskola monográfiája," 17.

115. Komoróczy, "Városképen, héber betűkből: Bevezetés," 28. In October 1821, the Jews of Pest petitioned the royal crown to be defined as a community in order to deal more effectively with intracommunal conflicts.

116. Büchler, *Zsidók Budapesten*, 366.

Chapter 4

1. Quoted by Ármin Beregi in Oszkár Jászi et al., eds., *A zsidókérdés Magyarországon* [The Jewish Question in Hungary] (Budapest: Huszadik század, 1917), 51.

2. Jenő Erdődi, "A pesti nagy árvíz és a magyar zsidóság" [The Great Flood of Pest and Hungarian Jewry], *Egyenlőség* (February 24, 1938): 10; Zsigmond Groszmann, "A száz év előtti nagy árvíz" [The Great Flood a Hundred Years Ago], *Egyenlőség* (March 16, 1938): 18.

3. James Wilde, "The Boatman of the Deluge: Miklós Wesselényi and the 1838 Flooding of Pest," *Hungarian Studies: A Journal of the International Association for Hungarian Studies and Balassi Institute* 1 (2005): 44.

4. Meredith Dobbie, Ruth Morgan, and Lionel Frost, "Overcoming Abundance: Social Capital and Managing Floods in Inner Melbourne during the Nineteenth Century," *Journal of Urban History* 46, no. 1 (2020): 35.

5. Two collections of essays, in particular, are especially noteworthy in this regard. Károly Némethy, *A pest-budai árvíz 1838-ban* [The Flood in Pest-Buda in 1838] (Budapest, 1938), was published on the centennial of the Flood. The other is Tamás Faragó, ed., *Pest-budai árvíz 1938* (Budapest: Fővárosi Szabó Ervin Könyvtár, 1988), published on the sesquicentennial of the event.

6. Thomas Bender and Carl E. Schorske, "Introduction: Budapest and New York Compared," in *Budapest and New York: Studies in Metropolitan Transformation,* ed. Schorske and Bender (New York: Russell Sage Foundation, 1994), 1–2.

7. Sándor Büchler, *A zsidók története Budapesten a legrégibb időktől 1867-ig jelentkorig* [The History of the Jews of Budapest Pest from Ancient Times until 1867] (Budapest, 1901), 326.

8. Michael K. Silber, "Budapest," in *YIVO Encyclopedia of Jews in Eastern Europe I,* https://yivoencyclopedia.org/article.aspx/Budapest.

9. Julia Richers, *Jüdisches Budapest: Kulturelle Topographien einer Stadtgemeinde im 19. Jahrhundert* (Koln, Weimar, Wien: 2009), 120–121.

10. Andrew C. Janos, *The Politics of Backwardness in Hungary, 1825–1848* (Princeton: Princeton University Press, 1982), 55.

11. József Patachich, *Szabad Királyi Pest Városának Leírása* (Pest: 1830, reprinted by Pranava Books, India, 2017), 138–139.

12. "Aufruf zur Unterstützung der durch die Wassernoth am 13., 14., und 15. März Verungluckten zu Pesth," *Allgemeine Zeitung des Judenthums* no. 50 (April 20, 1838): 200.

13. "Aufruf zur Unterstützung der durch die Wassernoth," 201.

14. J. H. Kohn, *Yemei Tzara ve-Nehama/Schilderung der Schreckentage zu Alt-Ofen durch die verheerende Donau-Überschwimmung* (Ofen, 1838), quoted in József Schweitzer, "Héber nyelvű krónika az 1838.ik évi árvíz eseményeiről," in *Széfer Le-Kavod Marjovszky Tibor— Tanulmánykötet Marjovszky Tibor 50. évi születésnápja alkalmából* (Budapest: B & V Bt., 2003), 212–216; reprinted as "Zsidók a nagy pest-budai árvíz idején," in *Fórrasok és dokumentumok a zsidók történetéhez Magyarországon* (Budapest: MTA Judaisztikai Kutatóközpont, 2005), 92–93.

15. Groszmann, "A száz év előtti nagy árvíz," 18.
16. Baron Miklós Wesselényi, "*Áz 'árvízi hájós' naplójából*" [The Diary of the "Boatman of the Danube"], *Magyar irodalmi ritkaságok* [Hungarian Literary Curiosities] no. 40, ed. László Vajthó, 14. Wesselényi's response to the Flood is discussed below.
17. János Trattner, *Jégszakadás és a Duna kiáradása Magyarországban* (Buda, 1838), quoted in *Zsidók Budapesten* I, 84.
18. *Liszt Ferenc árvízi hangversenyei Bécsben 1838/9* (Budapest, 1941), 76.
19. Viktória Czaga and István Gajáry, "Árvízkárosultak Budán: Újlak és Orszagút társadalma," in Faragó, *Pest-budai árvíz 1938,* 133, 140.
20. Mária Kéringer Patkóné, "Pest megye és az 1838. évi árvíz," in Faragó, *Pest-budai árvíz 1938,* 271.
21. According to Vera Bácskai, 72 percent of Pest Jews lived in Terézváros in 1838, while 22 percent—mainly more affluent Jews—lived in Lipótváros. Bácskai, "Társadalmi Változások Pesten az 1830–1840-es Években," in Farago, *Pest-budai árvíz 1938,* 208. Bácskai listed the number of Jews in Pest, not including day laborers and menial workers (who were often living there illegally) as 2,009 in 1809, 3,092 in 1819, 4,602 in 1829, 6,686 in 1837, and 13,355 in 1845. Ibid., p. 236.
22. *Hazai és Külföldi Tudósítások* [Local and Foreign Dispatches] no. 4, Saint George, 1838; quoted in Erdődi, "A pesti nagy árvíz és a magyar zsidóság," 10. The same dispatch reported that Jewish wholesaler Joseph Boscovitz and his wife personally donated an additional 100 loaves of bread plus money and meat.
23. *Hírnök* [Herald] (May 10, 1838), quoted in ibid.
24. *Hírnök* (April 1838), quoted in ibid.
25. Ibid., 85.
26. Lajos Nagy, *Budapest története III: a Török kiűzésétől a márciusi forradalomig* [The History of Budapest from the Expulsion of the Turks to the March Revolution] (Budapest: Akadémiai Kiadó, 1975), 296–301.
27. Miklós Asztalos, "Áz árvíz története—a részvét," in Némethy, *A pest-budai árvíz 1838-ban,* 140.
28. Ibid., 141.
29. Ibid., 149.
30. Ibid., 133.
31. Quoted in ibid., 86.
32. Asztalos, "Áz árvíz története—a részvét," 134.
33. Mihály Pásztor, *A Százötven Éves Lipótváros* [Lipótváros at One Hundred and Fifty] (Budapest: Székesfőváros Házinyomdája, 1940), 135–136.
34. Széchenyi, *Hitel* [Credit] (Pest: J. M. Trattner & István Károly, 1830), 164; see also Endre Arató, "The Emergence of the Hungarian Bourgeois Concept of 'Nation-Homeland,'" in *Annales Universitatis Scientiarum Budapestinensis de Rolando Eötvös Nominatae Sectio Historica* 19 (1978): 51.

35. Széchenyi, *Vilag* [World] (Pest: Füstkuti Landerer Nyomtató Intézetében, 1831), 101, quoted in Gábor Preisich, "Széchenyi Érdemei Budapest Fejlesztésében," *Magyar Tudomány* 36, no. 8 (1991): 1023.
36. Antal Zichy, ed., *Grof István Széchenyi hílapi cikkei* [Journal Articles of Count István Széchencyi, hereinafter *Articles*] (Budapest, 1893), I, 9–10.
37. Quoted in Endre Kerkápoly, "Széchenyi István közlekedésfejlesztési programja," *Magyar Tudomány* 36, no. 8 (1991): 973.
38. Ibid., 1025.
39. Széchenyi, *Hitel*, 235.
40. Mór Jókai, *Kárpáthy Zoltán* I, 16.
41. Mór Jókai, "Budapesti élet," *Budapesti Negyed* 57 (2007): 15.
42. Wesselényi, *Balítéletekről*, 80.
43. Wilde, "The Boatman of the Deluge," 45.
44. "Széchenyi to Baron Georg Sina," in *Széchenyi Pesti Tervei* [Széchenyi's Conceptions of Pest], ed. Vera Bácskai and Lajos Nagy, #73 (Budapest: Szépirodalmi könyvkiadó, 1985).
45. Ibid., #75.
46. Bertalan Szemere, "Pest jövendőjéről" [On the Future of Pest] (Budapest, 1840), 281.
47. Ibid., 283.
48. Ibid., 284.
49. Maté Tamáska, "The Industrialization of the Danube Cityscape: Danube Ports during the Concurrent Urban Development of Vienna and Budapest, 1829–1918," *Zeitschrift für Ostmitteleuropa Forschung* 67, no. 4 (2018): 556–557.
50. Szemere, "Pest jövendőjéről."
51. On Hungarian liberalism and England, Joshua Toulmin Smith, *Parallels between Constitution and Constitutional History of England and Hungary* (Boston: Ticknor, Reed, and Fields, 1851), 26.
52. "Az angol nemzet egyenjogúsíthatta a zsidó fajt. Mert ha például én egy palack tintát töltök egy nagy tóba, azért annak a vize nem romlik el és mindenki ártalom nélkül megihatja. A nagy angol elemben a zsidó elvegyülhet. Ugyanez áll Franciaországra nézve is. De ha a magyar levesbe az ember egy palack tintát önt, megromlik a leves és azt nem eheti meg az ember." Quoted in George Barany, "Magyar Jew or Jewish Magyar?"
53. Voltaire, "Letter VI: On the Presbyterians," *Letters on England* (1733), quoted online at https://www.gutenberg.org/files/2445/2445-h/2445-h.htm.
54. Quoted in Howard Lupovitch, *Jews at the Crossroads: The Expansion and Development of Traditional Jewish Society during the Golden Age of the Hungarian Nobility* (Budapest: CEU Press, 2007), 179–180.
55. Büchler, *A zsidók története Budapesten*, 429; Nathaniel Katzburg, "The Public Debate over Jewish Emancipation in Hungary during the 1840s" (Hebrew), *Bar Ilan Annual* 1 (1973): 285–287.

56. Law 15 of 1840, #54 and #56; #55 enumerated a complete list of days on which observant Jews were prohibited from engaging in business: "The list of holidays includes: Passover, Pentecost (*shavu'os*), Rosh Hashana ('usually in the month of St. Michael'), Yom Kippur, sukkot ('*Lauberhutten*, in the month of All Saints'), *shmini azeres* [*sic*], simchas tora [*sic*]."

57. Katzburg, "Public Debate," 288.

58. See Büchler, A *zsidók Budapesten,* 433; Nathaniel Katzburg, *Pinkas Ha-Kehilla: Hungariya* (Jerusalem: Yad Vashem, 1976), 22; Silber, "Budapest."

59. Katzburg, *Hungariya,* 192.

60. Géza Komoróczy, "Városképen, héber betűkből: bevezetés," *Ami látható és ami láthatatlan: Erzsébetváros zsidó öröksége* [What Is Visible and What Is Invisible] (Budapest, 2018), 26.

61. Komoróczy, "Városképen, héber betűkből: bevezetés," 27; *Pesti Divatlap* (April 22, 1848), 2.

62. Quoted in Komoróczy, "Városképen, héber betűkből: bevezetés," 28.

63. Ibid., 193.

64. On the "Jew Bill" see Robert Liberles, "The Jews and Their Bill: Jewish Motivations in the Controversy of 1753," *Jewish History* 2, no. 2 (1987): 29–36; Liberles, "From Toleration to '*Verbesserung*': German and English Debates on the Jews in the Eighteenth Century," *Central European History* 22, no. 1 (1989): 5–9.

65. Ágnes Deák, *From Habsburg Neo-Absolutism to the Compromise, 1849–1867* (Boulder, CO: Social Science Monographs, 2008), 127–128. Deák concluded: "Despite Vienna's centralizing intentions, the railway lines developed in a radial system in keeping with the central position of Pest-Buda, which corresponded to plans originally drafted in the Reform Era."

66. Károly Vörös, *Budapest Története IV: A Márciusi Forradalomtól az Őszirózsás Forradalomig* (Budapest: Akedémiai Kiadó, 1978), 135–138.

67. Ibid., 198; see also Richers, *Jüdisches Budapest,* 241–243.

68. Deák, *From Habsburg Neo-Absolutism to the Compromise,* 335.

Chapter 5

1. *The Jewish Chronicle,* January 14, 1898; reprinted in *Die Welt,* July 8, 1904.

2. A good recent biography on Herzl is Derek Penslar, *Theodore Herzl: The Charismatic Leader* (New Haven: Yale University Press, 2020); on the Pest Jewish Triangle, see Kinga Frojimovics, Géza Komoroczy, Viktória Pusztai, and Andrea Strbik, eds., *A zsidó Budapest: a város arcai* I (Budapest: MTA Judaisztikai Kutatócsoport, 1995), 148.

3. See my recent article on Neolog: Howard Lupovitch, "Neolog: Reforming Judaism in a Hungarian Milieu," *Modern Judaism* 40, no. 3 (2020): 329–330.

4. Ferenc Laczó, "Dual Identities: The Israelite Hungarian Literary Society, 1929–1943," *Jewish Studies at the Central European University* 7 (2009–2011): 127–145.

5. Mack Walker, *German Home Towns: Community, Estate, and General Estate, 1648–1871* (Ithaca, NY: Cornell University Press, 1998), 33.

6. In this sense, the situation in Budapest was comparable to Kiev and Warsaw, which were also

situated in close proximity to numerous small-town and village Jews who, aided by improved transportation, more easily made their way to the big city.

7. *Óbudai iratok* II/102 lists more than thirty Jewish communities in Pest County that paid the Toleration Tax in 1805. Nathaniel Katzburg provides population figures for many of these communities in Katzburg, *Pinkas Ha-Kehilla: Hungariya* (Jerusalem: Yad Vashem, 1976), 125 passim.

8. *Első magyar zsidó naptár és évkönyv 1848-ik szökőévre* [The First Hungarian Jewish Almanac and Yearbook for the Leap Year 1848, hereinafter *Első magyar zsidó naptár és évkönyv*] (Pest: Landerer and Heckenastnál, 1848), 140; the exact figures are 3,270 families and a total of 16,370 people.

9. Jewish occupations listed in the 1848 census include oil producers, brewers, glue makers, cigar makers, quill makers, matchstick makers, florists, apothecaries, mover, managers, bookkeepers/accountants, shop assistants, peddlers, pawnbrokers, grocers, fishmongers, day laborers, porters, artisans, rabbis and assistants, preachers, choir members, slaughterers, scribes/notaries, physicians, butchers, dentists, midwives, chiropodist, photographers, drawing teachers, calligrapher, musicians, minstrels, editors, teachers, dance masters, dry cleaners, innkeeper, domestic servants, and nannies.

10. "In-migrants," per Vera Bácskai, refers to those who migrate within a particular state, that is, without crossing a state boundary.

11. Károly Vörös, "A budapesti zsidóság két forradalom között, 1848–1918," *Zsidóság a dualizmus kori Magyarországon*, ed. Varga László (Budapest: Pannonia Kiadó, 2005), 41.

12. Katzburg, *Pinkas Ha-kehilla*, 188; *Első Magyar Zsidó Naptár és Évkönyv 1848-ik Szökőévre*, 124.

13. See Julia Richers, *Jüdisches Budapest: Kulturelle Topographien einer Stadtgemeinde im 19. Jahrhundert* (Koln, Weimar, Wien, 2009), 238–240.

14. Mihály Pásztor, *A százötven éves Lipótváros* (Statisztikai közlemények) (Budapest: Székesfővárosi házinyomdája, 1940), 50, 119. After the Flood, for example, the highest yearly rent in Lipótváros was 500 forints.

15. Michael K. Silber, "Budapest," in *YIVO Encyclopedia of the Jews in Eastern Europe,* https://yivoencyclopedia.org/article.aspx/Budapest

16. 1865 Statutes. Level 2 members paid 25 forints, Level 3 paid 40, and Level 4 paid 60. On the 1832 categories, see above p. 121.

17. See, for example, *Szefer Zichronot* [Gemeinde Protocol] PIH-I-2-4 *Zsidó Levéltár* [hereinafter PIH] #6 (1829); #11 (1830); #4 (1831).

18. 1832 Statutes #4.

19. Ibid., Part II–Part IX.

20. See, for example, *Szefer Zichronot* [Gemeinde Protocol] PIH- I-C-2 Magyar *Zsidó Levéltár* [hereinafter PIH] #35 (1843); #18 (1844); #28 (1846).

21. Vera Bácskai, *A vállalkozók előfutárai: Nagykereskedők a reformkori Pesten* (Budapest, 1989), 144–148; Michael K. Silber, "Ullmann Family," in *YIVO Encyclopedia of the Jews in Eastern*

Europe, https://yivoencyclopedia.org/article.aspx/Ullmann_Family. Literally a derivation of a Hebrew word meaning relationship, the meaning of this term was aptly characterized a decade ago by one historian as "a prestigious trait that could be acquired through marriage based on scholarly merit, wealth, or political status (i.e., holders of rabbinical or communal offices)," that is, a combination of affluence, education, and familial and political connections. See ChaeRon Freeze, "Yikhes," *YIVO Encyclopedia of Jews in Eastern Europe*, https://yivoencyclopedia.org/article.aspx/Yikhes (accessed May 27, 2020).

22. 1832 Statutes XIV–XV.

23. 1865 Statutes #3, #5.

24. 1865 Statutes #11–#16.

25. 1832 Statutes I; 1865 Statutes I–II.

26. Árpád Tóth, "Voluntary Society as Power Agency in Mid-Nineteenth-Century Pest: Urbanization and the Changing Distribution of Power," in *Who Ran the Cities? City Elites and Urban Power Structures in Europe and North America, 1700–2000*, ed. Robert Beachy and Ralf Roth (Aldershot: Ashgate, 2007); Robert Nemes, *The Once and Future Budapest* (DeKalb: Northern Illinois University Press, 2005); Tóth, *Önszervező polgárok: A Pesti egyesületek társadalomtörténete a reformkorban* (Budapest: L'Harmattan, 2005); Tóth, "Asszimilációs utak a késő rendi társadaomban: a Zsidóság szerepvállalásáról a reformkori pesti egyesületekben," 173–177.

27. Tóth, "Voluntary Society as Power Agency in Mid-Nineteenth-Century Pest," 179–181; Nemes, *The Once and Future Budapest*; Jacob Katz, *Tradition and Crisis: Jewish Society at the End of the Middle Ages* (Syracuse, NY: Syracuse University Press, 2000), 17–19.

28. See Howard Lupovitch, *Jews at the Crossroads: Tradition and Accommodation during the Golden Age of the Hungarian Nobility* (Budapest: CEU Press, 2007), ch. 3.

29. *Első magyar zsidó naptár és évkönyv*, 132.

30. *Első magyar zsidó naptár és évkönyv*, 131.

31. Ibid., 132.

32. Ibid., 133–134.

33. Joseph Vincesz Haufler, *Buda-Pest: Historisch-Topographische Skizzen von Ofen und Pest und deren Umgebungen: Mit Chromolithographirten Planen von Ofen und Pest und deren Umgebungen Sammt 12 Ansichten und Mehreren Historischen Illustrationen* (Pest: Verlag v Gustav, 1854), 178–179. An ophthalmology unit was added in 1863. Hungarian queen Erzsébet visited in 1884. The hospital moved to Aréna út in 1886.

34. *Első magyar zsidó naptár és évkönyv*, 134.

35. Quoted in István Csillag, "A régi pesti zsidókórhaz" [The Old Jewish Hospital in Pest], *Évkönyv: kiadja Magyar Izraeliták Országos Képviselete* 78 (1977): 96.

36. See Henrik Hollán, *A Rókus kórház története: adatok és személynevek a Szent Rókus közkórház és fiókjai alapításának és fejlődésének történetéből* [The History of the Saint Rókus Hospital: Documents and Personalities from the History of the Saint Rókus Public Hos-

pital and the Establishment and Development of Its Progeny], 27. On Semmelweis, see "Semmelweis Ignác," *Budapest Lexikon II* (Budapest: Akadémiai kiadó, 2007), 394–395.

37. Zsigmond Groszmann, "A régi pesti zsidókórház," *Egyenlőség*, May 6, 1933, p. 30.

38. Ibid., 31. The 353 patients admitted and treated in 1851, for example, ranged from two to ninety years old. The average stay was eighteen days, and the average cost per patient was 41 forints.

39. Ibid., 32.

40. Ibid., 33–34.

41. Ibid., 36.

42. Ibid., 36.

43. PIH #8 (1845); #22 (1846).

44. Groszmann, "A régi pesti zsidókórház," 37.

45. J. Lipót Berger, "Az óbudai izraelita hitközség iskolájának monográfiája" [A Study of the Óbuda Jewish Community School], in *A Magyar-Zsidó felekezet elemi és polgári iskoláinak monográfiája, ed.* Jónás Barna and Fülöp Csukási (Budapest, 1896), 245–259; Bernát Mandl, "A Pesti izr. hitközségi fiu-iskola monográfiája," in *A Magyar-Zsidó felekezet elemi és polgári iskoláinak monográfiaja,* ed. Jónás Barna and Fülöp Csukási (Budapest, 1896), 1–112.

46. József Patachich, *Szabad Királyi Pest Városának Leírása* (Pest: 1830, reprinted by Pranava Books, India, 2017), 32. In 1847, eleven Jewish girls attended a boarding and finishing school that had been set up in Pest for indigent girls in response to concerns regarding widespread impoverishment.

47. Eszter Götz, "Bóherek az Erzsébetvárosban," *Látható,* 56–57.

48. Mandl, "A Pesti izr. hitközségi fiu-iskola monográfiája," 34. Eight hours/week were allotted for Hungarian and Hebrew during the second half of the first grade, twelve hours/week during the second grade, eleven hours/week during the third grade, and three hours/week during the fourth grade.

49. PIH 1843 #6.

50. Mandl, "A Pesti izr. hitközségi fiu-iskola monográfiája," 40.

51. Ibid., 41–42.

52. See, for example, Ágnes Deák, *From Habsburg Neo-Absolutism to the Compromise* (New York: East European Monographs, Columbia University Press, 2009).

53. *Budapest Története* III, p. 330.

54. *Pester Lloyd*, March 4, 1850, p. 3.

55. Deák, *From Habsburg Neo-Absolutism,* 112ff.

56. Lajos Nagy, *Budapest Története III: a Török kiűzésétől a márciusi forradalomig* [The History of Budapest from the Expulsion of the Turks to the March Revolution] (Budapest: Akadémiai Kiadó, 1975), 335, 373 n. 33.

57. *Erstes Programm der Pester isr. haupt-u. Unterrealschul für Schuljahr 1856* (Pest: 1856), 29–30; Mándl, "A Pesti izr. hitközségi fiu-iskola monográfiaja," 45–47.

58. *Erstes Programm*, 40.

59. Ibid., 44.

60. Götz, "Bóherek az Erzsébetvárosban," 57; Lupovitch, *Jews at the Crossroads,* 164.

61. Götz, "Bóherek az Erzsébetvárosban," 347.

62. Pál Sándor, *Deák Ferenc kiadatlan leveleiből* (Budapest, 1992), 97–98.

63. Géza Komoróczy, "Városképen, héber betűkből: bevezetés," *Ami látható és ami láthatatlan: Erzsébetváros zsidó öröksége* [What Is Visible and What Is Invisible: The Jewish Heritage of Erzsébetváros] (Budapest, 2018), 27–28.

64. Mandl, "A Pesti izr. hitközségi fiu-iskola monográfiája," 72.

65. Zsigmond Groszmann, "A Pesti zsinagóga," *Egyenlőség*, December 12, 1915, p. 15.

66. Michael K. Silber, "The Social Composition of the Pest Radical Reform Society ('Genossenschaft für Reform im Judenthum'), 1848–1852," *Jewish Social Studies* 1, no. 3 (1995): 102–104.

67. Béla Bernstein, *A negyvennyolcas magyar szabadságharc és a magyar zsidók* (Budapest: Múlt és jövő Kiadó, 1998), 141.

68. Komoróczy, "Városképen, héber betűkből: bevezetés," 27–28.

69. Kálmán, "A Dohány utcai zsinagóga és orgonája építése, felújitása," *A Dohany utcai Zsinagóga 150 éve* (Gabbiano Print Nyomda és Kiadó, 2010), 67, 70. By comparison, the cost of the Leopoldstadter Temple in Vienna was more than 360,000 Austrian gülden, and the concurrent construction of an additional wing cost nearly an additional 65,000 gülden. Supplemental construction in 1862 added more than 70,000 gülden to the total cost. This massive sum was amassed though the annual sale of redeemable Temple bonds (*Tempel-Anleihen*), donations from community members, and a loan from Anselm Freiherr von Rothschild. "Original-Akten der IKG Wien," in *Jerusalem und Jüdische Zeitschriften. H. D. Karplus: "Der Leopoldstädter Tempel"* (The Central Archives for the History of the Jewish People).

70. "Napihírek és események," *Budapesti Hírlap,* Dec. 29, 1858, p. 2; *Kalauz*, Jan. 1, 1859, p. 16; see also Dénes Komárik, "A Dohány utcai zsinagóga építése," *Budapesti Negyed* 8 (1995/2). My thanks to Gábor Dombi for bringing these sources to my attention.

71. On sales of synagogue seats, see, for example, *Pest Izraelita hitközség jegyzőkönyve*, 1853/4, p. 248, #93–97. PIH I-Z-I 20236.

72. Charles Kecskeméti, *La Hongrie des Habsburg Vol. II: From 1790 to 1914* (Rennes: Presses Universitaires de Rennes, 2011), 205.

73. The construction of great synagogues in other major cities similarly took place at a time of wealth, security, and self-confidence. See Saskia Coenen Snyder, *Building a Public Judaism: Synagogues and Jewish Identity in Nineteenth-Century Europe* (Cambridge: Harvard University Press, 2013), 29–31 (Berlin), 211–214 (Paris).

74. Richers, *Jüdisches Budapest*, 233.

75. Snyder, *Building a Public Judaism*, 29–31 (Berlin), 211–214 (Paris).

76. Carsten Wilke, "Building the Great Synagogue of Pest: Moorish Revival Architecture and the European-Ottoman Alliance in the Crimean War," *Jewish Quarterly Review* III/3 (2021): 445.

77. Ludwig Forster, *Allgemeine Bauzeitung mit Abbildung* (1859), 3–6.

78. *Pester Lloyd,* May 8, 1863, p. 3.

79. *Magyar Sajtó,* May 11, 1863, p. 2.

80. Wilke, "Building the Great Synagogue of Pest," 444.

81. Dénes Komárik, "A Dohány utcai templom épitése," op. cit. *Zsidók Budapesten* I, 33–36.

82. Wilke, "Building the Great Synagogue of Pest," 448.

83. Vörös, "A budapesti zsidóság két forradalom között, 1848–1918," 46.

84. 1865 Statutes, #1–2.

85. Ibid., #4.

86. Ibid., #59.

87. PIH #11 (1869).

88. Groszmann, *Régi Zsinagóga,* 16–17.

89. On this, see the essays collected in Moshe Carmilly-Weinberger, ed., *The Rabbinical Seminary of Budapest, 1877–1977* (New York: Hermon Press, 1986).

Chapter 6

1. Illés Kaczér, *Ne félj szolgám Jákob* [Fear not My Servant Jacob], trans. Lawrence Wolfe (New York, 1953), 26–29; Mátyás Eisler, "A női és a zsidó egyéniség" [Women's and Jewish Character], *Izraelita Magyar Irodalmi Társulat* VIII (1907): 341.

2. This chapters draws on Julia Richers, "Der Pester israelitische Frauenverein," in Richers, *Judisches Budapest: Kulturelle Topographien einer Stadtgemeinde im 19. Jahrhundert* (Koln, Weimar, Wien, 2009), 303–332.

3. Julia Richers, "Johanna Bischitz, Katalin Gerő, and Budapest's Jewish Women's Association (1866–1943)," in *Gender, Memory, and Judaism*, ed. Judit Gazsi, Andrea Pető, and Zsuzsana Toronyi (Budapest: Balassi Kiadó, 2007), 129–130; on women and mainstream society generally see Marion Kaplan, "Tradition and Transition—The Acculturation, Assimilation, and Integration of Jews in Imperial Germany: A Gender Analysis," *Leo Baeck Institute Yearbook* 27 (1982): 3–26; Paula Hyman, *Gender and Assimilation in Modern Jewish History: The Roles and Representations of Women* (Tacoma: University of Washington Press, 1995).

4. Péter Hanák, "Polgárosodás és urbanizáció: Polgári lakáskultúra Budapesten a 19. Században" [*Embourgoisement* and Urbanization: Middle-Class Housing Culture in Nineteenth-Century Budapest], *Történelmi szemle* 27, no. 1–2 (1984): 127–128.

5. József Kőrösi, *Budapest főváros statisztikai havifüzetei kiadja Budapest székesfőváros statisztikai hivatala* (Budapest: 1881), quoted in Károly Vörös, "A budapesti zsidóság két forradalom között, 1849–1918," in *Zsidóság a dualizmus kori Magyarországon*, ed. László Varga (Pannonia Kiadó, 2005), 47.

6. Ibid., 47–48.

7. Ibid., 48–49.

8. László Varga, "Manfréd Weiss: The Profile of a Munitions King," in *Jews in the Hungarian Economy, 1760–1945: Studies Dedicated to Moshe Carmilly-Weinberger*, ed. Michael K. Silber (Jerusalem: Magnes Press, 1992), 196ff.

9. William O. McCagg, "The Role of the Magyar Nobility in Modern Jewish History," *East European Quarterly* 20, no. 1 (1986): 41–53; McCagg, *Jewish Nobles and Geniuses in Modern Hungary* (New York: Columbia University Press, 1972).

10. Richers, *Jüdisches Budapest*, 208.

11. Miklós Konrád, "Csalódott zsidók a magyar zsidóság aranykorában," in *Az érzelmek törté-nete,* ed. Anikó Lukács and Árpád Tóth (Budapest: Hajnal István Kör–Társadalomtörténeti Egyesület, 2019), 407–408.

12. Beth S. Wenger, "Jewish Women and Volunteerism: Beyond the Myth of Enablers," *American Jewish History* 79, no. 1 (1989): 16–17.

13. Ibid., 18. For further references on the division between public and private in Jewish communal life, see Wenger, "Jewish Women and Volunteerism," 18, n. 2; and Deborah Hertz's response to Dagmar Herzog, "Ethnic and Gender History Together: A Comment," *LBI Year Book* XLVI (2001).

14. Paula Hyman, "Culture and Gender: Women in the Immigrant Jewish Community," in *The Legacy of Jewish Immigration: 1881 and Its Impact* (hereinafter Hyman, "Culture and Gender"), ed. David Berger (New York, 1983) p. 158. Hyman's observations regarding the role of gender in the identity of first- and second-generation American Jews is a useful model for Hungarian Jews, many of whom were similarly first- and second-generation immigrants and entering the middle classes.

15. See Nathaniel Katzburg, *Pinkas ha-Kehillot: Hungariya* (Jerusalem: Yad Vashem, 1976). Even a casual glance through Nathaniel Katzburg's compendium of Hungarian Jewish communities finds a women's association in more than three-quarters of the communities included in this work. There are studies of individual women's societies, mainly as part of a jubilee or centennial celebrations. While virtually devoid of analysis, these works are an indispensable source, since the protocols on which they were based are rarely extant.

16. On the Judische Frauenverein in Vienna, see Marsha Rozenblit, *The Jews of Vienna, 1867–1914: Assimilation and Identity* (New York: SUNY Press, 1984), 183ff; Alison Rose, *Jewish Women in Fin de Siecle Vienna* (Austin: University of Texas Press, 2010), especially 53–54, 96–98, 230–232; and Elisabeth Malleier, *Jüdische Frauen in Wien 1816–1938* (Vienna: Wohlfahrt–Mädchenbildung–Frauenarbeit, 2003), 50ff; Katalin Gerő, *A szeretet munká-sai: A Pesti Izraelita nőegylet története, 1867–1937* [The Loving Works of the Pest Israelite Women's Society, 1867–1937] (hereinafter Gerő, *Pesti Nőegylet*) (Budapest, 1937), and Gerő's memoir, *Erfülltes Leben* (Leipzig, 1933).

17. Árpád Tóth, "A társadalmi szerveződés polgári és rendi normái: a pesti jótékony nőegylet

története 1817–1847" [The Civic and Operational Norms of a Social Organization: The History of the Pest Women's Association, 1817–1847], *FONS* 4 (1998): 425.

18. For a brief sketch of the PIN and its leadership and activities, see Richers, "Johanna Bischitz, Katalin Gerő, and Budapest's Jewish Women's Association," 123–141.

19. Gerő, *Pesti Nőegylet*. This work was written on the seventieth anniversary of the founding of the organization. While not citing sources, the author's main sources of information were the minutes of the weekly meetings.

20. Anna Perczel, "Az egyleti élet: egykor 'civil kezdeményezések,'" in *Ami látható*, p. 66.

21. Ibid., 79–81.

22. In many communities, weekly minutes were preserved in manuscript and sometimes published in some form or another, making it possible to get an inside look at these associations. As with much of historical literature, the most thorough examination of these minute books to date has been of German Jewish women's associations. See Maria Baader, "When Judaism Turned Bourgeois: Gender in Jewish Associational Life and in the Synagogue, 1750–1850," *Leo Baeck Institute Year Book* [Great Britain] 46 (2001): 113–123.

23. Perczel, "Az egylet élet: egykor 'civil kezdeményezések,'" SAME AS ABOVE 66; Perczel, *Védetlen Örökség: Lakóházak a zsidó negyedben* [Unprotected Heritage: Residential Buildings in the Jewish Quarter] (Budapest: Nemzeti Kulturális Alap, 2007), 52–53.

24. *Pester Lloyd,* October 7, 1867, p. 3; quoted in Gerő, *Pesti Nőegylet*, 29. The event also included a speech by Chief Rabbi Jacob Meisel, a performance by the cantor and choir, and a Hungarian language prayer composed and read by Rabbi Samuel Kohn.

25. The orphanage was bilingually named Pest Izraelita nőegylet leányárvaház and Madchenwaserhaus des Pesten Israelitische Frauenverein. Ibid., 25.

26. Gerő, *Pesti nőegylet*, 101.

27. Richers, "Johanna Bischitz," 127–128.

28. Gerő, *Pesti nőegylet*, 61.

29. Ibid., 129ff.

30. Gerhard Melinz and Susan Zimmermann, "Armenfürsorge, Kinderschutz, and Sozialreform in Budapest und Wien, 1870–1914," *Geschichte und Gesellschaft* 21 (1995): 340.

31. Ibid., 345.

32. Gerő, *Pesti nőegylet*, 85–86.

33. Ibid., 100.

34. Ibid., 189.

35. See, for example, Gerő, *Pesti nőegylet*, 96.

36. Moses Isserles on *Shulchan 'Aruch Orach Hayim* 282:3; *Babylonian Talmud Kiddushin* 34:a.

37. István Deák, "Chivalry, Gentlemanly Honor, and Virtuous Ladies in Austria-Hungary," *Austrian History Yearbook* XXV (1994): 3.

38. I am relying on the comprehensive study by Andor Máday, *A magyar nő jogaia múltban és jelenben* [The Rights of the Hungarian Woman in the Past and Present, hereinafter Máday,

Magyar Nő] (Budapest, 1913). The quote is from p. 53. According to Máday, "spiritual needs" referred both to religious as well as emotional needs. The *Tripartitum* was a massive compilation of laws given royal approval in 1608 by the Hungarian Diet. It remained the basis for subsequent legislation for more than two centuries.

39. Ibid., 52. This had particular significance with regard to the legal status of the clergy. As Máday points out, when noble privilege, which had been enjoyed by Roman Catholic bishops since the Middle Ages, was extended to Greek Catholic bishops, their wives were automatically considered noblewomen.

40. Ibid., 63.

41. Ibid., 92.

42. Ibid., 93.

43. Máday, *Magyar Nő*, 28.

44. Ibid., 137–138. Máday lists more than a dozen such pamphlets. Two initial pamphlets—"A Short Description of the Good Wife: The Most Cherished Treasure in the World," published in 1780, and "A Proof That Female Individuals Are Not People," which appeared in 1783—prompted a response in 1785 under the pseudonym Anna Carberi entitled "That Female Individuals Are People."

45. Ibid., 139.

46. Ibid., 139; see also Katalin Fehér, "Reformkori sajtóviták a nők művelődésének kédéséről" [Reform-Era Debates in the Press on the Question of Women's Education, hereinafter Fehér, "Reformkori sajtóviták"], *Magyar Könyvszemle* III, no. 3 (1995): 247.

47. János Fejes, *Die ungarische Staatsbürgerinn; ihre Pflichten und Rechte nach den ungarischen Gesetzen dargestelle* (Pest, 1812), quoted in Máday, *Magyar Nő*, 140–141.

48. Ibid., 141.

49. Joan Kelly, "Did Women Have a Renaissance?" *Women, History, and Theory: The Essays of Joan Kelly* (Chicago, 1984), 23.

50. Kossuth, *Beszédei* [Speeches], 122–123.

51. Quoted in *Theologische Gutachten über das Gebetbuch nach dem Debrauche des neuen Israelitischen Tempelvereins in Hamburg* (Hamburg, 1842), 47. On Chorin's outlook, see Howard Lupovitch, "Neolog: Reforming Judaism in a Hungarian Milieu," *Modern Judaism* 40, no. 3 (2020): 128–145.

52. This blending of noble and bourgeois mentalities was not anomalous to defining the status of women; rather it reflected a broader blending of these two outlooks, a process that was described by Péter Hanák as the "bourgoisification" of the nobility [*nemesség polgárosodása*] and by William McCagg as the emergence of a "feudalized bourgeoisie." See Hanák, "The Bourgoisification of the Hungarian Nobility—Reality and Utopia in the Nineteenth Century," *Études Historiques Hongroises* I (1985): 403–421; Péter Hanák, "Polgárosodás és asszimiláció Magyarországon a XIX. Században" [*Embourgoisement* and Assimilation in Hungary in the 19th Century], *Történelmi Szemle* [Historical Review] no. 4 (1974):

513–535; William McCagg, "Hungary's Feudalized Bourgoisie," *Journal of Modern Jewish History* 44, no. 1 (1972): 65–78.

53. Michael Silber, "The Entrance of Jews into Hungarian Society in *Vormärz*: The Case of the 'Casinos,'" in *Assimilation and Community: The Jews in Nineteenth-Century Europe*, ed. Jonathan Frankel and Steven J. Zipperstein (Cambridge: Cambridge University Press, 1992), 287–288.

54. Beáta Nagy, "'Az asszonyoknak egy szalónt kellett teremtenünk': Nők és klubélet a századforduló Budapestjén," *Nők a modernizálódó magyar társadalomban* (2006), 244–245.

55. Ödön Gerő, *Az én fővárosom* (Budapest, 1891), 41–42, quoted in Gábor Schweitzer, "Lapok az Abbázia kávéház történetéhez: az 1888-as alapítástól az 1944-es ideiglenes bezárásig," *Budapesti Negyed* 12–13, no. 2/3 (1996).

56. Milton Gordon, *Assimilation in American Life: The Role of Race, Religion, and National Origins* (Oxford: Oxford University Press, 1964), 246–250.

57. Shachar Pinsker, *A Rich Brew: How Cafés Created Modern Jewish Culture* (New York: NYU Press, 2019), especially 98ff.

58. Nagy, "Az asszonyoknak," 247.

59. Ibid., 248.

60. Ibid., 249–250.

61. Ibid., 248–249.

62. "Asszonyok a kávéházban" [Ladies in the Café], *Magyar Zsidó Nő*, January 14, 1901, p. 12.

63. Miklós Bartha, *Kazár földön* [In the Land of the Khazars] (Budapest, 1901). In contrast to Ruthenians, whom Bartha regarded as lacking any real cultural identity and thus more easily Magyarized, the Jews' deep connection to a foreign culture made them unable to assimilate into Magyar society. For a more detailed discussion, see Miloslav Szabó, "'Because the Words Are Not Deeds': Anti-Semitic Practices and Nationality Policies in Upper Hungary around 1900," *Quest: Issues in Contemporary Jewry* 3 (2012), accessed online at http://www.quest-cdecjournal.it/focus.php?id=299#_ftnref32.

64. Miklós Bartha, "A zsidó nők és a magyarosodás," *Magyar Zsidó Nő*, p. 11.

65. "Letter to Bartha," *Magyar Zsidó Nő* 1, no. 16, p. 15.

66. "Another Letter to Bartha," *Magyar Zsidó Nő* 1, no. 16, p. 16.

67. "Nyelvében él a nemzet," *Magyar Zsidó Nő* 1, no. 19 (August 24, 1900): 3.

68. Gerő, *Pesti nőegylet*, 195–196.

69. Melinz and Zimmermann, "Armenfürsoge," 351; ibid., 355.

70. Susan Zimmermann, "Wie sie Feministinnen wurden: Wege in die Frauenbewegungen in Zentraleuropa der Jahrhunderte," *L'homme: Zeitschrift für Geschichte* VIII, no. 2 (1997): 272. See also Zimmermann, *Die bessere Hälfte?: Frauenbewegungen und Frauenbestrebungen im Ungarn der Habsburgermonarchie 1848 bis 1918* (Vienna: Promedia Verlag, 1999).

71. Heves Kornél, "*Mit beszélt a karácsonyfa?*" [What did the Christmas Tree Say?], *Egyenlőség* (1893).

72. "Karácsonyfa," *Egylenlőség*, December 26, 1886, p. 4.

73. A similar sentiment was expressed in Grace Paley's short story "The Loudest Voice," in which a Jewish girl who is the daughter of immigrants is cast as the lead role of narrator in her local public school's annual Christian nativity play; her mother, rather than being dismayed that her daughter is playing Jesus, instead boasts that her daughter got the part because she has the loudest voice. See Paley, "The Loudest Voice," *The Grace Paley Reader: Stories, Essays, Poetry*, ed. Kevin Bowen and Nora Paley (New York: Farrar, Straus, and Giroux, 2017), 29–35.

74. "Karácsonyfa," 5.

75. "A Zsidók és a Karácsonyfa," *Egyenlőség*, December 29, 1893, p. 2.

76. Ibid., 3.

77. Todd Endelman, "The Checkered Career of Jew-King: A Study in Anglo-Jewish Social History," *AJS Review* 7–8 (1983): 96–97.

Chapter 7

1. Tamás Kóbor, *Ki agettóból* I [Out of the Ghetto] (Budapest: Franklin Társulat, 1911), 211.

2. Estimates of the size of the Budapest Orthodox community at its height in 1914 range from 20,000 to 50,000. To my mind, the most accurate calculation is that of Kinga Frojimovics, *Szétszakadt Történelem: Zsidó vallási irányzatok Magyarországon, 1868–1950* (Budapest, 2006), 126–127. The sizable Orthodox minority in Budapest, moreover, suggests a corollary to the "line of demarcation" with which historians delineated Hungarian Jewry's Orthodox and Neolog spheres of predominance. This line typically runs diagonally from northeastern to southwestern Hungary—the area above the line being predominantly Orthodox and below the line Neolog. Accordingly, Jewish communities were generally comprised either of a predominantly Orthodox or Neolog constituency, often with a small Orthodox or Neolog minority living in a community dominated by its rival camp. Budapest, exceptional in other ways as well among Hungarian Jewish communities, had a large contingent of Orthodox and Neolog Jews. Karády, "Religious Divisions, Socio-Economic Stratification and the Modernization of Hungarian Jewry after the Emancipation," in *Jews in the Hungarian Economy, 1760–1945: Studies Dedicated to Moshe Carmilly-Weinberger,* ed. Michael K. Silber (Jerusalem, 1992), 163–164.

3. Anikó Prepuk, "A neológ sajtó a zsidóság társadalmi befogadásáért a 19. század utolsó harmadában," *Budapesti Negyed* 16, no. 2 (2008): 2.

4. Miklós Konrád, "Music Halls and Jewish Identity in Budapest at the Turn of the Century," in *Jewish Space in East Central Europe: Day to Day History,* ed. Jurgita Šiaučiūnaitė-Verbickienė and Larisa Lempertienė (London: Cambridge Scholars Publishing, 2007), 145.

5. Nathaniel Katzburg, "Hungarian Jewish Historiography," in *The Rabbinical Seminary of Budapest, 1877–1977: A Centennial Volume,* ed. Moshe Carmilly-Weinberger (New York: Sepher-Hermon Press for the Alumni Association of the Rabbinical Seminary of Budapest, 1986), 217–218.

NOTES TO CHAPTER 7

6. For a concise definition of these terms, and the one used throughout this book, see Michael Silber, "The Emergence of Ultra-Orthodoxy: The Invention of Tradition," in *The Uses of Tradition: Jewish Continuity in the Modern Era,* ed. Jack Wertheimer (New York: Jewish Theological Seminary of America, 1999), 26n.4. Silber distinguished traditional Judaism from various forms of Orthodoxy, defining the former as an acceptance of tradition unself-consciously and without question and the latter as adherence to a tradition as part of a self-conscious reflexive conservative ideology. Thus, he notes, "the shift from a tradi-tional society to an Orthodox one ... was part and parcel of modernization and, as such, Orthodoxy must be viewed as a modern phenomenon." See also Adam Ferziger, *Exclusion and Hierarchy: Orthodoxy, Non-Observance, and the Emergence of Modern Jewish Identity* (Philadelphia: University of Pennsylvania Press, 2005), especially 2–6.

7. On the differences between these categories, see Daniel Bender, "'A hero ... for the weak': Work, Consumption, and the Enfeebled Jewish Worker, 1881–1924," *International Labor and Working-Class History* 56 (1999): 5; Michael Hanagan, "Artisans and Skilled Workers: The Problem of Definition," *International Labor and Working-Class History* 12 (1977): 28–29; Andrew Dawson, "The Parameters of Craft Consciousness: The Social Outlook of the Skilled Worker, 1880–1920," in *American Labor and Immigration History: 1877–1920s: Recent European Research*, ed. Dirk Hoerder (Urbana: University of Illinois Press, 1983), 136–140. My thanks to Elizabeth Faue for recommending these sources.

8. On this, see Ferziger, *Exclusion and Hierarchy,* 172–175; Ferziger, "Religious Zealotry and Religious Law: Rethinking Conflict and Coexistence," *Journal of Religion* 84, no. 1 (2004): 52ff.

9. Eötvös, *A zsidók emancipációja* (Pest, 1840), 25–26, 46–47.

10. Among the few Jewish participants were the painter Samuel Goldberger and Mór Fischer.

11. Julia Richers, *Jüdisches Budapest: Kulturelle Topographien einer Stadtgemeinde im 19. Jahr-hundert* (Koln, Weimar, Wien, 2009), 277.

12. Ödön Kertész, "A Százhatesztendős MIKÉFE első Negyedszázada," IMIT Évkönyéből; see also Richers, *Judisches Budapest,* 262ff.

13. Dávid Kemény, *A Magyar Izr. Kézmű és Földművelési Egylet hetvenéves működése* (Budapest, 1912), 13. Apart from Jakobovics and Bernát, officers included Jakab Bern, deputy director; L. M. Koppel, treasurer; Bernát Pollák, comptroller; Zsigmond Saphir, Jakab Schlesinger, scribes; and Antal Schiff. In addition, a 25-member board was elected that included Eliás Abeles, Mór Bloch (Ballagi), Náthán Braun (Barnai), M. A. Cahen, G. Frankl, H. Grünz-weig, Fülöp Jakobovics, Emánuel Kanitz, Jónás Kunewalder, Jakab Kern, L. M. Koppel, L. R. Landau, Ignác Lerner, Izrael Laszky, Vilmos Mandl, Bernát Pollák, Márk Pollák, Vilmos Práger, Dr. Zsigmond Saphir, Dr. Jakab Schlesinger, Mór Schulhof, Dr. Dávid Schwimmer, Veit Singer, M. A. Weisz, Rudolf Wodianer. Additional members: Simon Eigner, D. Fleischl, Mózes Heller, M. Schlesinger, L. Schőnwald, Lipót Schulhof, J. Schwartz.

14. Kemény, *A Magyar Izr. Kézmű- és Földművelési Egylet hetvenéves működése,* 43–44.

15. On the origins and development of the Lithuanian Kollel, see Shaul Stampfer, *Lithuanian*

Yeshivas of the Nineteenth Century: Creating a Tradition of Learning (London, 2012), especially chapter 11.

16. See the ReMA's gloss on *Orach Chaim* 688:1. Benjamin of Tudela, *The Itinerary of Benjamin of Tudela: Travels in the Middle Ages* (2004), 37–38. In modern Hebrew, *batlan* has a more pejorative meaning as a freeloader or bum.

17. Jerusalem Talmud, Megillah, 1:6.

18. ReMA on Yore Deah 246:1; Jonathan Eybeshütz, *Sefer Ya'arot Devash* (Jerusalem, 1983), Part I, Sermon 6, p. 137; *Takanot Mehrin* #16, p. 7.

19. Jacob Katz, *Tradition and Crisis: Jewish Society at the End of the Middle Ages* (Syracuse, NY: Syracuse University Press, 2000), 136–137; ibid., 128.

20. Volha Aliaksandrauna Sabeleuskaya, "Changing Conceptions of Leisure among the Jews of Western Belarus at the end of the 19th Century," *East European Jewish Affairs* 36, no. 2 (2006): 127–128.

21. "Budapesti Talmud Egylet," in *Magyar zsidó lexikon*, ed. Péter Újvari (Budapest, 1929), 158; Gábor Deutsch, "Egy cédrus Pozsonyból" [A Cedar from Pozsony], in *Magyar Zsidó Szemle*. My thanks to Rabbi Baruch Oberlander for bringing this source to my attention.

22. Katz, *Tradition and Crisis,* 157–159.

23. Andreas Reinke, "Gemeinde und Verein: Formen jüdischer Vergemeinschaftung im Breslau des 19. Und beginnenden 20. Jahrhunderts," in *Im Breslau zu Haus* (Hamburg, 2003), 143–144.

24. In this regard, recent studies of the tactics employed by Hasidic leaders in their infiltration of Polish Jewish communities provide a useful comparative perspective in analyzing the role of the Hevra Shas in the expansion and entrenchment of Orthodoxy in Budapest. The rapid spread of Hasidism resulted not only from the allure of Hasidic ideology or an emphasis on prayer over study per se, but also from the pivotal role of enlisting the support of local lay elites, infiltrating existing communal institutions, and creating new ones through which to diffuse Hasidic ideas and familiarize rank-and-file Jews with the allure of Hasidic prayers. Along these lines, the Hevra Shas reached full maturity once it had fashioned an alternate framework of communal institutions, attracted prominent rabbis, and secured the support of a coterie of affluent Jewish laity, akin to what Dynner characterized as "men of silk." In addition, like becoming a Hasid, joining the Hevra Shas provided the relative advantage that derived from greater access to the study of rabbinic text—an activity that enjoyed especially high status among observant Jews. See Glenn Dynner, *Men of Silk: The Hasidic Conquest of Polish Jewish Society* (Oxford, 2008), especially chap. 2; Dynner, "The Hasidic Conquest of Small-Town Central Poland, 1754–1818," *Polin: Studies in Polish Jewry* 17 (2004): 51–81; Yohanan Petrovsky-Stern, "Hasidism, Havurot, and the Jewish Street," in *Jewish Social Studies* 10, no. 2 (2004); Shaul Stampfer, "How and Why Did Hasidism Spread?" *Jewish History* 27 (2013): 201–219; see also Marcin Wodzinski, *Haskalah and Hasidism in the Kingdom of Poland: A History of Conflict* (Oxford, 2005), especially chap. 4; and Ilie Lurie, *The Habad Movement in Czarist Russia* (in Hebrew) (Jerusalem, 2006), 43ff.

25. Aron Fürst, "Budapest," in *'Arim ve-Imahot be-Yisrael: Mivzat Kodesh le-Kehilot Yisrael she-Nechervu Bidey 'arizim u-teme'im be-Milhemet 'Olam ha-Aharona,* Part II (Jerusalem, 1948), 164.

26. On Shomrei Ha-dat see, Jacob Katz, *Orthodoxy and Schism in Nineteenth-Century Central European Jewry* (Waltham, MA: Brandeis University Press, 1998), 57.

27. With regard to the latter, some historians have juxtaposed the ostensibly militantly Orthodox *Shomre ha-Dat* with the radically progressive *Genossenschaft für Reform im Judenthum,* phenomena that underlined the polarized character of Pest Jewry, as symptomatic of an early stage of the eventual schism between Orthodoxy and its nontraditional combatants.

28. These statutes were initially published in 1852. The earliest extant version was published in 1875, *Statuten die Budapester Talmud-Vereines* (hereinafter *Statuten* 1875) and then re-issued, this time in Hungarian, in 1898, *Budapesti Talmud-Egylet Alapszabályai* (hereinafter *Talmud-Egylet Alapszabályai*).

29. *Statuten* 1875, #3, 6.

30. *Budapesti Talmudegylet jegyzőkönye* [The Minute-Book of the Budapest Talmud Association, hereinafter Minute-Book] (August 23, 1874–May 17, 1885) (Mic #9805 JTSA Library), Protocol #130, September 28, 1874.

31. "Sussman," in Péter Újvári, *Magyar Zsidó Lexikon* (Budapest, 1929), 813.

32. Meir Eisenstadter, *Sheelot u-Teshuvot Imre Esh* on *Orach Chaim* #9.

33. Winkler, She-elot u-Teshuvot Levushe Mordechai, vol. 1 on Orach Chaim 14:5, quoted in Y. Y. Cohen, *Hachmei Hungariya ve-Hasifrut ha-Toranit Ba* (Jerusalem, 1997), 125.

34. Moses Schick, *She-elot u-teshuvot maharam shik* on *Yore de'a* #333.

35. In this regard, it is worth noting certain parallels between the Orthodox subcommunity in the 1870s and Pest Jewry as a whole a half-century earlier. Each grew in the span of a few decades from a small enclave into a sizable minority. Each was a small, marginalized minority: Pest Jewry with respect to the city of Budapest, Pest Orthodoxy with respect to Pest Jewry. Both were concentrated during their formative years in a specific part of the city—Terézváros—the major difference being that, while Budapest Jewry eventually expanded beyond these boundaries, Budapest Orthodoxy remained there. In terms of communal organization, both focused on the same three areas: synagogues, education, and charity. Finally, Pest Jewry in the 1830s and Pest Orthodoxy during the 1870s entered a period of rapid growth. Pest Jewry was minuscule at the end of the 1820s compared to Pest, but approached 20 percent of the total population a half-century later. Similarly, Pest Orthodoxy was a minuscule subset of Budapest Jewry in the 1870s and grew to between 15 and 20 percent of Pest Jewry by the First World War.

36. On the Pest Hevra Kadisha, see chapter 3 in this volume.

37. For an analysis of how these questions challenged Orthodox leaders elsewhere, see Robert Liberles, *Religious Conflict in Social Context: The Resurgence of Orthodox Judaism in Frankfurt Am Main, 1837–1877* (Praeger, 1985).

38. "Megjegyzések" [Reflections], *Egyenlőség* [Equality], October 7, 1888, p. 3 (italics mine).

39. *Budapesti Talmud Egylet*, 159.

40. Károly Vörös, "A budapesti zsidóság két forradalom között, 1849–1918," *Zsidóság a dualizmus kori Magyarországon: siker és válság*, ed. László Varga (Budapest: Pannonica, 2005), 43.

41. Kinga Frojimovics, Géza Komoróczy, Viktória Pusztai, and Andrea Strbik, eds., *A Zsidó Budapest: Emlékek, szertartások, történelem* (Budapest: MTA Judaisztikai Kutatócsoport, 1995), 182ff.

42. Ibid., 183.

43. Ibid., 184–185. On the Status Quo movement, see Howard Lupovitch, "Between Orthodox Judaism and Neology: The Origins of the Status Quo Movement," *Jewish Social Studies* 9, no. 2 (2003): 123–153.

44. See the appendix to Michael K. Silber, ed., *Shorashei ha-Pilug be-Yehadut Hungariya mimei Yoseph Ha-Sheni ad Erev Mahapechat 1848* [The Roots of the Schism in Hungarian Jewry from the Era of Joseph II until the Eve of the Revolution of 1848] (PhD diss., Hebrew University, 1979), 266–227.

45. See Howard Lupovitch, "Ordinary People, Ordinary Jews: Mór Jókai as Magyar Philosemite," in *Philosemitism in History,* ed. Jonathan Karp and Adam Sutcliffe (Cambridge: Cambridge University Press, 2011), 131–133.

46. On Sofer, see Adam Ferziger, "Sofer, Hayim ben Mordekhai Efrayim Fishel," in *YIVO Encyclopedia of the Jews of Eastern Europe* II, pp. 1774–1775; see also Ferziger, "Religious Zealotry and Religious Law," 49–53.

47. Chaim Sofer, *Sha'are Chaim* on Psalms 19:11.

48. On Sussman, see Gábor Deutsch, "Egy cédrus Pozsonyból" [A Cedar from Pozsony], 1–2; Baruch Oberlander, *Tel Talpiot: Kitve 'Eyt Torani* II (2001), 5–6; "Sussman," in *Magyar Zsidó Lexikon,* 813.

49. Haim Gertner, *The Rabbi and the City: The Rabbinate in Galicia and Its Encounter with Modernity, 1815–1867* [in Hebrew] (Jerusalem, 2013), 68.

50. Samuel C. Heilman, "The Many Faces of Orthodoxy," *Modern Judaism* 2, no. 1 (1982): 27.

51. *Egyenlőség,* November 29, 1899, p. 12.

52. L. D. Brandeis, "True Americanism" (1915), *Social Welfare History Project.* Retrieved from http://socialwelfare.library.vcu.edu/uncategorized/true-americanism-address-louis-d-brandeis-1915/.

53. On Mendelssohn and Weisl, see Zohar Shavit, "Train Up a Child: On the 'Maskilic' Attempt to Change the Habits of Jewish Children and Young Adults," *Journal of Jewish Education* 82, no. 1 (2016): 33–35. On Hochmuth, see Howard Lupovitch, *Jews at the Crossroads: Tradition and Accommodation during the Golden Age of the Hungarian Nobility* (Budapest: CEU Press, 2007), 198–203.

54. *A Budapesti Magyar Izr. Kézmű- és Földművelési Egylet Alapszabályai* [The Statutes of the Budapest Hungarian Israelite Crafts and Agriculture, hereinafter MIKÉFE Statutes] (Budapest: Schlesinger Ignácz Könyvnyomdája, 1889), #2.

55. Ibid., #3h–i.

56. Ibid., #3a–f.

57. These programs impacted children indirectly. Among the scholars whom the Hevra Shas trained came the nucleus of teachers at the new Orthodox schools that were founded at the turn of the twentieth century.

58. Pál Balázs, *Forgószélben: A Budapesti Orthodox Zsidóság és Iskolái* [In the Whirlwind: Budapest's Orthodox Jewry and Its Schools] (Budapest, 2009), 127–128.

59. Deutsch, "Egy cédrus Pozsonyból" [A Cedar from Pozsony], 4; "Sussman," in *Magyar Zsidó Lexikon*, 813.

60. "Vorstandes Schulcommissions Sitzung," *Izraelita hitkötség jegyőkönyve* [Protocols of the Pest Israelite Community] (December 1885), #26.

61. 1898 Statutes #3–#4. This instruction reappeared periodically in the minute books of the Hevra Shas. See also, for example, *Közgyűlési jegyzőkönyv/Protokolle der Budapester Talmudverein Schas Chevra* [Minute Book of the Budapest Hevra Shas, 1903–1945], Mic. #9806, #65, September 12, 1916.

62. Protokol #180, January 19, 1879; #254, 1883; #16, 1891.

63. "Trencséni Levél," *Egyenlőség*, January 9, 1891, p. 12.

64. *Budapesti Talmudegylet jegyzőkönye* #3 (1885).

65. "Budapesti orthodox hitközség," in *Magyar Zsidó Lexikon*, 156.

66. This partnership was further enhanced by familial ties: Sussman's son married Koppel Reich's daughter.

67. "Budapesti orthodox hitközség," 157.

68. József Kiss, "Reich Koppel: egy rabbi a felsőházból" [Koppel Reich: A Rabbi in the Upper House], *Múlt és Jövő* no. 2 (1993): 90–91.

69. 1898 Statutes #68; #65; #60.

70. Ibid., #69.

71. "A MIKÉFE," *Egyenlőség*, May 24, 1914, p. 16. In 1914, MIKÉFE paid out 163,054 in expenses and earned 104,516 in revenues and donations.

72. 1898 Statutes, #25.

73. *Budapesti Talmudegylet jegyzőkönye*, #16 (1910).

74. *Budapesti Talmudegylet jegyzőkönye*, JTSA Mic #9805, August 21, 1874–May 17, 1885, #138, November 16, 1875. Donations from women, all totaled, comprised 60 percent of all donations.

75. *Budapesti Talmudegylet jegyzőkönye*, August 20, 1907.

76. More about this in chapter 8 of this volume.

77. Menachem Friedman, "The Haredi (Ultra-Orthodox) Society: Sources, Trends, Processes," *Jerusalem Institute for Israel Studies Research Series* no. 41 (1991): 1.

78. Richers, *Jüdisches Budapest*, 338.

79. The conceptual category was coined in the last decade by Wei Li to distinguish between two Los Angeles neighborhoods: Chinatown (an immigrant enclave) and the Monterey Park

area of the San Gabriel Valley (an ethnoburb). Wei defined an ethnoburb as "an ethnic clus-
ter or residential area and business district in a large metropolitan area." Wei Li, *Ethnoburb:
The New Ethnic Community in Urban America* (Honolulu: University of Hawaii Press, 2012).

More precisely, Wei defined an ethnoburb as an area of a city where a particular ethnic group evinces a number of defining characteristics. First, the ethnic population of the
area in question is significant but not overwhelming; the ethnoburb has an easily identifi-
able "ethnic feel" but is not defined entirely by a particular ethnic group. Second, the ethnic population of an ethnoburb is comprised of a diverse cross section of the ethnic group:
immigrant and native, acculturated and unacculturated, parochial and cosmopolitan, and
multiple social classes. Third, although much or most of the ethnic group is favorably dis-
posed to embrace the culture of the mainstream, the members of this group sustain an "ethnic economy," that is, bookstores, clothing stores, restaurants, and local institutions that
cater to the particular cultural needs of the ethnic group. Fourth, an ethnoburb is a "fully
functioning community with its own internal socio-economic structures that are integral to national and international environments," thus allowing a particular ethnic group
to enjoy the "perceived perks of suburbia without the requirement that immigrants dis-
card or conceal their culture, language, and traditions." Finally, an ethnoburb has a constant give and take with the preexisting immigrant enclave; at times one complements the
other, at other times each regards the other with suspicion or even contempt. To date, little attempt has been made to apply this urban category to any ethnic group, city, or time
period other than the Chinese community of late twentieth-century Los Angeles. A useful and important first step is Bruce A. Phillips, "'Not Quite White': The Emergence of
Jewish Ethnoburbs in Los Angeles, 1920–2010," *American Jewish History* 100, no. 1 (2016):
73–104, and especially 74–78.

80. Alexander Vari, "Re-territorializing the 'Guilty City': Nationalist and Right-Wing Attempts to Nationalize Budapest during the Interwar Period," *Journal of Contemporary History* 47, no. 4 (2012): 711.

81. *A Magyar Szentkorona Országainak 1910-évi népszámlálása* (1920), quoted in C. A. Macartney, *A History of Hungary, 1929–1945* (New York, 1956), 18–19; and Stefan Barta, *Die Juden
Frage in Ungarn* (Budapest, n.d.), 62ff.

Chapter 8

1. Péter Hanák, "Az elpusztíthatatlan város: Budapest történelmi vitalitása" [The Indestructible
City: The Historical Vitality of Budapest], *Budapesti Negyed* 1, no. 1 (1993), accessed at
https://epa.oszk.hu/00000/00003/00001/fej01.htm. The Aster Revolution refers to the
movement led by Mihály Károlyi that replaced the monarchy with a liberal government.
The Red Revolution refers to the Communist overthrow of Károlyi's government by Béla
Kun and the Hungarian Communists. The Aster and Red Revolutions and their impact
on Budapest and Budapest Jewry are discussed below.

2. Nathaniel Katzburg, *Pinkas he-Kehilla: Hungariya* (Jerusalem: Yad Vashem, 1976), 64.

3. Even the putative continuity of the surge of antisemitism during the 1920s and 1930s is a matter of debate for historians. Some historians, such as Viktor Karády, Ignác Romsics, and Krisztián Ungváry, argue that the *Numerus Clausus* law of 1920 and the anti-Jewish laws of the late 1930s were separated by a decade or more of calm and stability; others, notably Mária Kovács, have suggested that the *Numerus Clausus* laid the groundwork for the later laws. See Karády, "Continuities of the 'Jewish Question' in Hungary since the Golden Age," in *The Holocaust in Hungary: Seventy Years Later*, ed. Randolph L. Braham and András Kovács (CEU Press: Budapest and New York, 2016), 46ff; Ignác Romsics, *A Magyar zsidóság története* (Budapest, 2015), 76ff; Krisztián Ungváry, *A Horthy-rendszer mérlege, Diszkrimináció, szociálpolitika és antiszemitizmus Magyarországon* (Pécs and Budapest: Jelenkor, 2013), 608; Mária M. Kovács, "The Problem of Continuity between the 1920 *Numerus Clausus* and Post-1938 Anti-Jewish Legislation in Hungary," *East European Jewish Affairs* 35, no. 1 (2005): 23–24.

4. "Dr. Mezey Ferenc beszéde a Magyar-Zsidó Múzeum megnyitásakor" [Dr. Ferenc Mezey's address at the opening of the Hungarian Jewish Museum] (January 23, 1916), *Évkönyv az Izr. Magyar Irodalmi Társulat* (Budapest: 1916), 372–373.

5. Alexander Vari, "Re-territorializing the 'Guilty City': Nationalist and Right-wing Attempts to Nationalize Budapest during the Interwar Period," *Journal of Contemporary History* 47, no. 4 (2012): 712.

6. Tibor Erényi, "Zsidók és a magyar politikai élet, 1848–1938" [Jews and Hungarian Political Life, 1848–1938], *Múltunk: Politikatörténeti folyóirat* IV (1994): 18.

7. L. Zsuzsa Nagy, *A budapesti liberális ellenzék* [The Liberal Opposition of Budapest], *1919–1944* (Budapest, 1972), 77–78.

8. Viktor Karády, "A zsidóság polgárosodásának és modernizációjának főbb tényezői a magyar társadalomtörténetben," in Karády, *Zsidóság, modernizáció, polgárosodás: tanulmányok* (Budapest: Cserépfalvi, 1997), 84–85. See also Gábor Gyáni, "Polgárosodás mint zsidó identitás," *Budapesti Könyvszemle–BUKSZ* (Fall 1997): 266.

9. Vari, "Re-territorializing the 'Guilty City,'" 712.

10. Quoted in ibid., 713.

11. C. Tormay, *Bujdosó könyv. Feljegyzések 1918–1919-ből*, vol. I (Budapest, 1923), 18.

12. Gábor Schweitzer, "Budapest, az ország vakbele: a magyar politikai közbeszéd történetéhez," *Budapesti Könyvszemle (BUKSZ)* (2005), 328–329; István Deák, "Budapest and the Hungarian Revolutions of 1918–1919," *Slavonic and East European Review* 46, no. 106 (1968): 130.

13. Vari, "Re-territorializing the 'Guilty City,'" 715.

14. István Deák, *Beyond Nationalism: A Social and Political History of the Habsburg Officer Corps, 1848–1918* (Oxford and New York: Oxford University Press, 1990); Erényi, "Zsidók és a magyar politikai élet," 14.

15. These sketches included not only heroic accomplishments on the battlefield but also remarks about the family and prewar life of the soldier.

16. "A Háború Körül," *Egyenlőség*, Sunday, October 18, 1914, p. 3.

17. Ibid., Sunday, March 12, 1916, p. 4.

18. "Von Nah und Fern," *Beilage zur Allegemeinen Zeitung des Judentums*, March 5, 1915, p. 4.

19. "József Főherceg a magyar zsidó katonákról," *Egyenlőség*, January 24, 1915, p. 1. Quoted by Avigdor Loewenheim, *Hanhagat ha-Kehilla ha-Yehudit shel Pest Be-Shanim 1914–1919: Ma'amada u-Pe'iluta be-Tzibbur ha-Yehudi* (PhD diss., Hebrew University of Jerusalem, 1990), 154–155.

20. "A magyar zsidóság és a hadikölcsön," *Egyenlőség*, November 22, 1914, p. 8.

21. *Judische Zeitung,* January 1, 1916, p. 2.

22. "Von Nah und Fern," *AZdJ,* December 31, 1915, p. 15. Sixty soldiers were interred there during the fall of 1915.

23. *AZdJ,* December 17, 1915, p. 16; *AZdJ,* February 18, 1916, p. 16.

24. Katalin Gerő, *A szeretet munkásai: a pesti izraelita nőegylet története, 1866–1937* (Budapest, 1937), 314–315.

25. "Háborús Peszach," *Egyenlőség,* April 11, 1915, p. 4.

26. *Egyenlőség's* weekly column "Pályzati hirdetmény" [Tender Announcement] provided a running list of these philanthropic acts.

27. *Egyenlőség,* August 19, 1916, p. 22.

28. *AZdJ,* October 27, 1916, p. 15.

29. *Fővárosi közlöny* [Capital Bulletin, hereinafter FK], February 26, 1915, p. 2.

30. Gerő, *A szeretet munkásai,* 310–312.

31. FK, October 23, 1914, p. 1.

32. Laura Umbrai, "A szegényétkeztetéstől a népétkeztetésig: a budapesti népkonyhák története az első világháború éveiben" [From Feeding the Poor to Feeding the People: The History of Public Kitchens in Budapest during the First World War], *Múltunk,* vol. 2 (2018), 162. Other Jewish public kitchens operating during the war were the following, all located in the Seventh District: the Ahavasz Reim/Szeret egyet kitchen adjacent to the Jewish Community Office at 12 Sip utca; the Bikur Cholim/ Beteglátogató egylet at 17 Károly körút; the PIN kitchens at 57 Dob utca and 14 Kertész utca; the kitchen run by the Budapesti Ortodox Bureau at 33 Wesselényi utca; and the kitchen run by the Országos Magyar Izraelita Közművelődési Egyesület [Hungarian Jewish Educational Association] at 17 Rákóczi út.

33. "Zsidó kertészek kellenek!" *Egyenlőség,* February 24, 1917, p. 6.

34. "A Magyar Zsidó kertészek—A MIKÉFE télepen," ibid., November 4, 1916, p. 8.

35. *AZdJ,* December 31, 1915, p. 16.

36. Loewenheim, *Hanhagat ha-Kehilla,* 153.

37. Quoted in Loewenheim, *Hanhagat ha-Kehilla,* 157.

38. Nathaniel Katzburg, "Ha-Miflaga ha-Antishemit be-Hungariya u-Mekoma be-Hayim ha-Politi'im bishnat 1883–1887" [in Hebrew], *Zion* 30, no. 1/2 (1965): 79–114.

39. Ibid., 90; Paul Hanebrink, *In Defense of Christian Hungary: Religion, Nationalism, and Antisemitism, 1890–1918* (Cornell University Press: Ithaca, 2009), 11–14.

40. Avigdor Loewenheim, "Yehudei Budapest ve-ha-Galicianim—Parasha mi-shnat 1904" [The Jews of Budapest and the Galicianers—an Episode from 1904], *Tsiyon* 53, no. 3 (1988): 303–312.

41. *Magyar Zsidó Szemle* [Hungarian Jewish Review] XXXII (1915): 172.

42. *AZdJ*, March 17, 1916, p. 4.

43. "A háború körül," *Egyenlőség*, October 14, 1914, pp. 5–6.

44. *Jüdische Zeitung*, January 1, 1915, p. 2.

45. Ibid., May 19, 1917, p. 2.

46. Sándor Bródy, "Zsidókról," *Fehér könyv* (1915): 67.

47. Ibid., 68.

48. Gábor Gyáni, *Parlor and Kitchen,* 162; Péter Hanák, *The Garden and the Workshop: Essays on the Cultural History of Vienna and Budapest* (Princeton: Princeton University Press, 2016), 12.

49. For a more detailed analysis of this episode, see Rebekah Klein-Pejsova, "The Budapest Jewish Community's Galician October," in *World War I and the Jews: Conflict and Transformation in Europe, the Middle East, and America,* ed. Marsha L. Rozenblit and Jonathan Karp (New York: Berghann Books, 2017), 112ff.

50. "Milliós alapitvány egy zsidó tanitónőképző létesitésére," *Egyenlőség,* July 28, 1917, p. 6.

51. *Egyenlőség,* February 2, 1920.

52. Even Theodore Herzl, in one of the last interviews he gave before his death, had discouraged Hungarian Jews from embracing Zionism (though he presciently suggested that eventually circumstances in Hungary would demand they do). Livia Bitton Jackson, "Zionism in Hungary: The First 25 Years," *Herzl Yearbook* 7 (1971): 285–320; Attila Novák, "Zionism in Hungary between the Two World Wars," in *In the Land of Hagar,* ed. Anna Szalai (Tel Aviv: Bet Hatefutzot, 2002), 133–140. On Herzl's interview with the editor of *Egyenlőség,* Miksa Szabolcsi, "Beszélgetés Herzl Drral," *Egyenlőség,* June 28, 1903, p. 3. For a more detailed analysis of this interview see Avigdor Loewenheim, "Teador Herzl ve-Yehude Hungariya: Sicha 'im Herzl mi-Shnat 1903" [Theodore Herzl and Zionism: A Conversation with Herzl from 1903], *Tsiyon* 54, no. 4 (1989): 461–467.

53. *Judische Zeitung,* February 11, 1916, p. 4. The mission of Achdut was "preserving and disseminating the Hebrew language." The group's new home was located at 36 Károlyi utca. Though the rooms in the schools were rent free, the organization was required to pay for heating and electricity. The committee elected in February 1916 was: President Adalbert Schonbach, Vice President Rabbi Manó Lieberman, Secretaries A. Südwarts and Martin Hirsch, Treasurer Armin Fabian, advisory board members Sara Heller, Szidy Redlinger, Lipót Leibovits (Pres. Mizrachi), Salomon Handler, Sándor Schlesinger, Dr. Mihály Glück (advocate), Rubin Diament, Desző Schwartz.

54. See, for an example of the former, the responses of Ferenc Mezey in ibid., 21–22; Lajos Szabolcsi, ibid., pp. 30–31 in *A Zsidókérdés Magyarországon: A huszadik század körkérdése* (Budapest, 1917); an example of the latter is Lajos Venetianer, ibid., 34ff. For a more in-

depth analysis of this exchange, see Guy Miron, "Introduction," in *Yehudim al Parashat Derachim: Siach ha-Zehut ha-Yahadut be-Hungariya beyn mishbar le-Hitchadshut, 1908–1926* [Jews at the Crossroads: Discourse on the Jewish Identity in Hungary between Crisis and Renewal], ed. Miron and Anna Szalai (Ramat Gan: Bar Ilan University, 2008), especially 27ff.

55. Ármin Beregi in ibid., 51.

56. Gerő, *Szeretet Munkásai*, 340; *Pesti Napló*, January 10, 1918, p. 7.

57. Loewenheim, *He-Kehilla*, 165.

58. István Deák, "Budapest and the Hungarian Revolutions of 1918–1919," *Slavonic and East European Review* 46, no. 106 (1968): 133; Gerő, *Szeretet Munkásai*, 338.

59. Ibid., 349.

60. Deák, "Budapest and the Hungarian Revolutions," 129.

61. "Az új szervezet," *Egyenlőség*, November 23, 1918, p. 8. The size of the loan depended on the scholarship and intellectual ability of the rabbi; ibid., 11.

62. *AZdJ*, February 14, 1919, pp. 4–5. The declaration was signed by Lajos Blau, Gyula Fischer, Mihály Guttmann, Simon Hevesi, Mór Klein, Lajos Venetianer, Mór Weiss, Ármin Balogh, Heinrich Bloch, Mór Dercsényi, and Vilmos Hausbrunner, and dated January 13, 1919.

63. Katzburg, *Pinkas ha-Kehilla*, 205.

64. Emily Gioielli, "'Home Is Home No Longer': Political Struggle in the Domestic Sphere in Post-Armistice Hungary, 1919–1922," *Aspasia* 11, no. 1 (2017): 58; Katzburg, "Budapest," in *Pinkas ha-Kehillot: Hungariya*, 206.

65. Katzburg, *Pinkas ha-Kehilla*, 206.

66. Gioielli, "Home Is Home No Longer," 64.

67. Ibid., 63.

68. This expression gained traction amid irredentist calls for Hungary to regain these lost territories, such as: "*Csonka Magyarország nem ország, nagy Magyarország mennyország!*" [Rump Hungary is not a country; Greater Hungary is paradise!].

69. Gioielli, "Home Is Home No Longer," 66–67.

70. For a more detailed summary, see "Hungary," in Ezra Mendelsohn, *The Jews of East Central Europe between the Two World Wars* (Bloomington: Indiana University Press, 1983), and "Hungary," in Joseph Rothschild, *East Central Europe between the Two World Wars* (Spokane and Tacoma: University of Washington Press, 1984).

71. Katzburg, *Pinkas ha-Kehilla*, 205–206.

72. Ibid., 207.

73. *Egyenlőség*, March 20, 1920, p. 4.

74. On the origins and specifics of the *Numerus Clausus*, see Mária A. Kovács, "A numerus clausus Magyarországon, 1919–1945," in *Jogfosztás—90 Éve: Tanulmányok a numerus claususról,* ed. Judit Molnár (Budapest, 2011), 29ff; Nathaniel Katzburg, *Hungary and the Jews: Policy and Legislation, 1920–1943* (Bar Ilan University Press, 1990). The law passed over the

objections of prominent members of parliament including Pál Sándor, Béla Fábián, Ernő Bródy (who were Jewish), and Károly Rassay (who was not).

75. *Egyenlőség*, February 21, 1920, p. 15; the reply appeared in ibid., April 24, 1920, p. 1.

76. Katzburg, *Pinkas ha-Kehilla*, 208.

77. On this see, Miklós Konrád, *Zsidóságon innen és túl: Zsidók vallásváltása Magyarországon a reformkortól az első világháborúig* [Judaism Within and Beyond: Jewish Conversion from the Reform Era until World War I] (Budapest: MTA, 2014), 224–226. For a less detailed version, see Konrád, "Mixing with Meshumads: Social Relations between Jews and Converted Jews in Modern Hungary," *Jewish Studies at the Central European University* IX, ed. András Kovács, Michael L. Miller, and Carsten L. Wilke (2017–2019), especially 29ff; William O. McCagg, "Jewish Conversion in Hungary in Modern Times," in *Jewish Apostasy in the Modern World*, ed. Todd Endelman (New York: Holmes and Meier, 1987), pp. 160–161.

78. "A Zsidók kiszorultak a középiskolából," *Egyenlőség*, September 4, 1920, p. 1.

79. "Újabb Iskolát állit fel a pesti zsidó hitköség," *Egyenlőség*, May 29, 1920, p. 9.

80. Ibid., 10.

81. "Zsidó Egyetem!" Ibid., September 4, 1920, p. 3.

82. "A Pesti zsidóság újjá szervezése," *Egyenlőség*, January 31, 1920, p. 6; ibid., March 27, 1920, p. 10.

83. Ibid., 11.

84. *Egyenlőség*, March 6, 1920, p. 14; ibid., February 21, 1920, p. 16; Katzburg, *Pinkas Ha-Kehilla*, 209.

85. "Zsidó kultur-matiné a Lipótvárosban," *Egyenlőség*, May 15, 1920, p. 6.

86. Katzburg, *Pinkas Ha-Kehilla*, 210.

87. Jenő Lévai, *Fekete Könyv a magyar zsidóság szenvedéseiről* [Black Book on the Sufferings of Hungarian Jewry] (Budapest: Officina, 1946), 9.

88. Ignác Romsics, *Bethlen István, Politikai életrajz* (Budapest: Magyarságkutató Intézet, 1991), 157.

89. Ibid., 157–158. The two rabbis were Immanuel Löw representing the Neolog Movement and Koppel Reich representing Orthodoxy.

90. Mór Szatmári, "Bethlen és a felekezeti béke" [Bethlen and denominational peace], *Egyenlőség*, July 8, 1922, pp. 3–4.

91. Romsics, *Bethlen István*, 159.

92. László Varga, "Ferenc Chorin," in *YIVO Encyclopedia of the Jews in Eastern Europe*, https://yivoencyclopedia.org/article.aspx/Chorin_Ferenc.

93. Ignác Romsics, "The Antisemitism of István Bethlen and Jewish Policy of the Horthy Era," in *The Holocaust in Hungary: Seventy Years Later*, ed. Randolph L. Braham and András Kovács (CEU Press: Budapest and New York, 2016), 30–31.

94. Katzburg, *Pinkas ha-Kehilla*, 209.

95. Judit Kónya, "Hungarian Rabbinic Responsa Regarding Local Decrees on Opening Shops on Saturdays," *Yad Vashem Studies* 42, no. 1 (2014): 87.

96. Kovács, "The Problem of Continuity between the 1920 *Numerus Clausus* and Post-1938 Anti-Jewish Legislation in Hungary."

97. Ágnes Adachi (née Ágnes Mandl), *Video Testimony for USC Shoah Foundation.*

98. Ivan Devai, ibid.

99. Frank Gipps, ibid.

100. Marianna Glazek, ibid.

101. Ibid., 32–33.

Chapter 9

1. Stern described these events in his diaries. See Nathaniel Katzburg, "Shmuel Stern Rosh kehillat pest: pirke zichronot, 1938–1939" [Samu Stern, Head of the Pest Kehilla: Recollections, 1938–1939], in *Publications of the Institute for the Study of the Holocaust* (Jerusalem, 1984), 204–206; see also Avigdor Löwenheim, "Stern Samu naplója elé" [From the Diaries of Samu Stern], *Múlt és Jövő* 3 (1994): 96–99.

2. Szabolcsi, "Vitéz Endre László," *Egyenlőség.*

3. András Kovács, "Jews and Jewishness in Post-War Hungary," *Quest: Issues in Contemporary Jewry* 1 (2010).

4. See, for example, https://bbj.hu/culture/-judafest-celebrates-jewish-fall-feasts_171249 for a description of this annual event.

Bibliography

Archival Sources

Central Archive for the History of the Jewish People (Hebrew University)

Óbudai iratok [Writings about Óbuda] I–VII

Óbuda Lajsztromozatlan iratok

Jewish Theological Seminary of America

Pinkas Kehilat Kodesh Oben Yashan (JTSA MS 8336)

Budapesti Talmudegylet jegyzőkönye (August 23, 1874–May 17, 1885) (JTSA Mic #9805)

"Vorstandes Schulcommissions Sitzung" Izraelita hitkötség jegyőkönyve [*Protocols of the Pest Israelite Community*] (December 1885)

Közgyűlési jegyzőkönyv/Protokolle der Budapester Talmudverein Schas Chevra [Minute Book of the Budapest Hevra Shas, 1903–1945] (Mic. #9806)

Magyar Zsidó Levéltár

PIH--I-Z-I Összeirátasok, 1825–1869, Hungarian Jewish Museum and Archives

   1. PIH-I-C-2 Jegyzőkönyvek/GemeindeProtocolle/Sefer Zichronot, 1805–1848

   2. PIH-I-Z-2 Másolati Könyv, 1849–1852

   3. PIH-Z-2 XIII Pesti Chevra Kadisha

Budapest Főváros Levéltára [Budapest Municipal Archive, BFL]

Intimata #6061

Miscellenia #7105

Printed Primary Sources

Bácskai, Vera, ed. *Források Buda, Pest, és Óbuda történetéhez* [Sources for the History of Buda, Pest, and Óbuda] I, 1683–1873. Budapest, 1971.

Bácskai, Vera, and Lajos Nagy, eds. *Széchenyi Pesti Tervei* [Széchenyi's Conceptions of Pest]. Budapest: Szépirodalmi könyvkiadó, 1985.

Bernstein, Béla. *A negyvennyolcas magyar szabadságharc és a magyar zsidók* [The 1848 Hungarian War of Independence and Hungarian Jewry]. Budapest: Múlt és Jövő Kiadó, 1998.

Domanovszky, Sándor, ed. *József Nádor élete és iratai* [The Life and Papers of Palatine Joseph]. Vols. I–II.

Eisler, Mátyás. "A női és a zsidó egyéniség" [Women's and Jewish Character]. *Izraelita Magyar Irodalmi Társulat* VIII (1907).

Első magyar zsidó naptár és évkönyv 1848-ik szökőévre [The First Hungarian Jewish Almanac and Yearbook for the Leap Year 1848]. Pest: Landerer and Heckenastnál, 1848.

Erstes Programm der Pester isr. haupt-u. Unterrealschul für Schuljahr 1856. Pest, 1856.

Gerő, Katalin. *A szeretet munkásai: A Pesti Izraelita nőegylet története* [Labors of Love: The History of the Pest Jewish Women's Association, 1867–1937]. Budapest, 1937.

Gerő, Katalin. *Erfülltes Leben.* Leipzig, 1933.

Hatvany, Lajos. "Magyar irodalom a külföld előtt." *Nyugat* 5 (March 1, 1910).

Haufler, Joseph Vincesz. *Buda-Pest: Historisch-Topographische Skizzen von Ofen und Pest und deren Umgebungen: Mit Chromolithographirten Planen von Ofen und Pest und deren Umgebungen Sammt 12 Ansichten und Mehreren Historischen Illustrationen.* Pest: Verlag v Gustav, 1854.

Herzl, Theodore. "Der Baseler Kongress." In *Theodore Herzls Zionistische Schriften*, edited by Leon Keller. Berlin, 1920.

Jászi, Oszkár, ed. *A zsidókérdés Magyarországon* [The Jewish Question in Hungary]. Budapest: Huszadik század, 1917.

Jókai, Mór. "Budapesti élet" [Life in Budapest]. *Budapesti Negyed* 57 (2007).

Jókai, Mór. *Kárpáthy Zoltán.* Akadémiai Kiadó, 1983.

Kemény, Dávid. *A Magyar Izr. Kézmű- és Földművelési Egylet hetvenéves működése* [The Seventy-Year Agency of the Hungarian Israelite Craft and Agriculture Society]. Budapest, 1912.

Klein, Gyula. "Az Óbudai Izr. hitközség történetéhez." *Magyar Zsidó Szemle* VIII (1891).

Kóbor, Tamás. *Ki a Gettóból* I–II [Out of the Ghetto]. Budapest: Franklin Társulat, 1911.

Kohn, J. H. *Yemei Tzara ve-Nehama/Schilderung der Schreckentage zu Alt-Ofen durch die verheerende Donau-Überschwimmung.* Buda, 1838.

Kohn, Sámuel. "Az óbudai zsidó hitközség a múlt század közepe felé." *MZsSz* VIII, pp. 255–259.

Lesznai, Anna. *Kezdetben volt a Kert* I–II [In the Beginning Was the Garden]. Budapest, 1966.

Máday, Andor. *A magyar nő jogai a múltban és jelenben* [The Rights of the Hungarian Woman in the Past and Present]. Budapest, 1913.

Magyar Zsidó Oklevéltár (Monumenta Hungariae Judaica) I–XVIII.

Mályusz, Elemér, ed. *Sándor Lipót főherceg Nádor iratai, 1790–95* [The Papers of Crown-Prince Palatine Alexander Leopold]. Budapest, 1926.

Mintz, Alexander. "Die Lage der Juden in Osterreich." *Protokoll des I. Zionistenkongresses in Basel vom 29. Bis 31. August 1897.* Prague, 1911.

Miron, Guy, and Anna Szalai, eds. *Yehudim al Parashat Derachim: Siach ha-Zehut ha-Yahadut be-Hungariya beyn mishbar le-Hitchadshut, 1908–1926* [Jews at the Crossroads: Discourse on the Jewish Identity in Hungary between Crisis and Renewal]. Ramat Gan: Bar Ilan University, 2008.

Némethy, Károly. *A pest-budai árvíz 1838-ban* [The Flood in Pest-Buda in 1838]. Budapest, 1938.

Pál, Sándor. *Deák Ferenc kiadatlan leveleiből.* Budapest, 1992.

Pásztor, Mihály. *A Százötven Éves Lipótváros* [Lipótváros at One Hundred and Fifty]. Budapest: Székesfőváros Házinyomdája, 1940.

Patachich, József. *Szabad Királyi Pest Városának Leírása.* Pest, 1830. Reprinted by Pranava Books, India, 2017.

Rapoport, Solomon Judah Loeb. *Bikkure Ha-'Ittim.* Prague, 1829.

Reglement für die Pester Israeliten yur Werwaltung ihrer religosen und ökönomishcen, sie allein betreffenden Gegenstande un Geschafte. Pest, 1832. "Introduction" #1, reprinted in *Ben Chananja* no. 22 (May 31, 1865): 362.

Schweitzer, József. "Héber nyelvű krónika az 1838.ik évi árvíz eseményeiről." In *Széfer Le-Kavod Marjovszky Tibor—Tanulmánykötet Marjovszky Tibor 50. évi születésnápja alkalmából,* 212–216. Budapest: B & V Bt., 2003. Reprinted as "Zsidók a nagy pest-budai árvíz idéjen." In *Fórrasok és dokumentumok a zsidók történetéhez Magyarországon,* 92–93. Budapest: MTA Judaisztikai Kutatóközpont, 2005.

Smith, Joshua Toulmin. *Parallels between Constitution and Constitutional History of England and Hungary.* Boston: Ticknor, Reed, and Fields, 1851.

Széchenyi, Count István. *Pesti Por és Sár* [The Dust and Mud of Pest]. Budapest, 1866. Reprinted by Fascimile Publisher, Delhi, 2020.

Széchenyi, István. *Hitel* [Credit]. Pest: J. M. Trattner & István Károly, 1830.

Széchenyi, István. *Világ* [World]. Füstkuti Landerer Nyomtató Intézetében. Pest, 1831.

Szemere, Bertalan. "Pest jövendőjéről" [On the Future of Pest]. Budapest, 1840.

Theologische Gutachten über das Gebetbuch nach dem Debrauche des neuen Israelitischen Tempelvereins in Hamburg. Hamburg, 1842.

Tormay, Cécile. *Bujdosó könyv. Feljegyzések 1918–1919-ből.* Vols. I–II. Budapest, 1923.

Trattner, János. *Jégszakadás és a Duna kiáradása Magyarországban.* Buda, 1838.

Vázsonyi, Vilmosné. *Az én uram.* Budapest: Genius Kiadó, 1931.

Wesselényi, Baron Miklós. *"Az 'árvízi hajós' naplója"* [The Diary of the "Boatman of the Danube"]. *Magyar irodalmi ritkaságok* [Hungarian Literary Curiosities] no. 40, edited by László Vajthó.

Wesselényi, Baron Miklós. *Balítéletekről* [On Prejudice]. Kolozsvár, 1833.

Newspapers and Periodicals

Pesti Napló (Budapest, 1850–1938)

Fővárosi Közlöny (1890–1938)

Egyenlőség (Budapest, 1881–1938)

Ben Chananja (Budapest, 1858–1869)

Allgemeine Zeitung des Judenthums (Leipzig, 1837–1938)

Wiener Morgenstern (Vienna, 1919–1927)

Jüdische Zeitung (Vienna, 1907–1920)

Zsidó Híradó (Budapest, 1890–1938)

Izraelita Magyar Irodalmi Társulat (1895–1938)

Magyar Zsidó Szemle (1884–1938)

Magyar Zsidó Nő (Budapest, 1900–1901)

Új Kelet (Cluj, 1918–1938)

Secondary Sources

Anshel, John, and Theodore Lavie, eds. *Pinkas ha-Kehillot: Romania* II. Jerusalem, 1980.

Arató, Endre. "The Emergence of the Hungarian Bourgeois Concept of 'Nation-Homeland.'" In *Annales Universitatis Scientiarum Budapestinensis de Rolando Eötvös Nominatae Sectio Historica* 19 (1978): 47–83.

B. Lukács, Ágnes. *Az 1831–32. Évi Magyarországi kolerajárvány néhány jellegzetessége* [Some Characteristics of the 1831–32 Cholera Epidemic in Hungary].

Bácskai, Vera. "Budapest and Its Hinterland: The Development of Twin Cities, 1720–1850." In *Capital Cities and Their Hinterlands in Early Modern Europe,* edited by Peter Clark and Bernard Lepett. Aldershot, 1996.

Bácskai, Vera. "Pesti Zsidóság 19. század első felében" [Pest Jewry during the first half of the nineteenth century]. *Budapesti Negyed* 8, no. 2 (1995).

Bácskai, Vera. *A vállalkozók előfutárai: Nagykereskedők a reformkori Pesten.* Budapest, 1989.

Balázs, Éva H. *Hungary and the Habsburg, 1765–1800: An Experiment in Enlightened Absolutism.* Tacoma: University of Washington, 1997.

Balázs, Pál. *Forgószélben: A Budapesti Orthodox Zsidóság és Iskolái* [In the Whirlwind: Budapest's Orthodox Jewry and Its Schools]. Budapest, 2009.

Barany, George. "'Magyar Jew or Jewish Magyar?': Reflections on the Question of Assimilation." In *Jews and Non-Jews in Eastern Europe, 1918–1945,* edited by Béla Vago and George L. Moss, 51–98. New York: John Wiley & Sons, 1974.

Barany, George. *Stephen Széchenyi and the Awakening of Hungarian Nationalism, 1791–1841.* Princeton: Princeton University Press, 1968.

Barna, Jónás, and Fülöp Csukási, eds. *A magyar-zsidó felekezet elemi és polgári iskoláinak monográfiája* [Monographs on the Elementary and High Schools of the Hungarian Jewish Denomination] I–II. Budapest, 1896.

Baron, Salo W. "The Impact of the Revolution of 1848 on Jewish Emancipation." *Jewish Social Studies* 11, no. 3 (1949): 195–248.

Baron, Salo W. "The Revolution of 1848 and Jewish Scholarship II: Austria." *Proceedings of the American Academy of Jewish Research* 20 (1951): 1–100.

Beachy, Robert, and Ralf Roth, eds. *Who Ran the Cities? City Elites and Urban Power Structures in Europe and North America, 1700–2000.* Aldershot: Ashgate, 2007.

Beizer, Mikhail. *The Jews of St. Petersburg: Excursions through a Noble Past.* Philadelphia: Jewish Publication Society, 1989.

Bender, Daniel. "'A Hero ... for the Weak': Work, Consumption, and the Enfeebled Jewish Worker, 1881–1924." *International Labor and Working-Class History* 56 (1999): 1–22.

Bender, Thomas, and Carl E. Schorske. "Introduction: Budapest and New York Compared." In *Budapest and New York: Studies in Metropolitan Transformation,* edited by Schorske and Bender. New York: Russell Sage Foundation, 1994.

Berger, J. David. "The *bet din*: An Institution Whose Time Had Returned." *Tradition: A Journal of Orthodox Jewish Thought* 27, no. 1 (1992): 58–67.

Berger, J. Lipót. "Az óbudai izraelita hitközség iskolájának monográfiája" [A Study of the Obuda Jewish Community School]. In *A Magyar-Zsidó felekezet elemi és polgári iskoláinak monográfiaja,* edited by Jónás Barna and Fülöp Csukási, 245–259. Budapest, 1896.

Bernát, György, and László Berza, eds. *Budapest Lexikon* I–II. Budapest: Akadémiai kiadó, 2007.

Büchler, Sándor. *A zsidók története Budapesten a legrégibb időktől 1867-ig jelentkorig* [The History of the Jews of Budapest Pest from Ancient Times until 1867]. Budapest, 1901.

Bur, Marta. "A balkáni kereskedők és a magyar borkivitel a XVIII. században" [Balkan Merchants and the Hungarian Wine-Export in the Eighteenth Century]. *Törtenelmi Szemle* 21, no. 2 (1978): 281–313.

Cohen, Y. Y. *Hachmei Hungariya ve-Hasifrut ha-Toranit Ba.* Jerusalem, 1997.

Csillag, István. "A régi pesti zsidókórhaz" [The Old Jewish Hospital in Pest]. *Évkönyv: kiadjaa Magyar Izraeliták Országos Képviselete* 78 (1977).

Dawson, Andrew. "The Parameters of Craft Consciousness: The Social Outlook of the Skilled Worker, 1880–1920." In *American Labor and Immigration History: 1877–1920s: Recent European Research,* edited by Dirk Hoerder, 135–155. Urbana: University of Illinois Press, 1983.

Deák, Ágnes. *From Habsburg Neo-Absolutism to the Compromise.* New York: East European Monographs/Columbia University Press, 2009.

Deák, István. *Beyond Nationalism: A Social and Political History of the Habsburg Officer Corps, 1848–1918.* Oxford and New York: Oxford University Press, 1990.

Deák, István. "Budapest and the Hungarian Revolutions of 1918–1919." *Slavonic and East European Review* 46, no. 106 (1968): 1–12.

Deák, István. "Chivalry, Gentlemanly Honor, and Virtuous Ladies in Austria-Hungary." *Austrian History Yearbook* XXV (1994): 1–12.

Deák, István. *Essays on Hitler's Europe.* Omaha: University of Nebraska Press, 2001.

Deák, István. "Historiography of the Countries of Eastern Europe: Hungary." *American Historical Review* 97, no. 4 (October 1992): 1041–1063.

Deák, István. *The Lawful Revolution: Lajos Kossuth and the Hungarians, 1848–1849.* New York: Columbia University Press, 1979.

Deák, István. "The Passing of the Habsburg Monarchy, 1914–1918." *Central European History* 1, no. 2 (1968): 187–190.

Dobbie, Meredith, Ruth Morgan, and Lionel Frost. "Overcoming Abundance: Social Capital and Managing Floods in Inner Melbourne during the Nineteenth Century." *Journal of Urban History* 46, no. 1 (2020): 33–49.

Dubin, Lois. "Port Jews Revisited: Commerce and Culture in the Age of European Expansion." *Cambridge History of Judaism VII* (2018): 550–575.

Dynner, Glenn. *Men of Silk: The Hasidic Conquest of Polish Jewish Society*. London: Oxford University Press, 2008.

Endelman, Todd. "The Checkered Career of Jew-King: A Study in Anglo-Jewish Social History." *AJS Review* 7–8 (1983): 69–100.

Engels, Renate. "Topografie des jüdischen Speyer im Mittelalter." *Europas Juden im Mittelalter.* Speyer, 2005.

Erdei, Ferenc. *Magyar Város*. Budapest: Akadémiai Kiadó, 1974.

Erényi, Tibor. "Zsidók és a magyar politikai élet, 1848–1938." [Jews and Hungarian Political Life, 1848–1938]. *Múltunk: Politikatörténeti folyóirat* IV (1994): 3–30.

Eulenberg, Salamon. *A Magyar Vasuti Jog.* Singer és Wolfner Könyvkereskedése, 1886.

Evans, R. J. W. *Austria, Hungary, and the Habsburgs: Central Europe c. 1683–1867.* Oxford: Oxford University Press, 2006.

Faragó, Tamás, ed. *Pest-budai árvíz 1938.* Budapest: Fővárosi Szabó Ervin Könyvtár, 1988.

Fehér, Katalin. "Reformkori sajtóviták a nők művelődésének kédéséről" [Reform-Era Debates in the Press on the Question of Women's Education]. *Magyar Könyvszemle* III, no. 3 (1995): 247–263.

Ferziger, Adam. *Exclusion and Hierarchy: Orthodoxy, Non-Observance, and the Emergence of Modern Jewish Identity.* Philadelphia: University of Pennsylvania Press, 2005.

Ferziger, Adam. "Religious Zealotry and Religious Law: Rethinking Conflict and Coexistence." *Journal of Religion* 84, no. 1 (2004): 48–77.

Friedman, Menachem. "The Haredi (Ultra-Orthodox) Society: Sources, Trends, Processes." *Jerusalem Institute for Israel Studies Research Series* no. 41 (1991), I–VIII.

Frojimovics, Kinga. *Szétszakadt Történelem: Zsidó vallási irányzatok Magyarországon, 1868–1950.* Budapest, 2006.

Frojimovics, Kinga, Géza Komoróczy, Viktória Pusztai, and Andrea Strbik, eds. *Jewish Budapest: Monuments, Rites, History.* Budapest and New York, 1999.

Frojimovics, Kinga, Géza Komoroczy, Viktória Pusztai, and Andrea Strbik, eds. *A zsidó Budapest: a város arcai* I–II. Budapest: MTA Judaisztikai Kutatócsoport, 1995.

Fürst, Aron. "Budapest." In *'Arim ve-Imahot be-Yisrael: Mivzat Kodesh le-Kehilot Yisraelshe-Nechervu Bidey 'arizim u-teme'im be-Milhemet 'Olam ha-Aharona,* Part II. Jerusalem, 1948.

Gál, Éva. *Az Óbudai uradalom a Zichyek földesurasága alatt, 1657–1766.* Budapest: Akadémiai Kiadó, 1998.

Gál, Éva. "Az Óbudai uradalom zsidósága a 18. században" [The Jews of the Óbuda Estate during the Eighteenth Century]. *Századok* 126, no. 1 (1992): 3–28.

Gates-Coon, Rebecca. "18th Century *Schutzherren*: Esterhazy Patronage of the Jews." *Jewish Social Studies* 47, no. 3/4 (1985): 189–208.

Gates-Coon, Rebecca. *The Landed Estates of the Eszterhazy Princes: Hungary during the Reforms of Maria Theresa and Joseph II.* Baltimore: Johns Hopkins University Press, 1994.

Geehr, Richard. *Karl Lueger: Mayor of Fin de Siecle Vienna.* Detroit: Wayne State University Press, 1993.

Gertner, Haim. *The Rabbi and the City: The Rabbinate in Galicia and Its Encounter with Modernity, 1815–1867* [in Hebrew]. Jerusalem, 2013.

Gioielli, Emily. "'Home Is Home No Longer': Political Struggle in the Domestic Sphere in Post-Armistice Hungary, 1919–1922." *Aspasia* 11, no. 1 (2017): 54–70.

Gluck, Mary. *The Invisible Jewish Budapest: Metropolitan Culture at the Fin de Siecle.* Madison: University of Wisconsin Press, 2016.

Gonda, Moshe Eliyahu. *A debreceni zsidók száz éve.* Haifa. 1970.

Gordon, Milton. *Assimilation in American Life: The Role of Race, Religion, and National Origins.* Oxford: Oxford University Press, 1964.

Groszmann, Zsigmond. *A pesti zsidó gyülekezet alkotmányának története.* Budapest: Országos Rabbiképző—Zsidó Egyetem Könyvtára, 1934.

Groszmann, Zsigmond. "A pesti zsinagóga" [Synagogues of Pest]. *Egyenlőség,* December 12, 1915.

Groszmann, Zsigmond. "A száz év előtti nagy árvíz." *Egyenlőség,* March 16, 1938, p. 18.

Grünvald, Fülöp. *A zsidók története Budán.* Budapest, 1938.

Guesnet, François. "Lodzer Juden im 19. Jahrhundert: Ihr Ort in einer multikulturellen Stadtgesellschaft." In *Annäherungen; Beiträge zur jüdischen Geschichte und Kultur in Mittel und Osteuropa,* edited by Stefi JerschWenzel and Günther Wartenberg. Leipzig, 2002.

Guesnet, François, and Glenn Dynner, eds. *Warsaw: The Jewish Metropolis: Essays in Honor of Antony Polonsky.* Leiden: Brill, 2017.

Gyáni, Gábor. "Polgárosodás mint zsidó identitás" [*Embourgoisement* as Jewish Identity]. *Budapesti Könyvszemle–BUKSZ* (Fall 1997): 107–113.

Hanagan, Michael. "Artisans and Skilled Workers: The Problem of Definition." *International Labor and Working-Class History* 12 (1977): 28–31.

Hanák, Péter. "The Bourgoisification of the Hungarian Nobility—Reality and Utopia in the Nineteenth Century." *Études Historiques Hongroises* 1 (1985): 403–421.

Hanák, Péter. "Az elpusztíthatatlan város: Budapest történelmi vitalitása" [The Indestructible City: The Historical Vitality of Budapest]. *Budapesti Negyed* 1, no. 1 (1993). https://epa.oszk .hu/00000/00003/00001/fej01.htm.

Hanák, Péter. *The Garden and the Workshop: Essays on the Cultural History of Vienna and Budapest.* Princeton: Princeton University Press, 2016.

Hanák, Péter. "Polgárosodás és asszimiláció Magyarországon a XIX. században" [*Embourgoisement* and Assimilation in Hungary in the 19th Century]. *Történelmi Szemle* [Historical Review] no. 4 (1974): 513–535.

Hanák, Péter. "Polgárosodás és urbanizáció: Polgári lakáskultúra Budapesten a 19. században" [*Embourgoisement* and Urbanization: Middle-Class Housing Culture in Nineteenth-Century Budapest]. *Történelmi szemle* 27, no. 1–2 (1984): 513–536.

Hanebrink, Paul. *In Defense of Christian Hungary: Religion, Nationalism, and Antisemitism, 1890–1918*. Ithaca, NY: Cornell University Press, 2009.

Heilman, Samuel C. "The Many Faces of Orthodoxy." *Modern Judaism* 2, no. 1 (1982): 23–51; no. 2, 171–198.

Hitzer, Bettina, and Joachim Schlör. "Introduction to God in the City: Religious Topographies in the Age of Urbanization." *Journal of Urban History* 37, no. 6 (2011): 819–827.

Hollán, Henrik. *A Rókus kórház története: adatok és személynevek a Szent Rókus közkórház és fiókjai alapításának és fejlődésének történetéből* [The History of the Saint Rókus Hospital: Documents and Personalities from the History of the Saint Rókus Public Hospital and the Establishment and Development of Its Progeny]. Budapest: Medicina, 1967.

Horel, Catherine. *Histoire de Budapest*. Paris: Fayard, 1999.

Hundert, Gershon David. "Jewish Urban Residence in the Polish Commonwealth in the Early Modern Period." *Jewish Journal of Sociology* 26, no. 1 (1984): 25–34.

Hundert, Gershon David. *The Jews in a Polish Private Town: The Jews of Opatów*. Baltimore: Johns Hopkins University Press, 2019.

Hundert, Gershon David. *Jews in Poland-Lithuania in the Eighteenth Century: A Genealogy of Modernity*. Berkeley: University of California Press, 2004.

Hyman, Paula. "Culture and Gender: Women in the Immigrant Jewish Community." In *The Legacy of Jewish Immigration: 1881 and Its Impact,* edited by David Berger, 157–168. New York, 1983.

Hyman, Paula. *Gender and Assimilation in Modern Jewish History: The Roles and Representations of Women*. Tacoma: University of Washington Press, 1995.

Hyman, Paula. *The Jews of Modern France*. Berkeley: University of California Press, 1998.

Janos, Andrew C. *The Politics of Backwardness in Hungary, 1825–1848*. Princeton: Princeton University Press, 1982.

Jones, Gwen. *Chicago of the Balkans: Budapest in Hungarian Literature*. London: Routledge, 2013.

Kaczér, Illés. *Ne félj szolgám Jákob* [Fear not My Servant Jacob], trans. Lawrence Wolfe. New York, 1953.

Kaplan, Marion. "Tradition and Transition—The Acculturation, Assimilation, and Integration of Jews in Imperial Germany: A Gender Analysis." *Leo Baeck Institute Yearbook* 27 (1982): 3–26.

Kárády, Viktor. "Les Communautés Juives: des Profiles Contrastes." In *Vienne-Budapest, 1867–1918: Deux Ages, Deux Visions, un Empire,* edited by Dieter Hornig and Endre Kiss. Paris, 1996.

Kárády, Viktor. "A zsidóság polgárosodásának és modernizációjának főbb tényezői a magyar társadalomtörténetben." In *Zsidóság, modernizáció, polgárosodás: tanulmányok,* edited by Kárády. Budapest: Cserépfalvi, 1997.

Kárády, Viktor. "Zsidóság Budapesten a 20. század első felében." *Budapesti Negyed* 16, no. 1 (2008).

Katz, Jacob. *Orthodoxy and Schism in Nineteenth Century Central European Jewry*. Waltham, MA: Brandeis University Press, 1998.

Katz, Jacob. *Tradition and Crisis: Jewish Society at the End of the Middle Ages.* Syracuse, NY: Syracuse University Press, 2000.

Katzburg, Nathaniel. *Antishemiyut be-Hungaryah, 1867–1944* (in Hebrew). Tel Aviv: Ha-Merkaz ha-Beynle'umit, 1992.

Katzburg, Nathaniel. "Ha-Hanhagah Ha-Merkazit shel ha-Kehillot be-Hungaryah 1870–1939." *Zion* 50 (1985): 379–395.

Katzburg, Nathaniel. "Ha-Miflaga ha-Antishemit be-Hungaria u-Mekoma be-Hayim ha-Politi'im bishnat 1883–1887" [in Hebrew]. *Zion* 30, no. 1/2 (1965): 79–114.

Katzburg, Nathaniel. "Hungarian Jewish Historiography." In *The Rabbinical Seminary of Budapest, 1877–1977: A Centennial Volume,* edited by Moshe Carmilly-Weinberger, 215–237. New York: Sepher-Hermon Press for the Alumni Association of the Rabbinical Seminary of Budapest, 1986.

Katzburg, Nathaniel. *Hungary and the Jews: Policy and Legislation, 1920–1943.* Haifa: Hermon Press, 1981.

Katzburg, Nathaniel. "Pál Teleki and the Jewish Question in Hungary." *Soviet Jewish Affairs* 2 (1971): 105–111.

Katzburg, Nathaniel. *Pinkas he-Kehilla: Hungariya.* Jerusalem: Yad Vashem, 1976.

Katzburg, Nathaniel. "The Public Debate over Jewish Emancipation in Hungary during the 1840s" (in Hebrew). *Bar Ilan Annual* 1 (1973): 282–301.

Katzburg, Nathaniel. "Redifut ha-Yehudim be-Hungarya." *Bar Ilan Annual* 3 (1975): 225–251.

Katzburg, Nathaniel. "Shmuel Stern Rosh kehillat pest: pirke zichronot, 1938–1939." [Samu Stern, Head of the Pest Kehilla: Recollections, 1938–1939]. *Publications of the Institute for the Study of the Holocaust,* 203–233. Jerusalem, 1984.

Kecskeméti, Charles. *La Hongrie des Habsbourg, Vol. II: de 1790 a 1914.* Presses Universitaires de Rennes, 2011.

Kelly, Joan. *Women, History, and Theory: The Essays of Joan Kelly.* Chicago: University of Chicago Press, 1984.

Kerkápoly, Endre. "Széchenyi István közlekedésfejlesztési programja." *Magyar Tudomány* 36, no. 8 (1991): 973–988.

Kesztenburg-Glatstein, Ruth. *Neuere Geschichte der Juden in Bohmischen Landern, vol. I, 1780–1830.* Tubingen: Mohr Sieback, 1969.

Király, Béla. *Hungary in the Late Eighteenth Century: The Decline of Enlightened Absolutism.* New York: Columbia University Press, 1969.

Kiss, József. "Reich Koppel: egy rabbi a felsőházból." [Koppel Reich: A Rabbi in the Upper House]. *Múlt és Jövő* no. 2 (1993).

Klein, Rudolf. *The Great Synagogue of Budapest.* Budapest: TERC, 2008.

Klein-Pejsova, Rebekah. "The Budapest Jewish Community's Galician October." In *World War I and the Jews: Conflict and Transformation in Europe, the Middle East, and America,* edited by Marsha L. Rozenblit and Jonathan Karp, 112–130. New York: Berghann Books, 2017.

Komoróczy, Géza. "Városképen, héber betűkből: bevezetés." In *Ami látható és ami láthatatlan: Erzsébetváros zsidó öröksége* [What Is Visible and What Is Invisible], edited by Gyöngyvér Török. Budapest: Erzsébetváros Polgármesteri Hivatala, 2013.

Konrád, Miklós. "Csalódott zsidók a magyar zsidóság aranykorában." In *Az érzelmek története,* edited by Anikó Lukács and Árpád Tóth, 405–421. Budapest: Hajnal István Kör–Társadalomtörténeti Egyesület, 2019.

Konrád, Miklós. "Disszimiláció az asszimilációpárti zsidóság körében 1848–1914." *AETAS* 36, no. 2 (2021): 94–104.

Konrád, Miklós. "A Dörgölődző Lipótváros." *Szombat* 33, no. 5 (2021): 8–11.

Konrád, Miklós. "A dualizmus mint magyar zsidó aranykor? Kortárs zsidó helyzetértékelések." In *Magyar-zsidó identitásminták,* edited by Dénes Iván Zoltán, 93–108. Budapest: Ráció, 2019.

Konrád, Miklós. "A galíciai zsidó bevándorlás mítosza." *Századok* 152, no. 1 (2018): 31–60.

Konrád, Miklós. "Jews and Politics in Hungary in the Dualist Era, 1867–1914." *East European Jewish Affairs* 39, no. 2 (August 2009): 167–186.

Konrád, Miklós. "Mixing with Meshumads: Social Relations between Jews and Converted Jews in Modern Hungary." In *Jewish Studies at the Central European University* IX, edited by Michael Miller, 25–42. Budapest, 2017–2019.

Konrád, Miklós. "Le Movement d'Embourgeoisement de la Noblesse et les Juifs dans la Hongrie du XIXᵉ Siecle." *Revue des Etudes Juives* 159, no. 1/2 (January 2000): 145–184.

Konrád, Miklós. "Music Halls and Jewish Identity in Budapest at the Turn of the Century." In *Jewish Space in East Central Europe: Day to Day History,* edited by Jurgita Šiaučiūnaitė-Verbickienė and Larisa Lempertienė. London: Cambridge Scholars Publishing, 2007.

Konrád, Miklós. "Orfeum és zsidó indentitás Budapesten a századfordulón." *Budapesti Negyed* 16, no. 2 (2008).

Konrád, Miklós. "Sportegyletek és antiszemitizmus a magyar zsidóság aranykorában." *Szombat* 31, no. 6 (2019): 4–7.

Konrád, Miklós. "Vallásváltás és identitás: A kitért zsidók megítélésének változásai a dualizmus korában" [Conversion and Identity: Changes of Attitude toward Converted Jews in the Period of the Dual Monarchy]. *Századok* 143, no. 3 (2009): 593–636.

Konrád, Miklós. "Zsidók az utcasarkon: A budapesti zsidó hordárok tündöklése és bukása." *Múlt és Jövő* [New Edition] 26, no. 3 (2015): 82–94.

Konrád, Miklós. *Zsidóságon innen és túl. Zsidók vallásváltása Magyarországon a reformkortól az első világháborúig.* Budapest: BTK, 2014.

Kónya, Judit. "Hungarian Rabbinic Responsa Regarding Local Decrees on Opening Shops on Saturdays." *Yad Vashem Studies* 42, no. 1 (2014): 83–109.

Kossuth, Lajos. *Országgzüllési beszédei* [Parliamentary Speeches] I–II. Pest: Heckenast, 1867.

Kovács, András. "Jews and Jewishness in Post-War Hungary." *Quest: Issues in Contemporary Jewry* 1 (2010). https://www.quest-cdecjournal.it/jews-and-jewishness-in-post-war-hungary/.

Kovács, Mária M. "The Problem of Continuity between the 1920 *Numerus Clausus* and Post-1938 Anti-Jewish Legislation in Hungary." *East European Jewish Affairs* 35, no. 1 (2005).

Laczó, Ferenc. "Dual Identities: The Israelite Hungarian Literary Society, 1929–1943." *Jewish Studies at the Central European University* 7 (2009–2011): 127–145.

Lee, Erica Kovács. *At America's Gates: Chinese Immigration during the Exclusion Era, 1882–1943.* Chapel Hill and London: University of North Carolina Press, 2003.

Lévai, Jenő. *Fekete könyv a magyar zsidóság szenvedéseiről* [Black Book on the Sufferings of Hungarian Jewry]. Budapest: Officina, 1946.

Li, Wei. *Ethnoburb: The New Ethnic Community in Urban America.* Honolulu: University of Hawaii Press, 2012.

Liberles, Robert. "From Toleration to '*Verbesserung*': German and English Debates on the Jews in the Eighteenth Century." *Central European History* 22, no. 1 (1989): 3–32.

Liberles, Robert. "The Jews and Their Bill: Jewish Motivations in the Controversy of 1753." *Jewish History* 2, no. 2 (1987): 29–36.

Liberles, Robert. *Religious Conflict in Social Context: The Resurgence of Orthodox Judaism in Frankfurt Am Main, 1837–1877.* Westport and London: Praeger, 1985.

Löewenheim, Avigdor. *Hanhagat ha-Kehilla ha-Yehudit shel Pest Be-Shanim 1914–1919: Ma'amada u-Pe'iluta be-Tzibbur ha-Yehudi.* PhD diss., Hebrew University of Jerusalem, 1990.

Löwenheim, Avigdor. "Stern Samu naplója elé" [From the Diaries of Samu Stern]. *Múlt és Jövő* 3 (1994): 96–99.

Löewenheim, Avigdor. "Teador Herzl ve-Yehude Hungariya: Sicha 'im Herzl mi-Shnat 1903" [Theodore Herzl and Zionism: A Conversation with Herzl from 1903]. *Tsiyon* 54, no. 4 (1989): 461–467.

Löewenheim, Avigdor. "Yehudei Budapest ve-ha-Galicianim—Parasha mi-shnat 1904" [The Jews of Budapest and the Galicianers—an Episode from 1904]. *Tsiyon* 53, no. 3 (1988): 303–312.

Loewenstein, Steve. *The Berlin Jewish Community: Enlightenment, Family, and Crisis, 1770–1820.* New York: Oxford University Press, 1994.

Lupovitch, Howard. "Beyond the Walls: The Beginning of Pest Jewry." *Austrian History Yearbook* 36 (2006): 40–64.

Lupovitch, Howard. "It Takes a Village: Budapest Jewry and the Problem of Juvenile Delinquency." In *Juvenile Delinquency and the Limits of Western Influence, 1850–2000*, edited by Lily Chang and Heather Ellis, 69–92. London: Palgrave Macmillan, 2014.

Lupovitch, Howard. "Jews and the Zichy Estate: A Case Study in Magnate-Jewish Relations." *Jahrbuch des Simon Dubnow Instituts* 7 (2008): 15–37.

Lupovitch, Howard. *Jews at the Crossroads: Tradition and Accommodation during the Golden Age of the Hungarian Nobility.* Budapest: CEU Press, 2007.

Lupovitch, Howard. "Neolog: Reforming Judaism in a Hungarian Milieu." *Modern Judaism* 40, no. 3 (2020): 128–145.

Lupovitch, Howard. "Ordinary People, Ordinary Jews: Mór Jókai as Magyar Philosemite." In

Philosemitism in History, edited by Jonathan Karp and Adam Sutcliffe. Cambridge: Cambridge University Press, 2011.

Lupovitch, Howard. "Traversing the Rupture: Antisemitism and the Holocaust in Hungary." *Patterns of Prejudice* 37, no. 4 (2003): 429–436.

Lupovitch, Howard, Antony Polonsky, and François Guesnet, eds. *Poland and Hungary: Jewish Realities Compared (Polin* 31). London: Littmann Library of Jewish Civilization, 2019.

Lurie, Ilie. *The Habad Movement in Czarist Russia* (in Hebrew). Jerusalem, 2006.

Macartney, C. A. *A History of Hungary, 1929–1945.* New York, 1956.

Malleier, Elisabeth. *Jüdische Frauen in Wien 1816–1938.* Wien: Wohlfahrt–Mädchenbildung–Frauenarbeit, 2003.

Mandfred, Hettlin, Andras Reinke, and Norbert Conrads, eds. *In Breslau zu Hause: Juden in einer mitteleuropaischen Metropole der Neuzeit.* Hamburg: Dölling and Gratz, 2003.

Mandl, Bernát. *Das Jüdische Schulwesen in Ungarn unter Kaiser Josef II (1780–1790).* Posen: Merzbach Buchdrakerei, 1903.

Mandl, Bernát. "A Pesti izr. hitközségi fiu-iskola monográfiaja." In *A Magyar-Zsidó felekezet elemi és polgári iskoláinak monográfiaja,* edited by Jónás Barna and Fülöp Csukási, 1–112. Budapest, 1896.

Matlekovics, Sándor. *Magyarország közgazdasági és közművelődési állapota ezeréves fennállásakor.* Vol. IX. Budapest, 1898.

McCagg, William. "Hungary's Feudalized Bourgeoisie." *Journal of Modern Jewish History* 44, no. 1 (1972): 65–78.

McCagg, William. "Jewish Conversion in Hungary in Modern Times." In *Jewish Apostasy in the Modern World,* edited by Todd Endelman, 142–164. New York: Holmes and Meier, 1987.

McCagg, William. *Jewish Nobles and Geniuses in Modern Hungary.* New York: Columbia University Press, 1972.

McCagg, William. "The Role of the Magyar Nobility in Modern Jewish History." *East European Quarterly* XX, no. 1 (March 1986): 41–53.

Meir, Natan. *Kiev, Jewish Metropolis: A History.* Bloomington: Indiana University Press, 2010.

Melinz, Gerhard, and Susan Zimmermann. "Armenfürsorge, Kinderschutz, and Sozialreform in Budapest und Wien, 1870–1914." *Geschichte und Gesellschaft* 21 (1995): 338–367.

Mendelsohn, Ezra. *The Jews of East Central Europe between the Two World Wars.* Bloomington: Indiana University Press, 1983.

Mendes-Flohr, Paul, and Yehuda Reinharz. *The Jew in the Modern World.* Oxford, 1995.

Mitteis, Heinrich. "Über den Rechtsgrund des Satzes 'Stadtluft macht frei.'" In *Festschrift Edmund Husserl: Zum 70. Geburtstag Gewidmet,* 342–358. Halle, 1929.

Moess, Alfréd. *Pest megye és Pest-Buda zsidóságának demográfiája, 1749–1846.* Budapest, 1968.

Nachama, Andreas, Julius H. Schoeps, and Hermann Simon, eds. *Jews in Berlin: A Comprehensive History.* Berlin: Berlinica Publishing, 2013.

Nagy, Beáta. "'Az asszonyoknak egy szalónt kellett teremtenünk': Nők és klubélet a századforduló Budapestjén." *Nők a modernizálódó magyar társadalomban* (2006).

Nagy, Iván. *Magyarország családai czímerekkel és nemzékrendi táblákkal* [The Families of Hungary with Coats of Arms and Genealogical Tables]. 13 vols. Pest: Ráth Mór, 1868.

Nagy, Katalin S. "A képzőművészpálya mint asszimilációs lehetőség a 19. század végén, 20. század elején." *Budapesti Negyed* 16, no. 2 (2008).

Nagy, Lajos. *Budapest története III: a Török kiűzésétől a márciusi forradalomig* [The History of Budapest from the Expulsion of the Turks to the March Revolution]. Budapest: Akadémiai Kiadó, 1975.

Nagy, Lajos. "A Terézváros kialakulása" [The Establishment of Terézváros]. *Tanulmányok Budapest Múltjából* (1956): 97–127.

Nathans, Benjamin. *Beyond the Pale: The Jewish Encounter with Late Imperial Russia*. Berkeley, Los Angeles, London: University of California Press, 2002.

Nathans, Benjamin. "Saint Petersburg." In *YIVO Encyclopedia of Jews in Eastern Europe*, https://yivoencyclopedia.org/article.aspx/Saint_Petersburg.

Nemes, Robert. *The Once and Future Budapest*. DeKalb: University of Northern Illinois Press, 2005.

Pásztor, Mihály. *A százötven éves Lipótváros (Statisztikai közlemények)*. Budapest: Székesfővárosi házinyomdája.

Peisner, Ignácz. *Budapest a XVIII. Században* [Budapest in the Eighteenth Century]. Budapest, 1900.

Penslar, Derek. *Theodore Herzl: The Charismatic Leader*. New Haven: Yale University Press, 2020.

Peremiczky, Szilvia. "Az emancipáció utáni Fin de siècle—Budapest és Gustav Mahler." *Budapesti Negyed* 16, no. 2 (2008).

Peterson, Heidemarie. "Kraków." In *YIVO Encyclopedia of Jews in Eastern Europe I*, https://yivoencyclopedia.org/article.aspx/Krakow/Krakow_before_1795.

Petrovsky-Stern, Yohanan. "Hasidism, Havurot, and the Jewish Street." *Jewish Social Studies* 10, no. 2 (2004): 20–54.

Pinsker, Shachar. *A Rich Brew: How Cafés Created Modern Jewish Culture*. New York: New York University Press, 2019.

Polonsky, Antony. "Warsaw." In *YIVO Encyclopedia of Jews in Eastern Europe*, https://yivoencyclopedia.org/article.aspx/Warsaw.

Praisman, Leonid. "Moscow." In *YIVO Encyclopedia of Jews in Eastern Europe*, https://yivoencyclopedia.org/article.aspx/Moscow.

Preisich, Gábor. "Széchenyi Érdemei Budapest Fejlesztésében." [Szechenyi's Merits in the Expansion of Budapest]. *Magyar Tudomány* 36, no. 8 (1991): 1023–1028.

Prepuk, Anikó. "A neológ sajtó a zsidóság társadalmi befogadásáért a 19. század utolsó harmadában." *Budapesti Negyed* 16, no. 2 (2008): 1–38.

Raj, Ferenc. *A History of Jews in Hungary under the Ottoman Domination, 1526–1686*. PhD diss., Brandeis University, 2004.

Reinke, Andreas. "Gemeinde und Verein: Formen jüdischer Vergemeinschaftung im Breslau des 19. Und beginnenden 20. Jahrhunderts." In *Im Breslau zu Haus*, 131–147. Hamburg, 2003.

Rethelyi, Mari. "The Wanderer's Gaze: Jewish Writers in the Urban Landscape of Budapest at the Turn of the 20th Century." *Jewish Culture and History* 21, no. 2 (2020): 131–155.

Richers, Julia. "Johanna Bischitz, Katalin Gerő, and Budapest's Jewish Women's Association (1866–1943)." In *Gender, Memory, and Judaism,* edited by Judit Gaszi, Andrea Pető, and Zsuzsana Toronyi, 125–144. Budapest: Balassi Kiadó, 2007.

Richers, Julia. *Jüdisches Budapest: Kulturelle Topographien einer Stadtgemeinde im 19. Jahrhundert.* Koln, Weimar, Wien, 2009.

Richers, Julia. "Zeiten des Umbruchs und der Liminalität: Lebenswelten Budapester Juden im Vormärz." In *Konzeptionen des Jüdischen,* edited by Petra Ernst and Gerald Lamprecht, 106–131. Innsbruck: Studien Verlag, 2009.

Romsics, Ignác. "The Antisemitism of István Bethlen and Jewish Policy of the Horthy Era." In *The Holocaust in Hungary: Seventy Years Later,* edited by Randolph L. Braham and András Kovács, 27–36. Budapest and New York: CEU Press, 2016.

Romsics, Ignác. *Bethlen István, Politikai életrajz.* Budapest: Magyarságkutató Intézet, 1991.

Romsics, Ignác. *A Magyar zsidóság története.* Budapest, 2015.

Rose, Alison. *Jewish Women in Fin de Siecle Vienna.* Austin: University of Texas Press, 2010.

Rosman, Moshe J. *The Lords' Jews: Magnate-Jewish Relations in the Polish-Lithuanian Commonwealth during the Eighteenth Century.* Cambridge, MA: Harvard University Press, 1990.

Rothschild, Joseph. *East Central Europe between the Two World Wars.* Spokane and Tacoma: University of Washington Press, 1984.

Rozenblit, Marsha. *The Jews of Vienna, 1867–1914: Assimilation and Identity.* New York: SUNY Press, 1984.

Sabeleuskaya, Volha Aliaksandrauna. "Changing Conceptions of Leisure among the Jews of Western Belarus at the End of the 19th Century." *East European Jewish Affairs* 36, no. 2 (2006): 127–140.

Schweitzer, Gábor. "Budapest, az ország vakbele: a magyar politikai közbeszéd történetéhez." *Budapesti Könyvszemle (BUKSZ)* (2005): 1–8.

Sennett, Richard. *Flesh and Bone: The Body and the City in Western Civilization.* London: W. W. Norton, 1996.

Shavit, Zohar. "Train Up a Child: On the 'Maskilic' Attempt to Change the Habits of Jewish Children and Young Adults." *Journal of Jewish Education* 82, no. 1 (2016): 28–53.

Siegmund, Stefanie. "Communal Leaders (*rashei qahal*) and the Representation of Medieval and Early Modern Jews as 'Communities.'" In *Jewish Religious Leadership: Image and Reality,* Vol. 1, edited by Jack Wertheimer, 333–370. New York: Jewish Theological Seminary, 2004.

Silber, Michael K. "Budapest." In *YIVO Encyclopedia of the Jews in Eastern Europe,* https://yivo-encyclopedia.org/article.aspx/Budapest.

Silber, Michael K. "The Emergence of Ultra-Orthodoxy: The Invention of Tradition." In *The Uses of Tradition: Jewish Continuity in the Modern Era,* edited by Jack Wertheimer, 23–84. New York: Jewish Theological Seminary of America, 1999.

Silber, Michael K. "The Entrance of Jews into Hungarian Society in *Vormärz*: The Case of the

'Casinos.'" In *Assimilation and Community: The Jews in Nineteenth-Century Europe*, edited by Jonathan Frankel and Steven J. Zipperstein, 284–323. Cambridge: Cambridge University Press, 1992.

Silber, Michael K., ed. *Jews in the Hungarian Economy 1760–1945: Studies Dedicated to Moshe Carmilly-Weinberger*. Jerusalem: Magnes Press, 1992.

Silber, Michael K. "The Making of Habsburg Jewry in the Long Eighteenth Century." In *The Cambridge History of Judaism. Vol. VII. The Early Modern World, 1500–1815*, edited by Jonathan Karp and Adam Sutcliffe, 763–797. Cambridge: Cambridge University Press, 2018.

Silber, Michael K., ed. *Shorashei HaPilug be-Yehadut Hungariya mimei Yoseph Ha-Sheni ad Erev Mahapechat 1848* [The Roots of the Schism in Hungarian Jewry from the Era of Joseph II until the Eve of the Revolution of 1848]. PhD diss., Hebrew University, 1979.

Silber, Michael K. "The Social Composition of the Pest Radical Reform Society ('Genossenschaft für Reform im Judenthum'), 1848–1852." *Jewish Social Studies* 1, no. 3 (1995): 99–128.

Snyder, Saskia Coenen. *Building a Public Judaism: Synagogues and Jewish Identity in Nineteenth-Century Europe*. Cambridge, MA: Harvard University Press, 2013.

Sorkin, David. "Port Jews and the Three Regions of Emancipation." *Jewish Culture and History* 4, no. 2 (2001): 21–36.

Sorkin, David. "The Port Jews: Notes toward a New Social Type." *Journal of Jewish Studies* 50, no. 1 (1999): 88–95.

Stampfer, Shaul. "How and Why Did Hasidism Spread?" *Jewish History* 27 (2013): 201–219.

Stampfer, Shaul. *Lithuanian Yeshivas of the Nineteenth Century: Creating a Tradition of Learning*. London: Littmann Library of Jewish Civilization, 2014.

Stone, Daniel. "Jews and the Urban Question in Late Eighteenth Century Poland." *Slavic Review* 50, no. 3 (Fall 1991): 531–541.

Szalai, Anna, ed. *In the Land of Hagar: The Jews of Hungary—History, Society and Culture*. Tel-Aviv: Beth Hatefutsoth, Nahum Goldmann Museum of the Jewish Diaspora; Ministry of Defense Publishing House, 2002.

Szapor, Judith. "Between Self-Defense and Loyalty: Jewish Responses to the *Numerus Clausus* Law in Hungary, 1920–1928." *Shoah: Intervention, Methods, Documentation*, 21–33. Los Angeles: Simon Wiesenthal Center, 2019.

Tamáska, Máté. "The Industrialization of the Danube Cityscape: Danube Ports during the Concurrent Urban Development of Vienna and Budapest, 1829–1918." *Zeitschrift für Ostmitteleuropa Forschung* 67, no. 4 (2018): 552–577.

Teller, Adam. *Money, Power, and Influence in Eighteenth Century Lithuania: The Jews of the Radziwill Estates*. Palo Alto, CA: Stanford University Press, 2016.

Teller, Adam. "Radziwill, Rabinowicz, and the Rabbi of Swierz: The Magnates' Attitude to Jewish Regional Autonomy in the 18th Century." *Scripta Hierosolymitana* 38 (1998): 246–276.

Tóth, Arpád. "'Nachäffen' oder zivilisatorisches Aufschließen? Die Pester Vereine des Vormärz und ihr Verhältnis zu westlichen Vorbildern." In *Vorbild Europa und die Modernisierung in*

Mittel- und Südosteuropa, edited by Flavius Solomo, Krista Zacj, and Juliane Brandt, 49–70. Berlin: LIT-Verlag, 2009.

Tóth, Arpád. *Önszervező polgárok: a pesti egyesületek társadalomtörténete a reformkorban* [Self-Organizing Citizens: A Social History of Associations in Pest during the Reform Era]. Budapest, 2005.

Tóth, Arpád. "A pesti Nemzeti Casino reformkori társadalmi összetételének tanulságai." In *História mezején. A 19. század emlékezete. Tanulmányok Pajkossy Gábor tiszteletére*, edited by Ágnes Deák and Orsolya Völgyesi, 45–56. Szeged: Csongrád Megyei Levéltár, 2011.

Tóth, Arpád. "A társadalmi szerveződés polgári és rendi normái: a pesti jótékony nőegylet története 1817–1847" [The Civic and Operational Norms of a Social Organization: The History of the Pest Women's Association, 1817–1847]. *FONS* 4 (1998).

Tóth, Arpád. "Voluntary Societies and Social Transformation in Hungary." *Szellem és Történelem* (2020): 571–581.

Tóth, Arpád. "Voluntary Society as Power Agency in mid-19th Century Pest: Urbanization and the Changing Distribution of Power." In *Who Ran the Cities? City Elites and Urban Power Structures in Europe and North America, 1700–2000*, edited by Robert Beachy and Ralf Roth, 161–177. Aldershot: Ashgate, 2007.

Ujvári, Hedvig. "Asszimiláció, nyelv és identitás problematikája a fiatal Max Nordaunál és Herzl Tivadarnál." *Budapesti Negyed* 16, no. 1 (2008).

Újvári, Péter. *Magyar Zsidó Lexikon*. Budapest, 1929.

Ungváry, Krisztián. *Bethlen István, Politikai életrajz*. Budapest: Magyarságkutató Intézet, 1991.

Ungváry, Krisztián. *A Horthy-rendszer mérlege. Diszkrimináció, szociálpolitika és antiszemitizmus Magyarországon*. Pécs and Budapest: Jelenkor, 2013.

Ury, Scott. "Lost and Found?: Jewish Historians, Jewish History, and Narrativization of Order in East European Cities." *AJS Review* 41, no. 1 (2017): 9–36.

van Rahden, Till, and Marcus Brainard, eds. *Jews and Other Germans: Civil Society, Religious Diversity, and Urban Politics in Breslau, 1860–1925*. Madison: University of Wisconsin Press, 2008.

Vari, Alexander. "Re-territorializing the 'Guilty City': Nationalist and Right-Wing Attempts to Nationalize Budapest during the Interwar Period." *Journal of Contemporary History* 47, no. 4 (2012): 709–733.

von Kessel, Peter, and Elisja Schulte, eds. *Rome and Amsterdam: Two Growing Cities in Seventeenth Century Europe*. Ann Arbor: University of Michigan Press, 1998.

Vörös, Károly. "A budapesti zsidóság két forradalom között, 1848–1918." In *Zsidóság a dualizmus kori Magyarországon*, edited by Varga László, 45–57. Budapest: Pannonia Kiadó, 2005.

Vörös, Károly. *Budapest Története IV: A Márciusi Forradalomtól az Őszirózsás Forradalomig*. Budapest: Akedémiai Kiadó, 1978.

Vörös, Kati. "How Jewish Is Jewish Budapest?" *Jewish Social Studies* 8, no. 1 (2001): 88–125.

Walker, Mack. *German Home Towns: Community, Estate, and General Estate, 1648–1871.* Ithaca, NY: Cornell University Press, 1998.

Wenger, Beth S. "Jewish Women and Volunteerism: Beyond the Myth of Enablers." *American Jewish History* 79, no. 1 (1989): 16–36.

Wilde, James. "The Boatman of the Deluge: Miklós Wesselényi and the 1838 Flooding of Pest." *Hungarian Studies: A Journal of the International Association for Hungarian Studies and Balassi Institute* 1 (2005): 27–50.

Wodzinski, Marcin. *Haskalah and Hasidism in the Kingdom of Poland: A History of Conflict.* Oxford: Littmann Library of Jewish Civilization, 2005.

Wyrozumski, Boüena. "New Sources for the History of Cracow during the Middle Ages." In *Kroke-Kazimierz-Cracow: Studies in the History of Cracow Jewry,* edited by Elhanan Reiner. Tel Aviv, 2001.

Zichy, Antal, ed. *Grof István Széchenyi hilapi cikkei* [Journal Articles of Count István Széchenyi]. Budapest, 1893.

Zimmermann, Susan. "Wie sie Feministinnen wurden: Wege in die Frauenbewegungen in Zentraleuropa der Jahrhunderte." *L'homme: Zeitschrift für Geschichte* VIII, no. 2 (1997): 272–306.

Zipperstein, Steven. *The Jews of Odessa: A Cultural History, 1794–1881.* Palo Alto, CA: Stanford University Press, 1991.

Zsuzsa, L. Nagy. *A budapesti liberális ellenzék, 1919–1944.* Budapest, 1972.

Index

Page numbers in *italics* indicate Figures or Tables.

About the Author

HOWARD LUPOVITCH IS PROFESSOR OF HISTORY AND DIRECTOR OF THE COHN-Haddow Center for Judaic Studies at Wayne State University. He is the author of *Jews at the Crossroads: Tradition and Accommodation during the Golden Age of the Hungarian Nobility* and *Jews and Judaism in World History*, and co-editor of *Polin*, vol. 31: *Poland and Hungary—Jewish Realities Compared*.